Environmental Law in Malta

Environmental Law in Malta

Simone Borg
Louise Spiteri
Chris Attard
David Chetcuti Dimech

This book was originally published as a monograph in the International Encyclopaedia of Laws/Environmental Law.

Founding Editor: Roger Blanpain
General Editor: Frank Hendrickx
Volume Editor: Kurt Deketelaere

Wolters Kluwer

Published by:
Kluwer Law International B.V.
PO Box 316
2400 AH Alphen aan den Rijn
The Netherlands
E-mail: lrs-sales@wolterskluwer.com
Website: www.wolterskluwer.com/en/solutions/kluwerlawinternational

Sold and distributed by:
Wolters Kluwer Legal & Regulatory U.S.
920 Links Avenue
Landisville, PA 17538
United States of America
E-mail: customer.service@wolterskluwer.com

ISBN 978-94-035-3947-8

e-Book: ISBN 978-94-035-3957-7
web-PDF: ISBN 978-94-035-3967-6

This title is available on www.kluwerlawonline.com

The Authors

Prof. Simone Borg studied Law at the University of Malta, where she obtained a doctorate degree in laws (LLD) in 1991 and later her Magister Juris degree in International Environmental Law in 1994. She completed her PhD at the International Maritime Law Institute (IMLI) of the International Maritime Organization in 2009. She worked for the public sector from 1991 to 2004, originally as a First Secretary with the Ministry of Foreign Affairs, then as head of the legal and multilateral affairs section within the ministry responsible for the environment. During this time, she was mainly responsible for negotiating Malta's position in international environmental multilateral agreements, the drafting of legislation and legal policymaking in environmental law. She coordinated the transposition of the environmental *acquis communautaire* during Malta's negotiations to become a European Union (EU) Member State. She also participated in various environmental consultancy projects with the EU and the United Nations. She was the first chairperson of Malta's Occupational Health and Safety Authority. Prof Borg is a resident full-time Lecturer and Head of the Environmental and Resources Law Department at the Faculty of Laws and a Visiting Lecturer at various international universities. She also works as a diplomat for the Government of Malta as ambassador at large for climate action. She has published books and various academic articles on Malta's environmental law, climate change, the conservation of living marine resources and ocean governance.

Dr Louise Spiteri pursued her studies at the University of Malta, where, in 1999, she was awarded the degree of Doctor of Laws. Two years later, in 2001, she was awarded the Magister Juris Degree in Public International Law. She started her work as a lawyer doing private practice at the Law Courts of Malta. In 2000, Spiteri joined the public sector, first as an environmental legal officer, where she participated in the drafting of Maltese law of the environment *acquis*, and has participated in various intergovernmental conferences and negotiating committees dealing with environmental issues as a legal advisor to the Government of Malta. She was also a legal advisor at the Attorney General's office for the Government of Malta, where she set up the EU relations and infringement office. In 2016, she was appointed as a Board Member of the newly established Environment and Resource Authority, and later between 2017 and 2020, she served as the CEO of the same Authority. Currently, she is a full-time resident Lecturer at the Environmental and Resource Law Department, and she carries out various research and legal practice, mainly in the field of environment and planning law.

Dr Chris Attard studied Law at the University of Malta, where he graduated with a Doctor of Laws (LLD) in 2007. He furthered his studies by specialising in international maritime law at the IMO International Maritime Law Institute. He graduated with a Master of Laws (LLM) with distinction in May 2008 and received the Professor Walter Muller Prize for best draft legislation project. Dr Chris Attard began practising as an Advocate in Malta and Gozo, focusing particularly on immigration law and international maritime law. He has been a resident academic at the University of Malta with the Department of Environmental and Resources Law, Faculty of Laws, since September 2011. Dr Attard also studied Law at the University of Oxford and is currently writing a PhD Thesis entitled *The Status of Submarine Cables and Pipelines under the Contemporary Law of the Sea* at the United Nations – IMO – International Maritime Law Institute.

David Chetcuti Dimech graduated with a Bachelor of Laws from the Faculty of Laws at the University of Malta and is currently pursuing a Master of Advocacy at the same University. He is expecting to graduate in March 2024. He has involved himself with Għaqda Studenti tal-Liġi (GħSL), the Malta Law Students' Society, where he has held the successive roles of editor (2019–2020), editor-in-chief of the Online Law Journal (OLJ) administered by the Society (2020–2021), and Publications Officer in charge of the OLJ and the publication of the Society's annual academic and peer-reviewed journal *Id-Dritt* (2021–2023). He has a strong interest in environmental matters and in constitutional and administrative law.

Table of Contents

List of Abbreviations

ASTM	American Society for Testing and Materials
BATs/EQs	Best Available Techniques (BATs), with reference to environmental quality standards
BCC	Bio-safety Coordinating Committee
CABE	Consultative and Advisory Board on the Environment
CAEA	Crimes Against the Environment Act
CE	Conformité Européenne (European Conformity)
CER	Certified Emission Reduction
CFC	Chlorofluorocarbon
CJEU	Court of Justice of the European Union
CITES	Convention on International Trade in Endangered Species of Wild Flora and Fauna
COCP	Code of Organisation and Civil Procedure
DPA	Development Planning Act
EC	European Community
EEC	European Economic Community
EEE	Electric and Electronic Equipment
EIA	Environmental Impact Assessment
ELV	Emission Limit Value
EPA	Environment Protection Act
EPD	Environment Protection Department/Directorate
EPRT	Environment and Planning Review Tribunal
ERUs	Emission Reduction Units
ETS	Emission Trading Scheme
EU	European Union
GMO	Genetically Modified Organism
IAS	Invasive Alien Species
IDEA	Institute of Design for Environmental Action
IMDG	International Maritime Dangerous Goods
IOPC	International Oil Pollution Compensation

List of Abbreviations

IPPC	Integrated Pollution Prevention Control
L.N.	Legal Notice
MARPOL	Marine Pollution
MCCAA	Malta Competition and Consumer Affairs Authority
MEPA	Malta Environment and Planning Authority
MRA	Malta Resources Authority
MSA	Malta Standards Authority
NGO	Non-government Organisation
NVZs	Nitrate Vulnerable Zones
ODZ	Outside Development Zone
OECD	Organisation for Economic Cooperation and Development
OHSU	Occupational Health and Safety Unit
PCBs	Polychlorinated Biphenyls
PCTs	Polychlorinated Terpheyls
PDS	Project Description Statement
PIC	Prior Informed Consent
PM	Particulate Matter
REACH	Registration, Evaluation, Authorisation and Restriction of Chemicals
SEA	Strategic Environmental Assessment
UNCLOS	United Nations Convention on the Law of the Sea
VOC	Volatile Organic Compound
WBRU	Wild Birds Regulation Unit
WEEE	Waste Electrical and Electronic Equipment

General Introduction

§1. General Information

I. Geography

1. The Republic of Malta[1] is made up of an archipelago of six islands. Malta, the largest, where the capital Valletta is situated, has an area[2] of about 246 km^2 and a shoreline of about 136.8 km, and Gozo is the second largest island, situated some 8 km to the northwest of the island of Malta. Gozo has an area[3] of about 67 km^2 and a shoreline of 45 km. Comino is one of the smaller islands; nevertheless, it has a small number of permanent residents. It lies between the islands of Malta and Gozo.[4] It has an area of about 6 km^2 and a shoreline of about 7.5 km.

The other islands, which are all uninhabited, are Cominotto, a fairly large islet-rock on the west side of Comino, St Paul's Islands or Selmunett on the northern side of the mainland of Malta. These two islands together are about 1 km in length and about 200 m wide. Finally, Filfla, a tiny islet, lies about 3 km off Malta's southern coast. It is about 400 m long and about 250 m wide. Filfla is a nature reserve.[5] Manoel Island, an island within Marsamxett harbour, separated from the mainland of Malta by a sea passage only a few metres wide, is considered to be part of the mainland. The Maltese Islands lie within the European continental shelf and are situated almost in the centre of the Mediterranean Sea.[6]

2. Malta has a Mediterranean climate with an average annual precipitation of 530 mm, with, broadly speaking, 70% of this amount occurring in the wet period,

1. Latitude 34.48 and 36.05° North; Longitude 14.11 and 14.35° East.
2. Length northwest to southeast 27.3 km; width southwest to northeast 14.5 km.
3. Length 14.5 km; width 7.2 km.
4. About 2 km to the northwest of Malta; about 1 km to the southeast of Gozo.
5. About 450 m long, 225 m wide. Access to it is prohibited except with a ministerial permit, which can be granted solely for scientific research reasons.
6. The distance from the southernmost tip of Sicily is 96 km; the nearest point in Tunisia is 288 km away and in Libya 320 km away. Malta is 1,826 km away from the Strait of Gibraltar and 1,510 km away from Port Said. Malta claims a territorial sea of 12 nautical miles, a contiguous zone of 24 nautical miles, and a fishing zone of 25 nautical miles from its baselines. Malta has not declared an exclusive economic zone, and the definition of its continental shelf remains suspended due to the fact that it has still not reached an agreement with the neighbouring countries on the matter. The delimitation of its shelf with Libya was determined by the International Court of Justice, when the two States decided to settle their dispute before it. *See ICJ Reports* 29.34 (1985).

namely during the months of October to March. The mean monthly temperature range is 12–26°C. The islands are very windy and sunny.

3. Malta has no natural resources other than the earth and limestone, which is quarried, and the sea. Natural water resources depend on percolating rainwater, which collects in limestone aquifers. Desalination supplements groundwater abstraction in order to satisfy the demand for water consumption. Original natural vegetation is very scarce. Considering their tiny size, aridity, over-population, and the limited range of habitats as a result thereof, the islands have a rich and diverse wildlife with around 2,000 species of plants and more than 3,000 species of animals recorded to date. A relatively large number of species are endemic. The main ecosystems are maquis, garigue and steppe. Others include patches of woodland, coastal wetlands, sand dunes, freshwater and rupestral communities, as well as those found in caves.

II. Population, Social and Cultural Characteristics

4. The Maltese population is really a mixture of populations, mainly the result of intermarriage between the various races and cultures which have, at one time or another, colonised the islands. In prehistory, the islands were settled by at least three different races of people. Despite foreign domination, the Maltese have succeeded in developing unique characteristics, especially a culture and a language, which differ from those of other countries that surround them. Evidence of human presence on the islands dates back to around 3,000 BC.

Mass emigration commenced by the beginning of the twentieth century and reached a peak around the 1960s[7] when it was even encouraged by the government of the day to ease the population problem, as Malta did not provide enough work for all its inhabitants. From the 1980s, emigration dropped to under 1,000 persons a year and has been decreasing steadily. Malta's population increased to 516,100 in 2020, an increase of 0.3%, compared to 2019, with net migration decreasing by 94.1%. During 2020, most of the net migration consisted of 1,237 European Union (EU) nationals and 336 Maltese nationals, with negative net migration registered for third-country nationals.[8]

5. The language of the Maltese Islands is Maltese, which has Semitic roots. There are no indigenous minorities, but immigration from the EU and third countries to support the workforce has grown exponentially in these last few years. The literacy rate is around 95%, although it varies according to the age group. In Malta, education is free and compulsory until the age of 16.

6. As issues relating to the environment have strong sociological implications, one must assess the relationship between the Maltese and the environment and all the implications connected therewith. The public expresses a strong interest in the

7. With around 9,000 emigrants each year.
8. Malta Economic Survey 2021, Executive Summary.

environment, and so do the politicians, although this interest is focused mainly on the need to curb urban development and embellishment issues rather than environmental protection per se. Nevertheless, there is an ever-growing impetus towards preserving the environment as an essential aspect of a good quality of life, and the sustainability of natural resources has been increasingly prioritised in the last five years. Above all, environmental non-governmental organisations (NGOs) have become increasingly active and well-organised. Environmental education, introduced in the mid-1990s, is provided in secondary and tertiary education. The environmental permitting system has been developing steadily since 2008, with a steady increase in integrated pollution prevention and control (IPPC) permits, operational environmental permits, and registrations. While environmental impacts as a result of agricultural activity seem to have declined overall due to the regulatory regime and good farming practices in the sector, the agricultural sector itself is in steady decline, and this may have negative environmental impacts such as land abandonment or alternative forms of development of agricultural land that have become increasingly attractive.

7. Consumer spending is strong, and one cannot say there is any form of culture to choose environment-friendly products, although targets on recycling and less energy-intensive equipment are changing this trend. Public health services are free of charge, and the welfare state provides a high standard of social services. Most Maltese own the houses they reside in. The household size of the Maltese Islands has been steadily decreasing in recent years. Consequently, there is a need for increased provision of services, amenities, housing, transport, and other needs which affect the natural and social environment, especially as a decrease in household size without a similar increase in household mobility will further impinge on the scarce land resources.[9] Maltese homes are, in general, fairly comfortable with appropriate sanitation facilities and many electrical appliances.

III. Legal and Political Structure

8. Malta is a Republic with a written constitution that has as its basic principles the basic rights and freedoms; namely, personal liberty, the right to a free trial, property rights, and freedom of opinion, of assembly, and of organisation. The Constitution guarantees that any person who alleges that his fundamental rights and freedoms have been, are being, or are likely to be contravened in relation to him,[10] may, without prejudice to any other action with respect to the same matter that is lawfully available, apply to the Civil Court, First Hall for redress. The Constitution also guarantees the separation of powers and upholds the social and cultural rights

9. Victor Axiak et al., *State of the Environment Report for Malta 1999*, 9 (Malta Council for Science and Technology 1999).
10. Or such other person as the Civil Court, First Hall, in Malta may appoint at the instance of any person who so alleges.

of any individual. These social and cultural rights are fundamental to the governance of the country and the aim of the State,[11] but they are not enforceable before a court of law.

9. The legislative power is vested in Parliament and is exercised by bills passed by the House of Representatives (the unicameral legislature) and assented to by the President of the Republic.[12] Such instruments are called Acts of Parliament. The Constitution is the supreme law of the land, followed by specific laws that are given superior status to other laws in the sense that their provisions prevail in the case of any inconsistency with other laws (excluding the Constitution).[13] It should also be noted that EU law has, in appropriate cases, a direct effect in Malta and is afforded the benefit of supremacy over national law. Parliament enacts laws through Acts of Parliament, which, if not being amending Acts, are referenced numerically in chronological order as Chapters of the Laws of Malta. The 'general law' is mostly found in the five Codes.[14] Parliament may delegate its legislative authority to the government, where it is specifically so stated in an Act of Parliament. Such legal instruments are referred to as subsidiary legislation and are generally published as Regulations under enabling Acts. Regulations appear as legal notices in the *Government Gazette* according to the date and year of issue. They are referenced numerically as subsidiary legislation, with the first digits bearing the Chapter number of the enabling Act under which they were published.

The Constitution also provides for certain instances where the President shall act in accordance with his own deliberate judgment.[15] The Head of Government is the Prime Minister, and Ministers charged with responsibility for any department of the government shall exercise general direction and control over the said government department. All Ministers bear parliamentary responsibility and are duty-bound to reply to questioning in parliamentary sessions, thus ensuring cohesion between the Legislature and the Ministries. Subject to the direction and control of the Ministries, a department may be brought under the supervision of a Permanent Secretary. Although the government in Malta is centralised, local councils have been established since 1993. Their power is still limited but is set to grow in the future. One of their main functions to date is waste collection and public cleansing.

10. The Constitution guarantees the independence of the Judiciary from the Legislature and the Executive, with the power to review legislation and to declare it null

11. Article 21, the Constitution of Malta.
12. Constitution Art. 72(2). The President, according to the Constitution, 'shall without delay signify that he assents'.
13. Of relevance to this publication are the European Convention Act, Ch. 319 of the Laws of Malta (which transforms the European Convention on Human Rights (ECHR) into Maltese law) and the European Union Act, Ch. 460 of the Laws of Malta (which makes EU law applicable in Malta).
14. These are the Criminal Code, Ch. 9 of the Laws of Malta, the Code of Police Laws, Ch. 10 of the Laws of Malta, the Code of Organisation and Civil Procedure, Ch. 12 of the Laws of Malta, The Commercial Code, Ch. 13 of the Laws of Malta, the Civil Code, Ch. 16 of the Laws of Malta.
15. Constitution s. 85. Examples include the dissolution of Parliament, the appointment and the removal of the Prime Minister, and the Leader of the Opposition.

and void if it is held to be inconsistent with any of the fundamental rights and freedoms of the individual or in the case of subsidiary legislation if it is beyond the scope of the enabling powers in the Parent Act of Parliament.

IV. Economic Characteristics

11. In the first half of 2021, economic activity in Malta grew by 6.9% in nominal terms and by 5.6% in real terms. During the first half of 2021, gross value added in nominal terms registered a growth rate of 6.3% over the same period in 2020. Major recovery was driven by the services sector and, to a lesser extent, by the industrial sector. The twelve-month moving average rate of inflation, as measured by the Retail Price Index, reached 0.78% in August 2021.

12. The Maltese labour market remained robust, even during the COVID-19 pandemic. The employment rate was 74.4%, as opposed to 73.0% in the second quarter of 2020. The at-risk-of-poverty and social exclusion rate for Malta stood at 19.9% in 2020, which was 0.9 percentage points lower when compared to 2019. External trade for Malta is essential in maintaining and improving economic activity, especially considering Malta's dependency on the importation and exportation of goods and services. This is reflected in a substantial increase in both imports and exports of goods in 2019 and the increase in the trade gap over the same period. As for the balance of payments, Malta has enjoyed a current account surplus during the past few years until 2020, when it was severely impacted by the COVID-19 pandemic and its effects on the tourism sector. This contributed towards a larger current account deficit of EUR 425.5 million over the period of January to June 2021.[16]

V. Main Environmental Problems

13. Like many other EU Member States, Malta has strived to reorganise its developmental policies to conform with the need of conserving a healthy environment. As a small island State, Malta's experience in this regard shows that far from being a rhetorical premise, sustainable development for small island States is indispensable. Malta has more than its fair share of environmental problems, but it has only been during these last three decades that public policy became aware of the need to address the problems which impinge upon the natural environment as a result of the brisk expansion in economic activity and the consequent changes in the lifestyle of the Maltese.

There are various socioeconomic drivers that have an impact on Malta's environment. The primary driver is Malta's population density, which increases significantly with seasonal tourism, and it is the root cause of the heavy demands for environmental and infrastructural services and, consequently, the negative impact

16. Malta Economic Survey 2021, Executive Summary.

on the environmental footprint. Population density also causes particular environmental management challenges, especially with respect to road traffic, noise, increased urbanisation, and general disturbances.

There is also a great deal of diversity occurring in the different demographic bands of the Maltese population. The actual native population of Malta is an ageing one. This poses different special needs with respect to consumption as well as investment patterns. In contrast with the decline in the Maltese population, the growth rate of the non-Maltese population has been exponential. These two growing segments of the population, namely the elderly and the non-Maltese, exert a demand for economic goods and social services that may leave an environmental footprint which may be different from that experienced in Malta so far. Combined with population density, land scarcity is another major driver with severe environmental impacts. Malta is the tenth smallest nation in the world, and this situation generates immense pressures caused by construction and the impact of development on virgin land when ironically, there are no successful incentives to promote the rehabilitation of old and vacant buildings. The rate of growth in domestic material consumption has increased at a faster pace than the rate of increase in real gross domestic product. This is indicative of a decline in resource productivity and highlights the urgent need to make more efficient use of resources.

Road transport is another matter of major concern due to the environmental and social impacts of private car use. Malta's car fleet has shifted towards fuel-efficient vehicles, but the use of the private car remains rampant and is one of Malta's biggest environmental challenges in terms of fighting greenhouse gas (GHG) emissions and air pollution, apart from social impacts like congestion and constraints to pedestrian mobility. Malta's tourism sector continued to increase until the start of the COVID-19 pandemic and is already showing signs of recuperating. Given the negative impacts of the pandemic, it will be challenging for this sector, which is a driver of the Maltese economy, to refocus its resurgence to quality rather than quantity to manage better environmental and infrastructural pressures. The increased importance of the tertiary sector within the Maltese economy, although less associated with resource extraction and negative environmental impacts, has driven a further demand for housing, transport, energy and infrastructure demands. According to the State of the Environment Report published by the Environment and Resources Authority (ERA), 'the challenge is to move activities – and infrastructure – from linear extractive/polluting systems to more circular and restorative systems'.[17]

Malta remains heavily dependent on imported fossil fuels (gas) for energy generation, with an increasing share of renewable energy in gross final energy consumption. Recent trends show greater efficiency in fuel usage, mainly due to increased efficiency of electricity production and the generation of energy via the Malta–Sicily interconnector. Any significant increase towards renewable energy generation can happen only if Malta develops offshore renewable energy, but geophysical constraints such as a deepwater continental shelf are a significant stumbling block.

---

17. State of the Environment Report 2018, Environment and Resources Authority, 2018.

A. *Land Use and Coastal Zone Management*

14. Like most islands, Malta's most arduous environmental problem is the misuse of land. The emerging needs of development and an ever-increasing standard of living have largely contributed to piecemeal land development, while a highly profitable building industry and a boom in tourism have exerted further pressure on the government to give up more and more land for urban use.

The coastal area of the Maltese Islands has played a very important role in both the social and economic development of the country and is probably the most important natural resource. The geological formations, in particular the natural harbours, have been extensively used in the past for defence and, lately, for commercial and tourism development. This has given rise to an expansion of settlements along coastal areas, which is mostly evident on the northeast coast. Of particular significance is the concentration of activities, including residential uses, in the Inner Harbour Region. Pressures for development and conflicting uses of these coastal areas are numerous. The most serious problems are major expansion of urban settlements, industrial installations, tourist development, waste and sewage pollution, abandoned agricultural land, active quarries, and threats to natural ecosystems.

Apart from the spread of urbanisation and the negative effects of the leisure industry, the other main problems related to land use include haphazard land reclamation in garigue areas for agricultural purposes when there exists a surplus of fallow land, which could be used alternatively, and the absence of a subject plan for the numerous quarries, which have fallen into disuse. Development Planning Law which regulates land use falls outside the remit of this monograph which focuses on environmental law, but references to it are made as necessary.

B. *Soil Erosion and Climate Change*

15. Soil erosion is also on the increase, mainly as a result of abandoned agricultural land and also as a result of increased aridity and consequent desertification, which appear to be Malta's major threat resulting from the impacts of climate change on the islands. The building sprawl has substantially decreased the number of catchment areas, thus resulting in a greater run-off. Due to a decline in agricultural activity, rubble walls and agricultural land is left to deteriorate. Regulations for the maintenance of rubble walls have been introduced to safeguard these rural structures as 'historical heritage'[18] and to acknowledge their fundamental role in preventing soil erosion. Similarly, water catchment and flood relief projects have greatly improved water harvesting these last few years.

18. L.N. 160/97 (S.L. 552.01), Rubble Walls and Rural Structures (Conservation and Management) Regulations.

C. Loss of Wildlife

16. Public policy and legislation aiming at the protection of habitats have vastly improved in the last decade through the publication of legislation aiming at the protection of natural habitats besides the species occurring in the wild that outline specific rules for the conservation of habitats and the establishment of specially protected areas that form part of the EU Natura 2000 network. No marine conservation areas have yet been established due to difficulties in reconciling the various interested parties. Land is managed according to various management practices, most of which are traditional.

Agriculture was, and to a certain extent still is, one of the most important land management practices of the Maltese Islands. It has influenced biodiversity in various ways, of which the most important are: erection of rubble walls to hold soil and avoid its loss through erosion; transportation of soil from different areas; and introduction of species for their agricultural or horticultural properties. The latter have indeed also led to a drastic reduction of woodlands on fertile valley-bed soils and close to villages. Hence, coastal woodlands found close to traditional fishing villages have been almost eradicated, and many endemic and indigenous species have long become extinct.

Deforestation is, in fact, also a kind of management practice which was widely resorted to in the past to reclaim land for agriculture. It may have been direct (i.e., to reclaim land for agriculture) or indirect (i.e., to obtain timber and firewood). On the contrary, afforestation is relatively recent and occurs in periods with a higher standard of living. For example, the most notorious afforestation scheme of the Maltese Islands, the creation of the *Buskett* woodland, was achieved during the period of the Knights of Malta (1530–1798). Analogously, afforestation projects have been carried out in the Maltese Islands since the Industrial Revolution, although they have increased drastically in the last thirty years. Unfortunately, very often, alien species were employed, notably acacias and eucalyptus trees, species which either became naturalised or were incompatible with the Mediterranean climatic conditions.

17. Animal husbandry and use of fire are other widely employed traditional management practices. Goats, sheep, cattle, and rabbits have been utilised for various reasons. Their most direct impact has been on the landscape with the reduction of forest cover to the more grazing-resistant maquis and garigue. This has led to the use of fire to clear the grazing-resistant vegetation and obtain more nutrient-rich soils. The combination of fire and grazing has led to drastic changes in the Maltese Islands, and further loss of tree cover is probably attributable to this combination of fire and grazing. Nowadays, due to improved socioeconomic aspects in the Maltese Islands, animal husbandry is on the decline, as are goat and sheep numbers. Nevertheless, burning is still a management practice of farmers to reclaim land for agriculture, obtain richer soils, and as a way to capture pests.

18. A high population density in itself creates a considerable stress on natural habitats and their biota. Local wildlife has also been exploited since time immemorial, and in most cases, the rate at which individuals are removed from the population is well above the rate at which they are replaced. Many species are over-exploited and are hence declining. Contributing factors include the use of indiscriminate methods of collection, such as fine mesh nets, which capture target and non-target species alike; collection for commercial purposes, as is the case of several species of wild flowers and reptiles; and collection for private use, as is the case of birds, which are shot to be stuffed and of species bearing decorative shells.

Due to the islands' aridity, freshwater communities are also over-exploited. Water sources have been diverted for human use, mainly irrigation and commercial exploitation. The abandonment of agriculture and changing agricultural practices are also resulting in a severe habitat loss, as dry stone walls and field verges provide important habitats. Some species associated with agricultural uses are threatened, if not extinct, while on the positive side, this has permitted the regeneration of maquis associations.

Sometimes ignorance and persecution are also a cause of loss of biodiversity. Disturbance due to human activities has also resulted in a continuously changing environment which favours the spread of alien species, often at the expense of indigenous flora and fauna.

D. *Waste Management*

19. In Malta, it is estimated that each family produces around 1,000 tonnes of waste each year. Construction waste, which accounts for 80% of waste generated annually, is now being legally addressed, and various initiatives to recycle it have been introduced. Malta's small size imposes a limit as to how much waste can be recycled or reused in an environmentally sound manner.

This situation accentuates the need for further cooperation with the international community, as waste export arrangements may be a good alternative. Malta is a Party to the Basel Convention on the Transboundary Movement of Hazardous Wastes and their Disposal. As waste collection has always been free of charge, introducing an environmentally friendly waste management culture with the general public and industry was not easy, but waste separation schemes introduced on a voluntary basis are increasingly being adhered to. A long-term Waste Management Plan 2021–2030 has been launched. The Plan has three key priority areas: waste prevention as a priority aiming at resource efficiency and to entice waste generators to minimise their waste by providing a range of measures to incentivise greener processes and nudge behavioural change towards smarter consumption patterns. The second key priority area is waste collection reform for unpreventable waste which is unpreventable, via efficient collection systems that will encourage source separation to minimise residual waste. The third key priority area is waste management and resource optimisation, which aims to support Malta's transition towards a more resource-efficient and circular economy.[19]

Compliance with EU legislation has also served to improve the management of waste, even if Malta's economies of scale render very costly and practically difficult to meet the recovery and recycling targets imposed by EU legislation. Despite these efforts, trends show that waste from households is still on the increase.

E. Pollution Control

20. EU legislation has served to increase coordination among the various entities regulating pollution control in Malta: namely the ERA, the Malta Resources Authority (MRA) and the Public Health Department, to mention a few. Legislation on integrated pollution control has also been introduced. EU air quality and water quality directives have filled in serious legal lacuna that existed previously, whereby particular sectors were either scarcely regulated or not regulated at all. Monitoring is carried out but not as intensively as necessary due to lack of human resources in the supporting structures. Although the situation is improving, the key limitation of the monitoring regimes carried out to date is that of continuity.

F. Data Collection, Administrative Cooperation, and Enforcement

21. One of the most serious shortcomings that are still being faced by environment policymakers is the lack of data or its fragmentation as it is housed in different public entities, which renders monitoring results more often than not incompatible. The setting up of the Malta Environment and Planning Authority (MEPA) through a merger between the Environment Protection Department (EPD) and the Planning Authority (PA) in 2002 served to eliminate duplication and lack of cooperation between the two different public entities that both had a regulatory role to play with respect to the protection of the environment. Nevertheless, the conflicts between developmental policies and environmental policies have, at times, remained even within MEPA itself.

In fact, in 2016, these two entities were once again demerged, and the PA and the ERA were established under two separate Acts of Parliament, namely the Development Planning Authority Act (Chapter 551 of the Laws of Malta) and the Environment Protection Act (EPA; Chapter 549 of the Laws of Malta). These Acts gave autonomy to the environment authority to have its own rules and procedures and to be a separate legal entity with various rights and obligations.

19. https://meae.gov.mt/en/Public_Consultations/MECP/Pages/Consultations/LongTermWasteManagementPlan20212030.aspx#:~:text=The%20Waste%20Management%20Plan%20sets%20out%20a%20number,as%20an%20update%20on%20where%20we%20stand%20today.

In daily practice, Memoranda of Understanding exist and regulate the roles between entities responsible for the environment with the aim of creating a one-stop-shop for operators, streamlining bureaucracy, and saving time. Due to the horizontal nature of environmental law and policy, this kind of integrated approach is not always as easy in practice.

§2. Historical Background

22. The first major step towards organised environmental awareness and conservation came with the enactment of the EPA in 1991, which provided the framework for the establishment of the EPD and the ministerial power to enact subsidiary legislation on a wide range of environmental issues, and which introduced criminal penalties for any person convicted of breaching such subsidiary legislation. The 1992 Development Planning Act (DPA), enacted a year later, provided for the setting up of a PA, which was responsible for development planning and policy as guided by the Structure Plan. The latter was in itself a legal instrument. For the first time ever, therefore, the development process was not left solely in the hands of landowners and developers, but there was an attempt to create a legal framework which had as its ultimate objective the reconciliation of developmental needs with the conservation of a healthy environment.

23. The EPA and the DPA were indispensable tools in turning the tide to force the politicians and policymakers of the day to adopt a more professional approach in their formulation of national strategies to protect the environment. Both the EPA and the DPA, in fact, served to introduce subsidiary legislation and guidelines to regulate and organise human activities in an environmentally friendly manner. Short-term priorities and the appeasement of sectoral interest groups, however, often led to the postponement of tough decisions in the 1990s that led to the exacerbation of certain problems such as waste management, habitat conservation, water resource management, and transport. The Maltese, in general, fail to realise that sound environmental standards have socioeconomic consequences for the population, which cannot be dispensed with or ignored simply because they are costly or inconvenient. Hence, although the 1991 EPA had as its basic characteristics the polluter pays and the preventive principles, as well as the precautionary approach and the concept of sustainable development, the subsidiary legislation issued thereunder did not do much to implement these characteristics and apply them in practice. Similarly, the DPA, when it set up the PA, attempted to organise and regulate development to render it sustainable; nevertheless, it was often accused of stalling development and impeding landowners from enjoying their property rights. The DPA was amended a number of times, while the 1991 EPA was repealed and replaced by a new Act in 2001. The Environment and Planning Development Act adopted in 2010 repealed and replaced both Acts and merged the PA and the environment department, and such a new entity started to be referred to as the MEPA.[20] Further changes

20. Vide Ch. 502 of the Laws of Malta.

occurred in 2016 when these two entities were demerged once again, and as indicated above, two separate Acts were adopted to set up these two Authorities.

24. The legislative framework relating to environmental protection in Malta was, until the beginning of the twenty-first century, lacking in providing a holistic approach to safeguard the environment. Although environmental policymaking in the second half of this decade has considerably improved, lack of enforcement is another major flaw that characterises Maltese law in general. Implementation, compliance, and enforcement in environmental law are still a challenge, and judicial remedies are lengthy procedures. The enactment of the 1991 EPA and all the other Acts in 2001, 2010, and more recently in 2016 served as the primary tool to give the legislator the required *vires* to issue subsidiary legislation as need be (i.e., to reflect the change in technological development and socioeconomic trends), to address general and specific situations, and, above all, to impose criminal responsibility with respect to any offences against the environment. It thus generated a sense of public responsibility towards the environment and introduced in Maltese legislation the concept of damages to the environment per se. Furthermore, with the enactment of the 2016 Act, this responsibility towards the protection of the environment has been strengthened, and both the regulator as well as operators and the public in general have been given both rules and obligations to promote and safeguard our surrounding environment at all times.

25. Environmental policymaking in Malta, however, can be traced back even earlier than the first EPA of 1991. The Government of Malta began to address the protection of environment per se in the late 1970s as a follow-up to the 1972 Stockholm Conference on the Human Environment and to the Barcelona Convention on the Protection of the Mediterranean Sea against Pollution. Environmental protection was then the responsibility of the Minister for Health, who set up a division for environmental protection within the Department of Public Health by appointing a small number of desk officers. In 1985, environmental protection became part of the portfolio of the Ministry for Education. An institute was established, namely the Institute of Design for Environmental Action (IDEA), which had as its mandate the synchronisation of all fields of environmental action to come up with a blueprint for the environment and which was to be representative of the State, the citizens in their individual capacity, and NGOs. This holistic approach was based on three strategic elements as the basis of a pyramidal structure: first, the promotion of aesthetics and health within society; second, this leads to a sense of security and peace as – third – the indispensable ingredients to achieve social stability and prosperity. The ultimate aim of IDEA was that these elements would not be compromised for the sake of political expediency.

26. In 1987, when a new government took office, environmental protection remained part of the portfolio of the Ministry for Education, but this time focus was laid particularly on the drafting of a law to do away once and for all with the fragmented and piecemeal regulation of environmental protection. This new law, the EPA of 1991, was an enabling law meant to be comprehensive by laying down the general legal principles relating to environmental protection. The adoption of the basic environmental legal principles had to be backed up by the setting up of structures and the conferment of powers for these structures to implement and enforce law. At the same time, its enabling provisions were meant to ensure flexibility such that regulations could be drafted to address sectoral environmental problems in detail, keeping up with the latest scientific information. The 1991 EPA also enabled the legislator to issue regulations to transform international obligations arising from international legal instruments to which Malta is a State Party. Perhaps the most innovative features of the 1991 EPA were the duties it bestowed on the government itself to act as the *bonus paterfamilias* in issues relating to the protection of the environment for the benefit of present and future generations. The duty to take the necessary remedial and preventive measures pertained to the government. It was not only the Minister for Environment who had the right to initiate legal proceedings in case of infringement of Regulations issued under the 1991 EPA, but also any Minister who is responsible for matters which the regulations in question address. The Minister responsible for environmental protection, however, always had the power to intervene if other Ministers did not.

As far back as 1991, the EPA provided for an action for environmental damages, apart from any criminal and civil action instituted against the offenders. The EPA also provides an official responsible for the environment to whom the Minister may delegate his powers. A year before the coming into force of the Act, in 1990, a Parliamentary Secretary for the Environment was appointed, whose functions are akin to those of a junior Minister. In 1992, the Secretariat for Environment Protection became part of a new Ministry for the Environment, which, apart from environmental protection, was also responsible for public works. In 1993, the official for environmental protection was appointed as the Director of the EPD. The Department thus became the administrative arm of the Secretariat for Environment Protection, supporting it by issuing policies and regulations and seeing to the enforcement of the same.

27. The Secretariat for the Environment ceased to exist in 1996, and the EPD came to form part of a new Ministry, namely the Ministry for Foreign Affairs and the Environment, following a change in government. As evident, the main reason for the coupling of environmental protection with foreign affairs was the particular nature of environmental protection which, as an issue, transcends national boundaries. The new Ministry appointed a group of experts to form part of the Consultative and Advisory Board on the Environment (CABE). The idea behind the CABE was for the Minister to have expert advice that was free from political pressures. The Ministry worked particularly on balancing the various interests in the sectoral aspects of environmental protection to ensure that the needs of social development are not undermined by strict environmental policies and vice versa. Furthermore, it sought to continue building upon the environmental education campaign and to ensure administrative coordination by drafting the Contingency Action Plan against Pollution and publishing the State of the Environment Report. It also commenced the process of reviewing the EPA to amend or redraft it and strengthen the EPD.

28. In 1998, following another change in government, the EPD became part of a new Ministry for the Environment, which also encompassed in its portfolio major construction projects and public works. This Ministry's mandate was in keeping with the particular historic moment Malta was facing, with its application for membership of the EU that occurred on 1 May 2004. Consequently, the main task of the Ministry and the Department for Environment Protection was the harmonisation of Malta's environmental legislation with that of the *acquis communautaire*. This entailed primarily the drafting of a new EPA and new Regulations and also embarking upon an ambitious capacity-building exercise such that the EPD would adequately deal with this new phase which Malta's environmental legislation was going through. The aim of the Ministry was to instil once and for all an integrated approach with respect to environmental protection, to ensure creative sub-divisions in the environmental sector, to promote environmental information and education, and to keep up with international developments on the subject.

29. A new EPA repealing the 1991 Act was promulgated in 2001. The 2001 EPA was the legal instrument via which the vast majority of the environmental *acquis communautaire* was transposed. It was also an enabling law which sought to update its predecessor by introducing new environmental concepts, such as public participation and access to information in environmental decision-making. It was more scientifically oriented and gave wider enabling powers to the Minister for the Environment. It institutionalised the Competent Authority for environmental protection, listing its functions[21] and established a non-executive Commission for Sustainable Development.[22] It also established an Environment Fund whose chair had the power to take an action for environmental damages on behalf of the government.[23] It bestowed upon the inspectors for environmental protection executive powers,[24] which, as stated above, have never been used, and introduced the possibility of out-of-court settlement procedures. Shortly after the 2001 EPA was enacted in September 2001, a new Competent Authority, namely the MRA, was established by law via the Malta Resources Authority Act[25] to regulate energy, water, and mineral resources. In December 2001, a merger between the PA and the EPD was announced, and the MEPA was established by law in 2002 as the Competent Authority for the purposes of the 2001 EPA. MEPA thus came to be regulated by both the EPA and the DPA. The DPA regulated its Development Planning Directorate, while the EPA regulated its Environment Protection Directorate. The EPA established what the functions of the Competent Authority regulating the environment were, but the structure of MEPA and its board and chairman continued to be regulated by the DPA.

30. In 2008, following a new legislature, MEPA was assigned to the Prime Minister's portfolio, while resources and climate change fell under the Ministry for Resources and Rural Affairs. This development was largely due to increased calls for the restructuring of MEPA by the general public, mainly due to discontent with

21. Article 7 of the 2001 EPA.
22. Article 8 of the 2001 EPA.
23. Article 24 of the 2001 EPA.
24. Article 25 of the 2001 EPA.
25. MRA Act (Ch. 423 of the Laws of Malta).

MEPA's role in granting controversial development permits and its over-bureaucratic character. This prompted the new legislature to embark on a restructuring process with the aid of a vast public consultation process that was supposed to be finalised by the end of 2007 but was not: the Bill for the Environment and Development Planning Act was endorsed by the Parliament only in the spring of 2010. The proposed changes aimed at allowing the organisation to focus on its core responsibilities and to implement better regulation in environmental and development planning. It was the government, through the Ministry responsible for environment and development planning, that would be responsible for policy decisions in these fields, although MEPA continued to act as adviser accordingly. An Environmental and Planning Policy Unit was set up within MEPA to ensure that government policy is implemented on a technical level. Environment and development planning formed part of the Prime Minister's portfolio, which was assisted by a Parliamentary Secretary. One of the major grounds for criticism levelled towards MEPA over the years was inconsistency in the application and interpretation of policy, particularly in the granting of development permits. The need has long been felt to streamline the development planning process, ensuring better interface between the myriad of policies as well as the need to update them according to current environmental and socioeconomic needs. Consequently, the authorities pledged that MEPA must invest in acquiring the most reasonably complete, updated, and correct information. The reform sought to provide better systems for public notification and participation. This included facilitating and defining access to planning-and/or environment-related information to ensure that the applicants and the general public are provided with a fair and adequate right of review to MEPA's decisions. Additionally, the reform aimed at guaranteeing better accountability at each decision stage. The reform, which was transposed within the Environment and Planning Development Act of 2010, was mainly related to the institutional setup and development planning procedures rather than environmental protection per se. In fact, most of the provisions of the 2001 EPA were retained, but the internal structure of MEPA reflected this merger between environment and development planning, something which was seriously lacking when the two separate directorates of the Authority were regulated by different Acts that were not originally intended for the same competent authority.

31. The adoption of the 2016 EPA, Chapter 549 of the Laws of Malta, set up the new ERA under its Article 6. This brought about a demerger, and MEPA ceased to exist. Instead, the PA and the new ERA were established as separate regulatory entities once more. An authority completely dedicated to the environment made it possible to invest in human resources, in more environmental research, and, most importantly, provided the new entity with its own budget completely dedicated to the safeguarding of the environment. ERA could also take environmental decisions via its Board, which consists of not less than eight and not more than ten members, of whom one shall be the Chairperson of the Authority.[26] The judicial arm in environmental matters was further strengthened with the setup of the Environment and Planning Review Tribunal (EPRT), established under Chapter 551 of the Laws of

26. EPA Art. 6(1).

Malta in 2016. The EPA of 2016 provides for the appointment of enforcement officers, and their role is spelt out within the Act itself. Furthermore, for the first time, environmental enforcement officers have been given the right to assist the police in the conduct of prosecution for offences under this Act and to plead the case on behalf of the prosecution.[27]

32. The EPA of 2016 reproduces the principal duty to protect the environment that featured in the EPAs of 1999 and 2001. Article 3 stipulates that:

> It shall be the duty of every person and entity, whether public or private, to protect the environment and to assist in the taking of preventive and remedial measures to protect the environment and manage natural resources in a sustainable manner.

Article 4 establishes this obligation on the government and provides a whole list of tasks to manage the environment in a sustainable manner, take preventive and remedial measures, disseminate environmental information, carry out environmental research, ensure the sustainable management of waste and biodiversity, combat all forms of pollution, environmental education, and the carrying out of plans and programmes for the enhancement of the environment. It is good to note that the provisions of Articles 3 and 4 are not directly enforceable in any court because these are principles. These principles are nevertheless declared to be fundamental to the Government of Malta and are to be employed in the interpretation of the other provisions of the Act or of any other law relating to matters governed by the Act.

33. Part III of the Act covers the administrative part; that is, the setup and functions of the Authority. The Authority is to be known as the ERA.[28] This part of the Act and subsequent procedural provisions were transposed mainly from other Acts establishing other authorities and mostly from the Act setting up the PA. The Authority acquired a separate legal personality and succeeded in the functions, assets, rights, liabilities, and obligations of the Competent Authority established under the provisions of Article 6 of the Environment and Development Planning Act and under the provisions of Article 3 of the Malta Resources Authority Act, in so far as such functions, assets, rights, liabilities, and obligations refer to the role of the Competent Authority established under the new EPA in relation to the protection and management of the environment and sustainable management of natural resources and the prevention, mitigation, offsetting, or remediation of adverse effects on the environment.

As for general functions, the Authority has to formulate and implement environmental laws and policies; carry out and/or commission surveys, studies, assessments, investigations, audits; monitor and promote research on any matter relating to the environment; provide information and issue guidelines to the public and to commercial and other entities; and respect national and international obligations and ensure their respective implementation. It also has the role of advising the Minister

27. EPA Art. 75(3).
28. EPA Art. 6.

responsible for the environment on international law and on the formulation of national policy in relation to matters regulated by the Act and on matters having a bearing on this, or to perform such other functions as may from time to time be assigned to it by the Minister. It has the power to permit, assess, investigate, audit, monitor, and take action on any activity, intervention, project, operation, or land use that may have an effect on the environment. The 2016 Act allowed for the first time environmental permits to be decided upon and issued by the Authority, specifically set up for the protection of the environment. Monitoring and enforcement are also led in an autonomous manner by the same Authority.

34. The Authority has its own internal administrative setup, and by virtue of Article 11, the Authority shall, after a public call, appoint a Chief Executive Officer, which shall be for a period of three years and may be extended for further periods of three years each. The Chief Executive Officer shall: be responsible for the implementation of the objectives of the Authority in the exercise of its functions and assume full responsibility for the overall supervision and control of the Directorates; with the approval of the Authority, assign to the Directorates such duties which are by, or in accordance with, the provisions of this Act vested in such Directorates; coordinate the workings of the Directorates; develop the necessary strategies for the implementation of the objectives of the Authority; advise the Authority on any matter it may refer to him or on any matter on which he considers his advice necessary or expedient; and carry out such other functions and duties as the Authority may assign to him from time to time. The Chief Executive Officer has the right to attend meetings of the Board of the Authority to report to the said Board. The Chief Executive Officer may be dismissed by the Authority at any time for a just cause, this being if the Authority determines that he has not achieved the targets and objectives that it has set for him.

35. The day-to-day running of the Authority is carried out by the Directorates. In fact, ERA is subdivided into three Directorates, which are the Environment Protection Directorate, the Compliance and Enforcement Directorate, and the Human Resources Directorate. The Environment Protection Directorate is further subdivided into three sections; namely, the assessment unit, the permitting unit, and the thematic units. The assessment unit carries out the task of a statutory consultant in the development process,[29] namely: development in protected areas under the EPA; development in outside development zone (ODZ) areas; project description statements (PDS); and environment impact assessments (EIAs). The permitting unit deals with four main categories of permitting, namely:

(1) nature permitting: CITES, trees, activities in protected areas, including development;
(2) small-scale industrial permitting: waste management activities, manufacturing, quarries; and

29. S.L. 552.13 identifies ERA as a Statutory Consultant and Ch. 552 nominates an ERA representative on the PA Board and Executive Council.

(3) large-scale industrial permitting: IPPC, landfills, farms, large-scale manufacturing, sewage treatment plants, petrol stations, fish farms; and
(4) low-impact activities: waste carriers, farms.

The Compliance and Enforcement Directorate's role and function is threefold:

(1) Education: Through inspections, they assume an educational role – preventing is better than remediating.
(2) Compliance: Monitoring of permits and monitoring in general. Chances for compliance are given to permit holders and operators to change operations.
(3) Enforcement: When compliance fails, enforcement measures are implemented.

The enforcement tools given under the new Act are the following:

- stop orders;
- compliance orders;
- administrative fines;
- out-of-court settlements;
- criminal prosecutions; and
- direct action.

36. Part V of the 2016 Act stipulates that the protection and effective management of the environment shall be regulated by plans, policies, and regulations, which are prepared and amended from time to time in accordance with the provisions of this Act. These include, for example, the National Strategy for the Environment, the Air Monitoring Plan, and the Waste Management Plan. Articles 53 and 54 bestow the Minister with the power to consult with the Authority to make regulations, rules, orders, lists, schedules, and any other instrument of like nature and includes the power from time to time to revoke, replace, amend, alter, or add to any such instrument as aforesaid.

37. Parts VI and VII of the Act are dedicated to the process of the permit system of the Authority and to the compliance and enforcement powers the Authority has. Article 58 stipulates that no person shall carry out any activity or operation, or be engaged in such activity or operation, relating to or affecting the environment unless such person is in possession of an authorisation from the Authority under this Act. The Authority's officers have the power to carry out inspections, in connection with the permit application process or any ancillary assessment or monitoring, for all authorisation types, including inspections preceding submission, during the processing of applications, and after the taking of a decision. An authorisation shall be granted for a limited period provided that the Authority may, on the application of the person holding the authorisation, extend the said authorisation to such further period or periods as it may consider reasonable. The ERA officers are given the power to inspect and monitor, together with the right of entry,[30] and as indicated above, they have various legal tools which allow them to take enforcement action. Any person who obstructs, threatens, attacks, or impedes any officer of the Authority in the exercise of his duties under this Act shall be guilty of an offence and shall, on conviction, be liable to imprisonment not exceeding three years, to a fine (*multa*) of not more than EUR 100,000, or both such fine and imprisonment.

38. As already indicated above, officers may issue a compliance or a stop order against an operator or against any other individual who is carrying out an activity which goes against any one of the provisions of this Act. Any person who feels aggrieved by any order served on him may, within fifteen days from the service of the order, appeal before the EPRT,[31] and this adjudicating body will decide whether the action taken should be upheld or whether it should be reconsidered by the Authority. Non-observance of such orders also carries with it a daily penalty of not more than EUR 150 for as long as the default lasts, and the Authority may recover such penalty from the said person as a civil debt owing to it.[32] Furthermore, all expenses reasonably incurred by the Authority in the exercise of its powers under this Article, or any other amount due to the Authority under any other provision of this Act or regulations made thereunder shall be recoverable as a civil debt by the Authority from the person against whom the order has been issued, or from any person responsible for the acts mentioned in the order, including an order for payment, or an applicant, subject to such right of recovery such person may have against any other person.[33]

39. Article 80 introduced the concept of administrative fines for environmental breaches. An administrative fine imposed shall not exceed EUR 100,000 for each contravention or EUR 1,500 for each day of non-compliance from the date of the notice of the imposition of the administrative fine given by the Authority. This provision also stipulates that if the infringement is committed by a body corporate and is proved to have been committed with the consent or involvement of, or to be attributable to, any gross negligence on the part of a person being a director, manager, secretary or other officer, however so described, of such body corporate or a person who was purporting to act in any such capacity then such person and such body corporate shall be responsible for the said infringement and shall be jointly and severally liable for the payment of any administrative penalty imposed by the Authority as a consequence thereof. The imposition of the administrative fine has to be followed through a rigorous procedure, and the person against whom such administrative penalty is imposed shall be given a reasonable opportunity to state any views and propose any possible remedies, and he also has the right to file an appeal in front of the EPRT against such decision.[34]

30. EPA Art. 71.
31. EPA Art. 76(9)–(13).
32. EPA Art. 78. Daily penalties are further regulated by L.N. 45/2018, Daily Fines (Environment) Regulations (S.L. 549.72).
33. EPA Art. 79.
34. EPA Art. 81.

40. The 2016 Act introduced on-the-spot fines and out-of-court settlements.[35] Officers may impose on-the-spot fines, not exceeding a maximum amount of EUR 1,000, for offences and to amounts as are prescribed in regulations issued by the Minister. Where the Authority believes that a person has committed an offence against this Act, the Authority may enter into an agreement in writing with such person describing the offence of which the person is accused, indicating the steps to be taken to remedy the offence and a penalty which is agreed to be paid in respect of that offence as shall be prescribed in regulations made by the Minister.[36]

41. Part VIII deals with environmental offences, which include: activities carried out without the required authorisation of the Authority, acts in contravention of any compliance or stop order, attempting to hinder, obstruct, threaten, molest, or interfere with any officer of the Authority (among other officers), or the making of false declarations. Such offenders shall be guilty and liable, on conviction, to a fine (*multa*) of not less than EUR 1,500 and not exceeding EUR 2,500,00 and may also incur a penalty of imprisonment for a term of not less than three months and not exceeding three years. Provided that, and without prejudice to such a maximum fine, the minimum fine (*multa*) to which an offender is liable is not to be less than the value of any work carried out without an authorisation or in violation of any conditions to which such authorisation was subject. The court, besides awarding the punishment, may confiscate the *corpus delicti* where applicable and shall order the offender to remove the causes of the offence and to undo anything which was done without an authorisation or to comply with the conditions imposed in the authorisation, as the case may be, within a time sufficient for the purpose, but in any case not exceeding three months from the date of the judgment, to be fixed by the court. If the offender fails to comply with any such order within the time so fixed, he shall be liable to a fine (*multa*) of not less than EUR 50 and not more than EUR 130, as the court may fix, for every day the default continues after the expiration of the said time, and the court may also order the modification, suspension, or revocation of any authorisation. Proceedings against any person for any offence as mentioned above shall be taken before the Court of Magistrates (Malta) or the Court of Magistrates (Gozo), as the case may be, as courts of criminal judicature in accordance with the provisions of the Criminal Code.[37]

42. Being an Authority, ERA did not only acquire autonomy to regulate and monitor the environmental legal regime, but it also acquired a budget of its own. In fact, one of the main tasks of the Human Resources Department is to manage the Authority's finances and also the necessary recruitment of officers needed for the function of the same Authority. The Authority Board shall so conduct the affairs of the Authority that the expenditure required for the proper performance of its functions shall, as far as practicable, be met out of its revenue. The Authority shall also be paid by the government out of the Consolidated Fund such sums as Parliament

35. EPA Arts 82 and 83.
36. The current regulations in force are L.N. 49/2019, Out of Court Settlement Regulations (S.L. 549.127).
37. EPA Art. 84.

may from time to time authorise to be appropriated to meet the costs of specified works or activities to be continued or otherwise carried out by the Authority. Subject to such directives as the Minister may give from time to time after consultation with the Minister responsible for finance, any excess of revenue over expenditure shall be applied by the Authority to the formation of reserve funds to be used for the purposes of the Authority. The Authority must keep proper accounts and other records in respect of its operations and must prepare a statement of accounts in respect of each financial year. The accounts of the Authority must be audited by an auditor or auditors appointed by the Authority and approved by the Minister. Also, every year the Authority has to present its estimates to Parliament so it can be allocated a budget.[38]

Like the previous Acts, the 2016 EPA has established the Environmental Fund. The Environment Fund is to be administered by the Authority, and it must be used to finance projects, programs, and schemes related to, and costs intended to achieve and manage, the aims and objectives of the Act, studies, as well as works which may be needed for that purpose or to remedy any harm caused to the environment, as the Minister in consultation with the Authority may prescribe.[39]

43. Finally, another innovative provision under the Act is that found under Article 70A dedicated to guardianship deeds. Under this provision, the Minister may, with the prior approval in writing of the Minister responsible for lands, enter by public deed into a guardianship contract with a local council or with an NGO whereby the custody and administration of immovable property are passed over to the local council or NGO, as the case may be, so that it may be used to secure an environmental objective, in accordance with the provisions of the Act and of such regulations as may be prescribed and with such conditions not inconsistent therewith as may be included in the deed. The guardianship deed shall state the term for which it is entered following careful consideration of the feasibility and scale of undertaking of each proposal.

44. The term 'environment' was included for the first time in the text of the Constitution of Malta through the Constitution of Malta (Amendment) Act, which was published on 21 June 2018 as Act XXII of 2018. It amended Article 9 of the Constitution of Malta, which established that 'the State shall safeguard the landscape, the historical and artistic patrimony of the nation', by including a new subparagraph (2) which provides:

> The State shall protect the environment and its resources for the benefit of present and future generations and shall take measures to address any form of environmental degradation in Malta, including that of air, water and land, and any sort of pollution problem and to promote, nurture and support the right of action in favour of the environment.

38. EPA Arts 19–30.
39. EPA Art. 32.

§3. Role of Government Institutions in the Shaping and Administration of Environmental Law and Policy

I. The Environment and Resources Authority

45. The setup of the ERA introduced an autonomous Authority with its own budget, legal personality and legal obligations to adopt and implement environmental rules, plans and policies. Despite such autonomy, it still has to work with other entities that also have a say in environmental issues. The ERA acquired a consultative role in various entities such as the PA and Heritage Malta. By law, it also achieved membership with voting rights on the Planning Authority Board and the Planning Authority Executive Council, and the Lands Authority Board.

The workings of the Authority, such as the State of the Environment Report, and other policies and plans like those of the PA must also pass through the scrutiny of the Standing Committee on the Environment, Climate Change and Development Planning established under Article 60 of the DPA, made up of five members appointed by the House, of whom three shall be members representing the government, one of whom shall be appointed as Chairperson, and the other two shall be members representing the Opposition. In fact, the major role of the Standing Committee is to review any other plan and policy referred to it by the Minister and report thereon to Parliament.

II. The Planning Authority

46. The DPA of 2016 (also referred to as 'New Planning Act' or '2016 Planning Act') gave a new identity to the PA and is now specifically concerned with the use of the land. In fact, Article 3 of the New Planning Act puts the onus on the government '*to enhance the quality of life for the benefit of the present and future generations, without compromising the ability of future generations to meet their own needs, through a comprehensive sustainable land use planning system*'. So, like in the case of the commitment towards a better environment, the government is committed towards good and sustainable planning.

Article 5 of the DPA 2016 provides that the PA shall consist of the Executive Council and the Planning Board. The Executive Council and the Planning Board are vested with different functions, and their respective roles are highlighted in Articles 38 and 64 of the Act. The various functions of the Executive Council are listed in Article 38(1) of the current Act and include, *inter alia*, the provision of a centralised office where all development applications are duly processed by case officers and recommended for either approval or refusal. The Council is also responsible for the carrying out of national mapping together with street alignments/levels. The said roles were previously assumed by the Planning Directorate within the MEPA. Moreover, the Council handles the coordination of enforcement complaints and enforcement operations, which functions were previously handled by the Enforcement Directorate. The Council has the power to issue discontinuance and removal orders as well as to issue scheduling and conservation orders. Plans and policies, minor modifications including planning control applications and development orders, are also formulated by the Executive Council. In the past, it was the MEPA Board which was responsible for these functions. The Council is made up of the Executive Chairperson, who is joined by six other members – the chairperson and deputy chairperson of the Planning Board ex officio, two independent members who shall be appointed by the Minister and two members appointed by the ERA. The latter shall only be present whenever the Executive Council is considering matters related to policies, scheduling and planning control applications. The Superintendent of Cultural Heritage shall be called in when the Council is considering scheduling, conservation orders and emergency conservation orders.[40]

The ERA is also represented on the Planning Board. The Planning Board consists of a chairperson chosen from among five independent members of known integrity and with knowledge and experience in different areas of interest. The other Board members are as follows: one member chosen from among the chairpersons of the Planning Commissions, two members of the House of Representatives nominated by the Prime Minister and the Leader of the Opposition, respectively, a member representing the ERA, a member nominated by environmental NGOs, three public officers and a member chosen by the Local Council who shall sit on the Board when a major project application lies within its boundary. ERA's role on the Board as a voting member is a step ahead compared to the role which the former Environment Directorate had within the MEPA, as this was limited to recommending planning applications for a decision without having a say in the final permit. The functions of the Planning Board are set out in Article 64(a)–(e) of the New Planning Act. Essentially, the Planning Board shall be responsible for the issuing of development permissions, taking over the decision role of the MEPA Board. As was the case with the previous legislation, planning decisions are still subject to an appeal before the EPRT, whose decision shall be final unless an appeal is made to the Civil Court (Inferior Jurisdiction) on a point of law decided by the Tribunal or on any matter relating to an alleged breach of the right of a fair hearing before the Tribunal. Moreover, the Planning Board is now tasked with additional powers, which previously fell outside the parameters of the MEPA's competence. These include the ability to dispense with or allow the relaxation of a requirement of building regulations and the examination of applications for the issuing of licenses of masons and consultants in the building industry. Nevertheless, the Planning Board shall be empowered to decide on such matters once the Minister so decides.[41]

Within the PA setup, there are also the Planning Commissions[42] which are the equivalent of the former Environment and Planning Commissions. The Commissions may determine all planning applications delegated to it by the Planning Board, except for those listed in Article 75 of the 2016 Planning Act. There may be as many number of divisions dealing with different types of applications as the Minister may from time to time prescribe. In contrast with the former Environment and Planning Commission, the number of sitting members was reduced from five to three. The members are appointed for a period of four years, which may be further extended to another four years and may be dismissed in the same manner as the independent

40. Article 36(2) of the Development Planning Act, 2016.
41. Article 35(5) of the Development Planning Act, 2016.
42. Article 65 of the Development Planning Act, 2016.

members sitting on the Planning Board. The quorum of the Commission shall be two, in which case the Chairperson has a second or casting vote.[43] To avoid situations wherein a casting vote would be necessary, the legislator included a supplementary member concurrently with the other three permanent members but who shall only take part in the deliberations when any of the permanent members cannot, for any reasonable cause, properly fulfil his duties. The DPA 2016 also saw the introduction of two Committees – the Agricultural Advisory Committee[44] and the Design Advisory Committee.[45] The PA, like ERA, in consultation with the Minister responsible for planning, has the power to issue regulations, plans and policies. The PA legal regime is strongly based on policies and plans. In fact, currently, the Strategic Plan for the Environment and Development, a key document on which planning policies are based, will begin a review process that will focus on 'intelligent planning and sustainable development'. ERA has a consultative role in this important process.

III. Other Public Institutions That Have a Role in Environmental Protection

47. The MRA[46] was established in 2001 and was responsible for minerals,[47] energy, including renewable energy, climate change mitigation and adaptation, the management of freshwater resources on the Islands, and the effluent of the public sewerage system. This responsibility was changed in 2015 with Act No. XXV of 2015. This Act provides for the establishment of a regulator to be known as the Regulator for Energy and Water Services and for the exercise by or on behalf of that Regulator of regulatory functions regarding services relating to energy and water and to make provision with respect to matters ancillary thereto or connected therewith. However, this Act shall not apply to matters relating to mineral resources, and this shall continue to be regulated by the MRA under the provisions of Article 43 of the same Act.

In 2014, the Energy and Water Agency was set up and legally established via L.N. 340/2016 within the Ministry for Energy, Enterprise and Sustainable Development. The Agency is tasked with formulating and implementing the government's national policies in the energy and water sectors, aimed at ensuring security, sustainability and affordability of energy and water in Malta. Among its various implementation tasks, the Agency also empowers various government entities to align their programmes and objectives to the national energy and water policies and also provides advice on the integration of renewable energy sources in their respective premises. In 2018, the government's commitment towards the better implementation of waste management for the attainment of a circular economy led to the setting up of the Resource Recovery and Recycling Agency. In 2021, an order (L.N. 256 of 2021)

43. Second Schedule Development Planning Act, 2016.
44. Article 66 of the Development Planning Act, 2016.
45. Article 67 of the Development Planning Act, 2016.
46. This Authority is set up by the Malta Resources Authority Act (Ch. 423 of the Laws of Malta).
47. Malta has no minerals except stone and is currently undertaking oil exploration.

was adopted in order to amend the Resource, Recovery and Recycling Agency (Establishment) Order of 2018 (principal order). Under this new order, the 'Resource, Recovery and Recycling Agency' started to be referred to as the 'Circular Economy Malta'.

In 2015, the Climate Action Act was published as Chapter 543 of the Laws of Malta and is Malta's main law on climate change. The Climate Action Act, as an enabling Act, specifies that it aims to contribute to the mitigation of climate change by limiting anthropogenic emissions of GHGs and protecting and enhancing GHG sinks and reservoirs. It also provides legal obligations for coherent and coordinated governance to deal with this challenge on a national level. The Act establishes a Climate Action Board as a body that represents government entities, the academia, business, and civil society, which ensures representation of all sectors of Maltese society in the fight against climate change, even by facilitating stakeholder dialogue. This Act also sets up a Climate Action Fund, which has a separate juridical personality and serves to act as the financial instrument which supports the implementation of the Act, namely measures to abate GHG emissions and to adopt carbon neutral technologies as well as to enhance sinks of such emissions while building a society, whose sectoral components are resilient to climate change.

48. Another Act and institutional setup which helps in promoting environmental enhancement is the Sustainable Development Act, Chapter 521, which was adopted in 2012 and amended by virtue of Act No. I of 2019. The purpose of this Act is to:

- mainstream sustainable development across the workings of the government;
- raise awareness about sustainable development issues and promote the adoption of sustainable practices across society; and
- foster increased participation of civil society as well as of all social actors in mainstreaming sustainable development.

The Sustainable Development Act provides for a system of coordination across public administration. It designates the Permanent Secretaries within each Ministry as Sustainable Development Coordinators and also provides for a Sustainable Development Focal Point in every government department, agency, or entity. The Act also establishes other bodies, such as the Guardian of Future Generations and the Sustainable Development Network, which aim to foster the exchange of views and national dialogue as well as oversee the implementation of sustainable development in Malta.

49. The Malta Maritime Authority, which forms part of Transport Malta, a governmental institution which encompasses transport control of the islands over sea, land, and air, is responsible for maritime affairs, which also include certain environmental aspects such as pollution control in internal waters and shipping standards. The maritime squadron of the Armed Forces of Malta is responsible for the maintenance of law and order in the territorial sea and the contiguous zone. The Public Health Department, which falls under the auspices of the Ministry of Health, is responsible for air quality and water quality from a public health perspective as well as for the reporting and monitoring of air and bathing water quality. The Occupational Health and Safety Authority (OHSA) is responsible for health issues and risks at the workplace. This may involve responsibility for the regulation of handling certain chemicals and other environmental quality issues. The Rural Affairs Department, falling under the auspices of the Ministry Minister for Agriculture, Fisheries, Food and Animal Rights, is responsible for agricultural policy, agro-industry, veterinary services, forestry, the importation and use of pesticides, and the management of certain natural resources such as soil and sand. The Department of Fisheries and Aquaculture, also falling under the auspices of the same Ministry, is responsible for marine life for harvesting purposes, fishing methods, and aquaculture. The Department for Civil Protection is responsible for coordinating matters during national emergencies, including environmental emergencies such as major oil spills. Set up by the Local Councils Act,[48] Local Councils have functions which impact the environment related to the provision for the collection and removal of refuse from public or private places, the maintenance of receptacles for the temporary deposit and collection of waste,[49] and the littering regulations. They also may make recommendations to any Competent Authority for or in relation to any planning or building scheme.

§4. Sources of Environmental Law

50. All legal sources in Malta are in written form. The Constitution is the supreme law of the land, followed by specific laws that are given superior status to other laws in the sense that their provisions prevail in the case of any inconsistency with other laws (excluding the Constitution).[50] It should also be noted that EU law has, in appropriate cases, a direct effect in Malta and is afforded the benefit of supremacy over national law. The 'general law' is mostly found in the five Codes, these being the Criminal Code, the Civil Code, the Code of Police Laws, the Code of Organisation and Civil Procedure (COCP), and the Commercial Code.

Acts of Parliament, also known as primary legislation, are enacted by Parliament. Primary legislation may enable and delegate power to Ministers to subsidiary legislation, usually in the form of regulations, which constitutes the bulk of the legal sources relating to environmental protection in Malta. Legislation, whether primary or subsidiary, is published in the *Government Gazette*.

Apart from the legal requirement under the Ratification of Treaties Act[51] that some treaties require an Act or a Resolution of Parliament, it is generally recognised that legal obligations arising from international legal instruments to which Malta is a Party must be transformed into national legislation to be enforceable by the courts as part of the law of the land. These environmental treaty obligations are transformed into national law via subsidiary legislation mainly published under the

48. Chapter 363 of the Laws of Malta. Local Councils are a body corporate established by law, considered to be an agency of the government.
49. *Ibid.*, s. 38.
50. Of relevance to this publication are the European Convention Act, Ch. 319 of the Laws of Malta (which transforms the ECHR into Maltese law) and the European Union Act, Ch. 460 of the Laws of Malta (which makes EU law applicable in Malta).
51. Chapter 304 of the Laws of Malta.

EPA. As most of the EU environmental *acquis communautaire* is made up of directives, subsidiary legislation is also used to transpose EU environmental directives. EU regulations are directly applicable by the courts and have a direct effect on Maltese subjects.

51. The main source of environmental law in Malta is the EPA, an enabling law that gives the Minister responsible for the environment the power to publish legislation according to the parameters set in its provisions. The EPA is in itself a framework Act meant to be supplemented by the vast number of subsidiary legislation that has been issued thereunder. It is based on a number of principles that enshrine the keystones of international and EU environmental law, namely: the government's ultimate responsibility for environmental protection and the sustainable use of natural resources, responsibility for environmental harm, the preventive approach and the precautionary principle, and the individual's access to environment information and participation in environment decision-making.

The EPA allows the Minister to issue subsidiary legislation in draft form and to subject it to public consultation for four weeks before it becomes law. During the consultation period, any person may send objections or make recommendations regarding the proposed draft legislation, which the Minister must then take into consideration. It is the Minister who has the final say in accordance with the Constitution since his powers to issue legislation have been directly delegated to him by Parliament. In emergency situations, the Minister may issue the legislation without prior consultation, but the public consultation period commences immediately after publication and is extended to six weeks.

As already indicated above, the EPA also provides for the institutional setup that is responsible for environmental protection. The Act refers to an authority that is mainly responsible for environmental protection and also establishes its functions. Currently, this is ERA. The EPA, however, empowers the Minister to bestow regulatory functions to any other public authority as appropriate to ensure that regulations issued thereunder are complied with and enforced. This was done to ensure that there would be no duplication of roles, given the horizontal nature of environmental issues. Such an arrangement permits, for example, that the OHSA is the regulator for certain harmful substances such as asbestos, the Malta Competition and Consumer Affairs Authority is responsible for type approval of machinery and biocides, the MRA is responsible for groundwater resources, and the Public Health Department is responsible for the bathing water quality.

52. The following are the most important sources of environmental law:

(1) General

The Criminal Code, Chapter 9 of the Laws of Malta.
The Code of Police Laws, Chapter 10 of the Laws of Malta.
The Civil Code, Chapter 16 of the Laws of Malta.
The Environment Protection Act, Chapter 549 of the Laws of Malta.
The Development Planning Act, Chapter 552 of the Laws of Malta.

The Environment and Planning Review Tribunal Act, Chapter 551 of the Laws of Malta
The Sustainable Development Act, Chapter 521 of the Laws of Malta
The Climate Action Act, Chapter 543 of the Laws of Malta
The Ports and Shipping Act, Chapter 352 of the Laws of Malta.
The Malta Resources Authority Act, Chapter 423 of the Laws of Malta.
The Occupational Health and Safety Act, Chapter 424 of the Laws of Malta.
The Civil Protection Act, Chapter 411 of the Laws of Malta.
The Ratification of Treaties Act, Chapter 304 of the Laws of Malta.
The Authority for Transport in Malta Act, Chapter 499 of the Laws of Malta.
The Malta Standards Authority Act, Chapter 419 of the Laws of Malta.
The Malta Competition and Consumer Affairs Authority Act, Chapter 510 of the Laws of Malta.
The Regulator for Energy and Water Services Act, Chapter 545 of the Laws of Malta.
The Convention on Biological Diversity (Incorporation) Regulations, L.N. 160/2002 (S.L. 549.27).
The Crimes Against the Environment Act Chapter 522, Laws of Malta

(2) Protection of Trees and Other Flora

The Antiquities Act, Chapter 54 of the Laws of Malta.
The List of Historical Trees having an Antiquarian Importance Order, G.N. 269/33 (S.L. 445.02).
The Conifer Trees (Preservation) Regulations, G.N. 328/49 (S.L. 10.22).
The Protection of the Wild Thyme Regulations, G.N. 85/32 (S.L. 10.10).
The Flora, Fauna and Natural Habitats Protection Regulations, L.N. 311/2006 (S.L. 549.44).
The Plant Quarantine Act, Chapter 433 of the Laws of Malta.
The Forest Law Enforcement, Governance and Trade Licensing Scheme Regulations, L.N. 115/2015 (S.L. 549.95).
The Timber and Timber Products (Placing on the Market) Regulations, L.N. 79/2015 (S.L. 549.94).
The Trees and Woodlands Protection Regulations, L.N. 258/2018 (S.L. 549.123).

(3) Protection of Fauna

Conservation of Wild Birds Regulations, L.N. 79/2006 (S.L. 549.42).
Conservation of Wild Birds (Falconry) Regulations, L.N. 249/2016 (S.L. 549.106).
Conservation of Wild Birds (Framework for Allowing a Derogation for the Control of Birds in the Interest of Air Safety) Regulations, L.N. 255/2013 (S.L. 549.85).
Conservation of Wild Birds (Framework for Allowing a Derogation Opening an Autumn Live-Capturing Season for Song Thrush and Golden Plover) Regulations, L.N. 303/2012 (S.L. 549.74).

Conservation of Wild Birds (Framework for Allowing a Derogation to Carry out Scientific Research on Seven Finch Species) Regulations, L.N. 394/2021 (S.L. 549.145).
Control of Invasive Alien Species of European Union Concern Regulations, L.N. 337/2017 (S.L. 549.119).
Framework for Allowing a Derogation Opening a Spring Hunting Season for Turtle Dove and Quail Regulations, L.N. 221/2010 (S.L. 549.57).
Importation of Skins of Certain Seal Pups and Derived Products Regulations, L.N. 335/2001 (S.L. 549.20).
Marine Mammals Protection Regulations, L.N. 203/2003 (S.L. 549.35).
Protection of Wild Rabbit Regulations, L.N. 207/2014 (S.L. 549.90).
Reptiles (Protection) Regulations, L.N. 76/1992 (S.L. 549.02).
Species Protection (Designation of Natural Species) Regulations, L.N. 25/2018 (S.L. 549.120).
Stony Sea Urchin Protection Regulations, L.N. 149/2023 (S.L. 549.157).

(4) Trade in species of Flora and Fauna

Trade in Species of Fauna and Flora Regulations, L.N. 236/2004 (S.L. 549.38)

(5) The Conservation of Fisheries

The Fisheries Conservation and Management Act, Chapter 425 of the Laws of Malta.
The Explosives Ordinance, Chapter 33 of the Laws of Malta.
The Territorial Waters and Contiguous Zone Act, Chapter 226 of the Laws of Malta.
Continental Shelf Act, Chapter 535 of the Laws of Malta.
Exclusive Economic Zone Act, Chapter 625 of the Laws of Malta.
Fishery Regulations, G.N. 206/1934 (S.L. 425.01).
Management of the Lampara Fishery Order, L.N. 407/2013 (S.L. 425.11).

(6) Nature Reserves

Establishment of the *Park Nazzjonali tal-Inwadar* Regulations, L.N. 343/2016 (S.L. 549.109).
Establishment of the *Majjistral*, Nature and History Park Regulations, L.N. 251/2007 (S.L. 549.48).
Filfla Nature Reserve Act, Chapter 323 of the Laws of Malta.
Fungus Rock (*Ġebla tal-Ġeneral*) Nature Reserve Regulations, L.N. 22/1992 (S.L. 549.01).
Il-Ponta tal-Qawra Nature Reserve Regulations, L.N. 240/2022 (S.L. 549.150).
Majjistral Nature and History Park Site Regulations, L.N. 217/2013 (S.L. 549.83).
Selmunett Islands (St. Paul Islands) Nature Reserve Regulations, L.N. 25/1993 (S.L. 549.03).

(7) Hazardous and Controlled Substances

Activities concerning the Professional Use of Toxic Products Rules, L.N. 350/2005 (S.L. 430.06).

Aerosol Spray Order, L.N. 70/90.

Access to Genetic Resources and the Fair and Equitable Sharing of Benefits Arising from Their Utilisation Regulations, L.N. 379/2016 (S.L. 549.111).

Biocidal Products (Implementation of Regulation (EU) No. 528/2012) Regulations, L.N. 348/2013 (S.L. 430.09).

Bio-Safety Coordinating Committee Regulations, L.N. 290/2002 (S.L. 549.31).

Bunkering (Fuels) Tax Act, Chapter 381 of the Laws of Malta.

Certain Fluorinated Gases Regulations, L.N. 93/2010 (S.L. 549.55).

Chemicals Co-ordinating Committee Regulations, L.N. 328/2002 (S.L. 549.34).

Contained Use of Genetically Modified Micro-Organisms Regulations, 2008, L.N. 127/2008 (S.L. 549.49).

Dangerous Substances Regulations, L.N. 306/2008 (S.L. 427.14).

Dangerous Substances and Preparations Regulations, L.N. 10/2007 (S.L. 427.28).

Deliberate Release into the Environment of GMOs Regulations, L.N. 485/2010 (S.L. 549.60).

Environment Protection (Control of Substances Depleting the Ozone Layer) Regulations, L.N. 133/95 (S.L. 549.06).

European Community Methods of Sampling for Official Control of Pesticide Residues in and on Products of Plant and Animal Origin Regulations, L.N. 479/2004 (S.L. 430.04).

Export and Import of Hazardous Chemicals Regulations, L.N. 27/2017 (S.L. 427.92).

Maximum Residue Levels of Pesticides of Produce of Plant and Animal Origin (Implementation of EC Regulation) Regulations, L.N. 14/2009 (S.L. 430.02).

Merchant Shipping Act, Chapter 234 of the Laws of Malta.

Ozone-Depleting Substances Regulation (EC) No. 2037/2000.

Petroleum (Importation, Storage and Sale) Ordinance, Chapter 25 of the Laws of Malta.

Petroleum Ships Entry and Discharge of Petroleum in Harbours, Regulations L.N. 13/96.

Pesticides Control Act, Chapter 430 of the Laws of Malta.

Plant Protection Products (Implementation) Regulations, L.N. 284/2011 (S.L. 430.07).

Prevention and Reduction of Environmental Pollution by Asbestos Regulations, L.N. 228/2001 (S.L. 549.18).

Port Regulations, L.N. 43/1966 (S.L. 499.01).

Protection of Workers from Risks Related to Exposure to Biological Agents at Work Regulations, L.N. 228/2003 (S.L. 424.25).

Prohibition of Importation of Asbestos Fibres Regulations, L.N. 129/1994 (S.L. 37.11).
Protection of Animals for Scientific Purposes Regulations, L.N. 124/2013 (S.L. 439.13).
Protection of Animals Used for Scientific Purposes Regulations, L.N. 161/2017 (S.L. 439.20).
Registration, Evaluation, Authorisation and Restriction of Chemicals (REACH) (Implementation) Regulations, L.N. 61/2008 (S.L. 427.66).
Registration, Evaluation, Authorisation and Restriction of Chemicals Enforcement (E-REACH) Committee Regulations, L.N. 207/2008 (S.L. 427.67).
Substances Depleting the Ozone Layer Regulations, L.N. 280/2010 (S.L. 549.58).
Sustainable Use of Pesticides Regulations, L.N. 489/2011 (S.L. 430.08).
White Phosphorus Matches (Prohibition) Ordinance, Chapter 38 of the Laws of Malta.
Work Places (Health, Safety and Welfare) Regulations, L.N. 52/1986 (S.L. 424.09).

(8) Land Use

Environment Impact Assessment Regulations, L.N. 412/2017 (S.L. 549.46).
Strategic Environmental Assessment Regulations, L.N. 497/2010 (S.L. 549.61)

(9) Waste Management

Abandonment, Dumping and Disposal of Waste in Streets and Public Places or Areas Regulations, L.N. 344/2005 (S.L. 549.40).
Authorisations (Suspension, Refusal and Revocation) Regulations, L.N. 195/2008 (S.L. 545.19).
Batteries and Accumulators Regulations, L.N. 311/2007 (S.L. 427.08).
Beverage Containers Recycling Regulations, L.N. 311/2020 (S.L. 549.134).
Deposit of Wastes and Rubble (Fees) Regulations, L.N. 128/1997 (S.L. 549.07).
Eco-Contribution Act, Chapter 473 of the Laws of Malta.
Extended Producer Responsibility Framework Regulations, L.N. 151/2021 (S.L. 549.141).
Industrial Emissions (Waste Incineration) Regulations, L.N. 14/2013 (S.L. 549.81).
Litter Act, Chapter 206 of the Laws of Malta.
Non-Alcoholic Beverages (Containers) Notice, L.N. 103/1994 (S.L. 549.05).
Regulations concerning Scavengers and the Removal of Refuse, G.N. 325/1899.
Restriction of Use of Hazardous Substances in Electrical and Electronic Equipment Regulations, L.N. 84/2013 (S.L. 427.57).

Restrictions on Placing on the Market of Lightweight Plastic Carrier Bags Regulations, L.N. 480/2020 (S.L. 549.139).
Restrictions on Placing on the Market of Single-Use Plastic Products Regulations, L.N. 481/2020 (S.L. 549.140).
Sewage Discharge Control Regulations, L.N. 139/2002 (S.L. 545.08).
Single-Use Plastic Framework Regulations, L.N. 237/2022 (S.L. 549.149).
Sludge (Use in Agriculture) Regulations, L.N. 212/2001 (S.L. 549.09).
Waste Management (Activity Registration) Regulations, L.N. 106/2007 (S.L. 549.45).
Waste Management (Electrical and Electronic Equipment) Regulations, L.N. 204/2014 (S.L. 549.89).
Waste Management (End of Life Vehicles) Regulations, L.N. 99/2004 (S.L. 549.36).
Waste Management (Landfill) Regulations, L.N. 168/2002 (S.L. 549.29).
Waste Management (Management of Waste from Extractive Industries and Backfilling) Regulations, L.N. 22/2009 (S.L. 549.50).
Waste Management (Packaging and Packaging Waste) Regulations, L.N. 277/2006 (S.L. 549.43).
Waste Management (Polychlorinated Biphenyls and Polychlorinated Terphenyls) Regulations, L.N. 166/2002 (S.L. 549.28).
Waste Management (Shipments of Waste) Regulations, L.N. 285/2011 (S.L. 549.65).
Waste Management (Ship Recycling) Regulations, L.N. 84/2019 (S.L. 549.131).
Waste Management (Supervision and Control of Shipments of Radioactive Waste and Spent Fuel) Regulations, L.N. 48/2009 (S.L. 549.51).
Waste Management (Waste Batteries and Accumulators) Regulations, L.N. 55/2010 (S.L. 549. 54).
Waste Regulations, L.N. 184/2011 (S.L. 549.63).
Water Services Corporation Act, Chapter 355 of the Laws of Malta.
Water Supply and Sewerage Services Regulations, L.N. 525/2004 (S.L. 545.14).

(10) Pollution Control

Marine Pollution:

Clean Air Act, Chapter 200 of the Laws of Malta.
Continental Shelf Act, Chapter 535 of the Laws of Malta.
Continental Shelf Regulations, L.N. 235/2015 (S.L. 535.02).
Dangerous Cargo Ships, Marine Terminals, and Facilities and Bunkering Regulations, L.N. 1/1996 (S.L. 499.12).
Designation of the Continental Shelf Area Order, L.N. 36/1971 & L.N. 113/1974 consolidated (S.L. 535.01).
Exclusive Economic Zone Act, Chapter 625 of the Laws of Malta.
Explosives Ordinance, Chapter 33 of the Laws of Malta.
Oil and Hazardous and Noxious Substances Pollution Preparedness, Response and Co-operation Regulations, L.N. 450/2020 (S.L. 226.03/ 499.69).

Oil Pollution (Liability and Compensation) Act, Chapter 412 of the Laws of Malta.
Permitted periods of Dark Smoke from Vessels Regulations, L.N. 32/1969
Marine Policy Framework Regulations, L.N. 73/2011 (S.L. 549.62).
Merchant Shipping (Prevention of Pollution from Ships) Regulations.
Ship-Source Pollution Regulations, L.N. 130/2008 (S.L. 226.01), L.N. 332/2003 (S.L. 234.32).
Territorial Waters and Contiguous Zone Act, Chapter 226 of the Laws of Malta.
Territorial Waters Regulations, L.N. 236/2015 (S.L. 226.02).

Water Pollution:

Groundwater (Prohibition of Discharge to Groundwater Bodies) Regulations, L.N. 81/2023 (S.L. 549.155).
Limit Values and Quality Objectives for Discharges of Certain Dangerous Substances into the Aquatic Environment Regulations, L.N. 221/2001 (S.L. 549.17).
Limit Values and Quality Objectives for Cadmium Discharges Regulations, L.N. 227/2001 (S.L. 549.15).
Limit Values and Quality Objectives for Mercury Discharges by the Chlor-Alkali Electrolysis Industry Regulations, L.N. 220/2001 (S.L. 549.14).
Nitrates Action Programme Regulations, L.N. 321/2011 (S.L. 549.66).
Pollution Caused by Certain Dangerous Substances Discharged into the Aquatic Environment Regulations, L.N. 213/2001 (S.L. 549.10).
Protection of Groundwater against Deterioration and Pollution Regulations, L.N. 108/2009 (S.L. 549.53).
Protection of Waters against Pollution caused by Nitrates from Agricultural Sources Regulations, L.N. 343/2001 (S.L. 549.25).
Quality of Fresh Waters Supporting Fish Life (Protection and Improvement) Regulations, L.N. 342/2001 (S.L. 549.24).
Quality Required for Shellfish Waters Regulations, L.N. 341/2001 (S.L. 549.23).
Quality Required of Surface Water Intended for the Abstraction of Drinking Water Regulations, L.N. 339/2001 (S.L. 549.21).
Regulator for Energy and Water Services Act, Chapter 545 of the Laws of Malta.
Urban Waste Water Treatment Regulations, L.N. 340/2001 (S.L. 549.22).
Values and Quality for Mercury Discharges by the Chlor-Alkali Electrolysis Industry Regulations, L.N. 220/2001 (S.L. 549.14).
Water Intended for Human Consumption Regulations, L.N. 17/2009 (S.L. 449.57).
Water Policy Framework Regulations, L.N. 345/2015 (S.L. 549.100).

Air Pollution:

Air Pollution by Ozone Regulations, L.N. 215/2001 (S.L. 549.11).
Ambient Air Quality Regulations, L.N. 478/2010 (S.L. 549.59).
Availability of Consumer Information on Fuel Economy and Carbon Dioxide Emissions in Respect of the Marketing of New Passenger Cars Regulations, L.N. 235/2002 (S.L. 549.30).
Cleaner and More Energy-Efficient Road Transport Vehicles Regulations, L.N. 175/2011 (S.L. 601.06).
Combating of Air Pollution from Industrial Plants Regulations, L.N. 211/2001 (S.L. 549.08).
Control of Volatile Organic Compound-VOC Emissions (Storage and Distribution of Petrol from Terminals to Service Stations) Regulations, L.N. 228/2016 (S.L. 549.52).
Industrial Emissions (Limitation of Emissions of Volatile Organic Compounds) Regulations, L.N. 12/2013 (S.L. 549.79).
Limitation of Emissions of Certain Atmospheric Pollutants Regulations, L.N. 303/2018 (S.L. 549.124).
Measures against the Emission of Gaseous and Particulate Pollutants from Internal Combustion Engines to be Installed in Non-Road Mobile Machinery Regulations, L.N. 55/2017 (S.L. 427.85).
Motor Vehicles Regulations, L.N. 128/1994 (S.L. 65.11).
Permitted Periods of Dark Smoke Regulations, L.N. 28/1969 (S.L. 200.01).
Permitted Periods of Dark Smoke from Vessels Regulations, L.N. 30/1969 (S.L. 200.02).
Quality of Fuels Regulations, L.N. 44/2008 (S.L. 545.18).
Reduction in Sulphur Content of Certain Liquid Fuels Regulations, L.N. 159/2002.
Vienna Convention for the Protection of the Ozone Layer and the Montreal Protocol on Substances that Deplete the Ozone Layer (Incorporation) Regulations, L.N. 226/2001 (S.L. 549.16).

Industrial Pollution:

European Pollutant Release and Transfer Register Reporting Obligations Regulations, L.N. 152/2007.
Industrial Emissions (Framework) Regulations, L.N. 9/2013 (S.L. 549.76).
Industrial Emissions (Integrated Pollution Prevention and Control) Regulations, L.N. 10/2013 (S.L. 549.77).
Industrial Emissions (Large Combustion Plants) Regulations, L.N. 11/2013 (S.L. 549.78).
Industrial Emissions (Titanium Dioxide) Regulations, L.N. 13/2013 (S.L. 549.80).
Limitation of Emissions of Certain Pollutants into the Air from Medium Combustion Plants Regulations, L.N. 101/2018 (S.L. 549.122).
Limitation of Emissions of Volatile Organic Compounds (Paints, Varnishes and Vehicle Finishing Products) Regulations, L.N. 152/2012 (S.L. 549.71).

Noise Pollution and Energy Control:

Product Safety Act, Chapter 427 of the Laws of Malta.
Assessment and Management of Environment Noise Regulations, L.N. 193/2004 (S.L. 549.37).
Noise Emission in the Environment by Equipment for Use Outdoors Regulations, L.N. 64/2002 (S.L. 427.19).

(11) Climate Change

Climate Action Act, Chapter 543 of the Laws of Malta.
Regulation (EU) No. 2018/842 of the European Parliament and of the Council of 30 May 2018 on binding annual greenhouse gas emission reductions by Member States from 2021 to 2030 contributing to climate action to meet commitments under the Paris Agreement and amending Regulation (EU) No. 525/2013 (Effort-Sharing Regulation)
European Union Greenhouse Gas Emissions Trading System for Aviation Regulations, L.N. 403/2012 (S.L. 423.51).
European Union Greenhouse Gas Emissions Trading System for Stationary Installations Regulations, L.N. 434/2013 (S.L. 423.50).
Geological Storage of Carbon Dioxide Regulations, L.N. 346/2011 (S.L. 549.68).
National System for the Estimation of Anthropogenic Greenhouse Gas Emissions by Sources and Removal by Sinks Regulations, L.N. 259/2015 (S.L. 543.01).

(12) Horizontal

Strategic Environmental Assessment Regulations, L.N. 418/2005 (S.L. 549.46).
Environment Impact Assessment Regulations, L.N. 114/2007 (S.L. 549.61).
Environment Protection (Preventive and Remedial Measures) Regulations, L.N. 1/1994 (S.L. 549.04).
Freedom of Access to Information on the Environment, Regulations, L.N. 116/2005.
Plans and Programmes (Public Participation) Regulations, L.N. 74 of 2006 (S.L. 549.41).
Prevention and Remedying of Environmental Damage Regulations, L.N. 280/2015 (S.L. 549.97).

53. The following are the international legal instruments to which Malta is a Party:

1948 The Convention on the International Maritime Organization, as amended.
1949 Agreement for the Establishment of a General Fisheries Council for the Mediterranean.
1951 The International Plant Protection Convention.
1954 International Convention for the Prevention of Pollution of the Sea by Oil.

1958 The Convention on the Continental Shelf.
1958 The Convention on the Territorial Sea and the Contiguous Zone.
1963 Treaty Banning Nuclear Weapon Tests in the Atmosphere, in Outer Space and Under Water.
1969 International Convention on Civil Liability for Oil Pollution Damage.
1971 The Treaty on the Prohibition on the Emplacement of Nuclear Weapons and Other Weapons of Mass Destruction on the Sea-Bed and the Ocean Floor and in the Subsoil Thereof.
1971 International Convention on the Establishment of an International Fund for Oil Pollution Damage.
1971 The Convention on Wetlands of International Importance Especially as Waterfowl Habitat.
1972 The Convention on the Prohibition of the Development, Production and Stockpiling of Bacteriological (Biological) and Toxic Weapons, and Their Destruction.
1972 The Convention on the Prevention of Marine Pollution by Dumping of Wastes and Other Matter.
1973 The Convention on International Trade in Endangered Species of Wild Fauna and Flora.
1974 The International Convention on the Safety of Life at Sea.
1976 The Convention for the Protection of the Mediterranean Sea Against Pollution and the 1996 Amendments to it.
1976 The Protocol for the Prevention of Pollution of the Mediterranean by Dumping from Ships and Aircraft.
1976 The Protocol concerning Cooperation in Combating Pollution of the Mediterranean Sea by Oil and Other Harmful Substances.
1976 The Protocol for the Protection of the Mediterranean Sea Against Pollution from Land-Based Sources.
1979 The Convention on Long-Range Transboundary Air Pollution.
1979 The Protocol to the Convention on Long-Range Transboundary Air Pollution on Long-Term Financing of the Cooperative Programme for Monitoring and Evaluation of the Long-Range Transmission of Air Pollutants in Europe (EMEP).
1979 The Convention on the Conservation of Migratory Species of Wild Animals (Bonn Convention).
1979 The Convention on the Conservation of European Wildlife and Natural Habitats (Berne Convention).
1982 United Nations Convention on the Law of the Sea (UNCLOS).
1985 The Vienna Convention for the Protection of the Ozone Layer.
1986 The Protocol Concerning Mediterranean Specially Protected Areas.
1987 The Montreal Protocol on Substances that Deplete the Ozone Layer.
1989 Convention on the Control and Transboundary Movement of Hazardous Wastes and their Disposal (Basel Convention).
1991 Convention on Environmental Impact Assessment in a Transboundary Context (ESPOO Convention).
1992 Convention on Biological Diversity.
1992 The United Nations Framework Convention on Climate Change.

1994 United Nations Convention to Combat Desertification in those Countries Experiencing Serious Drought and/or Desertification, particularly in Africa.
1995 UN Agreement Relating to the Conservation and Management of Straddling Fish Stocks and Migratory Fish Stocks.
1995 Protocol for the Prevention and Elimination of the Mediterranean Sea by Dumping.
1996 Protocol Concerning Protected Areas and Biological Diversity in the Mediterranean.
1996 Protocol on the Prevention of Pollution of the Mediterranean Sea by Transboundary Movement of Hazardous Wastes and their Disposal.
1996 Protocol for the Protection of the Mediterranean against Pollution from Land-Based Activities.
1997 Protocol to the United Nations Framework Convention on Climate Change (Kyoto Protocol as amended by the Doha Amendments).
1998 Convention on Access to Information, Public Participation to Decision-Making and Access to Justice in Environmental Matters.
2000 Protocol to the United Nations Convention on Biological Diversity on Biosafety (Cartagena Protocol).
2000 The European Landscape Convention (Florence Landscape Convention).
2004 Protocol on Pollutant Release and Transfer Registers (PRTR Protocol).
2010 The Nagoya Protocol on Access to Genetic Resources and the Fair and Equitable Sharing of Benefits Arising from their Utilization to the Convention on Biological Diversity (Nagoya Protocol).
2015 Paris Agreement to the United Nations Framework Convention on Climate Change (Paris Agreement).

Part I. Horizontal Issues

54. Environmental legislation that is cross-sectoral in scope is referred to as horizontal or procedural environmental law. It is mainly based on obligations emanating from the 1998 Aarhus Convention on Access to Information, Public Participation to Decision Making and Access to Justice in Environmental Matters. It is made up of a body of legislation that, although varied in subject, has a common objective, namely civilian participation. In this respect, environmental law is sui generis because it allows any person, whether natural or legal, to participate in decision-making and, in Malta's case, even in the drafting of legislation.[52] It provides the citizen with a right of review from any decision taken in this respect by a body with judicial powers. This applies whether the decision taken by the Competent Authority is a refusal for a permit or a decision taken regarding a project, public plan, or programme where the objections raised by the citizen were not taken into consideration. It automatically grants legal standing environmental to NGOs to make such claims as they may deem necessary, and in the case of a request for environmental information, it bestows this right to all citizens whether they have a direct interest or not. It also establishes the right to a claim for environmental damages, which are separate from the other claims for criminal responsibility and civil liability.

52. The Minister responsible for the environment is under an obligation to publish legislation in draft form for a priori public consultation, subject to certain exceptions such as for reasons of urgency or the fixing of offences and penalties. *See* Ch. 549 of the Laws of Malta, Art. 55.

Chapter 1. Environmental Impact Assessments (EIAs) and Strategic Environmental Assessments (SEAs)

55. The 2016 EPA (Chapter 549 of the Laws of Malta), which establishes the ERA, states that one of the functions of the said Authority is 'to carry out, review or request others to carry out environmental assessments, environmental audits and environmental monitoring of activities and works having an impact on the environment'.[53]

Article 54 of the 2016 EPA empowers the Minister to make regulations under the Act, which include regulations to 'establish, co-ordinate and enforce environment quality control systems and make provisions for the carrying out of assessments of environmental impacts and risks of both new and existing establishments as well as to provide for the effective prevention and remedying of environmental damage'.[54]

Within the purview of the 2016 EPA, and promulgated thereunder, one finds as subsidiary legislation, *inter alia*, the:

(1) Environmental Impact Assessment Regulations (S.L. 549.46).
(2) Strategic Environmental Assessment Regulations (S.L. 549.61).

The Environmental Impact Assessment Regulations transpose into Maltese law: Directive 2011/92/EU as amended by 2014/52/EU,[55] the 1991 UNECE Convention on Environmental Impact Assessment in a Transboundary Context (Espoo Convention) and its First and Second Amendments as well as the provisions of Regulation (EU) No. 347/ 2013.[56] The Strategic Environmental Assessment Regulations transpose into Maltese law: the provisions of Directive 2001/42/EC and incorporate, without prejudice, the provisions of the 2003 Kyiv Protocol.[57]

56. The 2017 Environmental Impact Assessment Regulations (2017 EIA Regulations) concisely define the environmental impact assessment ('EIA') as the process of identifying, predicting, evaluating, avoiding, and mitigating the relevant environmental effects of proposed projects and physical interventions prior to relevant decisions and commitments being made. Regulation 7 of the 2017 EIA Regulations further elaborates by stating that the EIA entails the identification,

53. 2016 EPA, Art. 8(2)(j).
54. 2016 EPA, Art. 54(2)(f).
55. Directive 2011/92/EU of the European Parliament and of the Council of 13 Dec. 2011 on the assessment of the effects of certain public and private projects on the environment (codification), as amended by Directive 2014/52/EU of the European Parliament and of the Council of 16 Apr. 2014.
56. Regulation (EU) No. 347/2013 of the European Parliament and the Council on guidelines for trans-European energy infrastructure, with regard to the co-ordination of environmental assessment procedures, arising from the requirements of Council Directives 2014/52/EU, 92/43/EEC, and other related Union legislation.
57. 2003 Protocol on Strategic Environmental Assessment to the '1991 UNECE Convention on Environmental Impact Assessment in a Transboundary Context', reproduced in Schedule III of S.L. 549.61.

description, and assessment in an appropriate manner of the direct and indirect significant effects of a project on the environment,[58] specifically:

(1) population and human health;
(2) biodiversity and ecology, with particular but not exclusive attention to species and habitats protected under other national and European Union legislation, including the Conservation of Wild Birds Regulations and the Flora, Fauna and Natural Habitats Protection Regulations;
(3) the physical environment, land, soil, water, air and climate;
(4) material assets, cultural heritage and the landscape; and
(5) the interaction between the factors referred to in paragraphs (1)–(4) above.

The EIA is a procedure or process whereby a local competent authority assesses the potential environmental impact(s) of proposed new development projects on the environment before such projects are allowed to proceed. Environmental permitting, on the other hand, is the process by which persons (legal or bodies corporate) or other entities are granted an environmental permit prior to carrying out an activity which is restricted by local environmental law (Chapter 549 and subsidiary legislation). In a nutshell, an environmental permit is needed when:

(1) an activity could pollute the air, water or land; or
(2) activities are to be carried out in a protected area; or
(3) an activity may affect a protected species of flora and fauna.[59]

The EIA and Environmental Permitting are not mutually exclusive. Although they are two separate and distinct processes, overlaps are possible. A development project which requires an EIA, and is completed, may still require an environmental permit should it, during its operation, carry out any activity (such as pollution or any other type of environmental harm) which is restricted by local environmental legislation.

57. A strategic impact assessment addresses specific impacts on the environment. The SEA should be implemented, insofar as possible, at the earlier stages, with the view of 'integrating environmental, including health, considerations into the preparation and adoption of plans and programmes and, to the extent appropriate, policies and legislation'.[60] The Strategic Environmental Assessment Regulations (S.L. 549.61) define the term 'strategic environmental assessment' as 'the

58. The term 'significant' is defined in Reg. 2 of the 2017 Regulations and requires consideration of both the aspects of context and intensity.
59. https://era.org.mt/era-topic-categories/applying-for-an-ep/ (accessed on 16 Jan. 2022). The following activities are also mentioned in ERA's non-exhaustive list: (i) industrial activities; (ii) waste management activities; (iii) quarries; (iv) operation of medium or large combustion plants; (v) activities relation to interventions on trees; (vi) activities in protected sites; (vii) activities on protected species or GMOs; (viii) trade or movement of protected species; trans-frontier shipment of waste; and /or (ix) extended producer responsibility.
60. 2003 Protocol on Strategic Environmental Assessment to the '1991 UNECE Convention on Environmental Impact Assessment in a Transboundary Context', Preamble.

preparation of an environmental report, the carrying out of consultations, the taking into account of the environmental report and the results of the consultations in decision making and the provision of information on the decision'.

The EIA, as seen above, is a reactive process – it is undergone as a reaction to a proposed project or a proposed physical intervention prior to consent (e.g., a development planning permit) being granted for its commencement.[61] It is also concerned with mitigating any possible adverse effects on the environment which the proposed project in question may pose. Proposing feasible alternatives to a particular project (or parts thereof) is part of the EIA process. Since the EIA process involves a 'cause and effect' analysis in relation to a particular project, the knowledge of the cumulative impacts on the environment at project level could be limited, especially if the proposed project is innovative, unique, or unprecedented.

An SEA, on the other hand, is a proactive process and is not usually tied to any project in particular. It features mostly in policy, planning and programme-making – and is regarded as a political instrument. While both identify the potential impacts on the environment, the SEA may be used as a tool in order for the State to adopt policies, plans, and programmes which are capable of benefitting the environment insofar as possible and emphasising the achievement of objectives which safeguard the environment with regard to the regulation of future activities. The scope of the EIA, therefore, is much narrower, although the 2017 EIA Regulations in Regulation 16 state that the EIA shall, with a view to avoiding duplication of assessments as well as to optimise the quality of the assessment, take into account the information contained in, and results of, other relevant environmental assessments and studies undertaken in terms of these regulations or under any other legislation, insofar as such information is relevant, reasonably available and still appropriate.[62]

61. *See* EIA Regulations, Art. 2, definition of 'EIA'.

62. *See also* EIA Regulations, Reg. 8(3) regarding taking into account the information found in already existing assessments (required by other legislation) in the interest of improved synergy and avoidance of duplication.

§1. THE MAIN STAGES OF THE EIA

58. The main stages of the EIA process are indicated in the chart below:

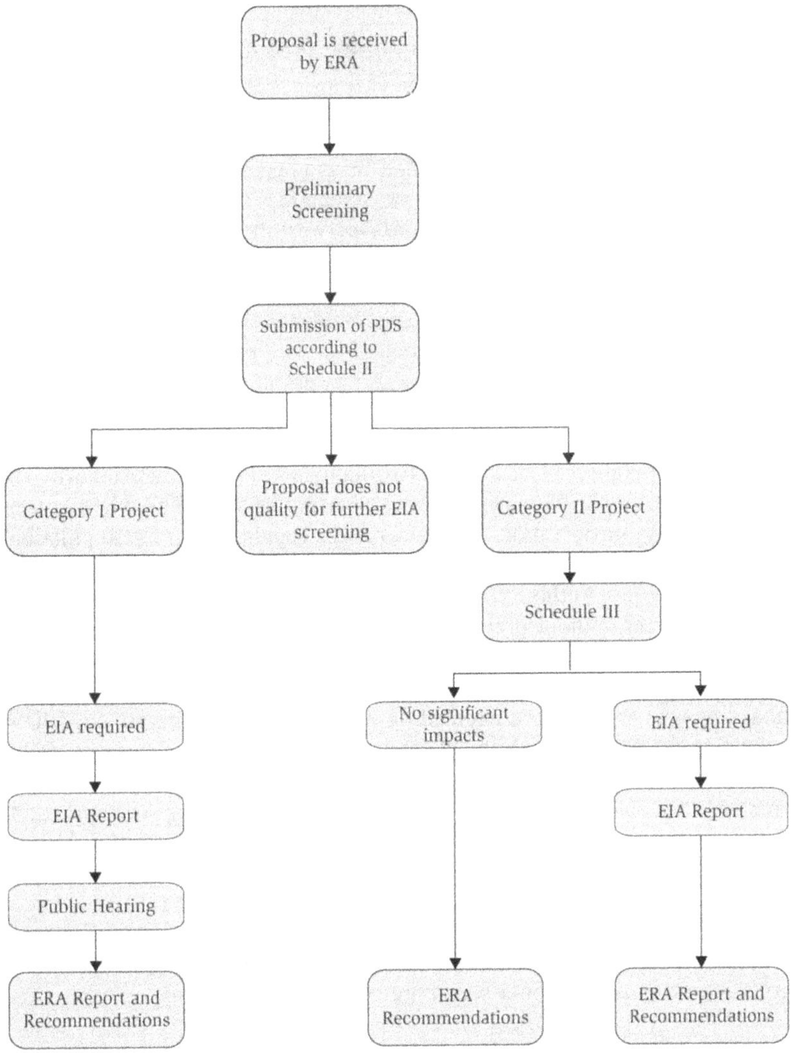

Source: ERA website – https://era.org.mt/era-topic-categories/eia-process/ (accessed on 9/3/2022).

I. Development Proposal

59. This is the first stage which commences the whole EIA process. Regulation 6(1) of the EIA regulations states that:

> Before any consent is given for a project likely to have significant effects on the environment due to, *inter alia*, its nature, size, scale, position or location, such project shall be subject to a requirement for development consent as well as an assessment of its effects on the environment in line with these regulations. No development consent shall be granted authorising any such project unless the required assessment or screening, as relevant, has been duly undertaken and completed in accordance with these regulations.[63]

The EIA process is, *inter alia*, to be integrated into the development consent procedure in order to synchronise compliance with both development planning regulations and the EIA Regulations with regard to each particular proposal or project as much as possible. This stage of the EIA process is referred to in the EIA Regulations as a preliminary screening process, which is carried out in order to determine whether a project submitted to ERA for its consideration falls under those Regulations. Regulation 11 of the EIA Regulations states that the Authority shall, at the earliest appropriate moment, undertake vetting to determine whether a project submitted for its consideration falls under these regulations. This Regulation shall apply irrespective of whether there currently is an application for development consent, as long as the Authority is satisfied that there is sufficient information for proper vetting and without prejudice to any additional considerations, issues, and objections that the Authority may have on the project. The outcome of such vetting may be communicated in writing to the developer or to the permitting authority, or both, as relevant. Should it be decided by the Authority that the project falls within the scope of the said Regulations, then a project description statement (PDS) will be required from the developer in order to determine whether the project being considered requires an EIA or whether further 'detailed screening' is required.[64]

60. Projects which fall within Category I of Schedule I of the EIA Regulations require an EIA.[65] Projects which fall within Category II of the said Schedule would need to undergo a 'detailed screening' process in order to determine whether or not they require an EIA.[66] The EIA Regulations also cater for the possibility of other projects requiring an EIA on a screening or case-by-case basis:

---

63. The term 'development consent' is synonymous with the term 'development permit' and is defined by Reg. 2 of the EIA Regulations as 'the decision of the permitting authority which entitles the developer to proceed with the project, as well as any equivalent consent arising from a development order or other instrument'.
64. This is also referred to in the EIA regulations as 'Mandatory Screening'.
65. EIA Regulations, Reg. 10(1).
66. EIA Regulations, Reg. 10(2).

> The Authority may require an EIA or screening for a project which is not included in Schedule I if it is of the opinion that the project may have significant environmental impacts and that a normal development consent application or an assessment other than provided by these regulations is not sufficient for their proper evaluation. In arriving at such requirement, the Authority shall have regard to the criteria set out in Schedule III.[67]

A PDS is therefore required for the Authority to examine the proposed project in detail. Regulation 12(1) of the EIA Regulations states that should the vetting undertaken by the Authority indicate that the project qualifies for an EIA or for screening, a PDS compliant with the provisions of Schedule II shall be required if the project is to be considered any further.

The PDS is 'a structured document containing a description of the site and the proposed project, in sufficient detail to enable an identification of the likely effects and implications on the environment'[68] and is to be submitted by the developer (or his appointed consultant) upon request by, or in agreement with, the Authority.[69] The PDS should:

(1) provide information on the characteristics of the project and its site and on the likely impacts on the environment, as detailed further in Schedule II of the EIA Regulations;
(2) take into account, where relevant, the available results of other environmental assessments;[70] and
(3) identify any characteristics or measures envisaged to avoid or prevent any significant adverse impacts on the environment.

The PDS may also include other relevant information as may be reasonably necessary or appropriate for proper screening while avoiding content that does not add value to, or which may distort, the screening or any eventual assessment. The Authority may also require any such information or content to be submitted, removed, corrected, or amended and may also direct that such changes be a part of the PDS or a separate document.[71] It is the developer who is responsible for the PDS in its entirety. Such responsibility includes ensuring the content of the PDS presents a complete and faithful representation of the project, the site, and the expected changes to any site affected by the project and its ancillary requirements.[72] In fact, the EIA Regulations ensure that the PDS duly reflects the final version of the project and shall be consistent with the relevant applications for development consent and

67. EIA Regulations, Reg. 10(3).
68. EIA Regulations, Reg. 2.
69. *Ibid.*, Reg. 12(2).
70. Such as those referred to in Reg. 8(1) of the EIA Regulations – i.e., including but not limited to: including but not limited to any assessment under: the Flora, Fauna and Natural Habitats Protection Regulations, the Strategic Environmental Assessment Regulations, the Industrial Emissions (Framework) Regulations, the Industrial Emissions (Integrated Pollution Prevention and Control) Regulations, the Water Policy Framework Regulations and other relevant legislation.
71. EIA Regulations, Reg. 12(3).
72. EIA Regulations, Reg. 14(3).

vice versa. One such safeguard, for example, is the case of project fragmentation. The EIA Regulations prevent the possibility of circumventing the application of their provisions by means of splitting a particular project into a series of smaller projects.[73] Upon finalisation, every PDS is to be made public on the Authority's website, clearly indicating, apart from the nature of the decisions to be taken, which are the respective authorities responsible for the EIA and the development consent process.[74] Regulation 13 of the EIA Regulations states that:

> Wherever relevant, projects that fall within the scope of these regulations shall require a sufficiently detailed and reasonably exhaustive initial appraisal of potentially suitable alternatives, on the basis of their technical merits, feasibility, and environmental implications and impacts, in the interest of streamlining and optimising the subsequent assessment process.

II. Environmental Impact Assessment or Screening

61. In accordance with Regulation 10 of the EIA Regulations, a project may take one of three main routes:

(1) Mandatory EIA[75] – such projects, which are listed in Category I of Schedule I of the Regulations, do not require screening – they automatically require an EIA. In such cases, one would proceed to 'scoping' and the formulation of the terms of reference.
(2) Mandatory Screening[76] – these projects, which are listed in Category II of Schedule I of the Regulations, would require screening in order to determine whether or not they are likely to result in 'significant environmental effects' and whether they should be subject to an EIA.
(3) Case-by-Case Examination[77] – certain projects, which are not listed in either Category I or Category II, may still require an EIA or Screening if the Authority is of the opinion that they may have significant environmental impacts and that 'a normal development consent application or an assessment other than provided by these regulations is not sufficient for their proper evaluation'.[78] There is also the possibility of projects not normally requiring an EIA but nonetheless require an examination due to the fact that they may 'in the Authority's opinion … produce significant environmental effects due to cumulating with other existing and/or approved projects'.[79]

73. EIA Regulations, Reg. 10(6).
74. *Ibid.*
75. EIA Regulations, Reg. 10(1).
76. *Ibid.*, Reg. 10(2).
77. *Ibid.*, Reg. 10(3) and (4).
78. EIA Regulations, Reg. 10(3).
79. *Ibid.*, Reg. 10(4).

The categorisation system (Category I or II) utilised in Schedule I of the EIA Regulations uses both qualitative and quantitative indicators in order to determine whether a project should be subject outright to an EIA or whether it should be screened in order to arrive at the conclusion as to the said project should require an EIA or not. The list of projects in Schedule I purports to be as comprehensive as possible but is by no means exhaustive. Should a project not feature in Schedule I, the Authority may examine it on a case-by-case basis in accordance with (3) above in order to determine whether such projects should undergo an EIA or should be screened in order to examine whether an EIA is, in fact, necessary.

62. Regarding screening, Regulation 14 of the EIA Regulations states that:

> The Authority shall undertake a screening on the basis of the information provided in the project description statement and any other information or investigations as deemed appropriate by the Authority. The screening shall determine whether a project falling within the scope of regulation 10 (but not covered by Category I of Schedule I) is likely to have significant environmental effects in terms of the relevant criteria listed in Schedule III, whether an environmental impact assessment is required, and whether any other provisions of these regulations should be applicable.

The Regulations provide the criteria to be applied by the Authority in the screening process relating to a particular project, which are listed in Schedule III of the Regulations. These branch out of three main categories:

(1) characteristics of the project – such as the nature, size and scale of the project, consumption of resources, production of waste, pollution potential, risks to human health;
(2) location of the project – mainly the environmental sensitivity of geographical areas likely to be affected by the project – types of land in relation to land use and whether there are, for example, any conservation areas present; and
(3) type and characteristics of the potential impact of the project on the environment – e.g., the nature, magnitude, intensity, complexity, duration, frequency, degree of reversibility.

63. Upon receiving the PDS from the developer, the Authority has thirty days[80] within which to conduct the screening process and to notify the said developer whether or not the project in question should be subject to an EIA. This is done by means of a formal decision known as the 'screening outcome',[81] which is to be

80. In cases relating to, *inter alia*, the nature, complexity, location or size of the project, the Authority may extend that deadline provided that it shall inform the developer in writing, giving reasons for the extension and indicating a reasonable date when the screening outcome is expected – EIA Regulations, Reg. 15(1).
81. EIA Regulations, Reg. 15.

made available to the public on the Authority's website.[82] If the screening concludes that no environmental impact assessment is required, the considerations and parameters influencing such screening may form an integral part of the Authority's recommendations on the project, the developer is informed accordingly, and it is then in the hands of the permitting authority to proceed with granting development consent.[83] Should it result from the screening process that the project in question requires an EIA, the Authority notifies this decision to the developer, who then has thirty calendar days from notification to either contest the decision before the Tribunal in accordance with Part X of the Regulations or to inform the said Authority in writing 'that he will undertake the EIA within a reasonable time period'.[84]

After receiving a written undertaking from the developer that he will carry out the EIA for the project in question, the Authority initiates a process known as 'scoping'.[85] Scoping is the process of defining the scope, extent, and level of detail of the EIA and includes the identification of environmental issues, baselines, geographical areas of influence, methodologies, alternatives and impacts to be considered, and the formulation of the terms of reference. The terms of reference for the EIA are formulated by the Authority, taking into account the above-mentioned screening outcome, and are based on the requirements enlisted in Schedule IV of the Regulations.[86] In a nutshell, the terms of reference indicate the information required by the Authority for reaching an informed conclusion on the significant effects of the project on the environment.

64. The EIA Regulations obligate the Authority to invite the following third parties to make recommendations and ancillary reasoned justifications on any relevant matters that merit inclusion in terms of reference within thirty calendar days of such notification:

(1) government entities as the Authority deems relevant;
(2) the local councils responsible for the localities where the project, including its ancillary infrastructure, is proposed to be sited;
(3) other local councils that, in the opinion of the Authority, are likely to be affected by the project or its ancillary infrastructure; and
(4) The public, and the public concerned.[87]

The Authority has the right to factor any recommendations in its terms of reference as well as to partly adopt or decline them as it deems most appropriate.[88] The

82. EIA Regulations, Reg. 15(3).
83. EIA Regulations, Reg. 14(3) – this is without prejudice to the applicability of Reg. 31 ('Supplementary provisions on development consent') and Reg. 32 ('Incorporation of environmental measures and safeguards in permits') of the said Regulations.
84. EIA Regulations, Reg. 15(2).
85. *Ibid.*, Reg. 16.
86. Schedule IV entitled 'Information for the EIA Report' of the EIA Regulations contains a set of thirteen requirements which the terms of reference should contain, as applicable.
87. EIA Regulations, Reg. 16(2).
88. *Ibid.*, Reg. 16(3).

Authority may also request further clarification or information from the aforementioned parties.[89] Prior to the finalisation of the terms of reference, either:

(1) one or more 'scoping meetings'; or
(2) one or more meetings between the Authority and the developer; may be held at the cost of the developer.[90]

The Regulations do not define 'scoping meetings'; however, the Regulations state that such meetings are requested by any of the above-mentioned parties due to the fact 'that the proposed project is of major significance because of its nature, scale, location, hazardous properties or other reasons'. The distinction between the two classes of meetings (1 and 2) is not entirely clear. First, the Authority and the developer fall within both classes of meetings. Second, the threshold of what exactly amounts to a project of 'major significance' is quite subjective. Third, both classes of meetings are collectively referred to as 'consultations' in Regulation 16(4).[91] One may reasonably deduce that a meeting held between the Authority and the developer with regard to a proposed project which is not 'of major significance' is, *a contrario sensu,* therefore, not a 'scoping meeting'.

Once the above consultations are closed, the Authority is tasked with formulating the 'draft terms of reference' for the EIA report. The said draft is then finalised according to Regulation 16(4), which states that the Authority shall give to the developer and the coordinator[92] if already appointed in accordance with these regulations, the opportunity to propose amendments thereto for the Authority's consideration. Thereafter, the Authority shall issue the final terms of reference for the assessment without prejudice to the provisions of these regulations and to any further requirements or modifications at a later stage in the light of the evolution and findings of the assessment itself.

A copy of the final terms of reference is then communicated to the developer and made public on the Authority's website. Even though the terms of reference document is final, the Regulations allow the Authority to adapt or modify the said terms of reference with 'due justification, at any time according to the environmental considerations relevant to the project',[93] and such changes shall be made public without delay.[94]

---

89. *Ibid.*
90. *Ibid.*
91. The EIA Regulations, in Reg. 2, collectively refers to 'Government entities, local councils or any other person, organisation or entity which the Authority might request the coordinator to consult, or which the Authority might consult' as 'consultees'.
92. For definition of 'coordinator', refer to Reg. 2 of the EIA Regulations which defines it as 'the consultant responsible for coordinating the environmental impact assessment'. 'Consultant' is in turn defined as 'an expert who is sufficiently competent in the relevant environmental field as may be required for the purpose of the environmental impact assessment'.
93. EIA Regulations, Reg. 16(6).
94. In no case later than fifteen days from the adoption or modification of the terms of reference.

65. It is the developer who is responsible for the commissioning of the EIA report in accordance with the EIA Regulations.[95] It is at this point that the Regulations contemplate the role of the 'consultant', who is engaged by the developer. This notwithstanding, Regulation 17(2) provides the consultants carrying out the EIA report shall be professionals, independent and impartial, and shall be duly competent experts in the respective areas of the assessment. The consultants shall be registered in accordance with the provisions of the Act once such registration mechanism enters into force and must also follow the regulations, procedures, rules, and guidelines established by the Authority and by the Registration Board. The consultants shall be led and managed by a coordinator, who shall be responsible for the overall content and presentation of the EIA report.

66. The Regulations define the term 'consultant' as an expert who is sufficiently competent in the relevant environmental field as may be required for the purpose of the EIA.[96] Moreover, the Regulations also create the role of 'coordinator', defined as 'the consultant responsible for coordinating the environmental impact assessment'.[97] Therefore, the coordinator is also a consultant, both of which are tasked with carrying out the EIA. All consultants involved in the EIA of a particular project shall be required to sign a declaration that they have no conflict of interest that may affect any aspect covered by the Regulations.[98] Such declaration shall follow the terms and specifications established by the Authority.[99] The Regulations also cater for a registration mechanism whereby all consultants are registered and accountable to the Registration Board and ultimately to the Authority.[100] The independent and impartial consultants, engaged by the developer, draw up the said report in accordance with the Regulations. The EIA report is meant to address the requirements and issues raised in the terms of reference and shall include at least:

- a description of the project, including information on the design, size and other relevant features;
- a description of the project site and its surroundings, including their environmental characteristics;
- a description of the likely significant effects of the project on the environment;
- a description of the features of the project and/or measures envisaged in order to avoid, prevent or reduce and, if possible, offset any likely significant adverse effects on the environment;
- a description of the reasonable alternatives studied, which are relevant to the project and its specific characteristics, and an indication of the main reasons for the option chosen, taking into account the effects of the project on the environment; and
- any additional information specified in Schedule IV as relevant to the project and to the environmental features likely to be affected.

---

95. EIA Regulations, Reg. 17(1).
96. *Ibid.*, Reg. 2.
97. *Ibid.*
98. EIA Regulations, Reg. 17(3).
99. *Ibid.*
100. EIA Regulations, Reg. 17(2).

The report may be in the Maltese or English language, or both, according to the exigencies of the parties involved. A non-technical summary of the above-mentioned requirements should also be included in a separate document, while technical studies shall be attached to the EIA report in the form of appendices or annexes. The names of the consultants and contributors involved in the preparation of the EIA report (including all ancillary technical studies, appendices and non-technical summaries) and other reports are to be listed in the final report. Their respective contributions and responsibilities must be identified.

67. Regulation 18(4), titled 'Quality control', centres around the responsibility of the consultants to ensure the professional and scientific integrity, veracity, coherence, concreteness, transparency, completeness, and effectiveness of the content, discussions, analyses, and recommendations in the EIA report. The Authority reserves the right to commission an independent assessment, such as in cases where it has 'any reasonable and significant doubt about the quality, sufficiency or impartiality of the EIA report or any part thereof'.[101] The developer or consultants may request information from government entities and local councils which they have in their possession and which may be relevant to the EIA. Furthermore, the Authority may seek from practically any entity 'supplementary information' other than that requested in terms of reference if it results that such information is relevant to reaching the reasoned conclusion on the project and its significant effects on the environment.[102]

III. Submission of the EIA Report and Inspection Period

68. Upon official submission of the EIA report to the Authority, notices indicating such submission shall be published by the developer in at least one daily or weekly newspaper in Maltese and one in English and by the Authority on the Authority's website.[103] As a rule, there is a minimum thirty calendar days' inspection period within which the EIA report can be read and during which written comments can be made to the Authority. The report is made available to the same consultees mentioned above (i.e., government entities, local councils, and the public) on the Authority's website, at the Authority's offices and, where appropriate, through any other additional means as the Authority may establish and may be inspected throughout the aforementioned inspection period on days and during such times as the Authority deems proper.[104] Following the expiry of the inspection period referred to above, the Authority 'shall arrange for a public hearing[105] to take place at a suitable venue, within the same locality in which the project is proposed

101. EIA Regulations, Reg. 18(7).
102. *Ibid.*, Reg. 18(1).
103. *Ibid.*, Reg. 19(1).
104. *Ibid.*, Reg. 19(2).
105. Regulation 20(7) of the EIA Regulations states that: 'Subject to regulation 10, the provisions of sub-regulations (1) to (6) shall not apply to environmental impact assessments carried out for projects other than those listed in Category I of Schedule I, unless the Authority considers that a public hearing should still be held.'

but not within the developer's property'. At least fifteen calendar days' notice of such hearing should be given by the Authority – whereby also the date, time, and venue of the said hearing are published on the Authority's website and newspapers.[106]

The coordinator shall ensure, as much as reasonably possible, that the relevant consultants are available for the hearing or that appropriate alternative arrangements are made for provision of adequate information and replies to the public present at the hearing.[107] The purpose of this hearing is to grant the opportunity to the general public to comment on, and enquire about, the EIA report as well as the proposed project and its impacts, and may request any relevant information and clarifications.[108] The comments, enquiries, and requests made by the public during the hearing are to be duly recorded by the Authority.[109] It is noteworthy that the Regulations allow the public the possibility of making written submissions up to seven calendar days after the public hearing.[110]

The submissions, comments, enquiries, and requests submitted or recorded during the inspection period of the EIA report or at the ensuing public hearing shall be collated into a report by the Authority and sent to the coordinator for his response.[111] During this stage, the Authority and the developer may liaise with each other, and additional considerations may be raised by the former while also allowing referral to public entities or the public concerned 'for information, comments or further guidance as it deems relevant'.[112] Should this consultation process produce material considerations, the EIA report may be further revised. The resulting version is considered the 'concluded EIA report'.[113] The concluded EIA report is submitted to the Authority by the coordinator in as many digital and printed copies as necessary. The report is then to be made available on the Authority's website not later than fifteen days from its finalisation.

69. The Authority analyses the concluded EIA report and prepares its own final assessment.[114] According to Regulation 31, the Authority may at any stage recommend to the permitting authority that permission for a proposed project falling within the scope of these regulations be refused, dismissed, or otherwise restricted in certain cases.[115] In so doing, it 'shall take a decision in public giving the opportunity to the applicant and the public to make comments and representations'.[116] The Authority's position shall be made publicly available on its website 'without delay'

106. EIA Regulations, Reg. 20(2).
107. *Ibid.*, Reg. 20(5)
108. *Ibid.*, Reg. 20(1).
109. *Ibid.*, Reg. 20(7).
110. *Ibid.*
111. *Ibid.*, Reg. 21.
112. *Ibid.*
113. *Ibid.*, Reg. 21(2)
114. *Ibid.*, Reg. 23(1); Reg. 23(3) states that: 'Wherever the available information is deemed by the Authority to be insufficient for acceptable decision-taking on the project or wherever the Authority deems that the risk factor or hazard factor or both are too high, the Authority shall adopt the precautionary principle.'
115. EIA Regulations, Reg. 31.
116. *Ibid.*, Reg. 23(1).

and not later than fifteen days from its finalisation. The Authority's assessment shall also include all relevant consultation submissions and replies, and minutes of the consultation meetings, as appendices or annexes. Such documents, together with any addenda, shall also be made publicly available.[117] Regulation 23(2) states that:

> In preparing and arriving at its final assessment, the Authority shall give due regard to the conclusions reached in the EIA report prepared by the consultants, including any relevant ancillary documentation, as well as to the comments received from the public concerned at any stage of the process pursuant to these regulations, and any other environmental considerations that may be relevant. As part of its final assessment, the Authority shall give adequately detailed reasons as to whether it agrees with or does not agree with the conclusions reached by the consultants in the report, in whole or in part.

Due consideration of, and clear reference to, the Authority's position shall be included in all relevant permit application reports compiled by the permitting authority in accordance with the provisions of the relevant legislation.[118] When a project successfully undergoes an EIA and development consent is granted, the Authority may recommend to the permitting authority to include any conditions and measures in the development consent. It may also recommend amendments to the project or specifications on any features of the project to ensure that the assessment outcome is duly fulfilled or to avoid, prevent or reduce and, if possible, offset significant adverse effects on the environment.[119] Such measures may include financial guarantees in favour of the authority, insurance against damage to the environment, as well as contributions to the Environmental Fund.[120] Other measures may include the submission of any data, information or documentation as well as environmental permitting requirements, other authorisations, and enforcement considerations.[121] Once the project is up and running, the Authority shall require monitoring of the relevant effects of the project on the environment in accordance with specifications and procedures as it deems most appropriate and effective in order to avoid, prevent or reduce and, if possible, offset significant adverse effects on the environment.[122] In accordance with Regulation 32A(1): 'When providing recommendations following the completion of an environmental impact assessment, the Authority shall duly take into account the comments received from the public and the public concerned in line with these regulations.' The position taken by the Authority in its final assessment, as well as any recommendations made by the Authority with regard to the same EIA, shall be duly taken into account by the permitting authority in its decision-making process.[123]

---

117. *Ibid.*
118. EIA Regulations, Reg. 23(1). This is without prejudice to Reg. 32A titled, 'Due consideration of public comments and of the Authority's position'.
119. EIA Regulations, Reg. 32(a).
120. *Ibid.*
121. *Ibid.*
122. *Ibid.*, Reg. 32(b); *see also* Reg. 32(c).
123. EIA Regulations, Reg. 32A(2).

IV. Transboundary Impact Assessments

70. The EIA Regulations, in Part VII (titled 'Transboundary Impacts'), impose certain obligations on Malta when it is aware that a project in its territory may have significant effects on the environment in another State or when another State that may be affected so requests in line with the provisions of the Directive[124] or Convention.[125] In such cases, in accordance with Regulation 25, the Minister shall notify that State, as soon as possible and not later than when the public in Malta is informed in accordance with these regulations and shall include the following information:

(1) information on the project and its location, together with the available information on the possible transboundary impacts;
(2) information on the nature of the possible decisions; and
(3) any other information which the Minister deems reasonable.[126]

71. The Minister shall also give that State (referred to as 'the interested State') thirty calendar days within which to indicate whether it wishes to participate in the environmental decision-making procedures, including the development consent procedure, the EIA and or scoping, as may be relevant.[127] If a State which has not been notified as per the above procedure considers that the environment under its jurisdiction is likely to be adversely affected by a project which is proposed to be carried out in Malta and which is within the scope of these regulations, the Minister shall, at the request of that State, exchange sufficient information for the purposes of holding discussions on whether there is likely to be a significant adverse transboundary impact.[128]

Should any interested State indicate to the Minister that it intends to participate in such procedures, the Minister shall, if he has not already done so, send to that State the required information as laid down in these Regulations and, once it is submitted to the Authority, the EIA report.[129]

The interested State/s may enter into consultations with the Minister regarding, *inter alia,* the following:

(1) the potential transboundary effects of the project;
(2) possible alternatives to the project, including the no-action alternative where relevant;

124. Directive 2011/92/EU of the European Parliament and of the Council of 13 Dec. 2011 on the assessment of the effects of certain public and private projects on the environment (codification), as amended by Directive 2014/52/EU of the European Parliament and of the Council of 16 Apr. 2014.
125. The Convention on Environmental Impact Assessment in a Transboundary Context (Espoo Convention) of the United Nations Economic Commission for Europe, and its First and Second Amendments.
126. EIA Regulations, Reg. 25(1).
127. *Ibid.*
128. *Ibid.*, Reg. 25(2).
129. *Ibid.*, Reg. 25(3).

(3) measures to prevent, reduce, eliminate or offset any significant transboundary impacts;
(4) monitoring of the effects of such measures and of the project;
(5) possible mutual assistance in preventing, reducing, eliminating or offsetting any significant adverse impact of the project; and/or
(6) any other appropriate matters as relevant to the project.[130]

72. The Minister and interested State(s) shall then agree on how the consultations are to take place. The latter are then to provide the Minister with information relating to the environment under its/their jurisdiction, which may potentially be adversely affected, where such information is necessary or relevant for the assessment.[131] The interested State(s) may arrange for the information to be made available, within a reasonable time, to the relevant authorities and the public in its/their territory such that they can forward their opinion within a reasonable time and participate effectively in the relevant environmental decision-making procedures before any consent for the project is granted.[132]

When the EIA is finalised, the Minister is bound to provide to the interested State/s information about:

(1) the final decision on the proposed project;
(2) the reasons and considerations on which the decision was based;
(3) the terms and conditions attached to the decision, including the relevant measures to avoid, reduce, or offset the major adverse effects;
(4) the public participation process; and
(5) any other ancillary information which the interested State may reasonably request in line with the Directive or the Convention or which the Minister deems appropriate.

The interested State may make such information available in an appropriate manner to the public concerned in its own territory. Should monitoring of a project or any other post-project analysis reveal any significant adverse transboundary impacts or any factors that may result in such impacts, the Minister shall immediately inform the interested State/s or vice versa, as relevant. The parties shall then enter into consultations on the measures that should be undertaken to prevent, reduce, eliminate or offset such impact, including any mutual assistance to this effect.[133] Regulation

130. *Ibid.*, Reg. 25(4). *See also* Reg. 25(7) which states that: 'If additional information on the significant transboundary impact of a project proposed in Malta, which was not available at the time a decision was made and which could have materially affected the decision, becomes available to the Minister or to an interested State before work on the project commences, the Minister shall immediately inform the interested State and vice-versa, as relevant. In such instances, any one or both parties may request that consultations be held on whether the decision needs to be revised.'
131. *Ibid.*, Reg. 25(4).
132. *Ibid.*, Reg. 25(5).
133. *Ibid.*, Reg. 25(9).

26 of the EIA Regulations deals with the converse situation – the Minister's right to be notified by another State about 'any project in that State which may have a potentially significant effect on the environment in Malta',[134] outlining the procedure to be followed, in a similar manner to Regulation 25. Part VII ends with provisions 'common to both reg. 25 and reg. 26',[135] as well as provisions on discussions with other States, settlement of disputes, as well as the possibility of entering into bilateral and multilateral agreements.[136]

73. Regulation 30 states that the procedures for notification, public participation, and availability of information to the public in the sphere of development permitting and development consent decisions shall be governed by the respective laws. However, where a development falls within the scope of this Regulation, the permitting authority shall clearly make available to the public, at the earliest possible stage and within reasonable time frames, details of the authorities responsible for taking the decision; those from which relevant information may be obtained; those to which comments or questions can be submitted; the time schedule for transmitting comments or questions; the nature of possible decisions; and where there is one, the draft decision.

Regulation 34 provides that 'appeals before the Tribunal, to challenge a decision, act or omission related to any matter regulated under these regulations, shall be applicable to all aggrieved persons including interested third parties referred to under the Environment and Planning Review Tribunal Act, and shall be made in accordance with the relevant rules and procedures laid down under the same Act'. Regulation 33(1) provides that any person who 'provides false, fraudulent or misleading information that may jeopardise, or render ineffective any assessment falling within the scope of these regulations or lead to processing errors; or causes any significant impact, risk or hazard to the environment, as a result of non-compliance, or unsatisfactory, incomplete or late compliance, with any provision of these regulations; or contravenes any order or instruction given by the Authority under these regulations, in respect of any aspect that may have an adverse impact on the environment, shall be guilty of an offence against the said Regulations'. Punishments may include fines, imprisonment or both and vary on first conviction[137] and second or subsequent convictions.[138] The court, besides awarding the said punishments, may order the offender to remove the causes of the offence and to rectify the situation within a stipulated time, at the latter's cost. A daily fine may be imposed in cases where the offender remains in default,[139] while the court may also order the

134. *Ibid.*, Reg. 26.
135. *Ibid.*, Reg. 27.
136. *Ibid.*, Reg. 28(1)–(3).
137. Fine (*multa*) of not less than EUR 2,500.00 and not more than EUR 230,000.00, or imprisonment for a term not exceeding two years, or both such fine (*multa*) and imprisonment.
138. Fine (*multa*) of not less than EUR 5,000.00 and not more than EUR 460,000.00 or imprisonment for a term not exceeding two years, or both such fine (*multa*) and imprisonment.
139. Fine (*multa*) of not less than EUR 50 and not more than EUR 130.

modification, suspension or revocation of 'any authorisation'.[140] Lastly, an administrative fine may be imposed on any person who contravenes or fails to comply with the Regulations,[141] which is payable to the Environment Fund established by Article 32 of the EPA.

140. EIA Regulations, Reg. 33(2).
141. *Ibid.*, Reg. 33(3) – the administrative fine *(multa)* shall not exceed EUR 100,000 for each violation.

Chapter 2. Public Participation and Access to Information

74. Public participation and access to information are important pillars under environmental law in Malta. In fact, the Environment Protection Act dedicates specific provisions to them. Namely, there is Article 4, which stipulates that one of the duties of the government towards the environment is to disseminate information on the environment and to facilitate the participation of the public in decisions that affect the environment.[142] It is also the duty of the Authority under Article 8(2)(d) to disseminate information. Article 57 of the same Act is specifically dedicated to access to information. It defines the right more fully and establishes the parameters regarding when and by whom such information may be requested. The Act also has dedicated provisions to public participation, namely Article 33, where certain decisions of the Authority have to be delivered in public, and Articles 51 and 54, which lay down the procedure for the adoption of regulations, plans and policies. Public participation is a legal requirement under these two Articles. In fact, the Minister is legally bound to publish draft subsidiary legislation for public consultation for a period of four weeks. When this time limit is reached, the Minister is to consider any notices of objection made by the public for or against the proposed legislation. This important exercise in public participation relating to environmental legislation allows the general public to participate in decision-making. In addition, ERA is consulted, and the Minister has the final say as to whether he accepts or rejects the objections made by the public and the recommendations made by ERA. It is good to note that the DPA (Chapter 504 of the Laws of Malta) largely mirrors those provisions found under the Environmental Protection Act just discussed.

While the two Acts provide for the legislative skeleton for the right to information and right of participation, these rights are truly fleshed out in the respective Regulations, which will be indicated below.

75. Directive 2003/35/EC of the European Parliament and of the Council, providing for public participation in respect of the drawing up of certain plans and programmes relating to the environment, was partially transposed in S.L. 549.41 through the Plans and Programmes (Public Participation) Regulations.[143]

These Regulations stipulate that it is the duty of the Competent Authority, being ERA, to make sure that the public is given early and effective opportunities to participate in the preparation and modification or review of plans or programmes. The process of ensuring the right of public participation is respected and is all-encompassing. The Regulations first state that the public is to be informed (be it by public notices or any appropriate means) of any proposals for plans, programmes, or the modification of existing ones. The public is then entitled to express comments and opinions before the decisions on the plans and programmes are made, and most importantly, these opinions and comments gathered through these public consultations are to be taken into consideration in the decision-making process. Subsequently, the competent authorities should inform the public of their decisions, including outlining the reasons and considerations taken to arrive at such decision,

142. Article 4(1)(d) of the EPA.
143. L.N. 74 of 2006 (S.L. 549.41).

including the information about the public participation process. These Regulations outline that reasonable timeframes shall be provided for the public to participate in the decision-making process.

76. The importance of these Regulations is that they create a basis or a skeleton structure on which the other legislation is to be built. For example, under the Industrial Emissions (Integrated Pollution Prevention and Control) Regulations (S.L. 549.77), which lay down the rules for the integrated prevention and control of pollution arising from certain industrial activities, public participation is obligatory.[144] The Regulations do not limit public participation to the granting of the actual permit, but they also extend post-granting of the permit. In fact, they put an obligation on the Competent Authority to make available information relating to the 'decision of granting of permit, reconsideration or updating of a permit'.

77. The Control of Major Accident Hazards Regulations,[145] which tackle the prevention of major accidents that involve dangerous substances and the limitation of their consequences for human health and the environment, also provides for public participation. In fact, Regulation 11(2) obliges every operator of an upper-tier establishment to ensure that 'all persons likely to be affected by a major accident receive regularly and in the most appropriate form, without having to request it, clear and intelligible information on safety measures and requisite behaviour in the event of a major accident'. Moreover, there is a further provision that a 'safety report' and an 'inventory of dangerous substances' are to be made available to the public upon request.

78. Under the Strategic Environmental Assessment Regulations (S.L. 549.61) and the Environmental Impact Assessment Regulations (S.L. 549.46), access to information and public participation form an integral part of the obligatory process under these two pieces of legislation. In both Regulations, one finds a rigorous process of how these two important pillars should be applied within a scheduled timeframe, which, if not respected, will render the whole process null and void.

79. The EU became a party to the Aarhus Convention in 2005, enshrining the first pillar of the Convention (access to information) in Directive 90/313/EEC, which has since been replaced by Directive 2003/4/EC on public access to environmental information. This Directive was transposed locally in S.L. 549.39, the Freedom of Access to Information on the Environmental Regulations.[146] The aim of these Regulations is to guarantee the right to access to environmental information held by or for public authorities. This includes ensuring that environmental information is made available and disseminated to the public. What is especially noteworthy in these Regulations are the definitions; first and foremost, there is a formal definition of 'public', which is to mean 'one or more natural or legal persons, and in accordance with national legislation or practice, their associations, organisations

144. Regulation 18
145. L.N. 179/2015 (S.L. 424.19).
146. L.N. 116 of 2005.

or groups'. This expands the notion of merely natural persons having the right to access information and creates a much wider net of stakeholders which is in line with the Aarhus Convention provisions. The Regulations also outline what constitutes 'environmental information', which again is essential in understanding what kind of information can be accessed.[147]

80. The Regulations (as in the Aarhus Convention itself) cover two aspects of the right to access information. On one part, there is the 'passive' side, whereby public authorities have a strict obligation to respond to requests for environmental information at their earliest – Regulation 4 provides a maximum of thirty days from receipt of request (unless the information requested is of such a complex nature to necessitate a further maximum of thirty days). Not only do the Regulations cater for a reasonable timeframe to address requests for information, but they also grant the applicant the facility to be provided with the information in the specific format requested. On the other hand, the Regulations also cover the 'active' aspect of such right, which encompasses the obligations relating to the provision of environmental information, through the collecting, updating, and disseminating of environmental information. Most notably, the Regulations outline the methods of updating such information to make sure that the information at hand is up-to-date and readily available in its 'best' form when requested. This includes updating the information as appropriate with texts of local and international legislation, policies and plans relating to the environment, progress reports on the implementation of such legislation and policies, reports on the state of the environment, any data which is pertinent to the environment, and any EIAs.

81. The Regulations continuously strive to make the process of accessing information as simple and as cost-effective for the applicant as possible. It is, in fact, enshrined in Regulation 8 of the same Regulations that the access to any public registers and examination *in situ* of the information requested must be free of charge. In the cases where the Competent Authority (being ERA) does request a charge for the provision of such information, the Regulations stipulate that the charge should be reasonable. Moreover, Regulation 11A ties in with the pillar of access to justice – here, the Regulations stipulate that in cases where the applicant decides to have recourse to the EPRT on matters relating to requests for environmental information, the Tribunal shall hold its first hearing within six days working from receipt of appeal. The six working days outlined in these Regulations confirm the commitment towards not only access of environmental information but also providing a solid system of redress within an expeditious timeframe.

82. Taking the above into consideration, one can firmly say that the Regulations create a holistic system which faithfully reflects the commitments put forward in the Aarhus Convention. Having said that, the Regulations (like the Aarhus Convention itself) do cater for those circumstances where the competent authority may refuse requests for environmental information. The reasons for refusal span from the

147. Vide Reg. 2.

request being manifestly unreasonable to being formulated in a too general manner, to the material requested being in the course of completion, and that request concerns internal communication.

83. These Regulations, however, provide ERA with no authority to seek redress against any public authority which refuses to provide the information so requested, even when the latter is obliged to do so under S.L. 549.39. Unlike other Regulations, ERA, therefore, cannot provide for its environment inspectors to take any action against such public authorities which do not comply with the Regulations. Compliance, or rather the lack of it, is not subject to enforcement.

Part II. Pollution Control

84. Before the promulgation of the 2001 EPA, there were a few pieces of legislation already regulating this environmental sector in a piecemeal and remedial manner. The 1967 Clean Air Act,[148] for example, was enacted to regulate air pollution caused by emissions of black smoke from chimneys and the engines of vessels. It is still in force, although there are now more specific pieces of legislation which regulate air quality. Transgression of its provisions leads to either a crime or a contravention, as the offence may be. The Act prohibits dark[149] smoke[150] emissions[151] from chimneys of any building by the occupier.[152] Emissions are exempted if they do not last longer than any period as specified by the Minister of Public Health by Regulations issued under the Act. Liability is not strict, and it would constitute a defence to claim that the contravention is due to some failure of the furnace or any apparatus linked to it, that the failure could not be reasonably foreseen and that the contravention could not reasonably have been prevented or minimised by action taken after the failure occurred.[153]

85. The 1991 EPA sought to regulate air pollution in a manner that was more preventive and in keeping with current air pollution legislation. More importantly, it established criminal responsibility if any of its provisions and any subsidiary legislation relating thereto were infringed. It defined pollution as 'the natural or artificial process resulting from the introduction of any contaminant into the environment'. Under this Act, it was the duty of the government to take preventive and remedial measures as may be necessary to address and abate the problem of pollution and any other form of environmental degradation in Malta and beyond, in accordance with the polluter-pays principle and the precautionary principle. In fact, the Minister responsible for the environment, among other things, could adopt Regulations which established standards, including maximum permitted levels in quantitative or qualitative terms, of discharge and emissions into the environment

148. Chapter 200 of the Laws of Malta.
149. Dark smoke is defined as such, 'when it compares to or is darker than Grade 2 under the Ringelmann Chart or as otherwise prescribed by Regulations issued by virtue of s. 13 of this Act'.
150. Smoke is defined as 'soot, ash, grit and gritty particles emitted in smoke'.
151. Defined as 'any structure or opening of any kind, from or through which, smoke or other matter foreign to normal air may be emitted' and defines a chimney of a building as 'including a chimney which serves a building but is separate therefrom'.
152. The word 'occupier' is rather ambiguous, as a factory is occupied, for example, by workers. The persons who ordered the activity that led to the emissions of dark smoke may, in fact, not occupy the building.
153. *See* Ch. 200 of the Laws of Malta, s. 3(3)(a–c).

of materials, substances or energy, and with regard to the use of any technology, equipment, matter, substance, method, or procedure in relation thereto. Furthermore, the Competent Authority had the function of establishing threshold levels of discharge from production, management, use, possession, or any other activity involving products, substances, and the production of or use of energy. The 1991 EPA also provided that, among other obligations, no person could carry out any activity related to pollution control, discharge, or cause or permit to be discharged such substance or energy as may be prescribed into the environment unless he is in possession of a licence from the Authority.

86. The 2001 EPA defined pollution in Article 2 as 'the direct or indirect introduction by man into the environment of substances, organism, genetic material or energy that cause or are likely to cause hazard to human health, harm to living resources or to ecosystems, or damage to amenities, or interfere with other legitimate uses of the environment'. It empowered the Minister via its enabling provisions under Article 9(2)(i) to issue regulations that ensure IPPC. The Regulations could have been published to: (i) establish systems which ensure such prevention and control; (ii) prescribe measures to control, prevent, manage or reduce pollution and degradation of the environment; (iii) control the keeping, management, trading in or use of substances and other activities which may cause or facilitate pollution; (iv) set standards including maximum of permitted levels in quantitative or qualitative terms, of discharge and emissions into the environment of materials, substances or energy and with regard to the use of any technology, equipment, matter, substance, method or procedure in relation thereto; (v) establish methodologies to be used in the monitoring of discharge and emission of substances and, or energy into the environment and to regulate the use of information gathered during such monitoring; (vi) prevent, control, reduce, remedy or otherwise manage situations which may lead to environmental emergencies and to prevent, control, reduce, remedy, or otherwise manage any adverse effects on the environment resulting therefrom. Infringements to the provisions of the EPA and the subsidiary legislation issued thereunder gave rise to a criminal offence apart from an action for civil damages and, where applicable, also environmental damages. Article 11(1)(c) of the 2001 EPA provided that no person could carry out any activity in relation to pollution control, discharge, or cause or permit to be discharged such substance or energy as may be prescribed into the environment without a licence from the competent authority. The enabling provisions of the 2001 EPA (that have been retained under the 2010 Bill) have allowed Malta to transpose without difficulty all the environmental *acquis communautaire* relating to pollution control. The enabling provisions of the 2001 EPA were retained in the subsequent Environment and Development Planning Act of 2010.

87. The pollution-oriented provisions of the 2001 EPA are now found in the new 2016 EPA with a few differences. Notably, the definition of pollution has been shortened to: the direct or indirect introduction by man, or due to natural processes, into the environment of substances, energy, organisms or genetic material that cause or are likely to cause hazard to human health, or harm to living resources or to the environment. Furthermore, the enabling provisions now specifically refer to the power of the Minister to issue Regulations to prevent, control, reduce, mitigate, remedy or otherwise manage situations which may lead to environmental emergencies.[154] The infringements regime has remained the same as in the 2001 EPA, combining criminal offences, actions for civil damages and environmental damages.

88. The discussion in the next chapters of this part focuses on the various pieces of subsidiary legislation that harmonise Maltese law on pollution control with the *acquis communautaire*.

Certain pieces of subsidiary legislation are all-pervasive, particularly where water and air pollution are involved. The two main pieces of legislation here are the Industrial Emissions (Framework) Regulations[155] and the Industrial Emissions (Integrated Pollution Prevention and Control) Regulations,[156] which both partly implement the provisions of the Industrial Emissions (Integrated Pollution Prevention and Control) (Recast) Directive.[157]

The former Regulations provide a framework for the integrated prevention and control of pollution arising from industrial activities, and the latter are partly implementing Regulations to the former. In the spirit of IPPC, both aim at preventing (or reducing where this is not practicable) emissions into air, water, and land in order to achieve a high level of protection of the environment taken as a whole. It should be noted, however, that they do not apply to research activities, development activities, or the testing of new products and processes. The specifics of these Regulations will be dealt with below, and it should be noted that certain Regulations will implement specific aspects of the Framework Regulations.

154. Environment Protection Act, Ch. 549 of the Laws of Malta, Art. 54(2)(k).
155. L.N. 9/2013 (S.L. 549.76).
156. L.N. 10/2013 (S.L. 549.77).
157. Directive 2010/75/EU of the European Parliament and of the Council of 24 Nov. 2010.

Chapter 1. Air Pollution

89. The subsidiary legislation transposing the environmental *acquis* on air quality is rather vast, and each set of Regulations corresponds to the various directives that make up this same sector under the EU's environmental *acquis*. There are, therefore, many pieces of subsidiary legislation, and to date, there has been no attempt to group them together by adopting a sub-sectoral approach. For better organisation, this chapter deals with the various legal sources of air pollution under the various headings denoting these same sub-sectors.

§1. Air Pollution from Industrial Sources

90. The Motor Vehicles Regulations of 1994[158] regulate emissions from motor vehicles. These Regulations are very general in nature and do not set any parameters as to what levels of pollutants emitted are permissible by law. The wording of these Regulations simply prohibits vehicles from emitting pollutants from their exhaust pipes[159] and that the exhaust be projected through the vehicle's silencer. Therefore, motorists are charged with committing such an offence only when the amount of emissions from exhaust pipes is visibly excessive.

91. L.N. 329/2002 on the Limitations of Emissions of Certain Pollutants into the Air from Large Combustion Plants Regulations transposed Directive 80/2001/EC of the European Council and Parliament and dated 21 October 2001. The Regulations applied only to combustion plants designed for the production of energy, with the exception of those which make direct use of the products of combustion in the manufacturing processes.

These Regulations were revoked and replaced by L.N. 172/2010, the Large Combustion Plants Regulations,[160] which transposed the same Directive.

Those Regulations were again revoked and replaced by L.N. 11/2013, the Industrial Emissions (Large Combustion Plants) Regulations.[161] These provide for the part-implementation of the IPPC (Recast) Directive, as well as for the implementation of the Industrial Emissions (Framework) Regulations. The new Regulations lay down rules for the limitation of atmospheric emissions from large combustion plants, applying to those with a total thermal input equal to or greater than $50MW_{Th}$, irrespective of the fuel source. Atmospheric emissions are sought to be reduced through these Regulations by discharging waste gases in a controlled way by means of a stack containing one or more flues. The stack height is to be calculated in a way to safeguard human health and the environment, using dispersion

158. L.N. 128/1994 (S.L. 65.11), issued under the Traffic Regulation Ordinance (Ch. 65 of the Laws of Malta).
159. *Ibid.*, Reg. 107 (private motor cars). Reg. 195, an identical provision applicable to buses, was revoked by L.N. 158/2009.
160. S.L. 549.56.
161. S.L. 549.78.

modelling software and procedures deemed appropriate by ERA. Waste gases themselves are the carrier gases together with any solid, liquid, or gaseous emissions discharged with it.

However, certain combustion plants are exempt from their provisions, such as reactors used in the chemical industry, post-combustion plants designed to purify waste gases by combustion,[162] and any technical apparatus used in vehicle, ship, or aircraft propulsion.

92. The Competent Authority is ERA, which must ensure that combustion plants falling within the scope of the Regulations comply with the emission limit values (ELVs) laid down in the various Schedules[163] for sulphur dioxide (SO_2), nitrogen oxides (NO_x), dust, and carbon monoxide (CO). Its role is that of overseer and supervisor, with the main obligations being imposed on the plant operators. It should be noted that although the caps are statutorily set, ERA has the power to impose stricter ELVs and even impose ELVs on exempt plants, in order to ensure compliance with regulations on ambient levels of atmospheric pollutants[164] and other regulations under the EPA or DPA that ERA deems relevant.

93. The ELVs vary depending on the type of fuel being fired and the date of its permit. The three types of fuel are solid, liquid, and gaseous. The time parameter depends on whether the plant in question was operating or permitted before certain dates.

If the plant was in operation or permitted prior to 7 January 2013, the permit must include conditions capping ELVs at the amounts set in Schedule I (if solid fuels), Schedule III (if liquid fuels), or Schedule V (if gaseous fuels). These ELVs are also applicable to plants permitted or in operation on or after 6 January 2011 (and therefore under the regimes of the previous Regulations).

Other plants, meaning those newly permitted or brought into operation under the regime of these Regulations, shall have permit conditions capping ELVs at the amounts set in Schedule II (if solid fuels), Schedule IV (if liquid fuels), or Schedule VI (if gaseous fuels).

It should be noted that the ELVs just mentioned are inapplicable to diesel engines (irrespective of fuel) and recovery boilers within installations for pulp production.

Plants firing solid or liquid fuels must also have permit conditions requiring compliance with ELVs for the heavy metals[165] in Schedule VII and the various dioxins and furans listed in Schedule VIII. Furthermore, if a plant is made up of multi-firing units involving the simultaneous use of two or more fuels, the permit conditions for compliance are to be established through a separate calculation to produce 'tailored' ELVs for a given plant.

---

162. When not operated as independent combustion plants.
163. The Schedules correspond to the type of plant and the date of its permit.
164. Particularly the Ambient Air Quality Regulations (S.L. 549.59).
165. These are: cadmium and thallium together; and arsenic, chromium, cobalt, copper, manganese, nickel, lead, antimony, and vanadium together.

Gas turbines are subject to a separate regime. If permitted before 7 January 2013, their permit conditions must set ELVs not higher than Schedule IX. If not, they must not be higher than those in Schedule X.

If the plant is modified or extended, the altered part is deemed to have been permitted under the new regime, meaning it must comply with the ELVs set out in Schedules II, IV, VI, and X, respectively, in terms of the total thermal output of the whole plant. It should be noted that in the case of modifications, this rule only applies if the change may have consequences for the environment and affect part of the plant having a rated thermal input of 50 MW $_{Th}$ or more. Nevertheless, the applicable limit value for CO shall not be higher than 100 mg/Nm $^{-3}$ in the case of any extension or modification.

Exemptions to the ELV rules could be obtained by operators by written declaration submitted to ERA by 1 October 2014, where the operator undertook to not operate the plant for more than 17,500 hours starting from 1 January 2016 and ending no later than 31 December 2023.

94. Each permit must contain conditions on procedures relating to malfunction or breakdown of the abatement equipment. In these scenarios, the operator must operate the plant using low-polluting fuels. However, if these are insufficient for the plant to keep within the set ELVs and twenty-four hours have elapsed from the failure, it must reduce or close down operations. ERA must be informed within forty-eight hours of the failure, and in any case, no plant shall have its cumulative duration of unabated operations exceed 124 hours per twelve months, except where the Director for Environment Protection deems there is an overriding need to maintain energy supplies or the plant with the breakdown would be replaced for a limited period by a worse plant.[166] Furthermore, the Director (and any officials to whom this role is delegated) may allow suspensions for a six-month maximum period from the requirement to comply with SO_2 ELVs in specific circumstances, mainly concerned with the maintenance of energy supplies and extraordinary extenuating circumstances (such as a serious shortage of low-sulphur fuel). In any case, the temporary derogation, ordered by ERA, must be published in the *Gazette* immediately.

95. The plant operator has monitoring and reporting obligations for ERA to ensure the ELVs are being respected. He must monitor the emissions of all pollutants in the various Schedules contained in the waste gases of the plant, with those of SO_2 , NO_X , dust, and CO being monitored continuously. He must also monitor the relevant process operation parameters of oxygen content, temperature, pressure, and water vapour content.[167] The installation and control of the monitoring equipment must be subject to control and annual surveillance tests. Furthermore, all sampling and analysis of pollution and process parameters, as well as reference measurement methods to calibrate automated measurement systems, are to be carried out in accordance with the European Committee of Standardisation standard

166. One which would cause an overall increase in emissions when compared to the plant with the breakdown.

167. Water vapour content need not be measured if the sampled exhaust gas is dried prior to analysis.

methods. If these are unavailable, ISO standards, or any national standard method from any of the EU Member States, may be used.

All monitoring results must be recorded, processed, and presented in such a manner as to allow ERA to verify the plant's compliance with ELVs of the permit.[168] ERA must be informed of the monitoring results in a timely manner, as stipulated in the permit.

The reporting obligations involve the operator forwarding an emissions inventory to the plant to ERA, which includes the energy input and loads of SO_2, NO_X, and dust (as total suspended particulates).[169] The inventory must also include specific plant details, including those relating to thermal output and total annual loads of pollutants, as set out in Schedule XIV.

96. The offences under these Regulations are the following: failure to comply with any lawful order in terms of any provision of the Regulations; contravening any restriction, prohibition or requirement imposed by or under the Regulations; acting in contravention of any provision of the same; or conspiring, attempting, aiding, or abetting any other person by whatever means, to perform any of the above.

A first conviction is liable to a fine (*multa*) of between EUR 23,000 and EUR 233,000, or imprisonment for a term not exceeding two years, or both. A second or subsequent conviction entails a fine (*multa*) of between EUR 46,000 and EUR 466,000, imprisonment for a term not exceeding two years, or both. The owner of a vehicle used in committing any offence mentioned is also liable in the same manner and degree, where applicable.

The court[170] must also order the convict to pay for the expenses incurred by the public entities (or other persons acting on their behalf) involved in the implementation of the Regulations and restitution of the environment as a result of the offence. It must also order the revocation of the permit and the confiscation of the *corpus delicti*. In any case, the provisions of Articles 21 and 30(1) of the Criminal Code apply, but the relevant disqualification can never be for less than a year.

97. L.N. 101/2018, the Limitation of Emissions of Certain Pollutants into the Air from Medium Combustion Plants Regulations,[171] transposes the provisions of Directive 2015/2193/EU on the same subject matter. The aim is to lay down rules to control emissions of SO_2, NOx, and dust into the air from those plants and thereby reduce emissions into the air and the potential risks they pose to human health and the environment. They also lay down rules to monitor CO emissions.

The Regulations apply to plants with a rated thermal input equal to or greater than 1 MW and less than 50 MW, irrespective of the fuel consumed. They also apply to 'combinations': the aggregation of two or more such plants, which are to be considered as a single medium combustion plant, and their rated thermal input is to be added together for the purpose of calculating the total rated thermal input of the

168. The permit must include a template to be followed by the operator.
169. The loads must be calculated by adding the mass of pollutant emitted by the combustion plant in question each day, on the basis of volumetric flow rates of waste gases.
170. The Court of Magistrates (Malta or Gozo) as a Court of Criminal Judicature. The Attorney General has a right of appeal from its decisions to the Court of Criminal Appeal.
171. S.L. 549.122.

plant. These plants fall under these Regulations even where the total rated thermal input is equal to or greater than 50 MW unless they form a large combustion plant.[172] The conditions to be fulfilled to be classified as a combination are: either the waste gases of the individual plants are discharged through a common stack, or the waste gases could, in ERA's judgment, be discharged like so, taking technical and economic factors into account. Certain plants are exempt from the provisions of these Regulations, such as those falling under the scope of other Regulations,[173] crematoria, any technical apparatus used in the propulsion of a vehicle, ship or aircraft, and post-combustion plants designed to purify the waste gases from industrial processes by combustion and which are not operated as independent combustion plants.

All plants falling under these Regulations must respect the minimum chimney height of 3 m above roof level.

98. All medium combustion plants must operate under a permit duly issued by ERA. No such existing plant with a rated thermal input greater than 5 MW is to operate without a permit, and the same is to apply to existing plants with a rated thermal input lesser than or equal to 5 MW. Operators of new plants are to notify ERA and apply for a permit prior to the commencement of operations, with deadlines to apply in the Regulations themselves.

The permit is to include the type, frequency, and format of information concerning events of non-compliance to be provided by operators to the competent authority, along with the information in the First Schedule, such as the plant's rated thermal input, yearly fuel burn by fuel type, and yearly waste gas flow rate. The application form itself is to be published and accessible from ERA's website. ERA may request a bank guarantee to ensure compliance with the permit conditions. Refusals must be accompanied by reasons.

Permits are for a fixed time and must include the timeframes to apply for a renewal. The renewal is to be applied for through a form provided by ERA, accompanied by any other relevant information requested and the permit fee.

Furthermore, permit conditions may be reviewed (added, amended, revoked, or substituted) in a number of cases: where the pollution caused by the installation is of such significance that the existing ELVs of the permit need to be revised or new values need to be included; where operational safety requires other techniques to be used; where it is necessary to comply with new or revised environmental legislation enacted under the Act; where the validity of a permit has elapsed; or as ERA deems fit in accordance with the Regulations.

Any planned change to the plant which would affect the applicable ELVs is to be informed to ERA without undue delay, such that, where appropriate, the permit is updated. The plant must not commence or resume operations prior to the issuance of the update.

---

172. This would be covered by the Industrial Emissions (Large Combustion Plants) Regulations (S.L. 549.78).

173. The Industrial Emissions (Large Combustion Plants) Regulations, Industrial Emissions (Waste Incineration) Regulations (S.L. 549.81), and Measures against the Emission of Gaseous and Particulate Pollutants from Internal Combustion Engines to be Installed in Non-Road Mobile Machinery Regulations (S.L. 427.85).

Plants covered by the IPPC Regulations are deemed to be compliant with the Medium Combustion Plants Regulations through compliance with those Regulations.

99. The ELVs set out in the Second Schedule must be observed without prejudice to the IPPC Regulations. The Schedule sets ELVs for SO_2, NO_X, and dust, depending on the fuel used, for a variety of plants as follows: existing plants with a rated thermal input equal to or greater than 1 MW and less than 5 MW, existing plants with a rated thermal input greater than 5 MW, existing engines and gas turbines, new plants and new engines and gas turbines. The Regulations establish specific cut-off dates by which the ELVs must be reached and not exceeded for each installation. Where a plant simultaneously uses two or more fuels, a specific formula needs to be applied to calculate the ELV for each pollutant.

It should be noted that certain plants may be exempt from observing the ELVs by ERA or are only bound to observe them by the Regulations from a specific cut-off date, depending on the nature of the plant. Furthermore, though the ELVs are statutorily established, ERA may apply stricter ones to individual plants in zones or parts of zones incompliant with the air quality limit values laid down in Ambient Air Quality Regulations,[174] provided that applying such ELVs would effectively contribute to a noticeable improvement of air quality. Derogations may also be granted to various plants for statutorily stipulated periods due to a sudden interruption in the supply of the relevant fuel where the plant only uses that fuel: these are either low-sulphur fuel or gas fuel.

100. The plant operator is to monitor emissions in accordance with Part 1 of Schedule 3, which lays down the frequency and methods of measurement for emissions. The monitoring results are to be recorded, kept, and processed in such a way as to enable the verification of compliance with the ELVs in accordance with the rules set out in Part 2 of the Third Schedule. The operator must also keep a record of the type and quantities of fuels used in the plant and of any malfunctions or breakdown of secondary abatement equipment, along with any records of non-compliance and measures taken to restore compliance. All this data and information is to be made available to ERA as soon as possible upon request, without undue delay. The operator must also provide ERA with all necessary assistance to enable it to carry out any inspections and site visits, take samples, and gather any information necessary for the performance of its duties for the purposes of these Regulations. ERA may also require the operator to submit periodic reports as part of the obligations arising out of the permit.

101. ERA's own duties under the Regulations mainly relate to ensuring the compliance of the operator and the meeting of ELVs; thus, a supervisory role. It must inspect and monitor all installations as it deems necessary to this end and set up a system of environmental inspections of installations to ascertain compliance with the Regulations. Furthermore, non-routine environmental inspections shall be carried out to investigate serious environmental complaints, serious environmental

174. As part of the development of air quality plans in those Regulations (S.L. 549.59).

accidents, incidents, and occurrences of non-compliance. ERA must require the operator of a non-compliant plant to take all necessary measures to secure compliance, and where this causes a severe degradation of local air quality, the operation of the plant is to be suspended until compliance is restored and ERA's confirmation it may resume operations.

ERA also has disclosure obligations. It must hold a register with information on each plant, which is to be made available to the public in accordance with the Freedom of Access to Information on the Environment Regulations.

102. It is an offence under these Regulations to: fail to comply with any provision of the same, or with permit conditions or lawful orders in terms of any of the same; operate a plant falling within these Regulations' scope without a permit; contravene a condition in an environmental permit; fail to comply with any notice issued under the EPA; provide incorrect values, data or other information pertaining to the relevant activity; fail to report a breach of a permit condition; or conspire, attempt to conspire, air or abet any other person by whatever means to contravene the provisions of the Regulations, or to fail to comply with any of the same or with a permit or lawful order issued under them, or to contravene any restriction, prohibition or requirement by or under them.

A first conviction is liable to a fine (*multa*) of between EUR 1,500 and EUR 3,000, imprisonment for a term not exceeding two years, or both. A second or subsequent conviction is liable to a fine (*multa*) of between EUR 3,000 and EUR 6,000, imprisonment not exceeding two years, or both. Furthermore, the court shall order any person who has been found guilty of committing an offence against these Regulations to pay for the expenses incurred by ERA as a result of the said offence, to undertake mitigation or prevention measures in order to address offence-related damages, the revocation of the permit issued by ERA and the confiscation of the *corpus delicti*, if applicable. Articles 23 and 30(1) of the Criminal Code are *mutatis mutandis* applicable; however, the disqualification from holding a licence, etc., shall not be for less than one year.

103. L.N. 78/2006, the Limitation of Emission of Volatile Organic Compounds (Paints, Varnishes and Vehicle Refinishing Products) Regulations, was a transposition of the EU Directive 2004/42/EC,[175] which amends Directive, 1999/13/EC. It was published under the EPA[176] and the Product Safety Act.[177] The Directive it

175. In reaction to this issue, the EU had adopted Directive 2001/81/EC, which established national emission ceilings for certain atmospheric pollutants, including VOCs. However, limit values for VOCs may differ significantly from country to country. Another issue was that VOCs in one Member State would affect the air quality in other Member States. To address such complications, the EU adopted another Directive, 2004/42/CE. This recent Directive aims to harmonise limit values for the content of VOCs in the products (paints, varnishes, and vehicle refinishing products) to ensure that these limits will not restrict the free movement of these products in the market. The Directive went into force on 30 Apr. 2004 and had to be transposed into national law by the 30 Oct. 2005.

176. Chapter 435 of the Laws of Malta.

177. Chapter 427 of the Laws of Malta.

transposed bears the same name as the Regulations and was concluded by the European Parliament and the Council of 21 April 2004.

These Regulations were revoked and replaced by new Regulations of the same name in 2012,[178] which transposed the same Directive. The Regulations relate to the limitation of emissions of volatile organic substances in certain paints and varnishes and vehicle refinishing products. The main purpose of the Legal Notice is to reduce the levels of air pollution (ground-level ozone or summer smog) by limiting the amount of solvents[179] contained in certain paints, varnishes, and vehicle refinishing products.[180] To achieve this, the Legal Notice lays down a number of standards which are to be complied with. These include a set of requirements, the proper manner of labelling the products, how monitoring should be carried out, and that there should be free circulation of such products if they fulfil all the requirements.

104. Product categories falling within the scope of the Regulations are listed in Schedule I and can be marketed in the EU only if they comply with the limit values in Schedule II. Furthermore, such products must be labelled as stipulated when placed on the market. A market surveillance system has also been developed to verify the volatile organic compounds (VOC) content of these products. In fact, there are stringent limits for maximum content limits of solvents. The Regulations make no direct reference as to which operators they are trying to target, but since they identify the products they regulate, the operators would be those people that trade in or otherwise make use of the mentioned products. However, they do provide for the grant of licences to buy and sell products that are not within Schedule II in a strictly limited quantity for purposes of restoration and maintenance of old buildings and old cars. This brings into the picture people working in property restorations and also sprayers and panel beaters restoring vintage cars. Manufacturers of the products must put up certain information on the packaging of the products, and hence they are affected too.

105. The competent authority is the Technical Regulations Division within the Malta Competition and Consumer Affairs Authority (MCCAA), which is responsible for ensuring conformity with this piece of legislation. It has to ensure that the products listed in Schedule I carry an appropriate label when placed on the market and must set up a monitoring programme jointly with the Environment Protection Directorate to verify compliance with the Regulations. In addition, the Competent Authority must also grant individual licences for the purchase and sale of the products mentioned above to be used for restoration and maintenance purposes, so long as it is furnished with certification from the authorised body to the effect that the thing is indeed regarded as being of historical and cultural value.

106. With regard to labelling, each label must indicate: the subcategory of the product and the relevant VOC limit values (in g/l) as indicated in Schedule II; and

178. L.N. 152/2012 (S.L. 549.71).

179. Solvents can also be referred to as volatile organic substances that react with sunlight to form ozone.

180. These products are set out in Annex I of the Legal Notice.

the maximum content of VOC (in g/l) of the product in a ready-to-use condition. When products are in their ready-to-use condition and comply with these conditions, they should not be restricted, prevented, or prohibited from being placed on the market on grounds dealt with in these Regulations.

107. A person is guilty of an offence under these Regulations if he: fails to comply with any order lawfully given through the Regulations; contravenes any restriction, prohibition or requirement imposed by or under the same; or conspires or attempts, or aids or abets, any other person by whatever means to commit any of the above.

A person convicted under these Regulations is liable to a fine (*multa*) of between EUR 23,000 and EUR 233,000, or imprisonment for a term not exceeding two years, or both, on a first conviction. On second or subsequent convictions, the offender shall be liable to a fine (*multa*) of between EUR 46,000 and EUR 466,000 or imprisonment for a term of not more than two years or both such a fine and imprisonment. In addition, if a person uses a vehicle to commit an offence under these Regulations, the vehicle's owner is held liable in the same manner and degree (where applicable).

The court[181] must order any person who has been found guilty to pay for expenses incurred by public entities and/or any persons acting on their behalf and who were involved in implementing these Regulations, as well as to pay for the restitution of the environment, as a result of the offence. The court may also order the revocation of the permit issued by the competent authority and the confiscation of the *corpus delicti*. Articles 23 and 30(1) of the Criminal Code apply *mutatis mutandis,* but the disqualification from holding or obtaining a licence, permit, or authority shall not be for less than one year for any case.

108. L.N. 234/2002, which adopted the IPPC Regulations, transposed the IPPC Directive as amended.[182] This piece of legislation was revoked and replaced by eponymous regulations: the Industrial Emissions (Integrated Pollution Prevention and Control) Regulations, which partly implement the Recast IPPC Directive as explained above. It must be read in conjunction with the Industrial Emissions (Framework) Regulations. The main objective of this piece of legislation is to prevent, or, where this is not practicable, to reduce, atmospheric pollution in water, air, and land, and thus create an obligation on industrial and agricultural activities having a high pollution potential. The Regulations impose the requirement to have a permit, which can only be granted if the required environmental conditions are met. These conditions include 'best available techniques' (BAT), which have to be operated by the industries and agricultural activities, and a list of pollutants which have

181. The Court of Magistrates (Malta or Gozo) as a Court of Criminal Inquiry. The Attorney General always has a right of appeal to the Court of Criminal Appeal from the relevant decision.
182. Council Directive 96/61/EC of the 24 Sep. 1996.

to be controlled. Schedule I provides a list of industrial activities to which the Regulations apply, some of which must reach the capacity thresholds set out therein to fall within their ambit.[183]

109. The main obligation imposed by the IPPC Regulations upon the operators is the requirement of a permit issued by the Competent Authority, which is ERA, for all the installations falling within the scope of Schedule I. The term 'integrated', as stated in the title of the Regulations, implies that the permit must take into consideration the whole performance of the installation in relation to the environment, mainly its pollution. Consequently, the application for a permit by the operator to the Competent Authority must contain not only a non-technical summary of some details but also separate descriptions of individual points; namely, a description of the installation; materials and energy used and generated; sources and nature of foreseeable emissions; proposed technology and techniques for preventing or reducing emissions; and measures planned to prevent or recover wastes generated. The applicant must also provide a description of the main alternatives (if any) and the measures planned to monitor emissions. These requirements enable the industrial installations subject to IPPC permits in accordance with the Regulations to identify ways to minimise as much as possible pollution produced by their activities.

110. For a person to be allowed to operate an installation as per Schedule I, the Competent Authority must be assured that appropriate measures are taken against pollution, no significant pollution is caused, waste production is avoided (and where this is not practicable, such waste is dealt with according to the appropriate regulations), energy is used efficiently, accidents are prevented, and, if any, their consequences are limited. The Competent Authority also must ensure that upon cessation of activities, the site is to be returned to a satisfactory state and that pollution risks are to be avoided.

111. Therefore, permits under these Regulations have to contain pollution standards, which must be set on the basis of BAT, with reference to environmental quality standards (EQS). The selection of BAT involves balancing the desirability of environmental protection against the cost of achieving it. The criteria for determining the BATs are found in Schedule III.

However, BATs in themselves are not set in stone. Therefore, ERA is under a responsibility to follow developments in BAT and the publication of any new or updated BAT conclusions, which are to be made available to the public concerned. Furthermore, ERA must encourage, where appropriate, the development and application of emerging techniques, particularly those identified in BAT reference documents. This is to be done taking into account any guidance of the European Commission on the matter.

EQS may also require stricter conditions than those achievable by the use of BAT. Hence, ERA must include the additional measures to be taken in the permit without prejudice to other measures which may be taken to comply with EQS.

183. For example, the energy industries, mineral industry, chemical industry, production of basic inorganic chemicals, and so forth.

112. If ERA grants the permit, the operator is bound to inform it of any change in the operation of the installation, including the transfer of the permit from one operator to another. The Regulations establish the criteria upon which the Competent Authority bases its decision as to whether or not to grant the permit. First and foremost, ERA analyses the eventual impact the installation in question would have on both the environment and human health. The applicant's suitability to undertake the proposed activity is also taken into consideration, giving importance to the operator's record of compliance with the law, his financial capacity to comply with all his obligations and liability, as well as his qualification, experience, and technical competence. The Competent Authority is also bound to verify both the measures proposed by the operator and the use of the best available technology, not entailing excessive costs.

Once a permit has been issued by the Competent Authority, the operators have significant responsibility for monitoring emissions and supplying it with data required to check compliance with the permit, which holds an operator legally responsible and accountable in terms of the installation. This ensures that the operator is in accordance with the Regulations and also with any other condition stipulated in the permit. The duty of the Competent Authority as the regulator is to undertake independent monitoring and inspections of the installation to check compliance with the set emission limits. This monitoring includes a systematic surveillance of the variations of a certain chemical or physical characteristic of an emission, discharge, consumption, equivalent parameter, technical measure, and so forth. Such monitoring should be based on repeated measurements or observations at an appropriate frequency in accordance with documented and agreed procedures. It is to be carried out in a manner that provides useful information. Information may range from simple visual observations to precise numerical data. Therefore, monitoring is mainly based on direct measurements, surrogate parameters, mass balances, other calculations, and emission factors.

113. It is ERA's obligation to decide on the validity of the permit issued. Thus, it shall periodically reconsider and, where necessary, update the permit conditions. The Competent Authority must also set ELVs for the polluting substances referred to in Schedule II in the permit. If ERA believes that the operator is breaching the conditions of a permit, enforcement options are available where an enforcement, suspension, or revocation notice can be served. The permitting enforcement and control procedures are required to be coordinated and negotiated. Above all, ERA has the responsibility to make the permit application, the decision, and the permit itself, together with the monitoring reports available to the public, as well as the overarching duty to allow effective public participation in the permit procedure from an early stage.

The Regulations require ERA to set up a system of environmental inspections of installations addressing the full range of relevant environmental effects from the installations concerned. Operators must assist ERA in any site visit to collect samples, perform inspections, etc., and each installation must be covered by an environmental inspection plan to allow for routine inspections by ERA.

114. A person shall be guilty of an offence under these Regulations if he: fails to comply with any provision in these Regulations, with any conditions laid down in the permit, or with any order lawfully issued in terms of the Regulations; acts in contravention of any of the provisions laid down in the Regulations; ignores any restrictions, prohibitions, or requirements imposed by or under the same; or conspires or attempts, or aids or abets any other person by whatever means, to perform any of the above.

If a person is convicted of an offence under these Regulations, he will be liable on a first conviction to a fine (*multa*) of not less than EUR 23,000 but not exceeding EUR 233,000, to imprisonment for a term not exceeding two years, or both. From the second conviction onward, a person shall be liable to either a fine (*multa*) of not less than EUR 46,000, but not exceeding EUR 466,000, to a term of imprisonment not exceeding two years, or both. If a person is found guilty of committing an offence by means of a vehicle, the owner of this vehicle (if not the same person committing the offence) shall be held liable in the same manner and punished to the same degree as the defendant.

The defendant shall be ordered by the court[184] to pay for the expenses incurred by ERA as a result of the offence. The court shall also order the revocation of the permit issued by ERA itself and the confiscation of the *corpus delicti*, which includes the vehicle used, if applicable. The disqualification from holding or obtaining a licence, permit, or authority under Articles 23 and 30(1) of the Criminal Code shall also apply to proceedings in respect of any offences committed against these Regulations. This disqualification shall, in no case, be for less than one year.

115. L.N. 152/2007, the European Pollutant Release and Transfer Register Reporting Obligations Regulations,[185] is to be read in conjunction with Regulation (EC) No. 166/2006 of the European Parliament and of the Council of 18 January 2006 concerning the establishment of a European Pollutant Release and Transfer Register and amending Council Directives 91/689/EEC and 96/61/EC, referred to in L.N. 152/2007 as the European Community (EC) Regulations. As the status of Regulations issued by the EU is higher than that of national legislation, L.N. 152/2007 specifies that the scope of these Regulations is twofold. First, to establish legally binding templates[186] for local operators to report releases and offsite transfers to ERA, as the Competent Authority, according to the prescribed time frames, and second, to have the necessary legal framework to establish penalties applicable to infringements of the provisions of the EC Regulation.[187]

116. Consequently, the operator of each facility listed in Annex I of the EC Regulations shall provide all the data referred to in Article 5 of EC Regulation 166/2006 within six months after the end of the reporting year for the first reporting year

184. The Court of Magistrates (Malta or Gozo) as a Court of Criminal Inquiry. The Attorney General always has a right of appeal to the Court of Criminal Appeal from the relevant decision.
185. S.L. 549.47.
186. In order to fulfil Art. 7 of Regulation (EC) No. 166/2006.
187. In order to fulfil the obligations of Art. 20 of the EC Regulation.

and within three months after the end of the reporting year for all subsequent reporting years. Data shall be submitted to the Competent Authority in electronic form as may be established from time to time by the Competent Authority. The first reporting year was 2007. An operator can apply for an extension of up to three months to the period allowed for reporting accordingly to the Competent Authority, provided appropriate justification is presented. The Competent Authority may grant an extension where it considers that this would be justified. When reporting, operators shall follow the guidelines established in the latest version of the Guidance Document for the Implementation of the European PRTR, published by the European Commission, and any template that may be published from time to time by notice in the Government Gazette by the Competent Authority.

117. Any operator shall be guilty of an offence under L.N. 152/2007 if he: does not meet the reporting obligations within the established time frames; does not prepare a complete report in the correct format determined by the Regulations; or if he reports incorrect values or data that are not quality assured, as prescribed in Article 9(1) of the EC Regulations. Any operator who commits an offence against L.N. 152/2007 shall be liable on a first conviction to a fine (*multa*) of not less than EUR 1,164.69 but not exceeding EUR 2,329.37; on a second or subsequent conviction, to a fine (*multa*) of not less than EUR 2,329.37) but not exceeding EUR 4,658.75 or imprisonment for a term not exceeding two years, or both such fine and imprisonment. Where there is a continuing offence against L.N. 152/2007, the court shall, in addition to the fine (*multa*) prescribed above, award an additional fine of not less than EUR 116.46 but not exceeding EUR 1,164.69 for every day, or part thereof, during which the continuance shall have subsisted, so however that the fine (*multa*) for the continuance of the offence and the fine (*multa*) awarded under Regulation 5 shall not exceed, in the aggregate EUR 23,293.73.

The court shall order any operator who has been found guilty of committing an offence against L.N. 152/2007 to meet his reporting obligations and to pay for the expenses incurred by the Competent Authority or other persons acting on its behalf involved in the implementation of the Legal Notice as a result of the said offence. The court shall also order the revocation of the permit issued by the Competent Authority and the confiscation of the *corpus delicti*. The court also orders the operator to bear all or part of the costs incurred due to any infringement action brought by the European Commission against Malta under these Regulations. Disqualification from holding or obtaining a license, permit, or authority shall, in no case, be for less than one year. Proceedings for an offence against these Regulations shall be taken before the Court of Magistrates of Malta (or Gozo) and shall be in accordance with the provisions of the Criminal Code regulating the procedure before the said courts as courts of criminal judicature. The Attorney General shall always have a right of appeal to the Court of Criminal Appeal from any judgment given by the Court of Magistrates of Malta (or Gozo) in respect of proceedings for any offence against these Regulations.

118. The Industrial Emissions (Titanium Dioxide) Regulations[188] order the prevention of the emission of acid droplets from installations producing titanium dioxide and require all emissions to stay below the limit values established in Schedule II. Limit values are established for emissions of: dust; gaseous sulphur dioxide and trioxide discharged from digestion and calcination;[189] and chlorine for installations using the chloride process. The operator must monitor the emissions into the air to verify compliance both with permit conditions and the Regulations, following Schedule III.

§2. Air Quality in General

119. Air Quality was regulated by five separate pieces of legislation up until 2010, each transposing an EU Directive on ambient air quality. The first was L.N. 216/2001,[190] which transposed the Air Quality Framework Directive.[191] This defined the basic principles of a common air quality strategy in order to assess ambient air quality, as well as establishing objectives for air quality to avoid, prevent, or reduce harmful effects on human health and the environment. The other four pieces of legislation each transposed one of the four daughter Directives of the Framework Directive, addressing specific pollutants having adverse effects on ambient air quality. These were: L.N. 224/2001,[192] L.N. 163/2002,[193] L.N. 11/2003,[194] and L.N. 292/2007.[195]

All these Regulations were revoked and replaced by the Ambient Air Quality Regulations,[196] which deal with the subject matter of all five pieces of legislation in a more holistic manner. They transpose: the aforementioned Directive 2004/107/EC; Directive 2008/50/EC on ambient air quality and cleaner air for Europe; and Commission Directive (EU) 2015/1480, amending Directive 2004/107/EC and establishing rules concerning reference methods, data validation and location sampling points for the assessment of ambient air quality.

The Regulations, dealing with so many atmospheric pollutants, necessarily adopted a classification methodology to refer to select categories of pollutants. This approach will be followed here too. The Regulations adopt three groups of

188. L.N. 13/2013 (S.L. 549.80).
189. Including acid droplets calculated as SO_2 equivalent.
190. Ambient Air Quality Assessment and Management Regulations.
191. Directive 96/62/EC.
192. The Limit Values for Nitrogen Dioxide, Sulphur Dioxide and Oxides of Nitrogen, Particulate Matter and Lead in Ambient Air Regulations, transposing Council Directive 1999/30/EC.
193. The Limit Values for Benzene and Carbon Monoxide in Ambient Air Regulations, transposing Directive 2000/69/EC.
194. The Ozone in Ambient Air Regulations, transposing Directive 2002/3/EC.
195. The Arsenic, Cadmium, Mercury, Nickel and Polycyclic Aromatic Hydrocarbons in Ambient Air Regulations, transposing Directive 2004/107/EC.
196. L.N. 478/2010 (S.L. 549.59).

pollutants, with ozone being a class of its own.[197] Group A pollutants are sulphur dioxide, nitrogen dioxide, oxides of nitrogen, particulate matter (PM_{10} and $PM_{2.5}$), lead, benzene, and carbon monoxide. Group B pollutants are arsenic, cadmium, nickel, and benzo(a)pyrene. Group C pollutants are benzo(a)anthracene, benzo(b)fluoranthene, benzo(j)fluoranthene, benzo(k)fluoranthene, indeno(1,2,3-cd)pyrene, and dibenzo(a,h)anthracene. Furthermore, 'ambient air' itself is understood to be outdoor air in the troposphere, excluding workplaces where provisions regulating occupational health and safety apply and to which the public does not have regular access.[198]

120. ERA, as the competent authority, must divide the Islands into zones and agglomerations for the purposes of these Regulations. An agglomeration is a type of zone so designated, which is a conurbation with either a population of over 250,000 inhabitants or a population of that amount or less but with a given population density per km^2 to be established by ERA itself. Therefore, reference to 'zone' here will include 'agglomeration'. Air quality is to be assessed and managed by ERA throughout all zones and agglomerations, and different zones may be established for different pollutants where this is considered appropriate.

The classification of zones is to occur in relation to the established assessment thresholds for Groups A and B and the long-term objectives for ozone. This classification is to be reviewed every five years in accordance with the procedure laid down in Section B of Schedule 2 for both group A and group B pollutants. However, it must be reviewed earlier in the event of a significant change in the activities relevant to the concentrations of both groups of pollutants in ambient air.

121. ERA is responsible for: the assessment of ambient air quality, ensuring the accuracy of measurements, the analysis of measurement methods, the coordination of Community-wide quality assurance programmes organised by the European Commission, cooperating with other Member States and with the European Commission, and the approval of measurement systems.

Sampling points for these measurements in each zone are not to be less than the minimum number established in Schedule 5, divided into points for Group A pollutants, Group B pollutants, and ozone, respectively. The data quality objectives to be achieved are set out in Schedule 1, while the reference methods to be used are prescribed in Schedule 10. The latter are to measure: concentrations of Group A pollutants in ambient air, concentrations of ozone in ambient air, and concentrations in ambient air and deposition rates of Group B pollutants.

The air quality studies are to be conducted in accordance with ERA's own guidance document, which are to be followed in all air quality studies required under

---

197. It should be noted that as for ozone, L.N. 215/2001 (S.L. 549.11), Air Pollution by Ozone Regulations, covers more or less the same subject matter as the Ambient Air Quality Regulations, with the same approach. They appear to have been subsumed into the latter, and will therefore not be tackled specifically.

198. The workplaces must be within the scope of the Work Place (Minimum Health and Safety Requirements) Regulations (S.L. 424.15).

any regulations issued under the EPA. ERA itself must compile an annual air quality report in order to assess compliance with the limit values, target values, long-term objectives, and national exposure reduction target in Schedule 7. If these aims are not achieved, or it is predicted that they will not be achieved, the Minister is to declare an Air Quality Management Area on ERA's advice. This is declared through an Air Quality Management Order, as stipulated in Schedule 13 and published in the *Gazette*.

One of ERA's fundamental statutory obligations, once the Order has been issued, is to prepare an Air Quality Action Plan for the area in question within twelve months from the publication of the Order. The aim is to keep the exceedance period as short as possible so as to mitigate the adverse impacts of higher-than-desirable levels of atmospheric pollutants and ensure compliance with the Schedule 7 requirements as soon as possible. Measures which may be included in the Action Plan are the rerouting or restriction of traffic flows, suspension of construction works in the area, and temporary suspension of commercial or industrial activity having an adverse impact on air quality (stone quarries, for example). These measures should take into account an integrated approach to the protection of air, water, and soil and not have a negative effect on any other Member State. Furthermore, they should be adopted on the strength of predictive modelling software to ensure their effectiveness in restoring the required localised ambient air quality. Should the exceedance occur in relation to more than one pollutant, an integrated Action Plan is to be prepared targeting all pollutants concerned. In any case, the Plan should ensure that the alert thresholds established in Schedule 8 are not exceeded in the zones in question.

Should ozone levels exceed the Schedule 8 alert thresholds, an Action Plan is only to be adopted if, following assessment, it results that the plan will result in a reduction of the risk, duration, or severity of the exceedance when taking national, geographical, meteorological, and economic considerations into account.

Prior to issuing the Action Plan, ERA is to consult the Air Quality Plan Subcommittee established under these Regulations. It is composed of a number of stakeholder representatives, such as the Director for Environmental Health, the CEO of the Transport Authority, a representative of the Malta Chamber of Commerce, Enterprise and Industry, a Local Councils Association representative, and a representative of environmental NGOs.

A short-term Air Quality Action Plan can also be drawn up for those zones for which there is a risk that the pollutant levels exceed one or more of the alert thresholds in Schedule 8.

In the case of significant transboundary pollution from neighbouring EU Member States causing an exceedance of any alert threshold, limit value, target value or long-term objective, ERA is to contact the competent authority of the relevant States in order to initiate the process under Article 25(1) of Directive 2008/50/EC. The aim is to cooperate and, where appropriate, draw up joint air quality plans in order to remove the exceedances through the application of appropriate but proportionate measures. ERA can also maintain dialogue with the respective competent authorities depending on the situation at hand where transboundary pollution is concerned.

122. Assessment thresholds are established in Schedule 2, prescribing both upper and lower thresholds for Group A and Group B pollutants, respectively. The long-term objectives of ozone are set out in Part III of Section D of Schedule 7. The method of assessment varies depending on how the respective concentrations in a given zone fare in relation to these standards.

Air quality is to be assessed by ERA in all zones with respect to Group A and B pollutants and ozone in accordance with the criteria in Schedule 3. The concentrations of Group A and B pollutants are to be assessed in zones in which their levels exceed the upper assessment threshold, while concentrations of ozone in zones are to be assessed where the long-term objectives have been exceeded during any of the previous five years of measurements during which fixed measurements were recorded. Group A substances and ozone are to be assessed using continuous measurements, whereas continuous measurements or random sampling can be used for Group B pollutants. These may be supplemented by modelling techniques or indicative measurements to provide adequate information on the spatial distribution of the ambient air quality.

Where the concentrations of Group A and B pollutants in a given zone are below the upper assessment thresholds but still higher than the lower assessment thresholds, these are to be assessed using a combination of fixed measurements and modelling techniques or indicative measurements. The method to determine whether concentrations are within this range is prescribed in Section B of Schedule 2.

Where concentrations of Group A and B pollutants in a given zone are below the lower assessment threshold, their concentrations are assumed – assessed through modelling techniques or objective estimation techniques. The method to determine whether concentrations are below this threshold is prescribed in Section B of Schedule 2.

Concentrations of benzo(a)pyrene in ambient air are assessed by monitoring for Group C pollutants at a limited number of measurement sites. These monitoring sites are to be co-located with the sampling sites for benzo(a)pyrene and shall be selected in such a way that the long-term trends can be identified, acting in accordance with Part II of Section B, Part II of Section C and Part I of Section D of Schedule 3.

Furthermore, the concentrations of Group A, B, and C pollutants, mercury, and ozone are to be measured at a rural background location away from significant sources of air pollution. ERA must also measure the total deposition of Group B pollutants, Group C pollutants, and mercury at the background site. The readings from the background station are to be used to assess the total mass concentration and the chemical speciation of $PM_{2.5}$ on an annual average basis. The data quality objectives in Parts I and III of Section A of Schedule 1 apply to the mass concentration measurements of PM, and Schedule 4 applies in its entirety.

Finally, ERA must measure the concentration of nitrogen dioxide at a minimum of 50% of the ozone sampling points required under Part I of Section C of Schedule 5 using continuous measurements.

As for ozone, the number of sampling points for its fixed measurement in those zones where, during each of the previous five years of measurement, concentrations were below the long-term objectives shall be in accordance with Part II of Section C of Schedule 5. At least one sampling point must be set up for ozone precursor substances as provided in Schedule 6. These are to include measurements for nitrogen oxides and appropriate VOCs.

123. The Regulations establish target values, critical levels or national reduction targets for the various pollutants as required. Target values are established for Group B pollutants in Schedule 7. A list of zones where these are exceeded must be drawn up, and ERA must specify the areas of exceedance and the contributing sources.

Critical levels of sulphur dioxide and nitrogen dioxide are established in Schedule 9 for the protection of vegetation, to be assessed in accordance with Section A of Schedule 3.

National exposure reduction targets are prescribed for $PM_{2.5}$ concentrations in Part II of Section B of Schedule 7. The target value prescribed is not to be exceeded; however, the Regulations do provide for margins of tolerance.

Target values for ozone are prescribed in Part II of Section D of Schedule 7. Where levels of ozone in ambient air exceed these values in a zone, the target values are to be achieved by dates set out in the same Schedule through a specific programme[199] and, if necessary, an Air Quality Plan. Where the levels are lower than the target values but still higher than the long-term objectives, reductions are to be achieved through cost-effective measures, which must nonetheless be consistent with the mentioned Plans and programmes. Where the long-term objectives are met, ozone concentrations are to be kept below those amounts, taking into consideration the transboundary nature of ozone pollution and meteorological conditions. The best ambient air quality compatible with a high level of environmental and human health protection is to be preserved.

124. ERA is to take any action it deems necessary, in accordance with the powers granted to it under the EPA, to make sure that the levels of Group A and B pollutants do not exceed the applicable limit values or target values prescribed by the relevant sections of Schedule 7 in those zones in which the ambient levels of these pollutants are below the applicable limit or target values. The best ambient air quality, compatible with sustainable development, is to be maintained throughout these zones.

ERA is also to take any action it deems necessary, always as empowered by the EPA, throughout the zones to ensure the limit values of specific pollutants are not exceeded, as prescribed in Schedule 7. These are: sulphur dioxide, PM_{10}, lead, and carbon monoxide; benzene and nitrogen dioxide; and Group B pollutants. However, the margins of tolerance in the same Schedule apply. Nevertheless, there are specific alert thresholds for concentrations of sulphur dioxide and nitrogen dioxide in ambient air prescribed by section A of Schedule 8.

125. The Regulations also require that the general public be informed by the media of any exceedances of the information and alert thresholds prescribed by Schedule 8 since this is essential to preserve human health. ERA itself must inform the general public, as well as all those specifically interested (such as environmental NGOs, consumer organisations and relevant industrial federations) of, among

199. Prepared pursuant to the National Emissions Ceilings for Certain Atmospheric Pollutants Regulations (S.L. 549.32).

other things, ambient air quality and air quality plans in line with the applicable provisions of the EU Directives. This is to be made available free of charge by means of any accessible media. It must also make the annual reports on pollutants available to the public in a like manner.

126. It is an offence against these Regulations to: fail to comply with any order lawfully given in terms of any provision of the Regulations; contravene any restriction, prohibition or requirement imposed by or under the same; or conspire, attempt, aid, or abet, any other person by whatever means to commit any of the aforementioned offences.

A first conviction entails a fine (*multa*) of between EUR 1,200 and EUR 2,300. A second or subsequent conviction entails a fine (*multa*) of between EUR 2,300 and EUR 11,600, imprisonment for a term not exceeding two years, or both. The owner of a vehicle used in the commission of an offence is, where applicable, liable in the same manner and degree as the actual offender.

The court[200] is bound to order any person so convicted to pay for the expenses incurred by the public entities and/or other persons acting on their behalf involved in the implementation of these regulations and restitution of the environment as a result of the said offence, the revocation of any permit issued by the competent authority and the confiscation of the *corpus delicti*. Furthermore, the provisions of Articles 23 and 30(1) of the Criminal Code apply, but the disqualification from holding a licence, permit, etc., shall not be for less than one year.

127. L.N. 211/2001, the Combating of Air Pollution from Industrial Plants Regulations,[201] is a transposition of the Council Directive 84/360/EEC of 28 June 1984 on the combating of air pollution from industrial plants and of the Long-Range Transboundary Air Pollution Convention to which Malta is a Party. The first eight articles are applied almost word for word from the Directive. Thus, the need for authorisation from the Competent Authority, which is ERA, ensures the proper management and operation of the industrial plants by issuing licences to those plants which satisfy the requirements laid down in the Regulations and any additional ones stipulated by the Competent Authority. The duties allocated to the authority in Regulation 5 are in compliance with section 5 of the EU Directive. The Legal Notice focuses on the licensing and inspection of industrial plants and the provision of measures and procedures designed to prevent or reduce air pollution from them. The categories of industrial plants that fall within the scope of the Regulations are the same as those listed in Annex I to Directive 84/360/EEC.[202]

200. The Court of Magistrates (Malta or Gozo) as a Court of Criminal Judicature. The Attorney General always has a right of appeal from its decision to the Court of Criminal Appeal.

201. S.L. 549.08.

202. The categories of plants listed under Annex I include the following: Energy industry, coke ovens, oil refineries, coal gasification and liquefaction, thermal power stations, production and processing of metals, roasting and sintering, integrated plants for production of pig iron and crude steel, ferrous metal foundries, etc. In Malta, the only industrial plants which qualify are the energy production plants, of which there are only two.

128. These plants need to obtain prior authorisation from the Competent Authority before commencing operations or before undergoing substantial alteration. The Competent Authority also may prescribe the technical conditions for operation. Enforcement of all preventive measures which are to be taken, including the application and adaptation of the best available technology to all plants, also falls under the responsibility of the Authority. The Competent Authority will provide for the process of authorisation for existing industrial plants in the individual categories and for monitoring compliance with the emission limits for those plants that have received permits. The Competent Authority must establish and maintain a database of granted permits. This database must be accessible to the public.

The Competent Authority has an obligation to only issue a licence to a plant if the operators fulfil their obligations under the Legal Notice; that is, taking all preventive measures against air pollution and ensuring that the operation of the plant will not result in significant air pollution, particularly from the emission of substances referred to in Annex II of the Legal Notice. The operators are to ensure that none of the ELVs shall be exceeded and that all air quality limit values applicable shall be taken into account. The operator, when applying for the authorisation to run a plant, must include a description of the plant containing all the necessary information which will enable the Competent Authority to make a decision.

The Legal Notice also gives a list of obligations of the Competent Authority, which may be carried out at its own discretion. Regulation 5, in fact, establishes that the Competent Authority may define certain areas as 'particularly polluted areas', for which it may prescribe more stringent ELVs, as well as 'specially protected areas', for which it may prescribe more stringent ELVs as well as more stringent air quality limit values. The Competent Authority also has the power to decide that, within these areas, specified categories of plants set out in Annex I may not be built or operated unless they meet certain conditions. An important duty of the Competent Authority concerns the public's right to know. That is, according to Regulation 7, it must ensure that all necessary measures are taken to ensure that applications and decisions are made available to the public within a reasonable time. The Competent Authority also has a duty to ensure that plants belonging to the categories listed in Annex I, which are already in existence at the time of coming into force of these Regulations, also adopt the best available technology. When determining whether the operator has employed the best possible technology, the Authority shall take into account: the plant's technical characteristics; its rate of utilisation and length of its remaining life; the nature and volume of polluting emissions from it; and the desirability of not entailing excessive costs for the plant concerned, having regard to its likely economic situation.

129. Any person who commits an offence against these Regulations shall, on conviction, be liable: On a first conviction to a fine (*multa*) of not less than EUR 1,165 but not exceeding EUR 2,329. On a second or subsequent conviction, to a fine (*multa*) of not less than EUR 2,329, but not exceeding or imprisonment for a term not exceeding two years EUR 4,659, or both such fine and imprisonment. Provided that whenever any person is found guilty of committing an offence under these Regulations by means of a vehicle, the owner of the said vehicle, where applicable, is held liable in the same manner and degree. Provided further that the court shall order any person who has been found guilty of committing an offence against these Regulations to pay for the expenses incurred by the public entities and/or other persons acting on their behalf involved in the implementation of these Regulations and restitution of the environment as a result of the said offence, the revocation of the permit issued by the police and the confiscation of the *corpus delicti*.

130. The 'Transport Topic Paper' prepared by then-MEPA, issued on 4 December 2003, sought to address issues related to transport. The paper was prepared as part of the Structure Plan Review process.[203] Some of the objectives of this paper have been adopted by L.N. 235/2002, the Availability of Consumer Information on Fuel Economy and Carbon Dioxide Emissions in respect of the Marketing of New Passenger Cars Regulations,[204] which transposes various EU Directives (the main Directive being 1999/94/EC) relating to the availability of consumer information on fuel economy and carbon dioxide (CO_2) emissions in respect of the marketing of new passenger cars. In fact, the Regulations also mention provisions of European Economic Community (EEC) Directives, being mainly 80/1268/EEC and 70/156/EEC, that are to be attached to the vehicle type-approval certificate or in the certificate of conformity. The objective of this Legal Notice is to ensure that information relating to fuel economy and CO_2 emissions of new passenger cars offered for sale or lease is made available to consumers in order to enable consumers to make an informed choice. The Regulations are mainly directed to consumers in general and for motor salespersons to provide the necessary information about new cars offered for sale or lease as regards fuel emissions and CO_2 emissions. This information has to be supplied with the new passenger car and thus has to be made available to the public at large (being the consumer).

131. Article 5 of L.N. 235/2002 states that the Competent Authority shall direct the publication of a guide to be made available to all consumers free of charge. This guide shall show information relating to fuel economy and CO_2 emissions. The Competent Authority uses the Council Directive to formulate the posters and the particular descriptions to be attached to such posters and also describes the formulation of the table, how it should be displayed, and what information should be presented.

132. There are four Annexes to the Legal Notice: Annex I describes the label on Fuel Economy and CO_2 emissions; Annex II describes the guide on fuel economy and CO_2 emissions, which is to be distributed to every consumer when purchasing or leasing a 'passenger car'; Annex III describes the poster to be displayed at the point of sale and also gives an example of a table showing the format that must be used and the data which must be recorded and made available to the consumer; and Annex IV gives the provision of data on fuel consumption and CO_2 emissions and

203. The Paper proposes an integrated transport strategy to ensure that the future of transport in Malta does not compromise quality of life.
204. S.L. 549.30.

also states that it must be easily read and understood and that the fuel consumption values should vary according to the make of the car.[205]

133. The directions of the Competent Authority are also shown in Articles 4–7. As the regulator, the Competent Authority gives strict directions to the operator at the point of sale and directs him to attach the labels (on fuel consumption and emissions) near each of the new passenger cars at the point of sale and in a visible manner. The Authority shall also be responsible for the compilation of the guide. The Authority also directs the operator at the point of sale to attach a poster visible on each new passenger car for sale or lease or at any point of sale. In Article 7, the Authority states clearly that any promotional material should contain information and data on fuel consumption and fuel emissions as laid down by Annex IV.

134. Any person shall be guilty of an offence under these Regulations if he: fails to comply with any provision of these Regulations or fails to comply with permit conditions or with any order lawfully given in terms of any provision of these Regulations; contravenes any restriction, prohibition, or requirement imposed by or under these Regulations; acts in contravention of any of the provisions of these Regulations; or conspires with or attempts to aid or abet any other person by whatever means – including advertising, counselling, or procurement – to contravene the provisions of these Regulations or to fail to comply with any such provisions, including any order lawfully given in terms of any of the provision of these Regulations, or to contravene any restriction, prohibition, or requirement imposed by or under the said regulations.

Any person who commits an offence against these Regulations shall, on conviction, be liable on a first conviction to a fine (*multa*) of not less than EUR 1,164.69 but not exceeding EUR 2,329.37. On a second conviction or subsequent convictions, to a fine (*multa*) of not less than EUR 2,329.37, but not exceeding EUR 4,658.75 or imprisonment for a term not exceeding two years, or both such fine and imprisonment. Provided that whenever any person is found guilty of committing an offence under these Regulations by means of a vehicle, the owner of the said vehicle, where applicable, is held liable in the same manner and degree. The court shall order any person who has been found guilty of committing an offence against these Regulations to pay for the expenses incurred by the Competent Authority as a result of the said offence, the revocation of the permit issued by the Competent Authority and the confiscation of the *corpus delicti*, if applicable.

Moreover, the presence on labels, guides, posters, or promotional literature and material referred to in Articles 4–7 of other marks, symbols, or inscriptions relating to fuel consumption or CO_2 emissions that do not comply with the requirements of these Regulations, is prohibited if their display might cause confusion to potential customers of new passenger cars.

135. L.N. 225/2001, the Limitation of Emissions of Volatile Organic Compounds Regulations, transposed Directive 1999/13/EC, the VOC Solvents Emissions Directive, and transformed Malta's obligations under the 1979 Convention on

205. This in accordance with the Council's Directive 80/181/EEC.

Long-Range Transboundary Air Pollution, concerning the control of emissions of VOCs in order to reduce their transboundary fluxes and the fluxes of the resulting secondary photochemical oxidant products, so as to protect human health and the environment from their adverse effects, into Maltese law.

These Regulations were replaced and revoked by eponymous regulations in 2010,[206] and these, in turn, were revoked and replaced by the Industrial Emissions (Limitation of Emissions of Volatile Organic Compounds) Regulations.[207] Previously, there was an overlap between the 2001 Regulations and the old IPPC Regulations, with the former setting minimum obligations and the latter more stringent ones for the installations falling within its scope. The latest Regulations removed this since they partly implement the recast IPPC Directive and the local Industrial Emissions (Framework) Regulations, leading to a more holistic approach. The purpose of these Regulations is hence to prevent or reduce the direct and indirect effects of emissions of VOCs into the environment, mainly into the air, and the potential risks to human health, as part of the overall IPPC framework.

136. These Regulations address a wide range of solvent-using activities, which are found in Schedule I,[208] where these operate above the solvent consumption thresholds in Schedule II. However, the activity includes the cleaning of the equipment but not the cleaning of products unless specified otherwise.

The competent authority is ERA, which has a largely supervisory role concerned with ensuring that certain specifications in the permit to operate applicable installations are complied with. The transitory provisions of the Regulations should be noted here. Permits issued under the revoked 2010 Regulations are to be construed as valid either until their term of expiry or until superseded by a permit under the new Regulations. Where the installation fell within the scope of the old 2002 IPPC Regulations, the new Regulations apply from 7 January 2014, while those not so covered fall under the new Regulations from 7 January 2015.

ERA is also under a specific duty to replace substances or mixtures required to carry hazard statements due to their content of VOCs classified as carcinogens, mutagens, or toxic to reproduction under Regulation (EC) No. 1272/2008 by less harmful substances or mixtures within the shortest time possible, where practicable. This duty entered into force on 1 June 2015.

137. Operators are to register installations falling within the scope of the Regulations, with ERA as the Competent Authority, before commencing operations. This duty arises from the Framework Regulations, with the VOC Regulations dealing with the permit specifications and the duty of ensuring them falling on ERA.

Generally, installations are to comply with either one of two things. The first alternative is compliance with the ELVs in waste gases and fugitive gases or with

206. L.N. 349/2010, Limitation of Emissions of Volatile Organic Compounds Regulations.
207. L.N. 12/2013 (S.L. 549.79).
208. Such as adhesive coating, various coating activities, dry cleaning using VOCs, and printing.

the total ELVs, and other requirements laid down in Schedules II and III.[209] The second is compliance with the specifications of the reduction scheme[210] found in Schedule V, provided that an equivalent emission reduction is achieved compared to that achieved through the application of the ELVs in the first option. If the limit values are not technically or economically feasible to adhere to for a specific installation, the operator is to demonstrate this to the satisfaction of the Competent Authority. Should an exemption be granted, the operator must show that the BATs are being used. Furthermore, all appropriate precautions are to be taken to minimise emissions of VOCs during start-up and shut-down operations.

Discharges of hazardous VOCs, as identified above, are subject to specific regulations depending on whether they are halogenated or not. Where the mass flow reaches or exceeds a specific flow rate, a determinate ELV must be complied with. Additionally, such emissions must be controlled under contained conditions as far as technically and economically feasible to safeguard public health and the environment.

Should an installation carry out two or more relevant activities which each exceed the Schedule II thresholds, ERA is to ensure emissions of hazardous substances comply with the rules mentioned above. As regards emissions of all other VOC substances, ERA must ensure either that each activity individually meets the respective requirements discussed above or that the total emissions of the installation do not exceed those in Schedules II and III.

138. It is ERA's duty to monitor emissions continuously for compliance where channels to which abatement equipment is connected and which, at the final point of discharge, emit more than an average of 10 kg/h of total organic carbon are operated. In other cases, measurements may be either continuous or periodic (consisting of at least three readings per exercise). However, measurements are not required in the case where end-of-pipe abatement equipment is not needed to comply with these regulations.

Operators must provide a yearly assessment of any data that would help ERA to verify compliance with the Regulations. They may also have to report whenever they may be requested to do so.

Compliance with ELVs is to be deemed, in the case of continuous measurements, if none of the averages over twenty-four hours of normal operation exceeds the ELVs, and none of the hourly averages exceeds the same by more than a factor of 1.5. Periodic measurements are subject to similar presumptions based on one monitoring exercise where the average of all readings does not exceed the ELVs, and none of the hourly averages exceeds the same by more than a factor of 1.5. As for emissions of VOCs deemed hazardous, verification is to occur on the basis of the sum of the mass concentrations of the individual VOCs concerned. Gas volumes may be added to the waste gas for cooling or dilution purposes where technically justified but shall not be considered when determining the mass concentration of the pollutant in the waste gas.

209. Schedule III deals specifically with ELVs for installations of the vehicle coating industry.
210. The specifics are contained in Schedule V; however, it is the operator's decision to opt for a suitable reduction scheme taking into account all requirements and formulae in the Schedule.

Where part of an existing installation undergoes a substantial change, it must comply with the requirements applicable to new installations.

139. ERA is to ensure publicity in practically all aspects of VOC emissions compliance. Applications for permits for new installations or for substantial changes to new installations requiring a permit are made available for an appropriate period of time for public inspection and comment before ERA reaches a decision on them. The results of emissions monitoring are likewise to be made available to the public. However, this right of the public is subject to restrictions in favour of grounds for refusal by public authorities to provide information as provided by law.[211]

ERA was required to apply a Solvent Management Plan under the 2001 Regulations, which established guidelines for the determination of compliance with the ELVs, Maximum Levels for Fugitive Emissions, Total ELVs, and the Reduction Scheme. For the determination of fugitive emissions when using the ELVs, the Plan provided a 'direct' method as well as an 'indirect' method. The Plan also identifies future emission reduction options and enables the provision of information regarding solvent consumption, emissions, and compliance with the Regulations to the public. Schedule IV of the new Regulations provides for a Solvent Management Plan as well, with one of its objectives being the verification of compliance of installations with the Regulations.

140. The offences under the Regulations are: failure to comply with any order lawfully given in terms of any provision of the Regulations; contravention of any restriction, prohibition or requirement imposed by or under the same; or conspiracy, attempt, aiding, or abetting, any other person by whatever means to commit any of the aforementioned offences.

Punishment for a first conviction entails a fine (*multa*) ranging from EUR 23,000 to EUR 233,000, a term of imprisonment not exceeding two years, or both. A subsequent conviction entails a fine (*multa*) of between EUR 46,000 to EUR 466,000, imprisonment for a term not exceeding two years, or both. If the offence is committed by means of a vehicle, the owner of the vehicle in question is to be held equally liable. The person found guilty is also to pay for any expenses incurred by public entities and/or other persons acting on their behalf involved in the implementation of these Regulations and restitution of the environment as a result of the said offence, the revocation of the permit issued by the police and the confiscation of the *corpus delicti*. Articles 23 and 30(1) of the Criminal Code are to apply when one infringes these Regulations, but the disqualification of a license, permit, or authority must not be for less than one year.[212]

141. L.N. 54/2009[213] on the control of VOC emissions resulting from the storage of petrol and its distribution from terminals to service stations regulations

211. Specifically under the Freedom of Access to Information on the Environment Regulations.

212. The competent Court is the Court of Magistrates (Malta or Gozo) as a Court of Criminal Judicature, with the Attorney General having a right of appeal to the Court of Criminal Appeal.

213. Control of Volatile Organic Compound-VOC Emissions (Storage and Distribution of Petrol from Terminals to Service Stations) Regulations.

transposed the European Parliament and Council Directive 94/63/EC of 20 December 1994. Its objectives, obligations, and eight schedules complied with those of the Directive and the United Nations Economic Commission for Europe (UNECE) Protocol to the Convention on the Long-Range Transboundary Air Pollution on the Control of Emissions of VOCs, which was put into force in September 1997.

This was revoked and replaced by the Control of Volatile Organic Compound-VOC Emissions (Storage and Distribution of Petrol from Terminals to Service Stations) Regulations[214] in 2016. They transpose the same Directive, as well as Directive 2009/126/EC[215] and Commission Directive 2014/99/EU amending it.

The Regulations establish obligations relating to the containment of gaseous compounds which evaporate from petrol so as to lessen the amount of vapours which evaporate in the air, thereby causing pollution. They apply to the operations, installations, vehicles, and vessels used for storage, loading, and transport of petrol from one terminal to another or from a terminal to a service station and to the dispensing of petrol to motor vehicle fuel tanks at service stations.

ERA is responsible for the enforcement of these Regulations.

142. The Regulations impose different requirements on the operator based on the facility being operated: terminal, mobile container, or service station.

Operators must communicate the information in Part A of Schedule I to ERA, which consists of the estimates of the mass of petrol lost from the storage installations at terminals, together with that lost from the loading and unloading of mobile containers at terminals, and the throughput of the terminal. These estimates have to be certified by an approved auditor. Furthermore, unless a terminal has a permit from ERA, it cannot be allowed to store, load, and unload petrol in Malta. This permit is to be granted only if an approved auditor certifies that: the storage installations at these terminals operate in accordance with the technical provisions of Schedule IV;[216] loading and unloading equipment at terminals is designed and operated according to the technical provisions of Schedule V;[217] and, all road tanker loading gantries at the terminal meet the technical provisions of Schedule VIII. However, the last two requirements need not be certified as regards terminals in existence at the time of promulgation with a throughput of less than 10,000 tonnes/year. Terminals are, in addition, forbidden from loading any mobile container with petrol unless registered. Furthermore, the operator is required to monitor the mean concentration of vapours in the exhaust from the vapour recovery unit according to a method approved by ERA – it will establish whether continuous or discontinuous measurements will be required. This concentration is not to exceed the hourly average of 35 g/Nm^3.

214. L.N. 228/2016 (S.L. 549.52).
215. On Stage II petrol vapour recovery during refuelling of motor vehicles and service stations.
216. In order to reduce the total annual loss of petrol from the storage installations of the terminal to below the target reference value of 0.01% mass by mass (m/m) of the throughput.
217. In order to reduce the total annual loss of petrol resulting from loading and unloading of mobile containers at terminals to below the target reference value of 0.005% mass by mass (m/m) of the throughput.

All mobile containers handling petrol have to be registered with ERA.[218] These mobile containers have to be compliant with the technical provisions of Schedule VII and must also be vapour tight, and the mobile container's vacuum or pressure valves must be vapour tight. However, these requirements are inapplicable to losses of vapours resulting from measuring options using dipsticks in relation to existing mobile containers and new mobile containers, which came into operation from 31 December 1995 to 31 December 1999. In any case, if, after the petrol unloading, the container is subsequently used for other products, ventilation may, after consultation with and permission from ERA, be allowed in a geographical area where emissions are unlikely to contribute significantly to environmental or health problems. This is insofar as vapour recovery or intermediate storage of vapours is not possible.

The operator of a service station is to communicate the information listed in Schedule I Part B[219] and the status of compliance with the provisions of Schedule IV to ERA. The permit requirements are the certification by an approved auditor that: loading and storage equipment at the service station is designed and operated in accordance with the technical provisions of Schedule VI Part A and that this loading and storage equipment is designed to reduce the total annual loss of petrol resulting from loading into storage installations at service stations to below the target reference value of 0.01% of the throughput mass by mass (m/m); and the station is compliant with Schedule VI Part B.[220] The permit is required to load petrol into storage installations and dispense petrol to a motor vehicle fuel tank. Furthermore, mobile containers are forbidden from unloading petrol into storage installations at any service station unless permitted. However, service stations with a throughput of less than 100 m^3/year are subject to certain exemptions, and certain other stations are also exempt from proving satisfaction of Schedule VI Part B.

143. The offences under the Regulations are: failure to comply with any order lawfully given in terms of any provision of the Regulations; contravention of any restriction, prohibition or requirement imposed by or under the same; or conspiracy, attempt, aiding, or abetting, any other person by whatever means to commit any of the aforementioned offences.

Any person who commits an offence against these Regulations shall, on a first conviction, be liable to a fine (*multa*) ranging from EUR 1,200 to EUR 2,300. A second or subsequent conviction results in a fine (*multa*) of not less than EUR 2,300 but not exceeding EUR 11,600 or imprisonment for a term not exceeding two years, or both. The owner of a vehicle used to commit the offence is, where applicable, to be held liable in the same manner and degree as the principal offender.

Furthermore, the court[221] is to order the person found guilty to pay for the expenses incurred by the public entities and/or other persons acting on their behalf

---

218. Including those retrofitted for bottom-loading, which are subject to specific rules in Schedule VIII.
219. This relates to the annual fugitive emissions from the loading of petrol into storage installations at service stations.
220. Regulating Stage II Petrol Vapour Recovery systems.
221. The Court of Magistrates (Malta or Gozo) as a Court of Criminal Judicature. The Attorney General always has a right of appeal from the decision to the Court of Criminal Appeal.

involved in the implementation of these Regulations and restitution of the environment as a result of the offence. It is also to order the revocation of the permit issued by the Competent Authority and the confiscation of the *corpus delicti*. Articles 23 and Article 30(1) of the Criminal Code *mutatis mutandis* apply to proceedings in respect of offences against these Regulations; however, the disqualification from holding or obtaining a license, permit or authority shall in no case be for less than one year.

144. L.N. 44/2008, the Quality of Fuels Regulations,[222] among other Directives, adopts EU Directive 1999/32/EC relating to a reduction in the sulphur content of certain liquid fuels and amending Directive 93/12/EEC.[223] Among other things, this Legal Notice relates to the reductions in the sulphur content of certain liquid fuels. The objective of enacting these national regulations was to reduce the emissions of SO_2 from the combustion of certain types of liquid fuels and, in the process, reduce the harmful effects which these emissions have on the environment and on human beings, as is clearly defined in the Directive itself. The Regulations list the method of sampling to be adopted, and this is representative of the parameters being tendered in the Directive itself, and it may be safely said that the whole relevant section is a literal transposition of the equivalent Directive provision. The national regulations also show a clear transposition of derogations allowed by the EU in cases where authorisation of heavy fuel oils with a sulphur content between 1.00% and 3.00% by mass may be allowed but only if it is ensured that air quality standards are respected, and the emissions do not contribute to critical loads being exceeded. The Regulations are more specific in obliging the applicant to request the issue of a permit from the Competent Authority for any combustion plant using heavy fuel oil with a sulphur concentration greater than that referred to in the same Regulations.

145. The Regulations define the term 'heavy fuel oil' as including any petroleum-derived fuel falling within CN code 2710 00 71 to 2710 00 78 or any petroleum-derived liquid fuel, other than gas oil, which by reason of its distillation limits falls within the category of heavy oils intended for use as fuel and of which less than 65% by volume distils at 250 degrees by the American Society for Testing and Materials (ASTM) D86 method.[224] Likewise, the term 'gas oil' means any petroleum-derived liquid fuel falling within CN code 2710 00 67 or 2710 00 68 or any petroleum-derived liquid fuel which, by reason of its distillation limits, falls within the category of middle distillates intended for use as fuel and of which at least 85% by volume distils at 350 degrees by the ASTM D86 method. The Regulations also regulate marine fuel, which means any petroleum-derived liquid fuel intended for use or in use on board a vessel, including those in use on board recreational craft when such vessels are at sea.

---

222. (S.L. 545.18).
223. The previous L.N. 159/2002 which transposed Directive 94/63 was repealed by L.N. 279/2009.
224. American Society for Testing and Materials in the 1976 edition of standard definitions and specifications for petroleum and lubricating products.

Limitations provided under these Regulations on the sulphur content of petroleum-derived liquid fuels shall not apply to fuels intended for research and testing, fuels intended for processing prior to final combustion, fuels to be processed in the refining industry, fuels used by warships and other vessels on military service, fuels used by vessels in order to secure the safety of the ship or for saving life at sea, and to fuels needed to be used in order to repair a damage sustained to a ship or to its equipment.

146. The use of heavy fuel oils with a sulphur content exceeding 1.00% by mass is not permitted. No combustion plant using heavy fuel oil with a greater sulphur content is to be operated without a permit issued by ERA with the responsibility for specifying the emission limits. Any person who fails to comply with any of these rules shall be guilty of an offence and shall be liable, on conviction, to a fine (*multa*) of not less than EUR 10,000, but not exceeding EUR 69,800 or imprisonment for a term not exceeding eighteen months, or both.

No gas oils, including marine gas oils, are to be used by any person if their sulphur content exceeds 0.10% by mass. Any person who fails to comply with this specific requirement shall be guilty of an offence and shall be liable on conviction to a fine (*multa*) of not less than EUR 10,000 but not exceeding EUR 69,800 or imprisonment for a term not exceeding eighteen months, or both.

147. Marine fuels are subject to specific regulation. The maximum sulphur content within the Maltese territory is 3.5% by mass, except if used/supplied to ships using emission abatement methods, as per the Regulations, operating in closed mode. The placing of marine diesel oils with a sulphur content exceeding 1.5% by mass on the market in Malta is prohibited. However, the use of marine fuels is prohibited in the areas of the Maltese territorial sea, internal waters, any exclusive economic zone[225] and any pollution control zones if the sulphur content of those fuels by mass exceeds 0.5% as of 1 January 2020. This rule applies to vessels of all flags, including those whose journey began outside the EU. It is the Master's duty to include fuel-changeover operations in the ship's logbook, and ERA is to ensure the availability of marine fuels in compliance with the Regulations. A ship found to be incompliant with these requirements may be subject to control orders by ERA or the Authority for Transport in Malta and must present a number of records and evidence, though it is not to be required to deviate from its intended course to secure compliance.

Where ships are at berth, the use of marine fuels with a sulphur content exceeding 0.1% by mass is prohibited, provided the crew shall be allowed sufficient time to complete any necessary fuel-changeover operation as soon as possible after arrival at berth and as late as possible before departure, the time of which is to be recorded in ships' logbooks. This is except where they are due at berth for less than two hours or where they switch off all engines and use shore-side electricity while at berth. In any case, the placing on the market of marine gas oils with a sulphur content exceeding 0.10% by mass is prohibited.

225. At the time of writing, Malta does not have an EEZ but government has expressed the intention to declare one.

Finally, ERA is to maintain a publicly available register of local marine fuel suppliers. These suppliers must document the sulphur content of all marine fuels sold in Malta in a bunker delivery note, along with a sealed sample signed by the receiving ship's representative. The fuel delivered must comply with the specification of the note, and furthermore, remedial action must be taken to ring any non-compliant marine fuel discovered into compliance. Infringing these obligations is an offence subject on conviction to a fine (*multa*) of between EUR 10,000 and EUR 69,800 or imprisonment for a term not exceeding eighteen months.

148. ERA has an obligation to carry out sampling to ensure fuel compliance with the above maximum sulphur contents. Sampling is to occur periodically with sufficient frequency and in such a way that the samples are representative of the fuel examined to be analysed without undue delay. The means of sampling, analysis and inspection of marine fuels are specifically provided for. However, generally, the Regulations leave it up to the discretion of the Authority in order to decide upon the frequency with which it must carry out sampling, and there is no specific provision establishing how and when the Authority is under obligation to compile its report on the annual statistics gathered with regard to sulphur content in liquid fuels.

Additionally, ERA or the Authority for Transport in Malta, as appropriate, is to allow the use of emission abatement methods[226] by ships of all flags in Maltese ports, territorial seas, internal waters, any exclusive economic zones, and any pollution control zones, as an alternative to using marine fuels meeting these Regulations. However, such ships are to continuously achieve reductions of SO_2 emissions that are at least equivalent to the reductions that would be achieved by using those fuels.[227] The method of approval of the methods depends on whether they fall under the Conformity Assessment of Marine Equipment Regulations[228] or not. Another alternative solution to those fuels is the encouragement of the use of onshore power supply systems by docked vessels by those Authorities.

The same Authorities may approve trials of ship emission abatement methods on vessels flying the flag of Malta, or in sea areas within Malta's jurisdiction, in cooperation with the competent authorities of other Member States. Here, compliance with the maximum sulphur content is not mandatory, so long as certain conditions are observed, such as notification of the trial to the Commission and relevant port State six months earlier, all ships involved achieve emission reductions which are at least equivalent to those which would be achieved through the sulphur limits for fuels specified in the Regulations, and there is an assessment of impacts on the marine environment, particularly ecosystems in enclosed ports, harbours and estuaries throughout the trial period.

149. Apart from specific penal clauses under specific regulations, these Regulations also provide for general penal clauses. These are: failing to comply with any

226. To comply with the criteria specified in the instruments referred to in the Fifth Schedule: those for biofuels, for exhaust cleaning systems, or for mixtures of marine fuel and boil-off gas.
227. Equivalent emission values shall be determined in accordance with the Fourth Schedule.
228. S.L. 427.60.

provision of these Regulations or with any order lawfully given in terms of them; or conspiring, attempting, aiding, or abetting the contravention of the same Regulations and orders.

Unless otherwise specifically provided elsewhere in the Regulations, the punishment is a fine (*multa*) of not less than EUR 10,000 but not exceeding EUR 69,800 or imprisonment for a term not exceeding eighteen months, or both. The owner of a vehicle used in committing the offence is, where applicable, to be held liable in the same manner and degree.

Together with this, the court[229] shall order any person who has been found guilty under these Regulations to pay for the expenses incurred by the public entities and/or other persons acting on their behalf, the revocation of the permit issued by the public entity, whichever it may be, and the confiscation of the *corpus delicti*. Articles 23 and 30(1) of the Criminal Code *mutatis mutandis* apply, but the disqualification from holding or obtaining a licence, etc., shall never be for less than one year.

The Regulations also provide for administrative fines, which may be issued by the Regulator for Energy and Water Resources against any infringer of the Regulations or person incompliant with any directive or decision of the Regulator in ensuring compliance with the same.

150. L.N. 291/2002, the National Emission Ceilings for Certain Atmospheric Pollutants Regulations, transposed the National Emission Ceilings for Certain Atmospheric Pollutants Directive 2001/81/EC of the European Parliament and of the Council of the EU dated 23 October 2001. This Directive was repealed by Directive (EU) 2016/2284 on the reduction of emissions of certain atmospheric pollutants. Article 10(2) of the Directive was implemented via L.N. 163/2017. Both Legal Notices were repealed by L.N. 303/2018,[230] which implemented the Directive in full along with the Protocol to Abate Acidification, Eutrophication and Ground-level Ozone to the Long-Range Transboundary Air Pollution (LRTAP) Convention, as amended.

The Regulations establish a set of national reduction commitments for emissions of SO_2,[231] NO_x, NMVOCs,[232] and ammonia (NH_3). These atmospheric pollutants cause acidification, eutrophication, and tropospheric ozone, which are transboundary phenomena where the pollutants move from one place to another; therefore, a collaboration between Member States is required in order to abate pollution. The sources of these four pollutants are human activities. For instance, sources of SO_2 are power stations, cars, incinerators, smelters, and oil refineries. NO_x arises from the combustion of biomass, nylon production, and nitrogen fertilizers in the soil. VOCs, which cause photochemical smog, result from unburned fuels, and the use

229. The Court of Magistrates (Malta or Gozo) as a Court of Criminal Judicature. The Attorney General always has a right of appeal from the decision to the Court of Criminal Appeal.
230. Limitation of Emissions of Certain Atmospheric Pollutants Regulations (S.L. 549.124).
231. Including all compounds expressed as such, like sulphur trioxide (SO3), sulphuric acid (H2SO4), and reduced sulphur compounds.
232. Non-methane volatile organic compounds.

of sprays and perfumes. The sources of NH_3 are livestock, fertilizers, and fossil fuel combustion. They also set a ceiling for $PM_{2.5}$. The Regulations apply to emissions from all sources occurring in Malta.

151. The competent authority is ERA, which has a number of obligations to ensure compliance with the national emission reduction commitments undertaken by Malta.

The national emission reduction commitments are to be published on ERA's website and calculated using the year 2005 as a baseline. The targets are at five-year intervals. The first targets were to be reached by 1 January 2020. The next set of targets is to be reached between that date and 1 January 2025, following a linear trajectory. For SO_2, NO_X, NMVOC, NH_3 and $PM_{2.5}$, the emission reductions are to be, respectively, 86%, 60%, 25%, 14%, and 38%. By 1 January 2030, the total anthropogenic emissions must, as a minimum, be limited to, respectively, as previously, the emission reductions of 95%, 79%, 27%, 24%, and 50%. Deviations from the linear trajectory for the period 2020–2025 may be allowed by ERA so long as the 2030 emission reduction commitments remain unprejudiced. The alternative trajectories must be appropriately described in the air pollution control programme. The reasons for ERA's inability to reach those targets must be included in the subsequent informative inventory reports, which are also to include any measures to be taken to realign the emission levels with those reduction targets. ERA is to apportion the total emission limits resulting from the national emission reduction commitments among the major contributors to the emissions of the respective pollutants in order to ensure compliance with the national reduction targets. The exempt emissions not to be taken into account in terms of compliance with the national targets are aircraft emissions beyond those released by during the landing and take-off cycle; emissions from international maritime traffic; and emissions of NO_X and NMVOC from activities falling under the 2014 Nomenclature for Reporting (NFR) as provided by the LRTAP Convention Categories 3B (manure management) and 3D (agricultural soils).

An air pollution programme is to be compiled, adopted, and implemented by ERA in collaboration with the Ministry responsible for the environment and any other relevant public body. Among the things it should cover as a minimum, laid down in Part 1 of the Second Schedule, is an air quality and pollution policy framework in which the context of the programme is developed. It should, among other things, include an assessment of the likelihood of impacts on air quality from emissions in Malta, in both Malta and neighbouring Member States, which may require transboundary consultations. It must also include the obligatory measures in Part 2 of the Second Schedule.[233] The programme must also be coherent with other relevant plans and programmes arising from obligations under both national and Union legislation. The first such programme was to be compiled by not later than 1 April 2019, and to be updated at least every four years. These updates are to be notified to the European Commission within two months. The programme is to be made publicly available on ERA's website.

233. These cover measures to control ammonia emissions, emission reduction measures for black carbon and $PM_{2.5}$ and, measures to prevent impacts on small farms.

ERA is also to prepare and update an annual national atmospheric emissions inventory for the pollutants in Table A to Schedule 1, which cover those in the broad categories of gaseous pollutants, PM, heavy metals, and persistent organic pollutants. A quadrennial spatially disaggregated national atmospheric emission inventories and large point-source inventories are to be prepared for pollutants in Table B to the same Schedule, along with a biennial national emissions projection for those pollutants. An informative inventory report is to accompany the national atmospheric emissions inventory and the national emissions projection. All inventories, projections, and reports are to be reported to the European Commission and the European Environment Agency by the reporting dates in Schedule I, which reporting must be consistent with the reporting to the Secretariat to the LRTAP Convention. These are to be made publicly available on ERA's website.

152. Aside from these obligations, ERA also has monitoring and record-keeping obligations.

The monitoring is to occur in relation to the negative impacts of air pollution on ecosystems based on a network of monitoring sites representative of freshwater, natural and semi-natural habitats, and forest ecosystem types, taking a cost-effective and risk-based approach. The competent authority must coordinate this programme with other monitoring programmes[234] and, if appropriate, the LRTAP Convention and ERA may, where appropriate, make use of data collected under those monitoring programmes. The location of monitoring sites and associated indicators and the monitoring data must be submitted to the European Commission and the EEA.

To collect information, ERA may prepare forms, questionnaires, and other records for the collection of information related to the activity of any sources deemed relevant to the compilation of any of the reporting obligations under the Regulations. The completion of forms, etc., the answering of questions and the provision of any information or records can occur notwithstanding any other law enjoining secrecy, so long as the provisions on restrictions on use and prohibition of disclosure of information in the same Regulations are observed.[235] The same rule applies to any person holding records which, in ERA's opinion, could lead to the compilation of the required inventories. Furthermore, ERA may request any public body to consult and cooperate with it for the purpose of assessing the potential of records of the authority as a source of information, which could contribute to the compilation of the inventories, and the public body must comply with any such request, in so far as resources permit.

234. Established under the Flora, Fauna and Natural Habitats Protection Regulations (S.L. 549.44), the Ambient Air Quality Regulations (S.L. 549.59), and the Water Policy Framework Regulations (S.L. 549.100).

235. These prohibit the communication, in any way, of collected information without consent, except: for the prosecution of an offence under the Regulations; to ERA's officers in the course of their duties under the EPA; and if the information is within the scope of the Freedom of Access to Information on the Environment Regulations.

153. The offences against the Regulations are: failure to submit data or any other information requested by ERA; submission of false data or information to ERA; or failure to comply with the relevant emission limits apportioned by ERA.

The punishments for the offences are fines (*multi*); however, the amount varies with each offence and may potentially run into the millions. The court[236] must additionally order any person who has been found guilty of committing an offence against the Regulations to pay for the expenses incurred by ERA or other public entities as a result of the said offence to undertake mitigation or prevention measures in order to address offence-related damages, if applicable, the revocation of any permit issued by the competent authority and the confiscation of the *corpus delicti*. The provisions of Articles 23 and 30(1) of the Criminal Code also apply, but the disqualification from holding a licence, etc., is not to be for less than one year.

154. L.N. 229/2001, the Measures against the Emission of Gaseous and Particulate Pollutants from Internal Combustion Engines to be Installed in Non-Road Mobile Machinery Regulations, transpose Directive 97/68/EC on emission standards and type-approval procedures for engines to be installed in non-road mobile machinery, as amended by Directive 2002/88/EC.

Eponymous Regulations[237] were promulgated in 2013 to transpose various Directives amending Directive 97/68/EC and other ancillary Directives. These were as exhaustive as the 2001 Regulations but contained no revocation clause in their regard. The 2013 Regulations were revoked and replaced by eponymous regulations[238] once again in 2017 to transpose Regulation (EU) 2016/1628. However, this latest piece of legislation is very short, providing merely for the Technical Regulations Division of the MCCAA as the approval authority and market surveillance authority within the meaning of the Regulation and the applicable penalties for infringement.[239] It should be noted that the 2013 Regulations were without prejudice to the transitional provisions in Article 58(1)–(4) of the EU Regulation. Therefore, the 2013 Regulations will still be dealt with here.

155. The Division, as the Competent Authority, must determine if the submitted application for type-approval of an engine family fully represents the engine family described in Schedule II, Appendix 2. If this does not fully represent the engine family, then an alternative and, if necessary, an additional parent engine has to be determined and approved by the Division. Once the Division receives the abovementioned application, it shall grant type-approval to all engine types or engine families which conform to the particulars in the information folder and which meet the requirements of these Regulations. It shall complete all applicable sections of the type-approval certificate (the model being given in Schedule VII) for each engine type or engine family that it approves and shall collect or verify the contents

236. The Court of Magistrates (Malta or Gozo) as a Court of Criminal Judicature. The Attorney General always has a right of appeal from the decision to the Court of Criminal Appeal.
237. L.N. 83/2013, Measures against the Emission of Gaseous and Particulate Pollutants from Internal Combustion Engines to be Installed in Non-Road Mobile Machinery Regulations.
238. L.N. 55/2017, Measures against the Emission of Gaseous and Particulate Pollutants from Internal Combustion Engines to be Installed in Non-Road Mobile Machinery Regulations (S.L. 427.85).
239. These are provided for under Part IV of the Product Safety Act, Ch. 427.

of the index to the information package. These type-approval certificates shall be numbered in accordance with the method described in Schedule VIII. The completed type-approval certificate and its attachments shall be delivered to the applicant.

The Division has the duty to issue revised pages of the information package when the particulars appearing in it have been changed. It shall also include marking each revised page to show clearly the nature of the change and the date of re-issue. The Division also has to issue a revised type-approval certificate which denotes an extension number and shall show clearly the reason for revision and the date of re-issue. The Division has to inform the manufacturer thereof and issue the documents aforesaid after the conduct of successful fresh checks when it is found that an amendment to an information package warrants fresh tests or checks. The Division may not refuse, or it shall only permit registration or placing on the market of new engines which meet the requirements of these Regulations.

The Division may also carry out additional controls of the identification numbers in conjunction with the control of conformity of production. If, at its request, the manufacturer is not able to verify the requirements, the approval granted in respect of the corresponding engine type or family pursuant to these Regulations may be withdrawn. The information procedure shall then be carried out as prescribed in Regulation 15. On the other hand, the Competent Authority shall refuse to grant type-approval for an engine type or engine family and shall also refuse to grant any other type-approval for non-road mobile machinery in which an engine is installed after the entry into force of these Regulations as stated in Regulation 11, which covers a wide array of engine types and families. It shall be refused if the engine fails to meet the requirements specified in these Regulations and where the emissions of gaseous and particulate pollutants from the engine do not comply with the limit values stated in Schedule I. Furthermore, the Competent Authority shall refuse to grant type-approval for an engine type or engine family and to issue the document.

The Division shall permit the placing on the market of engines these type-approvals after the dates laid down in Regulation 11 only if they meet the requirements of these Regulations and only if the engine is approved in compliance with the same Regulations. The specific dates for compliance with the Regulations have now elapsed, and now all categories must be in conformity with the Regulations. The Division is to ensure that the manufacturer complies with all corresponding obligations. The officials of the Division shall release for each engine in question a certificate of conformity on which a special entry has been made. If applicable, a consolidated document that contains all engine identification numbers in question may be used. The Division has to take the necessary measures to verify in cooperation with the approval authorities of other Member States that adequate arrangements have been made to ensure effective control of the conformity of production before it grants type-approval. This will help the production to be adequate and ensure that each production engine bearing a type-approval number pursuant to these Regulations continues to conform to the description as given in the approval certificate and its Annexes for the approved engine type or family.

Failure to conform to the approved type or family results where deviations from the particulars in the type-approval certificate or the information package are found to exist and where these deviations have not been authorised by the Division. Therefore, if it finds that engines accompanied by a certificate of conformity or bearing an approval mark do not conform to the type or family it has approved, it shall take the necessary measures to ensure that the engines in production again conform to the approved type or family. The approval authorities of other Member States shall advise the Division of the measures taken, which may, where necessary, extend to the withdrawal of type-approval. If the engines bearing a type-approval number do not conform to the approved type or family, the Division may request the other States which granted the type-approval to verify that engines in production conform to the approved type or family. Such action shall be taken within six months of the date of the request, and the Division shall inform the approval Authorities of other States within one month of any withdrawal of type-approval and of the reasons for such measures.

156. The operators falling within the scope of the Regulations are listed by law in Article 2, which includes all manufacturers. Under this Article, the word 'manufacturer' implies any 'person or body who is responsible to the competent authority for all aspects of the type-approval process and for ensuring conformity of production. It is not essential that the person or body is directly involved in all stages of the construction of the engine.

The operators are obligated under the Regulations to submit the application for engine or engine family type-approval to the Competent Authority, and such application shall be accompanied by an information folder. This engine has to be in conformity with the engine type characteristics described in Annex II, and it shall be submitted to the technical service responsible for conducting the approval tests. The person applying in respect of one engine type or engine family may not submit concurrently to the Competent Authority and to an approval Authority of another State. Thus, it shall be submitted on a separate application.

The applicant may not change the particulars appearing in the information package before the Competent Authority has granted the type-approval. The application for an amendment or an extension of a type-approval shall be submitted exclusively to the Authority if it had granted the original type-approval. The said application shall not be submitted to the approval Authority of another State once approved by Authority. The manufacturer has a duty to affix the relevant markings to each unit manufactured in conformity with the type-approval, which has to include the type-approval number. When the type-approval certificate is in accordance with the EU Directive and these Regulations, the manufacturer shall deliver with each unit manufactured detailed information on these restrictions on use and shall indicate any conditions for fitting it. If a series of engine types is delivered to one single manufacturer of machinery, the latter will be provided with only one such information document, at the latest on the delivery date of the first engine, which additionally lists the relevant engine identification numbers.

The operator is required to send on demand, and without delay to the Competent Authority, any requirements of these Regulations changed within forty-five days. This has to immediately follow each additional date which the Competent Authority may stipulate, and the operator is to make a list which contains the range of identification numbers for each engine type produced in accordance with the requirements of these Regulations since the last reporting was made, or since the requirements of these Regulations were first applicable. Furthermore, it is provided that such list shall contain particular information if the manufacturer ceases to produce an approved engine type or engine family and where such list is not required to be sent regularly to the Competent Authority, the manufacturer shall maintain such records for a minimum period of twenty years. He shall send to the Competent Authority which granted the type-approval a declaration specifying the engine types and engine families, together with the relevant engine identification codes for those engines he intends to produce from such date onwards, within forty-five days after the end of each calendar year and at each application date.

157. The Vienna Convention for the Protection of the Ozone Layer[240] and the Montreal Protocol on Substances that Deplete the Ozone Layer[241] form part of the laws of Malta by virtue of L.N. 226/2001, the Vienna Convention for the Protection of the Ozone Layer and the Montreal Protocol on Substances that Deplete the Ozone Layer (Incorporation) Regulations.[242] These Regulations were issued by the Minister for the Environment in accordance with the EPA of 2001. L.N. 226/2001 specifies that the Minister responsible for the environment may make transitional provisions as are considered necessary or expedient in connection with the Vienna Convention and its Protocol[243] with its subsequent four amendments.[244]

The fourth amendment to the Montreal Protocol also forms part of our law through Council Decision 2002/215/EC of 4 March 2002 concerning the conclusion of the Fourth Amendment to the Montreal Protocol on Substances that Deplete

240. Done at Vienna on the 22 Mar. 1985.
241. Done at Montreal on the 16 Sept. 1987.
242. S.L. 549.16.
243. The Vienna Convention for the Protection of the Ozone Layer is a multilateral environmental agreement that entered into force in 1987. It acts as a framework for international efforts to protect the ozone layer, but it does not include legally binding reduction targets for CFC use – the main chemical cause of ozone depletion. These targets are laid out in the accompanying Protocol to this Convention: the Montreal Protocol on Substances That Deplete the Ozone Layer. There are 191 Parties to the Vienna Convention and the Montreal Protocol, including Malta. Malta signed the Montreal Protocol on the 15 Sept. 1988, acceded to the Vienna Convention on 15 Sept. 1988, ratified the Montreal Protocol on 29 Dec. 1988, approved of the first amendment (London) to the Montreal Protocol on 4 Feb. 1994, and accepted the second (Copenhagen), third (Montreal) and fourth (Beijing) amendments on 22 Dec. 2003.
244. The four amendments to the Montreal Protocol reflected the need to accelerate the phasing out of certain substances. For example, in the London amendment, it was held that 1989 levels of certain CFCs were to be phased down 20% by 1993; 85% by 1997; and 100% by 2000. The 1986 levels of halons were to be phased down by 50% by 1995; 100% by 2000. The 1984 levels of carbon tetrachloride were to be phased down by 85% by 1995; 100% by 2000. Again, in the Copenhagen Amendment, CFCs were to be phased out by 1995 and halons by 1993. Carbon tetrachloride was to be phased out by 1995. The 1989 levels of halons were to be phased out by 35% by 2004; 90% by 2019; 100% by 2029. The third Montreal amendment introduced a ban on imports and exports of methylbromide to or from Montreal Protocol signatory countries. The most recent Beijing amendment introduced control measures for production for hydrofluorocarbons and imposed restrictions on trade with non-Parties for these hydrofluorocarbons. The amendment further introduced control measures for both production and consumption for one new group of substances, namely bromochloromethane.

the Ozone Layer.[245] L.N. 226/2001 was not the first attempt to create local regulations to tackle the global threat of ozone layer depletion. In fact, it was preceded by L.N. 70/1990 (the Standard Aerosol Spray Order), which phased out the use of chlorofluorocarbons (CFCs) in aerosol cans, and L.N. 133/1995 (regulations for the control of Ozone-Depleting Substances (ODS)),[246] which imposed strict conditions on the import of such substances. Between 1993 and 1995, the Ministry for the Environment also compiled a detailed National Country Programme for the definition of a strategy for the controlled phase-out of CFCs and other ODS.[247]

158. The Competent Authority, ERA, is responsible for ensuring the implementation of the obligations of the Convention and the Protocol, namely, the exchange of systematic observations, information, and research; the adoption of legislative or administrative measures and their international harmonisation; as well as cooperation between Parties and competent international bodies to implement the Convention and its Protocol.

159. In Malta, local research has identified industry areas which have been negatively impacted by the Montreal Protocol. These are namely: the local aerosol industry, the cosmetics packaging industry, the foam blowing industry, the manufacture of commercial refrigeration equipment, the domestic refrigeration sector, the mobile air-conditioning industry, and the unitary air-conditioning equipment industry.[248] However, adaptation in these industry areas has been rather swift, even after Malta was obliged to give up the special concessions that the Protocol makes to developing countries upon EU accession. This is in the sense that Malta could no longer avail itself of the advantageous terms of phasing out ODS by 2030 available to developing countries anymore but had to take on board complete phasing out of such substances by 2020. Within the local context, reduction in the use of ODS has not only been spurred on by the Vienna Convention and the Montreal Protocol but the reduction has also been affected by domestic environmental legislation that was

---

245. The Council Decision states that the Community became a party to the Vienna Convention and the Montreal Protocol by 99/540/EEC(3) due its environmental responsibilities, and approved the first, second, and third amendments to the Protocol by Decisions 91/690/EEC(4), 94/68/EC(5), and 2000/646/EC(6) respectively. The Council took into account that recent evidence shows that ozone layer protection requires a greater degree of trade control in ODS than was originally provided for in the Montreal Protocol, as amended in 1997. Evidence also indicated that further measures were required to control ODS production, particularly hydrochlorofluorocarbons and new substances. The Decision also states that the European Commission took part in the negotiation of the Fourth Amendment to introduce new controls to the Montreal Protocol, which was subsequently adopted by the Parties in December 1999 in Beijing. The Decision states that the Community has already adopted measures in this regard, particularly through Regulation (EC) No. 2037/2000, and must therefore undertake international commitments in that area. The Council therefore held that it is necessary for the Community to approve the Fourth Amendment, because its provisions relate to production and trade in controlled substances between the Community and other Parties, areas which fall squarely within the responsibility of the Community.
246. S.L. 549.06, Environment Protection (Control of Substances Depleting the Ozone Layer) Regulations.
247. Micallef, J.P., 'The Likely Impact of EC Law on Ozone Depleting Substances in Malta', Bachelor Thesis, 11 (2003).
248. *Ibid.*, 63–67.

implemented in the mid-1990s, as well as a vast spectrum of European regulations that came into force upon Malta's accession to the EU.[249]

160. In compliance with EU law and the Montreal Protocol on Substances that Deplete the Ozone Layer, Malta had to set targets to reduce and eventually eliminate consumption and production of a range of ODS. EC Regulation 2037/2000 on the Control of ODS had direct effect and direct applicability under Maltese law. This legal instrument controlled the ODSs; it set out controls for the production, trade, use, and recovery of ODSs. The EC Regulation could not be transposed into Maltese law, given its superior legal status. The EPA and L.N. 145/2007,[250] however, provided detailed requirements for the implementation of the requirements of the EC Regulation and a legal basis for inspections and penalties while also foreseeing the inclusion of new substances into the control scheme.

The Regulation was recast in 2009, as Regulation (EC) No. 1005/2009 of the European Parliament and of the Council of 16 September 2009, on substances that deplete the ozone layer (recast). Therefore, the local regulations transposing the old Regulation were revoked and replaced by the new Substances Depleting the Ozone Layer Regulations[251] to ensure the new Regulation's application in Malta.

161. ERA has several obligations to ensure the implementation of the EC Regulation, which emanates from Article 8 of the EPA, which states that it must give effect to any international treaty relating to any matter governed by the Act and to set up structures so as to carry out assessments of environmental risks of both new and existing establishments. It also has to establish, coordinate, and enforce environmental quality control systems. The presentation for collection, processing, comparison, and interpretation of data related to the environment prescribed is to enable the Authority to monitor and safeguard the quality of the environment. The Authority has to prescribe the techniques to be used in the monitoring of the environment and formulate objectives laid down in quantitative terms. With regard to IPPC, it has to establish systems that ensure such prevention and control, where it prescribes measures to control, prevent, manage, or reduce pollution and degradation of the environment.

ERA must issue licences and permits for the purposes of these Regulations under any conditions that it may deem fit. It may also, in carrying out the tasks assigned to it by these Regulations, request all relevant information from the personnel involved and from undertakings concerned. It is its duty to carry out any investigations necessary under these Regulations; moreover, it may conduct random checks and audits on imports, exports, shipments, storage facilities, users, and disposal facilities of substances. The ERA officials must label any containers filled with substances prior to their release from Customs. ERA may develop as appropriate and ensure the dissemination of guidance notes and documents for the purpose of ensuring the proper implementation of the EC Regulation.

249. *Ibid.*, 11.
250. Substances Depleting the Ozone Layer Regulations.
251. L.N. 280/2010 (S.L. 549.58).

162. The Operators that fall within the scope of the EC Regulation are all producers, importers, shippers, exporters, technicians, users (including retailers), and any persons involved in the destruction, recovery, reclamation, and recycling of the substances covered by the same Regulation. The operators' personnel shall possess the minimum qualification requirements, which take the form of a course with a duration and curriculum as defined and approved by ERA. On successful completion of this course, the licence and permit (valid for ten years) are issued by such Authority. The licence and permit may be reviewed, renewed, or terminated at any time by ERA. Under the EPA, no person shall carry out any activities unless he is in possession of this licence. Such personnel may also be subject to random audits by officials of the Authority. The operators involved who may only handle, use, or trade in substances falling within the scope of the EC Regulation have to be registered with the Competent Authority. Moreover, they are duly to fill out a logbook stating all amounts of controlled substances recovered, recycled, reclaimed, or destroyed during their day-to-day operations. For this purpose, every year before 31 January, each user and shipper of substances shall communicate to the Competent Authority the data, as specified in the Regulations, for each controlled substance in respect of the period 1 January to 31 December of the preceding year. ERA shall establish the format of this report, as a hard copy and an electronic version, in such manner that and also any other details as may be required from time to time by this authority by notice in the Government Gazette.

All owners or refrigeration technicians of fixed equipment with a refrigerating fluid charge of more than 3 kg and all entities involved in the recovery, recycling, reclamation, and destruction of controlled substances shall communicate to ERA, before 31 January of each year, for each specifically identified piece of equipment, for the period from 1 January to the 31 December of the previous year. They shall send copies of their logbooks to the Competent Authority for review. These copies shall be signed off by the official person in whose name the logbook was issued as a true copy of the original logbook in their possession. All shippers (including both importers and exporters) shall inform ERA about any upcoming shipment (import or export) at least fifteen working days in advance of the actual shipment that is carried out. All details shall be submitted according to the requirements of the format established for this purpose by such Authority. In addition, the retailer shall be responsible, as stipulated in Article 11 of the Regulations, for keeping and reporting information related to any sales or transfer by whatever means of these substances until the point of sale and when this responsibility will devolve to the new natural or legal persons involved.

163. The offences under these Regulations are the following: failure to comply with any provision stated by the EC Regulation or the Regulations; failure to comply with the permit conditions or with any order lawfully given in terms of any provision of the Regulations; contravention of any restriction, prohibition, or requirement imposed by or under the EC Regulation or the local Regulations; acting in contravention of any provision of the same instruments; or conspiring or attempting, or aiding or abetting, any other person to perform any of the above.

On a first conviction, one would be liable to a fine (*multa*) of not less than EUR 1,200 but not exceeding EUR 2,300 and where applicable, there can also be the revocation of such person's licence and confiscation of the *corpus delicti*. If there is a second or subsequent conviction, one shall be liable to a fine (*multa*) of not less than EUR 2,300 but not exceeding EUR 4,700 or imprisonment for a term not exceeding two years, or both, and where applicable, the revocation of such person's licence and confiscation of the *corpus delicti*.

Furthermore, where applicable, the court[252] shall order any person who has been found guilty of committing an offence mentioned above to pay for the expenses incurred by the Competent Authority as a result of the said offence and also to revoke the permit issued by the Competent Authority and confiscate the *corpus delicti*. The court shall also order the person so convicted to bear all or part of the costs incurred due to any relevant infringement action brought against Malta by the European Commission under the provisions of the EC Regulation or of the Treaty establishing the European Community.

Articles 23 and 30(1) of the Criminal Code also apply *mutatis mutandis*, so however that any disqualification from holding or obtaining a licence, etc., must not be for less than one year.

252. The Court of Magistrates (Malta or Gozo) as a Court of Criminal Judicature. The Attorney General always has a right of appeal from the decision to the Court of Criminal Appeal.

Chapter 2. Laws Addressing Climate Change

164. It may be said, to a certain extent, that Malta offers a particularly (almost) unique situation in respect of climate change legislation. Originally a non-Annex Party to the United Nations Framework Convention on Climate Change (UNFCCC), Malta was not bound by any quantified commitments to limit or reduce anthropogenic emissions of GHGs under the Kyoto Protocol to the UNFCCC. Following EU membership and its implementation of EU climate law, Malta voluntarily became an Annex I Party in December 2008. The proposal to amend Annex I to the UNFCCC by adding the name of Malta was approved at the fifteenth session of the Conference of the Parties (COP) at the end of 2009 in Copenhagen. Due to the fact that Malta had already assumed reporting obligations comparable to those of Annex I Parties as a result of its membership in the EU, this move to Annex I ensured coherence. Following the conclusion of the Paris Agreement in December 2015, the distinction between Annex and non-Annex Parties was removed as all Parties now have a pledge to reduce emissions under their National Determined Contribution (NDC). Malta shares a collective NDC with other EU Member States under the Paris Agreement.

§1. The Climate Action Act

165. Several pieces of legislation have been enacted over the years relevant to climate change; however, the landmark piece is arguably the Climate Action Act of 2015,[253] adopted to establish a framework for climate action. The Act recognises the reality of climate change and the need to combat it, as well as the duties of the government and guiding principles in this regard. Article 3 provides for the duty of every person, together with the government, to protect the climate and assist in the taking of preventive and remedial measures to do so.

The objectives of the Act are to provide for action on two concurrent fronts. The first is to contribute to the mitigation of climate change by limiting anthropogenic emissions of GHGs and protecting and enhancing GHG sinks and reservoirs. The second is to contribute to the prevention, avoidance, and reduction of the adverse impacts of climate change and the reduction of vulnerability, enhancement of resilience, and adaptation to the adverse effects of climate change.

The Act lays down a myriad of duties and obligations on the government, all stemming from the primary duty to 'protect the climate for present and future generations'. Sustainability is a guiding principle in this regard, as well as strong scientific reasons on the best ways to handle climate change. The government must also, to the extent possible, ensure that projects, policies, and programmes are designed around the reality of climate change, and it must cooperate with other States and stakeholders in climate action programmes, particularly within the Mediterranean Region. The specific duties and obligations are listed in Article 5. The Act

253. Chapter 543 of the Laws of Malta.

also contains specific guiding principles of climate action in Article 6. What is interesting to note is that contrary to the EPA and the Constitution, these provisions, which effectively constitute a 'declaration of principles', are not covered by a non-justiciability clause. This suggests climate change litigation, gaining in popularity worldwide, may well be possible locally under the Act and upheld by the courts.

166. The Act provides for two strategies in relation to climate change that must be prepared by the Minister responsible for climate change policy in consultation with any other competent Minister, civil society, environmental organisations, and the general public. These are to be laid on the table of the House of Representatives at least once every five years, together with their updates. A yearly report on the progress registered in meeting the respective targets under the strategies is also to be given to the House. The Minister must refer the reports, strategies and policies to the Standing Committee on the Environment, Climate Change and Development Planning.[254]

The first strategy is the national low-carbon development strategy under Article 7, aimed at monitoring actual and projected progress made by the government in limiting anthropogenic GHG emissions under the UNFCCC and meeting the GHG emission reduction targets Malta has as an EU Member State.

The second strategy is the adaptation strategy under Article 8. This aims at facilitating Malta's adaptation to climate change and preventing, avoiding, or reducing its adverse effects, as well as monitoring the government's progress in reducing vulnerability and enhancing resilience against it. It must also include information on the actual and projected impacts of climate change on Malta.

167. The supervisory and advisory body on climate change, as far as the Act goes, is the Climate Action Board, appointed by the Prime Minister in consultation with the Minister and composed of mainly ministerial appointees. The main disqualifications from office are a financial or other interest great enough to affect the discharge of the person's functions as a member of the Board and conviction of crimes affecting public trust, theft, or fraud, or of any offence under the Act.

The main roles of the Board are: supervising the implementation of the Act and regulations made under it; ensuring Malta's fulfilment of its UNFCCC and EU membership obligations; giving advice to the Minister on such implementation and fulfilment of obligations, as well as on climate change in general; and facilitating the government's adherence to the two strategies.

168. The Minister is empowered to make regulations to give better effect to the Act and generally ensure Malta fulfils its climate change obligations and duties. The full list is in Article 12. Any such regulations must, by derogation to the general rule, first be published as a draft in the Gazette, allowing any person four weeks to make representations to the Minister. The Minister may amend the draft based on the representations and then promulgate them.

Regulations may also be issued to lay down offences and administrative fines under the Act. The maximum punishment for each offence is capped at four years'

254. Established under Art. 60 of the DPA (Ch. 552).

imprisonment or a EUR 1,000,000 fine (*multa*). Continuing offences are capped at EUR 50,000 fines (*multi*) for each day the offence continues. Administrative fines are capped at EUR 1,000,000, without prejudice to any other sanctions made provision for, and the possibility of the fines constituting an executive title.

As of December 2021, the only regulations under the Act relate to a national system for the estimation of anthropogenic GHG emissions by sources and removals by sinks, to be discussed later.[255]

169. The Act envisages a Climate Action Fund,[256] as yet unrealised, to support the fulfilment of obligations under the Act, the UNFCCC and EU legislation and to provide financial support to the projected shift towards environmentally sound technologies, etc., for national requirements and developing countries in accordance with international treaty obligations and commitments.

The Fund is to have a separate legal personality from the government and is to be replenished from a number of sources laid down in Article 16, such as through the implementation of national measures relating to the reduction or limitation of GHG emissions.

§2. Emissions Trading

170. The concept of emissions trading and allowances was established in the EU through Directive 2003/87/EC,[257] which has been amended on numerous occasions to keep pace with developments in emission efficiency. This set up a European Union Emissions Trading Scheme, now System (EU ETS).

The Directive was originally transposed locally through the European Community Greenhouse Gas Emissions Trading Scheme Regulations of 2005;[258] however, the developments in EU legislation regarding emissions allowance trading for aviation and land-based installations, respectively, have led to the separation of these two aspects of the system under separate Regulations. The Regulations on stationary installations will be tackled first, followed by those on aviation.

The competent authority under both Regulations is the MRA, which is responsible for the overall implementation and administration of the System. Its responsibilities include the administration of the scheme, monitoring and reporting requirements, and procedures for the accounting of emissions, besides general provisions on enforcement. Some of these responsibilities are also imposed on operators of aircraft or installations participating in the System.

171. Before delving into the regulation of the ETS for installations and aviation, one should be familiar with the allowance system, which is the basis of the System.

255. *See* paras 182 et seq. below.
256. To be established by Order by the Minister.
257. Directive 2003/87/EC of the European Parliament and of the Council of 13 Oct. 2003 establishing a scheme for greenhouse gas emission allowance trading within the Community and amending Council Directive 96/61/EC, OJ L 275, 25 Jan. 2003. Herein called the 'Directive'.
258. L.N. 140/2005. This L.N. was revoked by L.N. 434/2013.

An allowance is defined as an allowance to emit one tonne of CO_2 equivalent[259] during a specific period. These are issued to each participating operator, both in the case of installations and aircraft and may be transferred between operators and with other persons. The operators are obliged to surrender their allowances by the stipulated deadline each year, equal in amount to the amount of emissions reported for the previous year. The surrendered allowances are then cancelled by the Authority. This aspect will be tackled for each of the Regulations separately.

Allowances may be issued freely or auctioned, but this will be tackled for each of the Regulations separately.

The ETS incorporates a system of project activity credits: Certified Emission Reduction (CER) and Emission Reduction Units (ERU). Operators are allowed to utilise these to partially meet their compliance requirements. This system is, however, being phased out, as will be seen in the discussions on the two local Regulations.

172. A Union Registry allows for the proper accounting of the issuance, transfer, surrender, and cancellation of allowances. The Authority is the national registry administrator in respect of operators holding accounts for installations and aircraft to which the Regulations apply. Each operator, of installation or aircraft, is required to have an operator holding account in respect of his installation or aircraft. The Authority is the person responsible for opening and administering the account in accordance with the relevant decisions and regulations adopted by the Commission pursuant to the Directive, and the operator/nominated authorised representative shall act in accordance with those same decisions and regulations. The Authority may prevent the transfer of allowances or other accounting units vis-à-vis any operator holding accounts whose operators fail to comply with their obligations until the non-compliance is rectified.

173. The monitoring and reporting of emissions is the fulcrum of the system. Reported emissions will determine the quantity of allowances that an operator must surrender each year. The monitoring plan, containing monitoring and reporting measures for emissions, must be submitted to the Authority, which must be kept informed of all deviations from the plan. This burdens the operator with stringent responsibilities to ensure the plan is being adhered to at all times and to submit an annual emissions report to the Authority. This report must be verified by an independent verifier,[260] which is to be made known to the Authority and National Accreditation Board – Malta[261] (NAB) by the operator in question.

Nevertheless, acceptance of the annual emissions report and its verification report lies with the Authority, which may perform additional checks to ensure all is in

259. Itself defined as one metric tonne of CO_2 or any other GHG listed in Sch. 2 of each of the Regulations, respectively, with an equivalent global warming potential.

260. Verifiers are to be accredited by a national accreditation body (the NAB), pursuant to Regulation (EC) No. 765/2008 and relevant decisions and regulations adopted by the Commission pursuant to the Directive.

261. Established by the National Accreditation Board (Malta) (Establishment) Regulations, L.N. 306/2007 (S.L. 419.07).

order before accepting it. Its decision must be communicated to the operator in writing. If the operator fails to submit an annual emissions report or submits a dissatisfactory one, the Authority is expressly empowered to determine the emissions for the activities performed during that year unless there is an express agreement with the operator providing otherwise. Here, the Authority is to be guided by the provisions of Schedules 3 and 4,[262] as well as the best data available and a conservative estimate that does not underestimate emissions.

Should the verification report highlight dissatisfactions, the operator must submit an improvement report to the Authority detailing how he has rectified, or plans to rectify, the non-conformities and implement the proposed improvements. There are also fines for failure to submit a monitoring plan and to monitor annual emissions, respectively.

174. The EU Greenhouse Gas Emissions Trading System for Stationary Installations Regulations[263] transpose the aspects of the Directive relative to the operators of installations (a stationary technical unit) situated in the Maltese territory, which carry out activities listed in Schedule 1 resulting in the GHG emissions specified therein. They also apply to any other legal body on which they place obligations.

The operators of those installations require a GHG emissions permit issued under the Regulations in order to perform any activity mentioned. This constitutes the authorisation to emit GHG through the installations. The permit is valid for the duration of the activity for which it is granted and is to be publicly available. Failure to operate under a permit entails hefty administrative fines based on the approximation of the emissions during that year to specified tonnes of CO_2 equivalents.

175. An operator is required to submit an application to the MRA for the issuance of the permit. The application shall provide details of the installation to be permitted, including emission sources. Furthermore, the operator is required to submit a monitoring and reporting plan to inform the Authority of the measures that will be undertaken to monitor and report emissions. Such a monitoring and reporting plan has to be consistent with the guidelines that the European Commission produces in the form of a Decision.

Once the Authority is satisfied that in respect of an installation, the operator is capable of ensuring continued compliance with the conditions of the Regulations, including having the capacity of implementing the monitoring and reporting plan as approved by it, it may issue the permit. To facilitate the permitting process, for itself so as to make the most efficient use of limited available resources, and for operators so as to minimise their burden, the Authority encourages continued cooperation through regular meetings and discussions between it and the operators, particularly in the process of preparing the application and the plans. This has been found to be effective in ensuring that once applications and plans are submitted, the approval is concluded rapidly.

---

262. Of each Regulation, respectively.
263. L.N. 434/2013 (S.L. 423.50).

The permits issued under L.N. 140/2005 and still valid are to continue to benefit the operator until their conditions are revised by the Authority.

176. The permit, besides containing a description of the activities and emissions from the permitted installation, will also confirm the monitoring and reporting requirements and include two important obligations. These are the reporting of verified GHG emissions specified for the permitted activity and the surrender of allowances equal to the total emissions of the installation, both for each calendar year.

An operator who holds a permit is also obliged to inform the Authority of any changes that take place in the nature or functioning of the installation or any extension to it, which would require an updating of the permit as relevant. It is important to note that the permit is directly linked to the installation. It is possible to transfer a permit from one operator to another through an application submitted and accepted by the Authority. In this case, the permit would be updated based on the extent of the transfer, and new ones would be issued accordingly.

177. A permit may be lost through surrender or revocation. In both cases, the Authority will issue a notice of revocation which will indicate the date the permit loses effect and any other information or obligations required.

Surrender occurs voluntarily when an installation ceases performing all of the activities covered by the permit. The operator must submit an application for surrender of the permit to the Authority, which may accede to it but on certain conditions. These relate to monitoring and verification of emissions, the relative allowance to be surrendered, and the surrender of any other outstanding allowances.

Revocation is imposed by the Authority, subject to reasons. It will entail the requirement of the reporting and verification of the emissions for any years for which they were not reported and verified and that of surrendering any outstanding allowances resulting therefrom.

178. Allowances are either issued freely or auctioned. The amount of each is determined by Annex 1 of the Directive in accordance with Chapter III of the Directive, except those provisions applicable to aircraft. Eligible installations are issued a quantity of free allowances by the Authority under the Directive. However, there are certain exceptions, such as electricity production (except from waste gases) and storage and transport of CO_2. The quantity of allowances not so issued is to be auctioned in accordance with the Directive and any relevant legislation. The revenue, after deducting the auctioning fees, goes to the Consolidated Fund. The allowances are to be sent to and kept in the Union registry. The information for Malta is to be sent to the registry by the Authority every five years.

179. The free allowances are to be issued yearly by 28 February. However, the installation must have been approved by the Commission for it to be eligible. The issuance of allowances generally is to be performed in accordance with the relevant decisions and regulations of the Commission pursuant to the Directive. No allowances are to be issued if the installation has ceased its operations, changed or surrendered its permit, or had it revoked. Allowances issued for the period beginning

1 January 2013 and subsequent periods are valid indefinitely, while those issued for the period beginning 1 January 2021 in a ten-year period are valid for emissions from the first year of that period onwards.

180. Surrenders and cancellations are to be carried out in accordance with the relevant decisions and regulations of the Commission pursuant to the Directive. To this end, the allowances issued by the competent authority of another Member State are to be recognised by the Authority. The surrendering period for allowances that ended on 31 December 2020 will not be considered since the date would have passed by the time this work is published. These are to be cancelled by the Authority of its own motion. Instead, the surrendering process for the new period starting on 1 January 2021 and subsequent periods will be considered, for which an operator must surrender allowances by the 30 April of each year. Contrary to preceding periods, the new period does not prohibit operators from surrendering allowances in respect of aviation activities listed in Annex 1 to the Directive in accordance with Chapter II of that Directive. However, there is no obligation to surrender allowances for emissions that have been verified as captured and transported for permanent storage to a permitted facility under Directive 2009/31/EC.[264] Since there is no provision requiring the Authority to cancel the allowances for the new period of its own initiative, the operator must himself request the Authority to cancel them.

Administrative fines are due to any operator failing to surrender the required allowances, which payment does not prejudice his obligation to surrender them.

181. The Regulations provide for the use of CERs and ERUs for the period from 1 January 2013 to 31 December 2020. Neither may be issued for reductions or limitations of GHG emissions with respect to activities falling within the scope of the Regulations.

182. Certain installations may, with the approval of the Minister, be excluded from the EU ETS, subject to equivalent measures to achieve a contribution to emissions reductions equivalent to the Regulations. These are small installations or reserve/backup units meeting certain specific requirements detailed in Regulations 26–28.

183. The EU Greenhouse Gas Emissions Trading System for Aviation Regulations[265] transpose the aspects of the Directive relative to the aircraft operators performing the aviation activities listed in Schedule 1, resulting in the emission of the GHG therein listed. These do not require a specific GHG emissions permit but instead require a valid operating licence granted by Malta in accordance with Regulation (EC) No. 1008/2008.[266] Aircraft operators may also be bound by these Regulations because Malta has been designated as their administering Member State via

264. Discussed in paras 193 et seq. below.
265. L.N. 403/2012 (S.L. 423.51).
266. Regulation (EC) No. 1008/2008 of the European Parliament and of the Council of 24 Sept. 2008 on common rules for the operation of air services in the Community (Recast).

Regulation (EC) No. 748/2009[267] by means of any measure taken by the Commission pursuant to the Directive or by the Authority in terms of the same Regulations. The lack of a GHG emissions permit, however, does not prevent the issuing of an operating ban if the aircraft operator in question fails to comply with the Regulations, notwithstanding enforcement measures taken against it to coerce compliance. The Authority here may request the Minister to request the Commission to impose such a ban after having consulted with the regulatory authority responsible for aviation.

184. The participation of aircraft operators in the ETS began in 2012, with an allocation system slightly different to that of installations. Free allowances are set at a benchmark by the Commission for each specified period, with the Authority being responsible for calculating the total allocation of Chapter II allowances and the allocation for each aircraft operator who applied for them. The process is set out in Article 4(6). The operator must apply for free allowances for the period ending 31 December 2020 under Chapter II of the Directive. This must be done by submitting verified tonne-kilometre data to the Authority for the aviation activities in Schedule 1 performed by the operator for the monitoring year. If the Authority is satisfied with the application, it must send it to the Commission for final approval. An aircraft operator satisfying certain criteria may also be allowed to benefit from free allowances in a special reserve for the purpose. The remaining allowances are then auctioned, which proceeds, after deduction of the auctioning fees, go towards the Consolidated Fund. All allowances issued to aircraft operators are to be held in the Union registry.

185. The operators are required to monitor their tonne-kilometre data for aviation activities. Thus, in applying for the free allowances, the operator must submit a monitoring plan to the Authority, which must then be implemented following approval. The data submitted is to be verified, and the verification must be accepted by Authority. It is empowered to perform its own checks before accepting it and may even request a revised tonne-kilometre report where it deems necessary.

186. The allowances are to be issued yearly by 28 February. Those issued for the period beginning 1 January 2013 and subsequent periods are valid indefinitely, while those issued as of 1 January 2021 for a ten-year period shall be valid for emissions from the first year of that period onwards. No allowances are to be issued if the installation has ceased performing an aircraft activity.

Two important changes occurred from 1 January 2021. First, the number of free allowances issued to aircraft operators shall decrease by 2.2% each year. Second, free allowances are no longer possible for the period beginning on that date.

187. Surrenders and cancellations are to be carried out in the same manner as with installations, including recognition of allowances by foreign competent

267. Commission Regulation (EC) No. 748/2009 of 5 Aug. 2009 on the list of aircraft operators which performed an aviation activity listed in Annex I to Directive 2003/87/EC on or after 1 January 2006 specifying the administering Member State for each aircraft operator.

authorities and administrative fines for default. However, aircraft operators may surrender both Chapter II and III allowances. The operative periods contemplated by the Regulations are those ending on 31 December 2020 and subsequent periods. The Authority may cancel the allowances surrendered during those periods of its own motion and may also cancel any allowances at any time at the request of the operator.

188. The Regulations provide for the use of CERs and ERUs for two periods: 1 January 2012 to 31 December 2012 and 1 January 2013 to 31 December 2020. None are to be issued for the limitation or reduction of GHG emissions with respect to aviation activities falling within the scope of the Regulations, however.

189. It is possible for the Authority to automatically derogate from the monitoring and reporting duties, verification duties and surrender duties in the Regulations in favour of specific operators satisfying certain conditions. These relate to emissions from flights to and from aerodromes outside the EEA and to and from certain aerodromes within the EU for each calendar year from 1 January 2013 to 31 December 2023. There are also derogations depending on the total annual emissions from aviation activities.

190. Appeals from decisions of the Authority under both Regulations fall within the jurisdiction of the Administrative Review Tribunal. Likewise, the decisions relating to the allocation of allowances are subject to publicity under the Freedom of Access to Information on the Environment Regulations,[268] but personal information is subject to the provisions of the Data Protection Act,[269] while information covered by professional secrecy is subject to the provisions of the Professional Secrecy Act.[270] Furthermore, the Authority is prohibited from disclosing any confidential information, even if commercially confidential, provided the commercially confidential information is made known as such to the Authority.

§3. The Monitoring Mechanism

191. Decision 280/2004/EC[271] provided the means for the EU and its Member States to monitor emissions of GHGs and demonstrate progress towards achieving respective quantified commitments to limit or reduce emissions. It has been repealed

268. L.N. 116/2005 (S.L. 549.39).
269. Chapter 586 of the Laws of Malta.
270. Chapter 377 of the Laws of Malta.
271. Decision 280/2004/EC of the European Parliament and of the Council of 11 Feb. 2004 concerning a mechanism for monitoring EC greenhouse gas emissions and for implementing the Kyoto Protocol.

and replaced by Regulation (EU) No. 525/2013,[272] which like its predecessor, sets monitoring and reporting obligations on Member States and is not transposed in national legislation.

192. The National System for the Estimation of Anthropogenic Greenhouse Gas Emissions by Sources and Removals by Sinks Regulations[273] are the first Maltese legislation providing for Malta's duties to set up such a system in accordance with international treaties to which it is a party and pursuant to the Regulation. They provide for the establishment and maintenance of a GHG inventory system, which is to be operated in accordance with the principles in Schedule 1 to the Regulations, the relevant decisions of the COP[274] and/or the COP/MOP,[275] and relevant decisions and regulations of the Commission pursuant to the Regulation. The Schedule reproduces the criteria expected from the EU in the operation of the inventory system. These must ensure the system is transparent, consistent, comparable, complete, and accurate, with each criterion explained. The Regulations contemplate two reports to be compiled by Malta: the inventory report and the actual report on national GHG emissions. It is the duty of the Minister responsible for climate change to lay the actual report before Parliament yearly, not later than two months from the submission of the GHG inventory report relating to that year. They must also be submitted to the Commission pursuant to the Regulation.

193. The overall responsibility of the inventory system rests with the Single National Entity,[276] which is to ensure the system is operated in accordance with the instruments listed above. The Entity has a number of responsibilities, notably the duty to ensure the timely submission of the national GHG inventory reports in accordance with the relevant decisions of the COP and/or the COP/MOP and the Regulation. It must also establish systems for the independent review, official consideration, and approval of those reports, as well as the definition and allocation of specific duties in the preparation process of the inventory itself.

194. An Inventory Agency is responsible for the annual preparation of the national GHG inventory report in accordance with the relevant decisions mentioned previously and within the deadlines established therein. This Agency is nominated by the Entity by order in the Gazette for such period as it may determine with the power to prolong, renew, or terminate such nomination by subsequent order at any time. The Agency is nominated to perform the functions listed in Schedule 2 to the Regulations and any other functions bestowed on it by the Entity.

The Second Schedule lays down the specific functions of the Agency relating to inventory preparation and management. These include the identification of key

272. Regulation (EU) No. 525/2013 of the European Parliament and of the Council of 21 May 2013 on a mechanism for monitoring and reporting greenhouse gas emissions and for reporting other information at national and Union level relevant to climate change and repealing Decision No. 280/2004/EC.

273. L.N. 259/2015 (S.L. 543.01).

274. The Conference of the Parties of the UNFCCC.

275. The COP serving as the meeting of the Parties to the Kyoto Protocol.

276. The Minister and such other body/person as the Minister may designate as such.

source categories, the preparation of estimates, and collect data. It must also elaborate an inventory quality assurance[277]/quality control[278] plan which describes specific quality control procedures to be implemented during the inventory development process and implement them.

195. Both the Entity and the Agency may identify data providers, which may be government agencies, to provide the data and information necessary for the preparation of the GHG inventory. They may also request such data and information from any Department, Authority, Agency, Corporation, or other body or person. The Entity and Agency may determine the format and the deadlines for the submission of that data and information.

§4. Other Legislation on Climate Action

196. The pieces of legislation described above may be considered the most important currently in force for Malta as a Member State of the EU. However, other legislation will have additional important input towards the country's contribution to the fight against climate change.

197. The EU has also set emission limitation obligations on its Member States in non-ETS sectors of the economy in order to meet its targets for reduced GHG emissions. The first piece of legislation was the Effort-Sharing Decision,[279] which provided for both emissions limitation and reduction. Its application came to an end in 2020, and consequently, a new Effort-Sharing Regulation[280] was promulgated to meet the EU's targets for emission reductions throughout the bloc, in line with the Paris Agreement of 2015. The Regulation, unlike the Decision preceding it, sets only quantified emission reduction targets for non-ETS emissions for each Member State not falling within the scope of the EU ETS. The aim is to reduce emissions from the non-ETS sectors by 30% by 2030 when compared to 2005 levels, laying

277. A planned system of review procedures conducted by personnel not directly involved in the inventory compilation development process, to verify that data quality objectives are met, ensure that the inventory represents the best possible estimate of emissions and sinks given the current state of scientific knowledge and data available, and support the effectiveness of the quality control programme.
278. A system of routine technical activities to measure and control the quality of the inventory as it is being developed, and designed to provide routine and consistent checks to ensure data integrity, correctness and completeness, identify and address errors and omissions, and document and archive inventory material and record all quality control activities.
279. Proposal for a Decision of the European Parliament and of the Council on the effort of Member States to reduce their greenhouse gas emissions to meet the Community's greenhouse gas emission reduction commitment up to 2020, COM (2008) 17 final Decision No. 406/2009/EC of the European Parliament and of the Council of 23 Apr. 2009 on the effort of Member States to reduce their greenhouse gas emissions to meet the Community's greenhouse gas emission reduction commitments up to 2020 OJ L 140, 5 Jun. 2009.
280. Regulation (EU) 2018/842 of the European Parliament and of the Council of 30 May 2018 on binding annual greenhouse gas emission reductions by Member States from 2021 to 2030 contributing to climate action to meet commitments under the Paris Agreement and amending Regulation (EU) No. 525/2013.

down annual GHG emissions targets for each MS for the period 2021–2030. The Regulation provides for the calculation of each annual legally binding target, based on a linear trajectory, with the annual limits contained in an Implementing Decision.[281] The overall target set for Malta is that of -19% in GHG emissions when compared to 2005 levels. However, Malta is allowed to use a limited amount of ETS allowances to offset emissions in the effort-sharing sectors, equal to 2% of the maximum percentage of 2005 GHG emissions as determined by the Regulation itself. This amounts to 204,120 tonnes of CO_2 equivalent.

198. Being a Regulation, there is no requirement for transposition into national legislation, although one would expect that the necessary implementing provisions that will ensure that Malta keeps on track with the set targets may require strengthening of already existing legislation in a number of sectors, the setting of additional new legislation, the setting of adequate national policy, and/or the mainstreaming of these emission limitation obligations into various other policy areas.

199. The effort-sharing sectors are the IPPC source categories of energy, industrial processes and product use, agriculture, and waste, as determined by Regulation (EU) 525/2013, and excluding GHG emissions from activities in Annex 1 to Directive 2003/87/EC. The Effort-Sharing Regulation is also inapplicable to GHG emissions and removals covered by Regulation 2018/841, and for its purposes, emissions for the IPPC source category '1.A.3.A civil aviation' are treated as zero. Some laws from varying sectors deemed useful for assisting Malta in meeting its effort-sharing targets will be discussed below. One of the so-called non-ETS sectors is transport. One of the relevant laws here is L.N. 235/2002,[282] which transposes the Car Labelling Directive[283] into Maltese law. The objective of this law is to ensure that information on the fuel economy and CO_2 emissions of new passenger cars is made available to consumers in order to enable them to make an informed choice. Also of some relevance is the application of passenger car-related taxes under the Motor Vehicles Registration and Licensing Act.[284] This is due to the fact that car registration taxes and annual circulation taxes are calculated by means of formulae that take CO_2 emissions into account. This could be a useful measure for reducing emissions from road transport since an incentive is created for consumers to go for more efficient vehicles. Another relevant law is the Clean Vehicles Directive,[285] which seeks to stimulate the market for clean road transport vehicles by requiring contracting authorities, entities, and operators to take environmental impacts into account when

---

281. Commission Implementing Decision (EU) 2020/2126 of 16 Dec. 2020 on setting out the annual emission allocations of the Member States for the period from 2021 to 2030 pursuant to Regulation (EU) 2018/842 of the European Parliament and of the Council.
282. L.N. 235/2002 (S.L. 549.30), Availability of Consumer Information on Fuel Economy and Carbon Dioxide Emissions in respect of the Marketing of New Passenger Cars Regulations.
283. Directive 1999/94/EC of the European Parliament and of the Council of 13 Dec. 1999 relating to the availability of consumer information on fuel economy and CO2 emissions in respect of the marketing of new passenger cars, OJ L 12, 18 Jan. 2000.
284. Chapter 368 of the Laws of Malta.
285. Directive 2009/33/EC of the European Parliament and of the Council of 23 Apr. 2009 on the promotion of clean and energy-efficient road transport vehicles, OJ L 120, 15 May 2009.

purchasing such vehicles. It thus promises to contribute to a reduction of GHG emissions from road transport. Having a modern, cleaner fleet would have a significant impact on emissions from public transport. It has been transposed locally as L.N. 175/2011.[286]

Industrial processes make up another non-ETS sector. Such processes result in emissions of fluorinated gases and are therefore regulated by L.N. 93/2010.[287] This Legal Notice provides various detailed rules for personnel involved with fluorinated GHGs. All such personnel have to be registered with the Competent Authority, which is ERA. These personnel have a number of obligations, such as the filling of logbooks and reporting information to the Competent Authority. Moreover, the Competent Authority is empowered to carry out any investigations necessary and to conduct random checks and audits. Some legislation also exists with respect to waste, which is yet another non-ETS sector. The disposal of solid waste is the major contributor to national emissions from this sector. Of relevance is L.N. 168/2002,[288] which transposes the Landfill Directive[289] into Maltese law. This Legal Notice provides general requirements for landfills in Schedule 1. Among such requirements is the taking of appropriate measures to control the accumulation and migration of landfill gas. Furthermore, legislation on packaging waste is also relevant for reducing GHG emissions from landfills since measures for preventing or reusing and recycling packaging waste reduce the final disposal of such waste in landfills. The relevant Legal Notice is L.N. 277/2006,[290] which transposes the Packaging Directive[291] into national legislation.

200. Another piece of legislation significant to climate change is L.N. 202/2018, the Limitation of Emissions of Certain Atmospheric Pollutants Regulations.[292] These implement Directive (EU) 2016/2284[293] and the Protocol to Abate Acidification, Eutrophication and Ground-level Ozone to the LRTAP Convention. The Regulations apply to emissions from all sources occurring in the territory of Malta. The Competent Authority is ERA, which is to publish the emission limits in tonnes equivalent to the emission reductions in the Regulations on its website, using the year 2005 as the baseline for its calculations following a linear trajectory.

201. The Regulations set reduction targets for the emissions of specific atmospheric pollutants to be reached by specific dates. The relevant anthropogenic emissions are those of sulphur dioxide, nitrogen oxides,[294] non-methane volatile organic

286. Cleaner and More Energy-Efficient Road Transport Vehicles Regulations (S.L. 601.06).
287. Certain Fluorinated Gases Regulations (S.L. 549.55).
288. Waste Management (Landfill) Regulations (S.L. 549.29).
289. Council Directive 1999/31/EC of 26 Apr. 1999 on the landfill of waste, OJ L 182, 16 Jul. 1999.
290. Waste Management (Packaging and Packaging Waste) Regulations (S.L. 549.43).
291. European Parliament and Council Directive 94/62/EC of 20 Dec. 1994 on packaging and packaging waste, OJ L365, 31 Dec. 1994.
292. S.L. 549.124.
293. Directive (EU) 2016/2284 of the European Parliament and of the Council of 14 December 2016 on the reduction of national emissions of certain atmospheric pollutants, amending Directive 2003/35/EC and repealing Directive 2001/81/EC.
294. Nitric oxide and nitrogen dioxide.

compounds, ammonia, and fine PM. The target periods are five years apart,[295] starting from 2020, and thus the next reduction targets to be reached are by the year 2025, and the final period ends in the year 2030. It is permissible for the 2025 targets to be altered so long as the final 2030 targets remain unchanged and are ultimately reached. The alteration is also subject to explanations and justifications appropriately described in the air pollution control programme set for Malta, which is to be prepared by ERA in collaboration with the Ministry responsible for the environment and any other relevant public body pursuant to Regulation 5. ERA is to set up a national atmospheric emissions inventory in accordance with the First Schedule to the Regulations. This is to be kept updated by ERA and reported as required to the European Commission and the European Environmental Agency (EEA) by the deadlines in the First Schedule, consistent with the reporting obligations to the Secretariat to the LRTAP Convention. Complimentary to this is ERA's obligation to monitor air pollution impacts on ecosystems. This monitoring programme is to be coordinated with others under specific pieces of environmental legislation[296] and the LRTAP Convention if appropriate. This information must also be reported to the Commission and EEA. The Regulations lay down procedures for collecting information relevant to the activities of any sources deemed relevant to the reporting obligations as well. ERA may also access records deemed relevant in this regard, notwithstanding anything in any other law enjoining secrecy, and can request the cooperation of public bodies as well.

202. Offences are in place in relation to the submission of data and failure to comply with the emissions limits, both of which are subject to severe fines (*multi*) depending on the gravity of the respective offences. The data submission punishments vary depending on whether the person has failed to submit data or information or has submitted false data. The fines for failure to comply with emissions vary depending on how much the limit has been exceeded. Recidivists and subsequent offenders are also afforded different treatment. All offenders are to be requested by the court to make good any expenses incurred by ERA or other public entities as a result of the offence and to remedy or mitigate its effects. The court must also suspend any licence issued by ERA and confiscate the *corpus delicti*. Certain provisions of the Criminal Code are also applicable with regard to these offences.

203. The fight against climate change involves not only CO_2 emissions reduction but also the safe storage and containment of CO_2 to remove excesses from the atmosphere. The EU has legislated in this regard through Directive 2009/31/EC,[297] transposed locally via the Geological Storage of Carbon Dioxide Regulations,[298]

295. L.N. 202/2018, Reg. 4.

296. The Flora, Fauna and Natural Habitats Protection Regulations, the Ambient Air Quality Regulations, and the Water Policy Framework Regulations.

297. Directive 2009/31/EC on the geological storage of carbon dioxide and amending Council Directive 85/337/EEC, European Parliament and Council Directives 2000/60/EC, 2001/80/EC, 2004/35/EC, 2006/12/EC, 2008/1/EC and Regulation (EC) No. 1013/2006.

298. L.N. 346/2011 (S.L. 549.68).

with the scope of establishing a legal framework for the environmentally safe geological storage of CO_2 to contribute to the fight against climate change. The purpose is the permanent containment of CO_2 in order to prevent, or at least eliminate as far as possible, the negative effects and risks to the environment and human health. The CO_2 must be stored in a licensed facility on the continental shelf of Malta[299] and not within the water column. The Regulations are inapplicable to geological storage of CO_2 with a total intended storage below 100 kilo tonnes undertaken for research, development or testing of new products and processes. The Competent Authority is the Office of the Prime Minister or such other body or person the Prime Minister may designate as such for different purposes under different provisions of the Regulations. It is the Authority's prerogative to select areas from which storage sites may be selected. The suitability of the geological formation for use as a storage site is to be determined through a characterisation and assessment of the potential storage complex and surrounding area, pursuant to the First Schedule to the Regulations. Nevertheless, the selection is to only occur if, under the proposed conditions of use, there is no risk of leakage and if no significant environmental or health risks exist.

204. The storage sites must have a permit granted by the Authority, which is kept in a register for that purpose. The Regulations lay down very stringent criteria to be met and the procedures to be followed for the granting of the permit. These are to ensure that the facility is effective in permanently storing CO_2 and avoiding any adverse effects through leakages, etc. One of the guarantees in place, pursuant to the Directive, is the review of the draft storage permits by the Commission, as well as the obligation on the authority to inform the Commission of its decision in relation to the particular application, with reasons if it diverges from the Commission's opinion on the matter. The operator of the facility is burdened with the responsibility of monitoring the facility and reporting to the authority yearly on its activities. The Regulations also provide for inspections and measures to be taken in the case of leakages or significant irregularities, including, as a last resort, the withdrawal of the permit. The operator remains responsible for monitoring, reporting and corrective measures after the closure of the facility, even if the closure occurred because the facility reached full storage capacity according to its permit.

205. The Regulations provide for a number of criminal offences. A compliance order may be issued against any person believed to be contravening the provisions of the Regulations or any licence conditions. Not abiding by the compliance order is an offence and, as such punishable with a fine (*multa*) of not less than EUR 1,000 and not more than EUR 60,000 for each day the failure subsists. The contravention of the provisions of the Regulations or any licence conditions is itself an offence, likewise punishable with hefty fines for each day the offence persists. There are also offences with respect to knowingly or recklessly failing to supply the information requested or required by the authority with respect to the Regulations. The offences relate to misleading information, failure to inform, hindrance of investigations and the like, and are punishable with hefty fines for each day the offence continues.

---

299. Within the meaning of the International Convention on the Law of the Sea.

Chapter 3. Water Quality and Pollution

§1. Marine Pollution

206. The earliest legal sources on marine pollution are those found in the Code of Police Laws,[300] which originally established marine pollution in harbours and wharves as a criminal offence. Section 227 of the Code of Police Laws prohibits the leaving in harbours or wharves of anything causing injury to public health or anything causing injury or which constitutes a 'nuisance'. It constitutes an offence to throw any 'rubbish or dirty liquid' which may cause a nuisance into the waters of any harbour or into the internal or territorial waters of Malta. This general provision is followed by a section which regulates the pollution of the marine environment in general; that is, not only in harbours or wharves but also wherever it occurs in the internal and territorial waters, but the discharges regulated by this provision are only those containing petroleum, oil, or mixtures thereof.[301] The responsibility for the offence depends on the source of the discharge, leakage, or running. If it emanates from a vessel, it is the owner or master of the vessel who is responsible. If, on the other hand, it emanates from an apparatus, it is the responsibility of the owner or person in charge of the apparatus, and if it emanates from any other place, it is the occupier or the other person in charge of such place who must bear the legal responsibility. The criminal offence arising as a result of the transgression of these provisions may be punished with a fine and/or imprisonment from one to six months. The perpetrator is also liable for any other damages and costs 'occasioned by the facts constituting the offence', which damages and costs, liquidated by the court, shall be paid to the Authority for Transport in Malta. It is interesting to note that such damages and costs may be awarded in the judgment of the criminal court and are executable in the same manner as if awarded following a civil action.

207. Another 'antique' piece of legislation is the Petroleum (Importation, Storage and Sale) Ordinance of 1889,[302] which regulates ships carrying a cargo, any part of which consists of petroleum. The owner or master of every such ship is to report to the Authority for Transport in Malta on the nature of such cargo and to give any other details as requested, while the agent of the ship (or if the agent does not comply, the importer or consignee) is to give the Authority three days' prior notice of the arrival of any such ship. Such ships are restricted from entering or discharging their cargo only in ports or bays, fixed by order for that purpose by the Authority. Also included is the right to take samples, the right to issue regulations with respect to ports, bays, and places where such ships may enter, be moored, or land their cargo, as well as any necessary precautions which should be taken in this regard.

300. Enacted in 1854 as Ch. 10 of the Laws of Malta.

301. Section 228 says, 'Discharges, leaks and the running of petroleum oil or any other mixture containing petroleum or oil into a harbour or the internal or territorial waters from any vessel of from any place on land/afloat or from apparatus used for transferring petroleum, oils from or to any vessel whether to or from a place on land or afloat, is prohibited.'

302. Chapter 25 of the Laws of Malta.

208. The Explosives Ordinance[303] prohibits the use of explosives for fishing purposes, thereby preventing marine pollution and the degradation of the marine environment from such activities. The penalty established is imprisonment for a term from one to nine years. It is also relevant to note that the Minister responsible for police may make regulations concerning the importation, storage, and sale of any explosive or inflammable substance not covered by other laws.

209. The Continental Shelf Act[304] empowers the Prime Minister to make regulations dealing with a variety of matters affecting marine pollution. Broadly, he may make regulations protecting the marine environment. He may also specifically provide for: the laying, maintenance and monitoring of submarine cables and pipelines; and the removal of artificial islands, installations, structures, or devices constructed, erected, or placed in, on, or above the continental shelf which has been abandoned or has fallen into disuse. These activities could result in inadvertent marine pollution and overall harm to natural marine resources. Furthermore, he may make regulations for the protection of the living resources of the sea and the natural resources of the continental shelf from harmful agents through prescribed measures to be taken in safety zones.[305] The continental shelf area is established by subsidiary legislation.[306]

210. The Continental Shelf Regulations[307] indeed greatly impact marine protection and pollution. Submarine cables and pipelines can only be lain or maintained, and surveys for their laying can only be conducted with a licence to that effect by the Prime Minister. Failure constitutes an offence liable to a fine (*multa*) not exceeding EUR 2,000,000, imprisonment not exceeding two years, or both. Likewise, a licence by the Prime Minister is required to operate an artificial island, etc., and the owner or operator of one which has fallen into disuse or is beyond repair shall inform the government forthwith thereof and remove it within the timeframe stipulated by government and in accordance with any conditions it imposes. Failure here is an offence liable to the same punishments mentioned previously.

The Regulations also regulate discharges and dumping. The discharge of any oil, or mixture containing it, into any part of the sea from a pipeline or due to any operations for the exploration of the seabed and subsoil or the exploitation of their natural resources in a designated area is an offence. The person deemed responsible is the one carrying on the operation unless he can prove the discharge was due to the act of a person there without his express or implied permission. The penalty is a fine (*multa*) of between EUR 5,000 and EUR 2,000,000. Dumping is the deliberate disposal of vessels, aircraft, platforms or other man-made structures, or of wastes or other matters therefrom, at sea.[308] Dumping onto the continental shelf is not to be

303. Chapter 33 of the Laws of Malta.
304. Chapter 535 of the Laws of Malta. It repealed the previous eponymous Act (Ch. 194).
305. An area around any artificial island, installation or structure, designated for the purpose of ensuring their safety as well as safety of navigation around them.
306. L.N. 36 of 1971 and L.N. 113 of 1974 consolidated (S.L. 535.01).
307. L.N. 235/2015 (S.L. 535.02).
308. Excluding: (a) disposal of wastes or other matter incidental to, or derived from, the normal operations of vessels, etc., at sea and their equipment, other than wastes or other matter transported by

carried out without the express prior approval of the government, which has the right to permit, regulate, and control such dumping after due consideration of the matter with other States, which by reason of their geographical situation may be adversely affected thereby. Contravening these rules is also an offence liable to a fine (*multa*) not exceeding EUR 2,000,000, imprisonment for a term not exceeding five years, or both.

Finally, marine scientific research is subject to stringent conditions to ensure minimal and necessary harmful effects on the marine environment. For example, the Prime Minister can choose to refuse permission to grant a licence for such research where the project involves drilling or coring into, or sampling from, the continental shelf, the use of explosives or the introduction of harmful substances into the marine environment. Furthermore, the project must comply with all applicable health, safety and environmental regulations and guidelines. The possible penalty for infringement is a fine (*multa*) not exceeding EUR 500,000. It should be noted that these regulations, among others, are also applicable to the territorial waters and internal seas of Malta by virtue of the Territorial Waters Regulations.[309]

211. The Exclusive Economic Zone Act[310] was passed in 2021 to allow the responsible Minister to establish an EEZ and environment protection area for Malta through Orders for the purpose. These areas would be subject to specific protection from the marine pollution perspective; however, to date, no such zone or area has been declared.

212. Act XVII of 1991, the Malta Maritime Authority Act,[311] set up the Malta Maritime Authority as an autonomous body made up of three Directorates: the Ports Directorate, the Merchant Shipping Directorate, and the Yachting Directorate. The functions of the Authority ranged from the regulation of ports and merchant shipping to yachting facilities and the enhancing of maritime affairs in Malta. The mandate of the Malta Maritime Authority included the responsibility for the running and upkeep of the ports in Malta and their approaches, as well as to provide any necessary facilities and services to that effect. It is responsible for all work relating to ports and to regulate and control merchant shipping. The Act has been renamed the Ports and Shipping Act by Act XV of 2009, the Authority for Transport in Malta Act,[312] which established the Authority for Transport in Malta as the legal successor to, *inter alia*, the Malta Maritime Authority. This Authority is itself a mega authority born of the merger of the MMA, the authority for land transport and the Civil Aviation Department. The Maritime Authority has therefore become a Directorate within the Authority for Transport, retaining the same functions and powers.

---

or to vessels, etc., at sea, operating for the purpose of disposal of such matter or derived from the treatment of such wastes or other matter on the same; and (b) placement of matter for a purpose other than the mere disposal thereof, provided that such placement is not contrary to the aims of the Regulations.

309. L.N. 235/2015 (S.L. 226.02).

310. Chapter 625 of the Laws of Malta.

311. Chapter 352 of the Laws of Malta.

312. Chapter 499 of the Laws of Malta.

References in this work to Malta Maritime Authority should be taken in this context, and the name may be used interchangeably with the Authority for Transport.

The jurisdiction of the Maritime Authority is limited to the internal waters and territorial sea by the Transport Act, as opposed to the Territorial Waters and Contiguous Zone Act, which bestows more extensive powers on the Prime Minister to regulate the marine environment, as jurisdiction therein is extended to the contiguous zone.[313] The Transport Act makes a cross-reference to the EPA, stating the Authority has, without prejudice to the EPA, the right to protect the environment and to prevent and control oil pollution or pollution by any other substance in any port or its approaches.[314] There is no definition of 'approaches' under the Act, but there are maps annexed to it which locate areas covered by this provision. This Authority also has the function, *inter alia*, to advise the government regarding the prevention and control of marine pollution.

213. The UNCLOS, a convention to which Malta is also a party, defines 'dumping' as the deliberate disposal of wastes or other matter from vessels, aircraft, platforms, or other man-made structures at sea. It does not include the disposal of wastes or other matter arising from normal operations or the placement of matter for any purpose other than disposal.[315] In other words, both discharges occurring in the normal operation of ships or platforms and accidental spillages do not constitute dumping. Incineration of waste is included,[316] while the issue of sub-seabed disposal remains unresolved. Malta fulfils its obligations in this regard through the provisions on dumping in the Continental Shelf Act, seen above.

214. The Oil Pollution Civil Liability and Compensation Act[317] provided for Malta's accession to the 1969 Convention on Civil Liability for Oil Pollution Damage and the 1971 Convention for the Establishment of an International Fund for Compensation for Oil Pollution Damage (IOPC Fund). It also appropriately transformed into municipal legislation the provisions of the 1969 Convention and its Protocol, such that the courts can enforce the international legal obligations in the Convention as part of the law of the land.[318] That Act was repealed and replaced by an eponymous Act[319] in 1999 to provide for accession to the 1992 Protocol amending the Liability Convention and the 1992 Protocol amending the Fund Convention. It also provides for Malta's denunciation of the original Liability Convention and Fund Convention.

215. In cases of liability, the First Hall of the Civil Court assumes jurisdiction whenever a claim is made for pollution damages resulting from an incident which

313. Chapter 226 of the Laws of Malta.
314. A provision previously found under the Maritime Authority Act.
315. *See* Art. 1(5) of UNCLOS.
316. Regulated by the London Convention for Prevention of Marine Pollution by the Dumping from Ships and Aircrafts.
317. Chapter 351 of the Laws of Malta.
318. As required by Art. 3(3) of the Ratification of Treaties Act, Ch. 304 of the Laws of Malta.
319. Chapter 412 of the Laws of Malta.

occurs in Malta.[320] The same court has to decide on the apportionment of monetary compensation from the fund.[321] It is the Registrar-General responsible for Merchant Shipping who is the Competent Authority to issue assurance certificates, required by the Liability Convention, to Malta-registered vessels and also to any vessel whose flag State is not a party to the Convention. It is up to the registrar to establish the conditions required for issuing the certificate of assurance and determining its validity in accordance with the provisions of the Convention.

216. The Act then goes on to implement the provisions of the Fund Convention and stipulates that any person who receives 'contributing oil'[322] must inform the Minister responsible for shipping within a definite time.[323] The Minister, in turn, is duty-bound to forward this information to the Director of the IOPC Fund. Again, it is the First Hall of the Civil Court which has jurisdiction over claims made against the IOPC Fund for compensation for incidents causing marine pollution occurring in Malta, including its territorial waters, or for any preventive and or responsive measures taken required to minimise harm in the territorial waters.[324] In turn, the IOPC Fund, by virtue of the Act, has the right to take legal action before the First Hall of the Civil Court against the polluters.

217. The Act reproduces the text of Articles I–XI of the Liability Convention (in the First Schedule) and Articles I to IV, VI–X and XII–XV of the Fund Convention (in the Second Schedule), making them part of the Law of Malta and enforceable as such. The Liability Convention relates to pollution damage and to preventive measures taken to prevent and minimise it. Liability rests with the owner of the ship at the time of the incident.[325] There are a number of exceptions to this, namely, fortuitous events, malicious intent of a third party, or the negligence of any Authority entrusted with maintaining navigational aids. Furthermore, if the person suffering the damage is wholly or partially responsible, either with malicious intent or as a result of his negligence, the owner is exonerated wholly or partially from his liability towards him. The burden of proof, in this case, rests with the owner. The Convention does not allow for compensation claims to be made against the servants or

320. This is understood to mean pollution damage sustained in the territorial waters, exclusive economic zone (so far Malta has none), the waters enclosed in Malta's contiguous zone claim and those superjacent to Malta's continental shelf claim.
321. In cases where the fund's resources do not suffice to satisfy the amount of monetary compensation which parties have a right to claim, it is up to the court to reduce, pro rata, the amount of compensation awarded to the parties.
322. The Fund Convention (Art. 3) defines contributing oil as crude oil and fuel oil. Crude oil crude oils as any liquid hydrocarbon mixture occurring naturally in the earth, whether it is treated for transportation or not. Crude oils may also have certain distillate fractions removed from them (topped crudes) or added to them (spiked/reconstituted crudes).
323. Such person will have up to 1 March of the year following the calendar year when the contributing oil is received.
324. Article 6 lays down the procedure: a judicial Act must be filed against the IOPC Fund, which is notified at the office of the Minister for shipping.
325. Where the incident consists of a series of occurrences, the liable owner is the one who owned the ship at the time when the incident first occurred.

the agents of the owner. The owner[326] is entitled to limit his liability by contributing to a fund unless the incident results from the actual fault or privity of the owner. Claims for compensation for pollution damage may be brought directly against the insurer of any other person providing financial security for the owner's liability for pollution damage. The 1971 Fund Convention established the Fund to provide compensation for pollution damage and to relieve ship owners in respect of the additional financial burden imposed upon them by the Liability Convention. The Fund shall pay compensation to any person suffering pollution damage if such person does not qualify for full and adequate compensation under the Liability Convention. The provisions of the Convention impose the obligation on any person who receives in total 150,000 tonnes of contributing oil in a contracting State during a stipulated time limit[327] to contribute to the Fund.

218. The Clean Air Act[328] prohibits dark smoke[329] from vessels.[330] Liability, which is strict,[331] rests on the vessel. Vessels belonging to the government for the purposes of its armed forces or any vessel in the service of the government employed in this manner are to be reported to the Clean Air Board set up under this Act. L.N. 30/1969 was issued under the Clean Air Act and establishes the permitted periods of dark smoke from vessels.[332]

219. Also relevant as a legal source for the regulation of marine pollution is the Territorial Waters and Contiguous Zone Act.[333] This is also an enabling Act, which bestows powers on the Prime Minister to make regulations to control and regulate the passage of ships through the territorial waters of Malta, as well for as the safety of navigation and the regulation of marine traffic, including the designation or establishment of sea lanes and traffic separation schemes for navigators. The Act also provides for regulations for the conservation of living resources of the sea; the prevention of infringement of laws or regulations affecting fisheries; the preservation of the environment; and the prevention, reduction, and control of pollution. Regulations may also provide for the arrest, detention, and service of ships to ensure compliance and any other necessary powers to secure compliance. It is also possible under this Act for the Prime Minister to establish punishments by means of fines or imprisonment in case of any contravention or non-observance of any regulations made under this section. This Act specifies that regulations under the Act may require warships, nuclear-powered ships, or ships carrying inherently dangerous or noxious substances to seek prior consent or notification from the Authorities for passage through the territorial waters of Malta. This Act affirms that nothing

326. Or any of his servants or agents, or any persons who have a right to subrogation.
327. *See* Art. 10.
328. Chapter 200 of the Laws of Malta.
329. Dark smoke is defined according to its comparison against a Ringelmann chart, while smoke itself is defined to include soot, ash, grit and gritty particles emitted as smoke.
330. Jurisdiction is limited to navigable waters in harbours and bays.
331. Clean Air Act, Arts 3(3)(a)–(c).
332. S.L. 200.02, Permitted Periods of Dark Smoke from Vessels Regulations.
333. Chapter 226 of the Laws of Malta.

under it affects any jurisdiction or power of the State, exercisable in accordance with international law outside territorial waters.

220. The Oil and Hazardous and Noxious Substances Pollution Preparedness, Response and Co-operation Regulations[334] were adopted under the Act. These establish a regulatory framework for the applicability of, and in accordance with, the International Convention on Oil Pollution Preparedness, Prevention and Co-operation (OPRC Convention) and the 2000 Protocol to the OPRC Convention relating to Pollution Incidents by Hazardous and Noxious Substances. They also provide for the applicability of the National Marine Pollution Contingency Plan[335] and for the requirement to have in place marine pollution response emergency plans for marine terminals, marine facilities, and ports.

The Authority for Transport is the competent authority tasked with the implementation, maintenance, updating, and enforcement of the National Contingency Plan. This applies to all marine terminals and marine facilities and to all ships while they are in the internal and territorial waters of Malta. The Authority is responsible for preparing pollution emergency plans for the ports under its jurisdiction, management, and control, which are to be in place within twelve months of the date of entry into force of the Regulations (which was 1 January 2021). They are to be revised within stipulated timeframes, except where major changes affecting their material validity or effectiveness occur. The Authority furthermore has a multitude of powers to ensure the fulfilment of the Act's objectives, such as: to actively participate in and approve the pollution emergency plans of marine terminals and facilities; to ensure the plans of the same are consistent with and part of the National Contingency Plan; and to organise periodical training and drills in pollution emergency and response. Each marine terminal and each marine facility must have its own pollution emergency plan, though joint plans are allowed between entities in the same port area. It is their duty to develop, implement, maintain, and update their plan and to appoint and maintain in position a person responsible for this. Operators of these terminals and facilities, and masters of ships in the Maltese territorial waters or contiguous zone, must report any polluting incident without delay. Failure of such an operator to comply with the provisions of the Regulations is an offence liable to a fine (*multa*) of between EUR 2,500 and EUR 100,000 for each offence, and in the case of a continuing offence to a further fine (*multa*) of between EUR 500 and EUR 1,500 for every day the offence persists. The Authority can also impose an administrative fine for non-compliance.

221. The Ship-Source Pollution Regulations[336] were adopted under the same Act. These Regulations implement Directive 2005/35/EC of the European Parliament and of the Council of 7 September 2005, as amended, on ship-source pollution and on the introduction of penalties for infringements. These Regulations filled in an important lacuna, which was left after the Marine Pollution and Prevention Act referred to in the next paragraphs was never brought into force. These Regulations

334. L.N. 450/2020 (S.L. 226.03/499.69).
335. This plan forms part of the Laws of Malta and is enforceable as such.
336. L.N. 130/2008 (S.L. 226.01).

apply to any ship in Maltese waters and any ship on the high seas provided that any discharge on the high seas may be reasonably expected to result in major harmful consequences in Maltese waters or to the coastline of Malta or related interests, including fishing. These Regulations do not apply to any warship, naval, or other ship owned or operated by a Member State and used, for the time being, only on government non-commercial service. However, any discharge of a harmful substance from any ship in the waters mentioned above constitutes a criminal offence, with the exception of those discharges which satisfy the conditions set out in Annex I, Regulations 15, 34, 4.1, or 4.3, or in Annex II, Regulations 13, 3.1.1, or 3.1.3, of the MARPOL Convention.[337] There is also an exception for any harmful substances from any ship on the high seas committed by the owner of the ship or by the master or other member of the crew acting under the master's responsibility if it satisfies the conditions set out in Annex I, Regulation 4.2 or Annex II, Regulation 3.1.2 of the MARPOL Convention.

222. It is indeed sad to note that the Marine Pollution (Prevention and Control) Act,[338] originally intended to transform the MARPOL provisions into national law, never came into force. The Act aimed at the prevention and control of marine pollution and pollution of other waters and to give effect to the provisions of international and regional conventions and protocols relating to the protection of the marine environment. The Act was divided into seven parts, addressing, among other things, the criminal and civil liability for various forms of marine pollution from differing sources. The Act was finally repealed and struck off the statute book by virtue of Act II of 2015. The MARPOL Convention is now dealt with in the other pieces of legislation seen.

223. The Dangerous Cargo Ships, Marine Terminals and Facilities and Bunkering Regulations[339] were issued under the Petroleum (Importation, Storage and Sale) Ordinance,[340] the Malta Maritime Authority Act[341] and the Bunkering (Fuels) Tax Act.[342] These Regulations regulate the movement, transfer, storage, and handling of dangerous cargoes, bunkers, ballast, and tank-cleaning operations on all ships and at all marine terminals and facilities within or connected to the internal and territorial waters of Malta. The Regulations allow any tanker carrying no more than 20,000 tonnes of volatile, dangerous cargoes into the Grand Harbour, provided it proceeds directly to the tank-cleaning berth and that it strictly complies with the conditions specified in the regulations regarding crude oil working[343] throughout its stay in the Grand Harbour. All crude oil working and tank-cleaning operations shall be carried out in strict compliance with relevant international instruments of law and

337. The International Convention for the Prevention of Pollution from Ships. It has been adopted under Maltese Law by means of the Merchant Shipping (Prevention of Pollution from Ships) Regulations, L.N. 332/2003 (S.L. 234.32).
338. Chapter 271 of the Laws of Malta.
339. L.N. 1/1996 (S.L. 499.12).
340. Article 7 of Ch. 25 of the Laws of Malta.
341. Article 28 of Ch. 352 of the Laws of Malta.
342. Article 7 of Ch. 381 of the Laws of Malta.
343. Detailed in Regs 27 and 28.

practice. After cargo operations are completed, the ship's tank may not be opened or cleaned while it is in internal or territorial waters, except in all places authorised by the Authority for Transport. Bunker barge operations in the territorial or internal waters of Malta shall only be undertaken by means of a licensed or authorised bunker barge. Outside port areas, bunker supply operations may only be conducted in anchorage areas designated by the Authority. The Authority may establish bunker areas and delineation of their boundaries. The penalty for non-compliance is a fine (*multa*) not exceeding EUR 9,317.49 for each offence.

224. The prior authorisation of the Authority is always required for any bunker barge to anchor in Malta's internal or territorial waters. Bunkering equipment must comply with international standards, while checklists detailed in Schedule B must be completed by the master of the bunker-receiving ship and the bunker barge prior to the commencement of and at each integral stage of every bunkering operation. The granting and renewal of licenses for bunker barges to operate within Malta's internal and territorial waters are subject to conditions laid down in the Regulations,[344] which include an insurance cover with respect to third-party damage, marine environment pollution damage, and clearance of pollution liabilities for an amount acceptable to the Transport Authority and by an insurer recognised by the Authority. The Regulations lay down that general operational resources and administrative and procedural requirements are in full compliance with relevant international legal instruments and codes of practice. Marine terminal and facility operations shall provide to the Authority detailed and updated information regarding safety and pollution prevention and control, including relevant operational data, equipment and personal resources, and general and specific procedures, as well as policies and plans in respect of pollution prevention and control. In addition, the operators shall also provide the Authority with full general details of a checklist on pollution prevention.[345] The Authority shall only consider issuing or renewing a licence to a marine terminal facility as a bunker operator when pollution control and removal equipment, resources, trained personnel, and approved procedures for any potential consequences of the most environmentally hazardous operations that can be undertaken at such place are wholly provided by the operator and approved by the same Authority.

225. The Regulations have five schedules. Schedule A is a specimen notice of the expected arrival and status of an oil, gas, or chemical ship or a ship carrying dangerous or potentially polluting packaged substances or solid bulk dangerous cargoes. Schedule B is a ship/shore safety checklist. Schedule C is a specimen of a hot work permit and cold work permit. Schedule D is a list of International Maritime Organisation conventions to which Malta has acceded. Schedule E provides fees for insurance and renewal of bunker operator's licenses and charges for inspection of bunker operator's facilities.

344. *See* Reg. 64 for more detail.
345. *See* Reg. 70.

226. The umbrella piece of legislation as regards marine pollution is the Marine Policy Framework Regulations,[346] transposing Directive 2008/56/EC on the indicative list of elements to be taken into account for the preparation of marine strategies. The aim is to establish a framework to take necessary measures to achieve or maintain good environmental status in the marine environment by the year 2020 at the latest. The Regulations aim to contribute to and ensure the integration of environmental concerns into the different policies, agreements and legislative measures which have an impact on the marine environment. However, they do not apply to activities, the sole purpose of which is defence or national security, although effort is to be made to ensure that these activities are conducted in a manner that is compatible, so far as reasonable and practicable, with the objectives of the Regulations. The Regulations apply to all marine waters. These are the waters, seabed, and subsoil on the seaward side of the baseline from which the extent of territorial waters is measured, extending to the outmost reach of the area where Malta has and, or exercises jurisdictional rights,[347] in accordance with UNCLOS and general international law; as well as coastal waters as defined by the Water Policy Framework Regulations,[348] their seabed, and their subsoil, in so far as particular aspects of the environmental status of the marine environment are not already addressed through those regulations or other legislation.

'Pollution' is given a specific definition under these Regulations. It means the direct or indirect introduction into the marine environment, as a result of human activity, of substances or energy, including human-induced marine underwater noise, which results or is likely to result in deleterious effects such as harm to living resources and marine ecosystems, including loss of biodiversity, hazards to human health, the hindering of marine activities, including fishing, tourism and recreation and other legitimate uses of the sea, impairment of the quality for the use of seawater and reduction of amenities or, in general, impairment of the sustainable use of marine goods and services.

The standard of 'good environmental status' is also defined as the environmental status of marine waters where these provide ecologically diverse and dynamic oceans and seas which are clean, healthy, and productive within their intrinsic conditions, and the use of the marine environment is at a level that is sustainable. More precisely, it is a state where the structure, functions and processes of the constituent marine ecosystems, together with the associated physiographic, geographic, geological, and climatic factors, allow those ecosystems to function fully and maintain their resilience to human-induced environmental change, and marine species and habitats are protected, a human-induced decline of biodiversity is prevented and diverse biological components function in balance.

227. The competent authority is ERA, whose duty is to develop and implement the marine strategy for Malta and ensure coordination in its own administrative

346. L.N. 73/2011 (S.L. 549.62).
347. At present, this extends to 25 nautical miles seaward from the baselines, since Malta claims an Exclusive Fishing Zone to that effect, though the government has recently expressed the intention to establish an EEZ.
348. *See* the next chapter.

setup to implement the Regulations holistically. The government's endorsement is, however, required for the marine strategy and programme of measures. The development and implementation of the strategy require an ecosystem-based approach to the management of human activities, the pressure of which should still be compatible with good environmental status and overall marine sustainability. On a broader level, developing the strategy requires ERA to duly account for the fact that Malta's marine waters form an integral part of the Ionian Sea and Central Mediterranean Sea marine sub-region of the Mediterranean. The strategy has two overall aims. First, the protection and preservation of the marine environment, which includes restoration of marine ecosystems where practicable. Second, to prevent and reduce inputs in the marine environment, with a view to phasing out pollution in accordance with the aims of the Regulations. The plan of action for the strategy is to include cooperation with other EU Member States sharing Malta's sub-region of the Mediterranean since the aim is a common approach to marine preservation. The coordination may also involve existing regional institutional cooperation structures and build upon them, such as the Convention for the Marine Environment and the Coastal Region of the Mediterranean Sea. The Regulations lay down the timeline for the preparation and implementation of the strategy to ensure the 2020 deadline is adequately met. However, if urgent action is required due to the critical state of the sub-region, Malta is to cooperate with the other relevant Member States to devise a plan of action, including an earlier entry into operation of programs of measures and, possibly, stricter protective measures. The strategy is to be kept up-to-date and reviewed every six years to ensure it is still fit for purpose. A brief interim report is to be published describing progress in the implementation of each programme of measures within three years of its publication. Furthermore, ERA all interested parties are to be given early and effective opportunities to participate in the Regulations' implementation in accordance with Union legislation, as well as publish and make available to the public summaries of specific aspects of the strategy: assessment and determination of good environmental status, environmental targets, monitoring programmes, and programmes of measures. The Freedom of Access to Information on the Environment Regulations also apply to these Regulations.

228. ERA has assessment and monitoring obligations under the Regulations. An initial assessment of Malta's marine waters was to be made on which to base the strategy (and which must be reviewed as described above). It was to take account of three broad data sets: ecological,[349] anthropogenic[350] and socioeconomic.[351] The analysis is to take into account elements regarding coastal, transitional, and territorial waters covered by relevant provisions of existing legislation, in particular, the Water Policy Framework Regulations. They shall also take into account or use as their basis other relevant assessments, such as those carried out jointly in the context of Regional Sea Conventions, so as to produce a comprehensive assessment of

349. Analysing the essential features and characteristics, and environmental status, of the waters, based on the indicative list of elements in Table 1 of Schedule I.

350. Analysing the predominant pressures and impacts, including human activity, on the marine environment, based on the indicative list of elements in Table 2 of Schedule II.

351. An economic and social analysis of the use of marine waters and the cost of degradation of that environment.

the status of the marine environment. Transboundary impacts and effects are also to be taken into account. Coordinated monitoring programmes are to be established and implemented on the basis of this assessment to keep the environmental status of marine waters under constant surveillance. This is to be based on the indicative list of elements in Schedule II, the list in Schedule IV, and the environmental targets. The programmes are to be built upon and compatible with the Habitats and Birds Directives. A programme of measures required to achieve or maintain good environmental status in Malta's Mediterranean sub-region is to be devised by ERA on the basis of its initial assessment, the environmental targets, and accounting for the types of measures in Schedule V.[352] It is also to take account of other relevant EU Directives and international agreements to ensure coherence – for example, marine protected areas. The measures must be cost-effective and technically feasible, based on impact assessments, and have a view towards sustainability. Furthermore, ERA must account for the potential risk of damage to marine waters beyond Malta to minimise the risk and, if possible, negate it.

229. ERA must determine good environmental status and establish environmental targets for the strategy. Good environmental status is to be determined at the marine sub-region level on the basis of the qualitative descriptors in Schedule I.[353] The strategy's ecosystem approach means adaptive management techniques must be applied. The qualitative descriptors are to be used as the basis for determining a set of characteristics of good environmental status for Malta's marine waters by reference to ERA's initial assessment. Here, ERA is to account for the indicative lists of elements in Table 1 of Schedule II, particularly physical and chemical features, habitat types, biological features and hydromorphology. ERA is to establish a comprehensive set of environmental targets and associated indicators for Malta's marine waters on the basis of the initial assessment, with the endorsement of the Minister responsible for the environment. The purpose is to guide progress towards achieving good environmental status in the marine environment. Account must be taken of the indicative lists of pressures and impacts set out in Table 2 of Schedule II and of characteristics set out in Schedule III. Furthermore, ERA is to bear in mind relevant environmental targets already existing under national, EU or international law in respect of the marine sub-region to ensure all are mutually compatible.

ERA may identify exceptions where the above-mentioned targets and status cannot be achieved. The reasons are twofold: they may not be achievable in every respect or within the relevant time schedule. Instances of the former are: natural causes; force majeure; action or inaction for which Malta is not responsible; and modifications or alterations to the physical characteristics of marine waters brought about by actions taken for reasons of overriding public interest which outweigh the negative impact on the environment, including any transboundary impact. The only contemplated instance of the latter is through natural conditions, which do not allow timely improvement in the status of the marine waters concerned. These are all to

352. These include input and output controls, distribution controls, overall management, and mitigation and remedial tools.
353. Examples are maintenance of biodiversity, non-harmful levels of non-indigenous species, contaminant levels at no-pollution-effect levels.

be clearly identified in the programme of measures and do not exempt ERA from taking appropriate ad hoc measures to pursue the environmental targets and achieve/ maintain good environmental status.

§2. Freshwater Pollution

230. Malta's legislation on the subject used to be very limited, as Malta has no freshwater resources. There are a few perennial springs, but even these sometimes dry up in the hot summer months. Groundwater is extracted for drinking and agricultural purposes, but nowadays, farmers also use water from sewage treatment plants, while drinking water is mainly produced by reverse osmosis plants located around the islands. The more recent legislation on the subject is tackled in the next section since it forms an integral part of water management on the semi-arid Maltese Islands.

231. The Code of Police Laws, under Article 151, lays down that any person shall avoid causing, through his negligence, any rubbish, mud, or other noxious or offensive matter to enter into any fountain, aqueduct, or any other place used for the preservation of public water, or any putrid water of other offensive matter to run into a public water source or in any other thing whereby public water is rendered foul or unwholesome. The Code also prohibits any person from throwing or negligently allowing to flow any rubbish or any polluted or dirty water, or any other offensive matter into the public wastewater pit.

§3. Water Management

232. The EPA of 2001 provided in its part on definitions that 'environment' means the whole of the elements and conditions, natural or man-made, existing on earth, whether together or in isolation, and in particular, the air, water, and land. This definition was retained in the 2016 EPA. Also notable is the presence of a definition of 'water' in the Regulator for Energy and Water Services Act:[354] when used in relation to any practice, operation or activity regulated by that Act, it includes drainage and sewage services but not bottled table water. The Malta Resources Authority Act,[355] which set up the MRA, provided for the separation of the MRA's regulatory and operational functions as regards water management. The Water Services Corporation[356] continued to be the operator, while the Directorate for Water Resources Regulation was established and vested with regulatory functions for water resources. The MRA Act was repealed and replaced in that respect by the REWS Act, which also established the Regulator for Energy and Water Services (REWS). REWS is now the single regulatory authority at national level for the purposes of Directive 2019/944/EC and Directive 2009/73/EC.

354. Chapter 545 of the Laws of Malta.
355. Chapter 423 of the Laws of Malta.
356. Established under Ch. 355 of the Laws of Malta, Water Services Corporation Act.

233. Today, REWS has the duty to ensure the proper and sustainable use of all water resources in the Maltese Islands while respecting hydro-environmental and socioeconomic constraints. Being also responsible for economic regulation, REWS encourages the national water utility to improve its efficiency and service standards while ensuring fair and reasonable pricing of its services to the consumer. Due to the strategic importance in having a reliable water supply, REWS is aiming to secure, in the long term, the most proper use of all water resources, both conventional and non-conventional ones, while ensuring environmental protection. As one of the main bodies responsible for the formulation of water regulations and policies, REWS, sometimes together with ERA, reviews existing legislation and continues to work on the transposition of EU Directives into Maltese law. In fact, there are different Competent Authorities for the various Legal Notices that make up Maltese Law on water quality. These include ERA, REWS, the Unit,[357] and the Public Health Department.

234. During Malta's negotiations to become a member of the EU, the Water Framework Directive[358] (WFD) was still being prepared. As a result, Maltese law on water quality transposed this Directive as a framework law and also the various water quality directives[359] that it has integrated and will eventually repeal. Consequently, L.N. 194/2004, the Water Policy Framework Regulations, which transposed the WFD, aimed at establishing a management structure for water policy, with the following main objectives: expanding the scope of water protection to all waters, surface waters, and groundwater; achieving 'good status' for all waters by a certain deadline; combining an approach of ELVs and quality standards; getting the citizen involved more closely; and rationalisation of legislation. Amendments to the Directive by various other EU Directives led to the repeal[360] of the 2004 Regulations and their replacement by eponymous Regulations in 2015[361] in order to reflect the new aims of, and positions at, EU law on the subject. These will be dealt with at a later stage below.

235. L.N. 203/2002, the Protection of Groundwater against Pollution caused by Dangerous Substances Regulations, transposed Council Directive 80/68/EEC on Groundwater. This Directive was repealed by Directive 2006/118/EC on the protection of groundwater against pollution and deterioration, leading to the corresponding repeal of the 2002 Regulations[362] and their replacement by the Protection of

357. The Sustainable Energy and Water Conservation Unit, established by L.N. 50/2014, the Sustainable Energy and Water Conservation Unit (Establishment as an Agency) Order.
358. Directive 2000/60/EC.
359. Such as the Dangerous Substances Directive 76/464/EEC, which was transposed by L.N. 213/2001 and Urban Waste Water Treatment 91/271/EEC, which was transposed by L.N. 340/2001, Directive 82/176/EEC on limit values and quality objectives for mercury discharges by the chlor-alkali electrolysis industry, transposed by L.N. 220/2001; 83/513/EEC on limit values and quality objectives for cadmium discharges transposed by L.N. 221/2001; 86/280/EEC on limit values and quality objectives for discharges of certain dangerous substances transposed by L.N. 227/2001.
360. Without prejudice to anything done or omitted to be done thereunder.
361. L.N. 345/2015, Water Policy Framework Regulations (S.L. 549.100).
362. By Act XXV of 2015, the Regulator for Energy and Water Services Act.

Groundwater against Pollution and Deterioration Regulations.[363] The new Directive establishes a regime which sets underground water quality standards and introduces measures to prevent or limit inputs of pollutants into groundwater. The Directive establishes quality criteria that take account of local characteristics and allow for further improvements to be made based on monitoring data and new scientific knowledge. The Directive thus represents a proportionate and scientifically sound response to the requirements of the WFD as it relates to assessments on chemical status of groundwater and the identification and reversal of significant and sustained upward trends in pollutant concentrations. Member States will have to establish the standards at the most appropriate level and take into account local or regional conditions. These are also the aims of the local Regulations.

The Regulations apply to both the direct and indirect introduction of pollutants into groundwater as a result of human activity, meaning they tackle pollution from both point and diffuse sources. Direct introduction occurs without percolation through the ground or subsoil; indirect introduction occurs after such percolation. Groundwater itself means all water which is below the surface of the ground in the saturation zone and in direct contact with the ground or subsoil. The Regulations also apply to all measures to prevent the deterioration of the status of all groundwater bodies, with the Framework Regulations applying unless inconsistent with the Groundwater Regulations. The Competent Authority is the Unit, and where the Framework Regulations apply, the Ministry for Energy and Health. The Unit's duties of publicity are implemented through obligations to publish results, assessments, etc., in the river basin management plans in accordance with the Framework Regulations.

236. The criteria for assessing groundwater chemical status are the groundwater quality standards and threshold values. The former are detailed in the First Schedule, indicating the values of nitrates and active substances in pesticides.[364] However, more stringent threshold values will be established in accordance with the Regulations where, for a given groundwater body, it is considered that the quality standards could result in: a failure to achieve the environmental objectives of the Framework Regulations for associated bodies of surface water; in any significant diminution of the ecological or chemical quality of such bodies; or in any significant damage to terrestrial ecosystems which depend directly on the body of groundwater. The threshold values are to be established by the Unit in accordance with the procedure set out in Part A of the Second Schedule for the pollutants, groups of pollutants, and indicators of pollution which, within the Maltese territory, have been identified as contributing to the characterisation of bodies or groups of bodies of groundwater as being at risk, taking into account the list contained in Part B of the Second Schedule.[365] The list of threshold values must be amended as new information on pollutants arises in order to protect human health and the environment. The

363. L.N. 108/2009 (S.L. 549.53).

364. Including their relevant metabolites, degradation, and reaction products.

365. Part B of Schedule II indicates pollutants and their indicators for which the Unit must establish thresholds, such as arsenic, lead, nitrites, trichloroethylene, and parameters indicative of saline or other intrusions.

criteria for establishing a groundwater body as one of good chemical status are also provided. The procedure for assessing groundwater chemical status is laid down in the Regulations. The choice of monitoring sites is to satisfy the requirements of the Framework Regulations to ensure representative monitoring data and a holistic overview of the site's status, and the Unit must take all measures in accordance with those Regulations to protect aquatic ecosystems, terrestrial ecosystems and human uses of groundwater dependent on the part of the body of groundwater represented by the monitoring point or points at which the value for a groundwater quality standard or the threshold value has been exceeded, where a body of groundwater is classified as being of good chemical status.

237. The Unit is to identify any significant and sustained upward trend in concentrations of pollutants, groups of pollutants, or indicators of pollution found in bodies or groups of bodies of groundwater identified as being at risk and define the starting point for reversing that trend in accordance with the Fourth Schedule. Such trends are any statistically and environmentally significant increase in concentration of a pollutant, group of pollutants, or indicator of pollution in groundwater for which trend reversal is identified as being necessary in accordance with the Regulations.

Trends which present a significant risk of harm to the quality of aquatic ecosystems or terrestrial ecosystems, to human health, or to actual or potential legitimate uses of the water environment are to be reversed through a programme of measures as required in the Framework Regulations. The starting point for a trend reversal is to be calculated as provided in the Regulations. Additional trend assessments may be carried out to assess the impact of existing plumes of pollution in groundwater bodies that may threaten the objectives in the Framework Regulations, particularly those resulting from point sources or contaminated land, to ensure they do not expand, deteriorate the chemical status of the bodies, or present a risk for human health or the environment.

238. The Unit must prevent and/or limit inputs of pollutants into groundwater through a programme of measures. This must include all necessary measures to prevent inputs of hazardous substances[366] and all necessary measures to limit inputs of non-hazardous substances nevertheless deemed by the Unit to present an existing or potential pollution threat.[367] Wherever technically possible, it must take into account the pollutant inputs from disseminated sources of pollution which have an impact on the chemical status of groundwater.

239. The penalties incurred for discharging pollutants into groundwater sources are more attentively regulated through the Groundwater (Prohibition of Discharge to Groundwater Bodies) Regulations.[368] The pollutants for the purposes of these

366. Taking account of substances identified or considered as hazardous by the Framework Regulations.
367. To ensure they do not cause deterioration or significant and sustained upward trends in the concentrations of pollutants in groundwater, taking account, at least, of established best practice, including the Best Environmental Practice and Best Available Techniques.
368. L.N. 81/2023 (S.L. 549.155).

Regulations are: those substances listed in Schedule VIII to the Water Policy Framework Regulations;[369] pollutants listed in the First Schedule to the Protection of Groundwater Against Pollution and Deterioration Regulations;[370] those substances or indicators of pollution referred to in items 1, 2 and 3 of Part B of the Second Schedule to the Protection of Groundwater Against Pollution and Deterioration Regulations; heat (unless the activity resulting in the discharge of heat has been expressly authorised or permitted); and any other substance at concentrations exceeding the natural background levels of the receiving body of groundwater.

There are two main classes of offences under the Regulations. The first is where any person undertakes, or causes to be undertaken, any activity which consists of or results in a direct discharge of pollutants to groundwater, which is punishable by a fine (*multa*) not exceeding EUR 1,000. The second is where any person undertakes, or causes to be undertaken, any activity of disposal or tipping for the purpose of disposal, which activity consists of, or results in, or may lead to, the indirect discharge to groundwater of pollutants, unless the activity has been expressly authorised or permitted. This is punishable with a fine (*multa*) not exceeding EUR 750. If either of these offences is committed where the discharge to groundwater occurs within a groundwater safeguard zone, he will instead, on conviction, be liable to a fine (*multa*) of not less than EUR 5,000 and not more than EUR 10,000. It should be noted that it is not an offence if any prohibited activity is directed at the artificial recharge or augmentation of bodies of groundwater in accordance with Regulation 12(3)(f) of the Water Policy Framework Regulations for which prior authorisation has been obtained.

Notwithstanding the aforementioned punishments, the Court may also order the decommissioning and, or sealing of any structure or infrastructure located above or underground used in carrying out the activity to be undertaken at the offender's expense and may further order the confiscation of any equipment used in the carrying out of said activity. If the activity takes place at the ground surface, the Court shall, notwithstanding any punishment to which it may impose on the offender, order any necessary environmental remediation, including any required removal and disposal, to be carried out at the offender's expense. It can also make other orders pursuant to specified provisions of the Criminal Code.

240. L.N. 221/2001, the Limit Values and Quality Objectives for Cadmium Discharges Regulations,[371] transposes Directive 83/513/EEC and is one of the main legislative tools for the protection of water quality. These Regulations complement L.N. 213/2001, which addresses pollution caused by certain dangerous substances discharged into the aquatic environment. As stated in its title, L.N. 221/2001 was designed to regulate the handling of cadmium through the industrial process involved in its use or production. The limit values which are to be complied with and the monitoring procedures for discharges are laid down in Annex I. Since the concentration of cadmium depends on the volume of water involved, differing between different processes and plants, the limit values, which are expressed in

369. L.N. 435/2015 (S.L. 549.100).
370. L.N. 108/2009 (S.L. 549.53).
371. S.L. 549.15.

terms of the quantity of cadmium discharged in relation to the quantity handled, must always be complied with. Second, L.N. 221/2001 establishes where such limit values are to be applied. Where wastewater containing cadmium leaves the industrial plant, the parameters shall apply as established under the Regulations, but where such wastewater is treated outside the industrial plant at a treatment plant for the removal of cadmium, the Competent Authority may permit the limit values to be applied at the point where the waste waters leave the treatment plant.

The Competent Authority may also grant authorisations for new plants only if those plants apply the standards corresponding to the best technical means available when this is necessary for the elimination of pollution. There is also the requirement that authorisations are reviewed every four years. It is up to the Competent Authority to ensure that the regulations on limit values and quality objectives of cadmium discharges are being followed. However, it is also the responsibility of the industrial plant operators to ensure that the regulations and limits applicable to their industrial plant are complied with.

241. The Competent Authority under these Regulations is the Department for Environment Protection, under the guidance of the Director for Environment Protection. The main responsibility of the Competent Authority under these Regulations is that of monitoring the aquatic environment affected by industrial discharges. If such discharges affect the waters of other States, it must cooperate with other Competent Authorities in Malta and abroad with the intention of harmonising monitoring procedures. The functions of the Competent Authority have to be carried out while ensuring that limit values and quality objectives for cadmium discharges are followed. As mentioned before, the limit values are set down in Annex I to the Legal Notice. Annex IV then deals with the monitoring process for quality objectives. These are determined by the intended use of the area affected. However, it has to be kept in consideration that the main purpose is that of eliminating all pollution. Annex III(1) gives the reference method of analysis to be used in determining the presence of cadmium, while the accuracy required in the measurement of effluent flow is given in Annex III(2).

242. A person is guilty of an offence under these Regulations if he: fails to comply with any order lawfully given in terms of any provision of the Regulations; or if he contravenes any restrictions, prohibitions, or requirements imposed by or under the Regulations. Such person will be liable on a first conviction to a fine (*multa*) between EUR 1,164.69 and EUR 2,329.37. On a second or subsequent conviction, he would be liable to a fine between EUR 2,329.37 and EUR 4,658.75, or imprisonment up to two years, or both. Any person found guilty also has to pay for expenses incurred by the public entities or other persons acting on their behalf involved in the implementation of these Regulations and suffers the revocation of the permit and the confiscation of the *corpus delicti*. Since such an offence constitutes a crime under the Criminal Code, procedures are taken before the Court of Magistrates (Malta or Gozo) as courts of criminal judicature.

243. The 2004 Water Policy Framework Regulations[372] transposed the Water Framework Directive, which establishes a framework of action for the protection of inland surface waters, transitional waters, coastal waters, and groundwater. The new 2015 Water Policy Framework Regulations[373] perform the same function with the same aims and also transpose new Directives amending the original WFD. These are: Article 32 of Directive 2009/31/EC,[374] Directive 2013/39/EU,[375] Commission Directive 2009/90/EC,[376] and Directive 2014/101/EU.[377] These Regulations attempt to adopt a holistic approach with respect to the whole field of water management, from protection to supply, to quality, to monitoring and analyses. The Competent Authority varies depending on the water body concerned: the Ministry for Energy and Health for inland waters; ERA for coastal waters. Nevertheless, ERA is still responsible for those surface waters found in areas protected by scheduling declarations[378] and for surface waters located in areas hosting protected species or other areas of ecological and scientific importance.[379] The division of competence gains importance in determining who is responsible for taking the necessary measures to ensure the environmental objectives established for each water type are met.

244. The definitions section is very important to understand when assessing the role and scope of the Regulations. The different types of 'waters' are particularly relevant. 'Surface waters' means inland waters (except groundwater) and transitional and coastal waters. 'Coastal waters' are surface waters on the landward side of the baselines, plus waters one nautical mile seaward of the baselines, extending up to the outer limit of transitional waters where appropriate. 'Inland waters' are all those standing or flowing waters on the land's surface and groundwater on the landward side of the baselines. 'Groundwater' means all water below the surface of the ground in the saturation zone and in direct contact with the ground or subsoil. 'Transitional waters' are bodies of surface water in the vicinity of the mouths of water catchments which are partly saline due to proximity to coastal waters but are substantially influenced by freshwater flows. Important also is the definition of pollution: the direct or indirect introduction, as a result of human activity, of substances or heat into the air, water, or land which may be harmful to human health or the quality of aquatic ecosystems or terrestrial ecosystems directly depending on aquatic ecosystems, which result in damage to material property, or which impair or interfere with amenities and other legitimate uses of the environment. 'Pollutant', in turn, means any substance liable to cause pollution, particularly those listed in Schedule VIII. The emissions and discharges concerned, therefore, are those that affect water, whether via point or diffuse sources, irrespective of where they originate from. The Competent Authorities are legally bound to prevent the deterioration

372. L.N. 194/2004.
373. L.N. 345/2015 (S.L. 549.100).
374. On the geological storage of carbon dioxide.
375. On environmental quality standards for priority substances and certain other pollutants, with the aim of achieving good surface water chemical status.
376. Laying down technical specifications for chemical analysis and monitoring of water.
377. To include an amended Annex V.
378. Under the EPA or the Filfla Nature Reserve Act.
379. Under, or according to the provisions of, the EPA.

of the status of all the bodies of water[380] and to implement the measures necessary to reverse any significant and sustained upward trend in the concentration of any pollutant resulting from the impact of human activity in order to reduce progressive pollution.

245. Administratively, Malta and Gozo are one water catchment district[381] for the purposes of the Regulations, with administrative arrangements for proper implementation being the responsibility of the competent authorities. They must also ensure that the requirements for achieving the environmental objectives, and the programme of measures, are coordinated for the whole catchment district.

The authorities must undertake: an analysis of characteristics; a review of the impact of human activity on the status of surface waters and on groundwater; and an economic analysis of water use for the district. These must be updated every six years and carried out in accordance with the technical specifications contained in Schedules II and III. A register must be kept of all areas within the district designated as requiring special protection under specific legislation for the protection of their groundwater and surface water or for the conservation of habitats and species depending directly on water. This is to include: all water bodies used, or intended for, the abstraction of drinking water for human consumption, providing an average of more than 10 m^3 a day and all protected areas covered by Schedule IV. Furthermore, water catchment management plans must be produced for the district, with the information detailed in Schedule VII, to be published and reviewed every six years. Publicity requirements are tied to the plan and extend to the implementation of the Regulations generally, particularly through the involvement of interested parties, even at the planning level.

246. The programmes of measures in the catchment management plans are to be made operational through environmental objectives, depending on the water at hand. If surface waters, the competent authority must implement the necessary measures to prevent the deterioration of their status and to protect, enhance, and restore all such bodies with the aim of achieving good surface water status. If the bodies are artificial or heavily modified, it must take the necessary measures to protect and enhance them. The end aim, in any case, is the progressive reduction of pollution from priority substances[382] and the ceasing/phasing out of emissions, discharges, and losses of priority hazardous substances. If groundwater, the competent authority must implement the measures necessary to prevent or limit pollutant input and to prevent deterioration of its status, as well as those required to protect, enhance, and restore groundwater bodies with the aim of achieving good groundwater status, particularly by balancing groundwater abstraction and recharge. It must also take the necessary measures to reverse any significant and sustained upward trend in the concentration of any pollutant resulting from the impact of human activity in order

380. According to the type of water resources falling under their responsibility.
381. An area of land and sea composed of one or more neighbouring water catchments together with their associated groundwaters and coastal waters. Water catchments are areas of land over which surface run-off flows through a sequence of watercourses into the sea from a single exit.
382. Listed in Schedule X, with some identified as ‘priority hazardous substances’.

to progressively reduce pollution of groundwater. The deadline to achieve good water status for ground- and surface waters was November 2015. However, where more than one objective applies to a given water body, the most stringent one is to apply. Furthermore, the deadlines may be extended for the purpose of phased achievement of the objectives for a given body, and the competent authority may aim to achieve less stringent objectives for specific bodies when they are so affected by human activity or their natural condition is such that the achievement of the objectives would not be feasible or would be disproportionately expensive. The grounds for which this dispensation applies are laid down exhaustively in the Regulations.[383] Likewise, the grounds and instances where breaches of the Regulations are not to be deemed to have occurred are laid down at law.[384] In any case, the attainment of the objectives in one waterbody must not permanently exclude or compromise their achievement in other waterbodies within the same catchment district.

247. Programmes of measures must be adopted for each district, accounting for the aforementioned analyses and aimed to achieve the required environmental objectives. Each must include 'basic' measures and, where necessary, 'supplementary' ones. Basic measures are the minimum requirements laid down exhaustively at law,[385] such as: measures aimed at implementing legislation aimed at water protection; measures to prevent or control point and diffuse pollution sources; prohibitions of direct discharges of pollutants into groundwater; and measures to eliminate pollution of surface waters. Supplementary measures are adopted and implemented in addition to the basic ones to further achieve the environmental objectives. A non-exhaustive list of these is provided in Part B of Schedule V. Furthermore, all appropriate steps, such as reviews of permits[386] and monitoring programmes, must be taken where monitoring or other data indicates the objectives for a specific waterbody are unlikely to be achieved. The programme of measures is to be updated and reviewed every six years. Surface water status, groundwater status, and protected areas must be monitored by a programme to establish a coherent and comprehensive overview of water status for the whole catchment district. The authority must adhere to the technical specifications and standardised methods for analysis and monitoring of water status prescribed in Schedules V and XI. The programmes are to cover: for surface waters – volume and level/rate of flow to the extent relevant for ecological and chemical status and ecological potential, and the ecological and chemical status and ecological potential; for groundwater – chemical and qualitative status; for protected areas – the relevant programme must be supplemented by the specifications contained in the legislation under which that area has been established. A combined approach is adopted for point and diffuse sources of discharges into surface waters. One of three approaches must be adopted: emission controls based on BATs; the relevant ELVs; or for diffuse sources, the controls

383. *See* Reg. 5(5).
384. *See* Regs 5(6) and (7) generally, and Reg. 5(1) for coastal waters.
385. *See* Reg. 12(3).
386. The authorities are given considerable powers to alter or revoke permits or serve remedial notices on permit holders where the attainment of the environmental objectives for a specific body are at stake.

including BATs as appropriate, provided the controls and limit values are construed according to the IPPC Regulations, among others, and the regulations listed in Schedule IX.[387]

248. The offences under the Regulations are: failure to comply with their provisions or with any order lawfully given in their terms; contravention of any prohibition, restriction or requirement imposed by or under them; acting in contravention of any of their provisions; and conspiring or attempting, or aiding or abetting, any other person by whatever means to perform any of the aforementioned. A first conviction entails a fine (*multa*) of between EUR 1,164.69 and EUR 4,658.75. A second conviction entails a fine (*multa*) of between EUR 4,658.75 and EUR 58,234.33, imprisonment for a term not exceeding six months, or both. The court[388] must also order the person to pay for the expenses incurred by the competent authority due to the offence, the revocation of the permit, and the confiscation of the *corpus delicti*. Articles 23 and 30 of the Criminal Code apply mutatis mutandis in this respect.

249. The Urban Waste Water Treatment Regulations[389] transpose Council Directive 91/271/EEC of 21 May 1991. These Regulations relate to the collection, treatment, and discharge of urban wastewater and the treatment and discharge of wastewater from certain industrial sectors. The Regulations are mainly directed at all the relevant authorities which are concerned with the treatment of urban wastewater and which have a major say in the prevention of damage done to the environment by it. The objective of these Regulations is to protect the environment from the adverse effects of the above-mentioned wastewater discharges. According to the interpretation section of these Regulations, 'domestic waste water' means wastewater from residential settlements and services, which originates predominantly from the human metabolism and from household activities, while 'industrial waste water' means any waste water which is discharged from premises used for carrying on any trade or industry, other than domestic waste water and run-off rainwater. So, the aim of these Regulations is the collection and treatment of wastewater, whether domestic or industrial. The requirements for domestic wastewater treatment are found in Annex I(B), while the requirements for industrial water treatment are found in Annex II(C).

250. Several obligations are imposed on EPD as the Competent Authority.[390] It shall ensure that all agglomerations are provided with collecting systems for urban wastewater. This, however, depends on the population. The two types of populations which fall under this Article are those with a population equivalent of more than 15,000 and those with a population equivalent of between 2,000 and 15,000. The collecting system shall satisfy the requirements of Annex I(A). Moreover, the

387. Dealing with ELVs and environmental quality standards.
388. The Court of Magistrates (Malta or Gozo) as a Court of Criminal Judicature, with a right of appeal of the Attorney General to the Court of Criminal Appeal.
389. L.N. 340/2001 (S.L. 549.22).
390. Under the direction of the Director for Environment Protection.

discharge of urban wastewater into receiving waters, which are considered 'sensitive areas', requires the EPD to ensure that collection systems are provided for agglomeration of more than 10,000 population equivalent. Where the establishment of collecting systems is not justified either because it would produce no environmental benefit or because it would involve excessive cost, individual systems or other appropriate systems which achieve the same level of environmental protection shall be used. Staggered dates were laid down for the coming into force of the regulations vis-à-vis the various wastewater treatment plants on the Islands. Compliance by all plants was reached by 31 October 2006.

The Competent Authority must ensure that urban wastewater entering collecting systems is subject, before discharge, to secondary treatment or an equivalent treatment according to these categories: all discharges from agglomerations of more than 15,000 population equivalent, all discharges from agglomerations of between 10,000 and 15,000 population equivalent, and discharges to freshwater and estuaries from agglomerations of between 2,000 and 10,000 population equivalent. Staggered dates were laid down for the coming into force of these obligations, with the latest date for compliance being 31 March 2007. Discharges from urban wastewater treatment plants shall satisfy the relevant requirements of Annex I(B). Another responsibility of the Competent Authority is that the load expressed in population equivalent is to be calculated on the basis of the maximum average weekly load entering the treatment plant during the year, excluding unusual situations such as those due to heavy rain.

The Competent Authority must identify sensitive areas according to the criteria laid down in Annex II of the Regulations. In addition, it must ensure that urban wastewater entering collecting systems is subject to more stringent treatment than that described above for all discharges from agglomerations of more than 10,000 population equivalent before discharge into sensitive areas. Discharges from urban wastewater treatment plants which are situated in the relevant catchment areas of sensitive areas and which contribute to the pollution of these areas shall be subject to the obligations just described. Furthermore, the Competent Authority shall ensure that the identification of sensitive areas is reviewed at intervals of no more than four years. It must also ensure that areas identified as sensitive shall meet the above requirements. Additionally, the Competent Authority does not have to identify sensitive areas for the purpose of these Regulations if it implements the treatment established under the same.

The Competent Authority may identify 'less sensitive areas', and such identification shall be reviewed at intervals of not more than four years from when they were identified. Additional responsibilities are for it to ensure that urban wastewater entering collecting systems is subject, before discharge, to appropriate treatment in the following cases: for discharges to freshwater and estuaries from agglomerations of less than 2,000 population equivalent and for discharges to coastal waters from agglomerations of less than 10,000 population equivalent. The Competent Authority must ensure that the urban wastewater treatment plants built to comply with the requirements of Regulations 5–8 are designed, constructed, operated, and maintained to ensure sufficient performance under all normal local climatic conditions. When designing the plants, seasonal variations of the load shall be taken into account. Furthermore, without prejudice to any other laws and authorisations, the

Competent Authority must ensure that the discharge of industrial wastewater into collecting systems and urban wastewater treatment plants satisfies the requirement of Annex I(C), and discharges from urban wastewater treatment plants made within agglomerations of 2,000 to 10,000 population equivalent in case of discharges of freshwaters and estuaries shall satisfy the relevant requirements of Annex I(B). Moreover, it must ensure that treated wastewater is reused whenever appropriate. Disposal routes must minimise the adverse effects on the environment. Further duties are to ensure that, before discharge, biodegradable industrial wastewater from plants belonging to the industrial sectors listed in Annex III, which does not enter urban wastewater treatment plants before discharge to receiving waters, respects conditions established in prior regulations and/or specific authorisation by the Competent Authority or appropriate body, in respect of all discharges from plants representing 4,000 population equivalent or more. Also, the Authority shall set requirements appropriate to the nature of the industry concerned for the discharge of such wastewater.

The Competent Authority must ensure that the disposal of sludge from urban wastewater treatment plants is subject to general rules or registration or authorisation. Furthermore, the disposal of sludge to surface waters, by dumping from ships by discharge from pipelines or by other means, is phased out. Until the elimination of the forms of disposal, the Competent Authority shall ensure that the total amount of toxic, persistent, or bioaccumulable materials in sludge disposed of to surface waters is licensed for disposal and progressively reduced. The Competent Authority and any other appropriate bodies, as may be notified by order by the Minister in the Government Gazette, shall monitor discharges from urban wastewater treatment plants to verify compliance with the requirements of Annex I(B) in accordance with the control procedures laid down in Annex I(D), along with amounts and composition of sludges disposed of to surface waters. The Competent Authority shall monitor waters subject to discharges from urban wastewater treatment plants and direct discharges in cases where it can be expected that the receiving environment will be significantly affected. In the case of a discharge, subject to the provisions of Regulation 6 and in the case of disposal of sludge to surface waters, the Competent Authority shall monitor and carry out any other relevant studies to verify that the discharge or disposal does not adversely affect the environment. The Competent Authority shall ensure that every two years, the relevant authorities or bodies publish situation reports on the disposal of urban wastewater and sludge in their areas. Besides this, the Competent Authority shall determine the methods and formats to be adopted for reporting under the Regulations.

251. The criminal offences under these Regulations are: failure to comply with any order lawfully given in terms of any provisions of the Regulations; contravening any restriction, prohibition, or requirement imposed by or under the same; or conspiring or attempting, or aiding or abetting, any other person by whatever means, to fail to comply with any order lawfully given in terms of any of the provisions of the same, or to contravene any restriction, prohibition, or requirement imposed by or under them. Any person who commits an offence against these Regulations shall, on conviction, be liable on a first conviction to a fine (*multa*) of not less than EUR 1,164.69 but not exceeding EUR 2,329.37. On a second or subsequent conviction, to a fine (*multa*) of not less than EUR 2,329.37 but not exceeding EUR 4,658.75 or imprisonment for a term not exceeding two years, or both. The court shall order any person who has been found guilty of committing an offence against these Regulations to pay for the expenses incurred by the public entities and/or other persons acting on their behalf involved in the implementation of these Regulations and restitution of the environment as a result of the said offence, the revocation of the permit issued by the police and the confiscation of the *corpus delicti*. The revocation of any permit held by the offender may in no case be for less than one year. Proceedings for an offence against these Regulations shall be taken before the Court of Magistrates of Malta (or Gozo). The Attorney General shall always have a right of appeal to the Court of Criminal Appeal from any judgment given by the Court of Magistrates of Malta (or Gozo) in respect of proceedings for any offence against these Regulations.

252. The Pollution Caused by Certain Dangerous Substances Discharged into the Aquatic Environment Regulations[391] are a transposition of EU Directive 76/464/EEC of 4 May 1976, which was one of the first water-related directives to be adopted by the EU. The original Legal Notice came into force on 1 May 2004, upon Malta's accession to the EU. On 15 February 2006, the EU codified Directive 76/464/EEC and its subsequent amendments into Directive 2006/11/EC. This codification led to clarification and rationalisation of legislation; it also takes into account the adoption of the Water Framework Directive and the international conventions on the protection of water courses and the marine environment.

253. The Regulations regulate the discharge of polluting substances into inland surface waters, territorial waters, inland coastal waters, and groundwater. Therefore, this is an umbrella regulation which controls pollution in the waters which fall within the jurisdiction of Malta. The definition of pollution here is:

> the discharge by man, directly or indirectly, of substances or energy into the aquatic environment, the results of which are such as to cause hazards to human health, harm to living resources, and to aquatic organisms, damage to amenities, or interference with other legitimate use of water. Moreover, the same Article also defines the term discharge as being the introduction into the waters mentioned above, of any substances in List I and List II. The term discharge, in this legislation, does not cover the discharges of dredging, operational discharges from ships in territorial waters, and the dumping from ships in territorial waters.[392]

254. The main waters which are under threat of pollution in Malta are the groundwater and coastal waters. According to the State of the Environment Report of 2018, issued by ERA, the principal threats to groundwater quality are point pollution incidents involving unlawfully discharged substances, nitrate contamination from agricultural fertilizers, contamination from human and animal wastes, and high

391. L.N. 213/2001 (S.L. 549.10).
392. *Ibid.*, Reg. 2(1).

chloride concentrations associated with localised seawater intrusion as a result of over-abstraction. Twelve out of the fifteen bodies of groundwater in Malta have been identified as having poor qualitative status. With regard to coastal water, the Report indicates Malta's coastal waters are in good chemical status with respect to most pollutants. The notable exception is mercury, which was the most common contaminant detected, and concentrations exceeded the annual average EQS. Lead and Nickel, two other heavy metals, exceeded the established EQSs for the water column occasionally.[393]

255. As this legislation controls the discharge of polluting substances, it deals with point-source pollution, that is, pollution coming from a single location, such as a discharge pipe attached to a factory. When point-source pollution enters the environment, the place most affected is usually the area immediately around the source. In order to provide effective protection of the aquatic environment, this legislation establishes List I and List II substances. Substances in List I are certain individual substances selected mainly on the basis of their toxicity, persistence, and bioaccumulation, with the exception of those which are biologically harmless or which are rapidly converted into substances which are biologically harmless. Substances which fall under List II are organohalogen compounds and substances which may form such compounds in the aquatic environment, organophosphorus compounds, organotin compounds, mercury, cadmium, substances which possess carcinogenic properties, persistent mineral oils, and hydrocarbons of petroleum origin, which are persistent synthetic substances which may float, remain in suspension, or sink and which may interfere with the use of the waters.[394] Through the adoption of these Regulations, Malta is required to eliminate pollution of surface waters from these substances since their presence in water may result in adverse effects on water quality and human health even at trace concentrations. The Department for Environment Protection must lay down quality objectives for substances within List I, principally on the basis of the toxicity, persistence, and bioaccumulation of the said substances in living organisms and in sediment, taking into account the difference in characteristics between saltwater and freshwater.[395]

256. List II substances consist of substances belonging to the families and groups of substances in List I for which controls referred to in Article 7 of the Legal

393. 'State of the Environment Report 2018, Chapter 5: Marine and Fresh Waters', ERA.

394. List I substances pose health risks to humans and to the aquatic environment, due to their physio-chemical and toxicological properties.

395. Moreover, the European Commission issued ELVs and quality objectives for a number of List I substances, and these have also been transposed into the following Maltese Legal Notices: L.N. 218/2001, Limit Values and Quality Objective for Hexachlorocyclohexane Discharges Regulations; L.N. 219/2001, Limit Values and Quality Objectives for Mercury Discharges by Sectors Other than the Chlor-Alkali Electrolysis Industry Regulations; L.N. 220/2001, Limit Values and Quality Objectives for Mercury Discharges by the Chlor-Alkali Electrolysis Industry Regulations; L.N. 221/2001, Limit Values and Quality Objectives for Cadmium Discharges Regulations; L.N. 227/2001, Limit Values and Quality Objectives for Discharges of Certain Dangerous Substances into the Aquatic Environment Regulations.

Notice have not been determined.[396] Substances within List II also have an adverse effect on the aquatic environment. For the relevant pollutants of List II, the Department must establish pollution reduction programmes, including water quality objectives, according to Regulation 8 of the L.N. 213/2001. These programmes of reduction shall be implemented by requiring authorisation of discharges based on emission standards. These emission standards determine the maximum allowable concentration and maximum quantity in a discharge.

257. The objective of the Regulations is the elimination of pollution in the waters, indicated in the same[397] by the dangerous substances in the families and groups of substances in List I. Furthermore, this legislation also aims at diminishing pollution in the same waters by the dangerous substances in the families and groups of substances in List II. To reach this goal, the Department is to adopt limit values which the emission standards should not exceed, quality objectives for water, methods of measurement, and the time limits with which existing discharges should comply.

258. The Regulations set out a number of obligations in order to reduce and eliminate the pollution caused by dangerous substances discharged into the aquatic environment. Any person who discharges into the indicated waters is required to hold a licence issued by the Competent Authority. The Regulations make it clear that this authorisation to discharge into the aquatic environment must be given prior to the actual discharge. However, there is an exception in the case of an existing discharge, where the person carrying out the discharge must comply with the conditions laid down in the licence within a stipulated period. The licence issued by the Authority lays down emission standards with regard to discharges of any such substance into the waters or into any sewer. Moreover, the licence is granted for a limited period only; however, it may be renewed while taking into account any changes in the limit values, which the emission standards may not exceed for the various dangerous substances included in the families and groups of substances within List I.

The Authority has the obligation to apply a system of zero-emission to discharges into groundwater within List I. This law imposes an obligation on the authority to lay down emission standards in a licence when it is granted. These emission standards shall determine the maximum concentration of a substance permissible in a discharge and the maximum quality of a substance permissible in a

396. The following metalloids and metals and their compounds: zinc, copper, nickel, chromium, lead, selenium, arsenic, antimony, molybdenum, titanium, tin, barium, beryllium, boron, uranium, vanadium, cobalt, thallium, tellurium, and silver. Biocides and their derivatives not appearing in List I. Substances which have a deleterious effect on the taste and/or smell of the products of human consumption derived from the aquatic environment, and compounds liable to give rise to such substances in water. Toxic or persistent organic compounds of silicon, and substances which may give rise to such compounds in water, excluding those which are biologically harmless or which are rapidly converted in water into harmless substances. Inorganic compounds of phosphorus and elemental phosphorus. Non-persistent mineral oils and hydrocarbons of petroleum origin. Cyanides, fluorides. Substances which have an adverse effect on the oxygen balance, particularly NH_3 and nitrates.

397. Namely, surface waters, territorial waters, coastal waters, and groundwater.

discharge during one specified period of time or more.[398] The Authority is also given the discretion to impose more rigorous emission standards by taking into account, in particular, the toxicity, persistence, and bioaccumulation of the substance concerned in the environment into which it is discharged. In addition, the Authority is granted the power to take appropriate steps to ensure that the conditions of the licence are fulfilled and, if necessary, it can also prohibit the discharge. Besides, the Authority has the discretion not to grant a licence if the person who is effecting the discharge declares that he is unable to comply with the required emission standards or if this situation is evident to the Authority.

259. The Competent Authority has a number of functions to perform in compliance with the Regulations. It is to take the necessary measures to eliminate pollution of inland surface water, territorial waters, internal coastal waters, and groundwater by the dangerous substances which are present in the groups of substances in List I of the Annex. It must take the necessary adequate measures to reduce pollution of those waters by the dangerous substances in the groups of substances in List II of the Annex. The Competent Authority is to issue prior authorisations to any person who discharges any substances included in List I into those waters. The licence issued by the Competent Authority has to provide for emission standards with regard to the discharges of any substances into those waters. The Competent Authority has the function to apply a system of zero-emission to discharges of substances in List I into groundwater.[399] The Competent Authority is to grant the authorisation licence to lay down emission standards to determine the maximum concentration of a substance permissible in a discharge. Where there is a case of dilution, the limit value provided for in Regulation 7(1)(a) shall be divided by the dilution factor.

The Department is also to determine the maximum quantity of a substance permissible in a discharge during one specified period of time. This quantity may be expressed as a unit of weight of the pollutant per unit of the characteristic element of the polluting activity. Another function of the Competent Authority when granting a licence is to impose more stringent emission standards than those resulting from the application of the limit values enlisted in Regulation 7, taking into consideration the toxicity, persistence, and bioaccumulation of the substance(s) concerned in the environment into which it is discharged. The Competent Authority is obligated to refuse to grant a licence if the person who discharged any substance declares that he is unable to comply with the required emission standards or if this situation is evident according to the Competent Authority. Furthermore, if the emission standards are not complied with, it must take appropriate steps to ensure that the licence conditions are fulfilled, and, in certain cases, the discharge should be prohibited.

The Competent Authority has the duty to lay down the limit values which the emission standards may not exceed for the dangerous substances included in List I. It is also to establish quality objectives for the substances in List I. It is of major

398. Regulation 6 of L.N. 213/2001.
399. This is an important provision in Reg. 5(1) of L.N. 213/2001.

importance that these objectives are laid down principally on the basis of the toxicity, persistence, and bioaccumulation of the aforementioned substances in living organisms and in sediment, taking into account the difference in characteristics between saltwater and freshwater. Another function to be adhered to by the Competent Authority is that of the establishment of programmes for the reduction of pollution in the waters.[400] It is to require that any person who discharges any substances within List II into the waters shall be in possession of a licence by the said Authority in which emission standards are laid down. The Competent Authority is to take all appropriate steps to implement measures adopted by it so as not to increase the pollution of waters to which the Regulations do not apply. The Competent Authority further has the function to prohibit all acts which intentionally or unintentionally circumvent the provisions laid down in the Regulations. The Department is also responsible for drawing up an inventory of the discharges into inland surface water, territorial waters, internal coastal waters, and groundwater, which may contain substances within List I to which emission standards are applicable.

260. The punishments against any person who commits any offence which goes against the Regulations are laid down in Regulations 13 and 14. Regulation 13(a) provides that when a person is liable on a first conviction, he must pay a fine (*multa*) of not less than EUR 2,329 and on a second or subsequent conviction, he is subject to a fine (*multa*) of not less than the above-mentioned amount but not to exceed EUR 4,658 or else to imprisonment for a term not exceeding two years, or both such fine and imprisonment. Furthermore, when a person is found guilty of committing an offence against the Regulations by means of a vehicle, the owner of the vehicle is to be held liable in the same manner and degree. Furthermore, the court shall order the person who has been found guilty of any offence against the Regulations to pay for the expenses incurred by the public entities and/or other persons acting on their behalf involved in the implementation of the same and restitution of the environment as a result of the offence. The court shall also order the revocation of the permit issued by the police and the confiscation of the *corpus delicti*. Proceedings for an offence against these Regulations should be taken before the Court of Magistrates of Malta (or Gozo) and shall be in accordance with the Criminal Code regulating the procedures before the aforementioned courts as courts of criminal judicature. Acting in compliance with the Criminal Code, the Attorney General always has a right of appeal to the Court of Criminal Appeal from judgments delivered by the Court of Magistrates in relation to proceedings for offences which breach these Regulations.

261. The Limit Values and Quality Objectives for Discharges of Certain Dangerous Substances into the Aquatic Environment Regulations[401] transpose Council

400. Regulation 2(2) of L.N. 213/2001. Thus, these programmes shall be implemented and apply methods referred to in Reg. 2(3).
401. L.N. 227/2001 (S.L. 549.17).

Directive 86/280/EEC on limit values and quality objectives for discharges of certain Dangerous Substances, which was enacted to minimise the production of Dangerous Substances.[402] The obligations of the Competent Authority,[403] according to Annex I, include the taking of samples from the discharge of an industrial plant over a period of twenty-four hours. Then the quantity of the substances discharged is to be calculated over the result that emerges over a period of one month. Regulation 3(2)(b) states that the substance can be treated after it is treated before being discharged. Therefore, the Competent Authority is to treat the final discharge into the environment to see if the industrial plant is discharging enough substances within the limits specified in the Regulations. Licences or permits issued by the Competent Authority must be reviewed every four years and must comply with the provisions of these Regulations. The Competent Authority may grant permits or licences for new plants only if those plants apply the standards corresponding to the best technical means available when that is necessary for the elimination of pollution. The Competent Authority shall seek to ensure that the measures taken do not result in an increase in the pollution of other media, notably soil and air, by these substances.

262. The Competent Authority is responsible for monitoring the aquatic environment affected by discharges from industrial establishments and other sources of significant discharges. In the case of discharges affecting the territorial waters of Malta and of other States, the Competent Authority concerned cooperates with the Competent Authorities of Malta and other States with a view to harmonising monitoring procedures. The Competent Authority with respect to substances to which specific reference is made in Annex II[404] draws specific programmes to avoid or eliminate pollution from significant sources of these substances, including multiple and diffuse sources, other than sources of discharges subject to such other regulations in force establishing limit value rules or emission standards. The programmes include the most appropriate measures and techniques for the replacement, retention, or recycling of the substances. The specific programmes had to be implemented not later than five years after the date of entry into force of the Regulations.

263. A person is guilty of an offence against the Regulations if he fails to comply with any of their provisions or with any order lawfully given in terms of any such provision. He will also be found guilty if he contravenes any restriction, prohibition, or requirement imposed by or under these Regulations. A person is also guilty if he conspires or attempts, or aids, or abets, any other person by whatever

402. This Directive specifically makes reference to the Council Directive 76/464/EEC of 4 May 1976 on pollution caused by certain dangerous substances discharged into the aquatic environment of the Community which contains a list of Dangerous Substances.

403. The term 'Competent Authority' means the Department for Environment Protection under the guidance of the Director for Environment Protection, and such other body or person as the Minister responsible for the environment may, by order in the *Government Gazette*, prescribe, and different bodies or persons may be designated as a Competent Authority for different provisions and different purposes of these Regulations.

404. Such as carbon tetrachloride, DDT, pentachlorophenol, and chloroform.

means, including advertising, counselling, or procurement, to contravene the provisions of these Regulations or to fail to comply with any such provisions, including any order lawfully given in terms of any of the provision of the same, or to contravene any restriction, prohibition, or requirement imposed.

Any person who commits an offence against these Regulations shall, on conviction, be liable on a first conviction to a fine (*multa*) of not less than EUR 1,165 but not exceeding EUR 2,329. On a second or subsequent conviction, to a fine (*multa*) of not less than EUR 2,329 but not exceeding EUR 4,659, or imprisonment for a term not exceeding two years, or both such fine and imprisonment. The court will also order any person who has been found guilty of committing an offence against these Regulations to pay for the expenses incurred by the public entities and/or other persons acting on their behalf involved in the implementation of these Regulations and restitution of the environment as a result of the said offence, the revocation of the permit issued by the police and the confiscation of the *corpus delicti*. A person found guilty of an offence against these Regulations would not be able to obtain a licence from the Competent Authority regarding the matters of these Regulations at least one year after conviction.

264. The Quality of Water Intended for Human Consumption Regulations,[405] enacted under the Food Safety Act,[406] fully transposed the provisions of the Drinking Water Directive.[407] These were revoked and replaced by the Water Intended for Human Consumption Regulations,[408] which transpose the same Directive and the amendments made to it by Council Directive 2015/1787. The scope of these Regulations is to protect human health from adverse effects of any contamination of water intended for human consumption by ensuring that it is wholesome and clean and, at the same time, set up a regime that provides protection to persons consuming the water. These Regulations give a definition of the 'source' from where water is abstracted, and this includes the outlet of water treatment works, a borehole, a pumping station, a blending point, or a service reservoir, whether permanent or not. Many of the sources mentioned are sources from where underground water is abstracted. The Regulations also apply to water supplied by a water supplier. Certain types of water are exempt from their provisions, such as mineral waters designated as such by the Superintendent and waters which are medicinal products within the meaning of Council Directive 65/65/EEC.

These Regulations are another legal tool whereby the conservation of underground water, which is the only type of freshwater resource in Malta, is safeguarded from diffuse source pollution. This fact is not directly specified in the Regulations, but the Competent Authority is responsible for ensuring that the consumer receives good-quality drinking water. Water quality safeguards are imposed from the stage when water is still at source. Furthermore, these Regulations want to protect the consumer by also obliging water suppliers to take the necessary measures to protect this natural resource.

405. L.N. 23/2004.
406. Chapter 449 of the Laws of Malta.
407. Council Directive 98/83/EC.
408. L.N. 17/2009 (S.L. 449.57).

265. The Competent Authority is the Superintendent of Public Health, which, together with water suppliers, is responsible for carrying out all the necessary measures to ensure the best quality of water intended for drinking. In fact, the Superintendent shall take necessary measures to ensure that regular monitoring of the quality of water intended for human consumption is carried out in order to guarantee that the water supplied to the consumer meets the requirements of the Regulations. On the other hand, it is the responsibility of water suppliers to adopt programmes in order to monitor all water intended for human consumption. Water suppliers are also required to prepare and maintain a record of water supply zones, which establish sampling frequencies, in order to ensure compliance with these Regulations, which information shall be made available to the public. For better controls, the Competent Authority may determine that water suppliers publish an annual report of their operations.

266. The Quality Required of Surface Water intended for the Abstraction of Drinking Water Regulations[409] to transpose Directive 75/440/EC on the sampling and measurement procedures for the waters. The Regulations establish quality requirements which must be met by surface water after the application of the proper treatment. 'Surface water' is defined here as freshwater used or intended to be used for the abstraction of drinking water. Surface water does not include groundwater, brackish water, and water intended to replenish water-bearing beds. The Regulations ensure the quality and safety of drinking water by establishing a number of criteria which must be met. Since Malta has no permanent surface water resources, the implementation of these Regulations is limited.

267. The Regulations establish criteria upon which the safety and quality of drinking water is to be determined. Surface water is assigned limiting values, according to which it is then divided into three categories: A1, A2, and A3. The three categories, in turn, correspond to methods of treatment and different qualities of water. REWS (the Competent Authority) has the ability to lay down, at any time, more stringent values than those laid down in the Regulations. It is also given the power, in discharging its obligation to ensure that surface water conforms to the applicable values, to take 'all necessary measures'. The same latitude is allowed with respect to the duty of ensuring the continuing improvement of the environment and surface water.

268. The duties of the Competent Authority according to the Regulations include setting the values (these may be more stringent than those laid down in the regulation) applicable to surface water for all the parameters, taking in all necessary measures to ensure that surface water conforms to the values, as well as to ensure the continuing improvement of the environment by drawing up a systematic plan of action. It is also responsible for defining the frequency of sampling and the analyses of each parameter, as well as defining the methods of measurement and the extent of abstraction. The Competent Authority may exceptionally allow the use of lower-quality water by means of suitable processes, including blending, provided that it

409. L.N. 339/2001 (S.L. 549.21).

publishes the grounds for such exceptions on the basis of a water resources management plan. The Regulations provide that the Competent Authority may change parameters in the case of floods and other natural disasters, meteorological or geographical conditions or in the case when surface water undergoes natural enrichment, and these changes must be published by the Competent Authority by notice in the Government Gazette.

269. Any person shall be guilty of an offence against these Regulations if he: fails to conform with any of these provisions and lawful orders; contravenes any prohibition imposed by these Regulations; or conspires, aids, or abets any other person by any means possible to act in contravention of such provisions, lawful orders, and restrictions. The penalties imposed for such infringement are a fine (*multa*) of not less than EUR 23,290 but not exceeding EUR 232,900 on a first conviction, while on a subsequent conviction, the penalty will be a fine (*multa*) of not less than EUR 116,450 but not exceeding EUR 465,800. Moreover, another penalty could be imprisonment for a term not exceeding two years or both a fine and imprisonment. The court shall order any person who has been found guilty of committing an offence to pay for the expenses incurred by the Competent Authority or any public entity or persons acting on their behalf. The court shall also order the confiscation of the *corpus delicti*.

The provisions of Article 23 and of sub-Article (1) of Article 30 of the Criminal Code shall apply to proceedings in respect of offences against these Regulations, meaning that the disqualification from holding or obtaining a license, permit or authority shall in every case be for over a year. Proceedings for an offence against these Regulations shall appear before the Court of Magistrates of Malta (or Gozo), and such proceedings shall be in accordance with the provisions of the Criminal Code regulating the procedure before the said courts. The Attorney General always reserves the right of appeal to the court of criminal appeal from any judgment given by the Court of Magistrates of Malta (or Gozo) in respect of proceedings for any offence against these Regulations.

270. The Limit Values and Quality Objectives for Mercury Discharges by the Chlor-Alkali Electrolysis Industry Regulations[410] are a transposition of the European Council Directive 82/176/EC bearing the same name of 22 March 1982. It establishes limit values and quality objectives for mercury discharges by the chlor-alkali electrolysis industry, which had to conform to quality objectives as specified in the Regulations. These quality objectives were revoked in 2011. To date, there are no such industries in Malta, so there can be no implementation of this Legal Notice.

271. The Legal Notice lays down the limit values and quality objectives for mercury discharge from industrial plants. It establishes the reference method of measurement, which allows for the determination of mercury content in discharges within the aquatic environment. It further provides for a monitoring procedure,

410. L.N. 220/2001 (S.L. 549.14).

which is to ensure that such limit values and objectives are followed. The limit values, the time limits which must be complied with, and the monitoring procedure for discharges are laid down in Annex I. The limit values applicable are established mainly on the basis of toxicity, persistence, and bioaccumulation, always taking into account the best technical means available. It further laid down the quality objectives for mercury emission into the aquatic environment, which were determined according to the same qualities as the limit values, taking into account the difference in characteristics between saltwater and freshwater. These were dealt with specifically in Annex II, now revoked.

The Competent Authority, which is the Department for Environment Protection, may grant authorisations for new plants only if such comply with certain standards and make use of the best technical means possible for preventing mercury discharges. The reference method of analysis for determining the presence of mercury is given in Annex III. The accuracy required for such measurement is also given in Annex III. The Competent Authority must monitor the effects of industrial discharges on the aquatic environment.

272. Annex I caters for the different connotations of the words 'Limit Values', which are found throughout the Directive. It is a stringent provision which deals with the time limits by which the countries have to comply in regulating their position in relation to mercury discharges, and it also tackles the issue of how discharges are to be monitored. It sets the limit values for the level of concentration of mercury which should not be exceeded. The Annex specifies the exact limit values and how they are to be calculated in a table which must be strictly complied with by all Member States. The limit values expressed may not be greater than those expressed as maximum quantities divided by water requirements per tonne of installed chlorine production capacity. Annex I also provides for a monitoring procedure which seeks to act as a check in order to ensure that the discharges made by this industry comply with the emission standards fixed by this same Annex. As set down in the Directive, the procedure consists in taking a sample of the discharge over a period of twenty-four hours every day and calculating the mercury content in that sample. Additionally, such monitoring should also provide for measuring the total flow of the discharge over twenty-four hours. After such processes, the quantity of mercury discharge for a month is determined by adding the total mercury discharge every day and dividing them by the installed chlorine capacity.

Annex III lays down the method of calculating the mercury content in the waters, the flesh of fish, sediments, and shellfish, and Annex IV requires that for every authorisation granted, the Competent Authority is bound to specify the restrictions, the monitoring procedure, and deadlines for ensuring compliance with the quality objective(s) concerned. It is imperative that such samples must be properly representative of the quality of the aquatic environment in the area affected by the discharges. Additionally, the saltwater fish analysis must be carried out on a sufficiently representative number of samples and species.

273. The chlor-alkali industries must obtain prior authorisation from the Competent Authority, and furthermore, the licence issued by the Competent Authority must lay down emission standards with regard to discharges of any such substance into the applicable waters[411] and, where necessary, in sewers. In the case of discharge which is already present, the person responsible for such discharge shall comply with the conditions laid down in the licence within the period stipulated therein, which usually does not exceed the limits laid down in accordance with Regulation 7. The licence may be given to whosoever has references to the standards corresponding to the best technical means available for preventing discharges of mercury by the Competent Authority. The Competent Authority may allow the use of other methods if and only if the limits of detection, accuracy, and precision of such methods are as superior as those listed in Annex III.1 to these same Regulations. The monitoring of the aquatic environment affected by industrial discharges shall be within the responsibility of the Competent Authority, and if the case may arise that the discharges affect the relevant waters, it must cooperate with other States to synchronise the monitoring procedures.

274. It is an offence against these Regulations to: fail to comply with any order lawfully given in terms of any provision of the Regulations; or contravene any restriction, prohibition, or requirement imposed by or under the same.

Any person found guilty of an offence against the Regulations shall, on conviction, be liable: on a first conviction to a fine (*multa*) of not less than EUR 1,165 but not exceeding EUR 2,329; and, on a second or subsequent conviction, to a fine (*multa*) of not less than EUR 2,329 but not exceeding EUR 4,659 or imprisonment for a term not exceeding two years, or both. Any person who has been found guilty of committing an offence against these Regulations is to pay for the expenses incurred by the public entities and/or other persons acting on their behalf involved in the implementation of these Regulations and restitution of the environment as a result of the said offence, the revocation of the permit issued by the police, and the confiscation of the *corpus delicti*. Proceedings will be carried out before the Court of Magistrates (whether in Malta or Gozo). The Attorney General has the absolute right to appeal to the Court of Criminal Appeal from any judgment given by the Court of Magistrates (whether in Malta or Gozo) in respect of proceedings for any offence against these Regulations.

275. The Protection of Waters against Pollution Caused by Nitrates from Agricultural Sources Regulations[412] aim to reduce, and as far as possible, water pollution caused or induced by nitrates from agricultural sources. It transposes the Nitrates Directive 91/676/EEC and establishes the requirement of a code of good agricultural practice. Moreover, it provides for the identification of waters polluted by nitrates from agricultural sources and the identification of the land areas contributing to the nitrate pollution and the designation of these lands as Nitrate Vulnerable Zones (NVZs). In addition, it prescribes that there shall be the establishment and implementation of action programmes in relation to designated NVZs. The objective of these Regulations, like the Nitrates Directive, is to reduce water pollution caused or induced by nitrates from agricultural sources and prevent further such pollution.

411. Namely, surface waters, territorial waters, and coastal waters.
412. L.N. 343/2001 (S.L. 549.25).

276. The Competent Authority, which is the Department for Environment Protection, had the duty to identify waters affected by pollution and, within a two-year period, following the coming into force of these Regulations,[413] designate as a vulnerable zone all known areas of land in Malta which drain into the waters and which give rise to pollution. Annex VI was subsequently added in 2004, designating all of Malta as an entire NVZ. The Department is also responsible for revising or adding the designation of vulnerable zones as appropriate, and at least every four years, an inspection has to be held for any changes and factors not taken into consideration within the previous designation. The Competent Authority is not restrained from identifying specific vulnerable zones as action programmes are established and applied for such purposes. The Competent Authority was also obligated, within a period of two years following the coming into force of such Regulations, to establish a code or codes for good agricultural practice, to be followed by farmers on a voluntary basis; and to set up, where necessary, a programme containing training and information for farmers promoting the application of the code or codes of good agricultural practice.

277. The first Maltese Code of Good Agricultural Practice was published by the Competent Authorities in 2011. It consists of guidelines for the handling of animal husbandry and manure, fertilisation, and irrigation processes, plant protection, and furthermore, guidelines for practising field cropping.[414]

As established by the Nitrate Directive, action programmes have to be established for the protection and testing of NVZs, and this is reflected in the Regulations. Since Malta has adopted a whole-territory approach with regard to such designated vulnerable zones, the action programmes have to cover all the islands in the Maltese archipelago. However, as disclosed in these Regulations, different action programmes may be implemented for different designated vulnerable areas. Action programmes must take into consideration: scientific and technical data, with special reference to respective nitrogen contributions originating from agricultural and other sources and environmental conditions in the relevant regions of the Competent Authority concerned.

278. Action programmes must be implemented within four years of their establishment and must consist of those measures which the Competent Authority has laid down in the Codes of Good Agricultural Practice. The Competent Authority shall, moreover, in the framework of the action programmes, take such additional measures or reinforced actions as it considers necessary if, at the outset or in the light of experience gained in implementing the action programmes, it appears to it that the measures will not be sufficient for achieving the objectives. The action programme, as revised from time to time, is to be published in the Government Gazette.

In addition, the Competent Authority is responsible for drawing up and implementing monitoring programmes to assess the effectiveness of established action

413. 14 Jan. 2003, via L.N. 24/2003.
414. *The Maltese Code for Good Agricultural Practice*, published by the Ministry for Rural Affairs and the Environment.

programmes. This must include the monitoring of the nitrate content of waters (surface waters and groundwater) to establish the extent of nitrate pollution in the waters from agricultural sources. Groundwater here includes all water which is below the surface of the ground in the saturation zone and in direct contact with the ground or subsoil. Such action programmes shall be reviewed and, if necessary, revised every four years.

279. The Regulations lay down that the Competent Authority is to monitor the nitrate concentration in freshwaters over a period of one year for the purpose of designating and revising the designation of vulnerable zones. They go into detail with regard to surface waters and groundwater. Surface water sampling stations and/or other sampling stations should at least be monitored monthly and more frequently during flood periods, while sampling stations which are representative of the groundwater aquifers should be examined at regular intervals. The monitoring programme is to be repeated every four years, according to the circumstances, due to the nitrate concentration. If the nitrate content is stable,[415] then the monitoring programme shall be carried out every eight years. The Competent Authority has the duty to review the eutrophic state of the fresh surface waters, estuarial, and coastal waters every four years.[416]

The guidelines for the monitoring process may be published. Furthermore, the Competent Authority is bound to publish a report containing information to demonstrate compliance with the Regulations.

280. This Legal Notice also includes several Annexes. Annex I regulates the criteria that need to be followed so as to ensure good quality of water. The first criterion is that the surface freshwater, particularly that which is intended to be used as drinking water, should be in regulation with the Quality of Surface Water Intended for the Abstraction of Drinking Water Regulations[417] with regard to nitrate content if NVZs are not yet established. The second criterion is that if such groundwater contains or could contain more than 50 mg/l of nitrates, this should be identified as an NZV if such zone was not yet identified. Moreover, areas containing natural freshwater lakes, other freshwater bodies, estuaries, coastal waters, and marine waters found to be eutrophic or in the near future could become so and should be identified by the Competent Authority if action programmes are not taken. When applying such criteria, the Competent Authority should consider the physical and environmental characteristics of the waters and land, the understanding of the effects of nitrogen compounds found in water and soil, and the impact of these actions.

281. Annex II of these Regulations provides that the Code(s) of Good Agricultural Practice should be established and published for those working, even voluntarily, in the business of agriculture. The main objective of such Code(s) is to reduce pollution by nitrates and take account of conditions in the different regions of the

415. Below 25 mg/l and no new factor likely to increase this has appeared.
416. Article 7(1)(c) of L.N. 343/2001.
417. L.N. 339/2001 (S.L. 549.21).

Community. Such Code(s) shall establish periods when the land application of fertilizer is inappropriate, guidelines on the land application of fertilizer to steeply sloping ground, and the land application of fertilizer to water-saturated, flooded, frozen, or snow-covered ground. It should also set the conditions for land application of fertilizer near water courses, the capacity and construction of storage vessels for livestock manures, including measures to prevent water pollution by run-off and seepage into the groundwater and surface water of liquids containing livestock manures and effluents from stored plant materials such as silage. Furthermore, it establishes procedures for the land application, including rate and uniformity of spreading, of both chemical fertilizer and livestock manure that will maintain nutrient losses to water at an acceptable level.

It is the responsible Authority that draws up such Code(s) and ultimately publishes it for those concerned. Annex II lists items which the Code may include within such publication, such as land use management, including the use of crop rotation systems, the maintenance of a minimum quantity of vegetation cover during rainy periods, which could result in taking up nitrogen from the soil contributing to the nitrate pollution of water, the establishment of fertilizer plans and lastly, the prevention of water pollution from run-off and the downward water movement beyond the reach of crop roots in irrigation systems.

282. Annex III of this Legal Notice prescribes the measures that must be included in Action Programmes. These refer to: the prohibition of certain types of fertilizers in certain periods; the storage capacity of livestock manure; and when one is applying fertilizers, certain characteristics have to be taken into consideration, such as soil conditions, climate conditions, agricultural practices, including crop rotation systems, and the foreseeable nitrogen requirements of the crops. These measures also address the supply of nitrogen from the soil and fertilisation according to the amount of nitrogen present in the soil at the moment when the crop starts to use it to a significant degree (outstanding amounts at the end of winter), the supply of nitrogen through the net mineralisation of the reserves of organic nitrogen in the soil, the additions of nitrogen compounds from livestock manure, and additions of nitrogen compounds from chemical and other fertilizers. These measures will ensure that a specified amount of livestock manure applied to the land each year shall not exceed 170 kg N per hectare. The Competent Authority, for the first four-year action programme, may allow an amount of manure up to 210 kg N, but after the first four-year programme, it may fix specified amounts, even different from those already mentioned, so as not to prejudice the achievements of the objectives of this Legal Notice and must be justified according to long growing seasons, crops with light nitrogen uptake, high net precipitation in the vulnerable zone, and soils with exceptionally high de-nitrification capacity. Annex VI describes the reference methods of measurement. In the case of chemical fertilizers, nitrogen compounds shall be measured using a method which is permissible by the Competent Authority, and when it comes to freshwaters, coastal waters, and marine waters, the nitrate concentration shall be measured according to the Quality of Surface Fresh Water Regulations.[418]

283. The fifth annex in this Legal Notice deals with the information to be contained in the compliance reports to be published by the Competent Authority. It has the duty to issue a report containing a map showing the waters in question and the location of the designated vulnerable zones. It must contain a summary regarding the designation of the vulnerable zones, including a statement regarding the considerations which led to the designation of each vulnerable zone. There must also be a summary of the action programme, such as a summary of the results of the monitoring programme and the assumptions made by the competent authority about the likely timescale within which the waters are expected to respond to the measure in the action programme, along with an indication of the level of uncertainty incorporated in these assumptions.

284. Offences against these Regulations are to: fail to comply with any order lawfully given in terms of any provisions of these Regulations; contravene any restrictions, prohibition or requirement imposed by or under the same; conspiring or attempting, or aiding, or abetting, any other person by whatever means to contravene the provisions of the same or to fail to comply with any order lawfully given in terms of any of their provisions, or to contravene any restriction, prohibition or requirement imposed by or under the said Regulations. Any person found guilty of contravening the Regulations will be liable on a first conviction to a fine (*multa*) of not less than EUR 1,164 but not exceeding EUR 2,329. On a second or subsequent conviction, to a fine (*multa*) of not less than EUR 2,329.27 but not exceeding EUR 4,658.75, or imprisonment for a term not exceeding two years, or both. The court shall order any person who has been found guilty of committing an offence against these Regulations to pay for the expenses incurred by the public entities and/or other persons acting on their behalf involved in the implementation of these Regulations and restitution of the environment as a result of the said offence, the revocation of the permit issued by the police and the confiscation of the *corpus delicti*. Subsequent to such conviction, the necessary licences will be forfeited, and persons applying for a new licence will not be considered for a period of one year from conviction of the offence(s). Proceedings for conviction shall place before the Court of Magistrates of Malta (or Gozo) as courts of criminal judicature, and these shall be in accordance with the provisions contained in the Criminal Code. Moreover, the Attorney General shall always retain a right of appeal from any judgment given by the courts mentioned above.

285. The Nitrates Action Programme forms the substance of the Nitrates Action Programme Regulations,[419] which further ensure compliance with Council Directive 91/676/EEC. The main aim of the Regulations is the reduction of pollution of natural water resources by nitrates, and to this end, the Competent Authority must

418. L.N. 342/2001 (S.L. 549.24).
419. L.N. 321/2011 (S.L. 549.66).

draw up guidelines and relevant manuals of procedure to ensure compliance with the Regulations. They apply to all agricultural activities taking place on any holding[420] in Malta; however, certain types of production units are exempt from these Regulations for *de minimis* reasons. Nevertheless, should these exempt practices be abused or pose a threat in terms of nitrate pollution, the exemption will no longer avail them. The Competent Authority is the Directorate responsible for agriculture, which is vested with the administration and implementation of the Regulations. It must conduct all the necessary administrative checks, collection of data, verification of records and on-the-spot checks on the holding to ensure compliance. The farmer is to permit any authorised person to enter his land for the purpose of monitoring the implementation of the Regulations or of assessing their effectiveness in reducing water pollution caused or induced by nitrates from agricultural sources and preventing further pollution. The inspector can ask for any documentation or record reasonably required to these ends. The Department must also draw up and maintain a National Nitrates Database containing information such as: registered persons responsible for agricultural land and/or holdings or using fertilisers; information concerning the holdings and/or agricultural land; information concerning the landscape and land management practices; and findings of the Department's monitoring and controls. Any person responsible for agricultural land and/or holdings must register as such with the Department. Only these persons, registered as making use of fertiliser, may be permitted by it to apply fertilisers. These persons are also legally presumed to be responsible for the premises complying with the Regulations and are the persons to whom a breach is to be attributed. Furthermore, all importers, distributors and resellers of fertiliser must be registered with the Department.

286. The Regulations place great responsibilities on farmers. Administratively, they must keep adequate and updated management records, to be made readily available for inspection on the Department's request, to be completed on a yearly basis and kept for a minimum of five years. The Regulations specify the information to be contained in the reports, which spans details of the farmer and agricultural area, cropping regimes, livestock information and fertiliser information. All sales, purchases, or movements of livestock manure or of organic or inorganic fertiliser must be adequately recorded and retained in the Farm Management Records. Holdings with a continuous area greater than one hectare under irrigated cultivation must have a Nutrient Management Plan drawn up for them in terms of Schedule III.[421] Furthermore, all animal holdings and passageways are to be suitably covered at all times. A yearly fertiliser plan must be prepared by farmers responsible for agricultural activities taking place on a holding, irrespective of whether he applies fertiliser or not.[422] This is to be compiled by a qualified technical advisor as approved

420. All production units managed by a farmer.
421. Schedule III details the information and approaches to be adopted in the Nutrient Management Plan.
422. Fertiliser means any substance containing a nitrogen compound applied on land to enhance vegetation growth, except substances confirmed by nitrogen test to have nitrogen content of 0.05% or less.

by the Department,[423] and no fertiliser is to be applied to crops prior to the preparation of a complete plan. The plan will be valid if: the crop plan is not altered for a maximum of three years[424] and the soil test used as its basis is performed every three years. It must determine the crop fertilisation requirement for each crop type on each production unit of the holding for the year and establish safe methods for fertiliser land application, in particular calculating the optimum amount of nitrogen fertiliser required in relation to each crop on each production unit of the holding for that year, taking into account the crop's nutrient requirements and the amount of nitrogen available from soil and water based on adequate soil and water analysis. The land application of organic and inorganic fertiliser is prohibited between 15 October of one year and 15 March of the following year. However, that of inorganic fertiliser may be permitted by the Director if a demonstrable crop nitrogen requirement is notified to him by the farmer, accompanied by relevant proof. An exemption may also be granted owing to justified circumstances by notice in the Gazette. Nevertheless, land application of both fertiliser types is always permitted in closed systems with a concrete platform if the location complies with certain distance requirements tied to fertiliser application. Land application of slurry is, in all cases, prohibited.

Land application of fertiliser is also prohibited in these specific scenarios: where the surface of the field slopes to a degree of 7% or greater, taking into account factors such as proximity to watercourses, soil condition, ground cover and rainfall, or if there is a significant risk of causing water pollution; where the land is located or is in a manner which would make it likely that the nitrogen fertiliser will directly enter a watercourse or any underground water body; or where the land is water-saturated or flooded, and such prohibition shall remain in force until such land remains saturated or flooded. Furthermore, there is an outright ban on fertiliser application: to any type of natural water courses; within a minimum distance of 5 m of natural watercourses; within 5 m of springs, galleries, gallery shafts, boreholes and karst features; within 30 m of any borehole used for public water supply; or within 100 m of the coast. The Regulations also regulate the storage facilities for livestock manure – among other requirements, livestock manure must be stored in a leak-proof, covered storage clamp connected to a cesspit, which itself must be leak-proof, covered and of sufficient capacity to collect all urine and washings for at least fifteen days. Deep-litter systems[425] may be used for ovines and caprines subject to veterinary approval. They also deal with holdings producing soil improvers or soil conditioners to ensure such soil does not cause increases in water nitrogen levels.

287. The Regulations contemplate both administrative penalties and criminal sanctions for contravention of their provisions. The Department may serve an enforcement notice on a farmer it believes to have so contravened the Regulations,

423. A public register detailing these persons is to be published yearly.
424. Crop alterations must result in an update to the plan throughout the three years.
425. An animal housing system whereby repeated layers of straw, sawdust or other dry similar materials are spread for the animals to use as bedding and to defecate in. As the litter is soiled, new layers of litter are continuously added by the farmer.

requiring him to carry out such works or take such steps as the Director may determine in order to remedy or to prevent the continuation or repetition of any contravention to which the notice relates. The specified period for compliance must not be of less than twenty-eight days. Any decision of the Department or Director in this regard is subject to review by the Administrative Review Tribunal. In the case of criminal offences, the Department may impose an administrative penalty instead of initiating criminal proceedings. Should the person admit the offence and pay within the established timeframe, no criminal proceedings are to be taken. If he refuses or asks that the case be tried before the Courts, the Court of Magistrates, as a court of criminal judicature, will take cognisance of the case.[426]

The offences are: failure to comply with any provision of the Regulations or any order lawfully given thereby; failure to comply with a duly served enforcement notice; contravening any restriction, prohibition or requirement imposed by or under the Regulations; acting in contravention of any provision of the same; or conspiring or attempting, or aiding or abetting, any other person to perform any of the above. A first conviction is liable to a fine (*multa*) of between EUR 800 and EUR 1,700. A second conviction entails a fine (*multa*) of between EUR 2,500 and EUR 10,000, imprisonment for a term not exceeding two years, or both. The owner of a vehicle used to commit the offence shall, where applicable, be held liable in the same manner and degree as the actual offender. The court must furthermore order the person found guilty to pay for the expenses incurred by the public entities and, or other persons acting on their behalf involved in the implementation of these regulations and restitution of the environment as a result of the said offence, the revocation of any permit or licence[427] and the confiscation of the *corpus delicti*.

288. The Quality of Fresh Waters Supporting Fish Life (Protection and Improvement) Regulations[428] are a transposition of the EU Directive 78/659/EEC bearing the same name. The main objectives are: to guard or improve the value of running or standing freshwaters which are capable of supporting fish; to diminish or eliminate pollution in order to prevent species found in these freshwaters from being exposed to danger; and to protect indigenous species as well as those which are advantageous for water management purposes since these offer a natural diversity. This allows the natural biodiversity of freshwater ecosystems and habitats to be sustained and flourish. Furthermore, the Regulations aim to ecologically and economically assist fish populations in order to prevent certain species of fish from becoming extinct. The Regulations also require the Competent Authority, which is the Department for Environment Protection, to identify, monitor, and protect high-status sites and to prevent the consumption of contaminated fish, which could lead to potential health implications. In reality, Malta does not have freshwater supporting fish that are used for human consumption, nor does it have any freshwater bodies that it shares with other States because it is an archipelago.

426. The Attorney General has a right of appeal from such decisions to the Court of Criminal Appeal.
427. The court must impose a prohibition on their re-issue of not less than one year.
428. L.N. 342/2001 (S.L. 549.24).

289. The Competent Authority is primarily obligated to designate the waters to which the Regulations are to apply and to set measures to comply with specified water quality parameters, which are listed in the Annex. The implementation of these parameters had to be abided by March 2007, that is, within five years after the Legal Notice came into force. The Competent Authority, in fact, is obligated to present to the EU Commission a status report on the waters allocated and their central features. Designated freshwater bodies may eventually be revised, and hence new parameters may be established. If such parameters are not followed, information is to be given as a justification for this derogation. An important feature of this information is that of taking a certain number of samples in order to guarantee the quality of waters that support freshwater fish.

290. The assessment of water quality in the designated freshwater bodies must be carried out according to the methodology laid down in Annex I. If alternative methods are used, the results that ensue will have to correspond or be analogous to those in Annex I. Methodologies used must not jeopardise the quality of the designated freshwater bodies by increasing pollution. According to Directive 78/659/EC, the Competent Authority must, before applying these parameters, classify designated waters into two types: salmonid waters – these waters are capable of supporting fish belonging to species such as salmon, trout, grayling, and whitefish; and cyprinid waters – these waters are capable of supporting fish which belong to species such as cyprinids, pike, perch, and eel. These are, however, of no relevance to Malta since these species do not occur in freshwater bodies. To ensure a good water quality status, the list of parameters controls temperature,[429] pH level, oxygen levels,[430] and the occurrence of nitrates. The parameters vary depending on the type of water in question (i.e., either salmonid or cyprinid). Under each heading, there are two values listed, one being mandatory and the other being a mere guide. When setting up these values, the Competent Authority is to adhere to the rigidity of the mandatory rules (Column I) while also respecting the guidelines (Column G). While the rigidity of these values cannot be reduced, it can nevertheless be rendered more stringent by the Competent Authority.

291. The Competent Authority is to fix specific sampling points, the space from one point to another where pollutants are released, and the depth at which the samples are to be taken. Programmes are to be established to diminish contamination of water as well as to ensure that the allocated waters conform with the parameters of Annex I, being both Columns I and G. Water sampling must be carried out by the Competent Authority and must conform to the values which are set by the Authority. Floods or other natural disasters should not be taken into consideration

429. There is an obligation that the temperature be kept at 10°C during breeding stages of certain species which require cold water for reproduction. This temperature can only be applied to those waters which contain such species. Abrupt changing in temperature is to be avoided. The sampling for assessing temperature is to take place on a weekly basis.

430. When the oxygen concentration falls, implementations are to be carried out provided that the Competent Authority is able to prove that such course of action will not harm the development of the fish population. The sampling is to take place monthly with the exception that if there are major disparities on a daily basis, a minimum of two samples in one day are required.

when calculating percentages. However, the Competent Authority is to examine the circumstances and ascertain whether this lack of conformity with the values is a matter of chance. Depending on the circumstances, suitable measures will be taken. On the other hand, where the quality of the designated waters is significantly higher, the frequency of the sampling may be decreased. It may also be decided that there is no need for further sampling due to no risk of pollution or deterioration. Derogation from these Regulations is permitted due to natural causes such as inclement weather or particular geographical conditions. These derogations are only permitted with respect to parameters concerning temperature, pH level, and suspended solids. Derogations are also allowed when natural enrichment occurs in the designated waters, meaning that by a natural process, soil substances are combined with a body of water. Technical and scientific progress may require that the Competent Authority bring into effect certain amendments.

292. It is a criminal offence to breach the provisions of these Regulations. This occurs when a person fails to conform to a legal order based on the provisions of these Regulations or when there is instigation to conspire, or assistance or back up to a person to contravene these legal orders or any action that goes against the provisions of these Regulations. The person convicted for the first time must pay a fine (*multa*) of not less than EUR 1,165 and not more than EUR 2,329. If the same person is subsequently convicted, the fine is increased from EUR 2,320 to EUR 4,659. Such person may also be subject to imprisonment for not more than two years. Expenses incurred by public entities as a result of the offence must always be paid, regardless of the number of convictions. Furthermore, if the offender had any permits, these are to be revoked by the police for at least one year. The *corpus delicti* is also to be confiscated. Proceedings take place either in front of the Court of Magistrates of Malta or else in front of the Court of Magistrates of Gozo. The Attorney General shall always have a right to appeal with respect to these Regulations.

293. The Quality Required of Shellfish Waters Regulations[431] transpose Council Directive 79/923/EEC, which was substantially amended by Directive 2006/113 EC[432] of the European Parliament and the Council on 12 December 2006. The Regulations address the quality of shellfish waters; that is, the waters suitable for the development of shellfish (bivalves and gastropod molluscs[433]). It applies to those coastal and brackish waters which need protection or improvement in order to allow shellfish to develop and to contribute to the high quality of shellfish products intended for human consumption.

Like the Directive, the Regulations establish parameters applicable to designated shellfish waters as well as indicative values, mandatory values, reference methods of analysis, and the minimum frequency for taking samples and measures. These parameters are set for pH, temperature, salinity, and the presence or concentration

431. L.N. 341/2001 (S.L. 549.23).
432. Directive 2006/113 EC codifies Directive 79/923/EEC, which it replaces: it is a formal amendment that aims to bring together the original Directive and its subsequent amendments in one single legislative act without altering its fundamental provisions.
433. Invertebrates having a soft unsegmented body usually enclosed in a shell.

of certain substances (dissolved oxygen, hydrocarbons, metals, organohalogenated substances, etc.). The following proportions of samples must conform to the established values: 100% of the samples for the parameters 'organohalogenated substances' and 'metals'; 95% of the samples for the parameters 'salinity' and 'dissolved oxygen'; and 75% of the samples for the other parameters.

In the event of non-compliance with the limit values or the established criteria, the Competent Authority must establish whether this is the result of chance, a natural phenomenon, or pollution and must take appropriate measures. These measures may, on no account, lead to increased pollution of coastal and brackish waters.

294. ERA is the Competent Authority and is responsible for monitoring, protecting, and improving the quality of shellfish waters. Annex I to the Regulations sets the applicable parameters to the waters designated by the Competent Authority. The Authority is to set values for the parameters listed in Annex I. The Authority cannot set values which are less stringent than those set in Annex I; it must ensure compliance with the Pollution Caused by Certain Dangerous Substances Discharged into the Aquatic Environment Regulations[434] when dealing with discharges of metals and organohalogenated substances. The Competent Authority has the discretion to designate the shellfish waters and to make additional designations. It may opt to revise what it had considered to be designated waters under the condition that the revision must be made due to unforeseen factors at the time of designation. It must also establish programmes that reduce pollution and ensure that the designated waters conform to values set in Annex I within six years after the designation. ERA may consider the waters to be in conformity with the Regulations if the samples ensure that conformity is taken at the minimum frequency at the same sampling point over twelve months. Non-conformity is not regulated by the Regulations if it results from a disaster or an emergency. If, when taking samples, the Competent Authority finds the quality of the waters to be 'appreciably' higher than the values set in Regulation 3 and Annex I, the frequency of the sampling may be reduced. Furthermore, if there is no risk of deterioration in the quality, the Authority may decide that no sampling is necessary.

The Authority must determine why the sample is not in conformity with the parameters set by the Regulations, and once determined, it is to adopt the appropriate measures to ensure compliance. It must determine and fix the sampling point, together with the distance from the nearest point where pollutants are discharged and the depth at which the sample ought to be taken. An important detail is that the fixing of the sampling point must be carried out, in particular, on the basis of the local environmental conditions. This means that the Authority must take special care as to where it places the sampling point, not according to a standard procedure but according to the individual requirements of the environment of the designated water. The Regulations require that sampling methods must ensure that the results obtained are equivalent or comparable to those laid down in these Regulations.

The implementation of the measures in pursuance of the Regulations must not lead to increased pollution of coastal or brackish waters, whether direct or indirect. The Competent Authority may set more stringent values for designated waters than

434. L.N. 213/2001 (S.L. 549.10).

those laid down in the Regulations and may also lay down provisions relating to other parameters. This provision is indicative that these Regulations are a minimum course of action that needs to be taken. Indeed, it does not allow for action, which is less stringent (except in a few exceptional cases). ERA may derogate from the parameters in Annex I because of exceptional weather or special geographical conditions so that the values in Annex I are not met. It is to adopt amendments as are necessary for adapting to technical and scientific progress. It has an obligation to publish information regarding the waters designated (in summary form), information regarding the revision of the designation of certain waters, and the provisions enacted to establish new parameters. The Competent Authority is also to publish what measures it is taking to comply with the Regulations, its reasons for doing so, and the period when it is to do so. It is responsible for publishing, on a regular basis by notice in the Government Gazette, information relating to designated waters, the revision of the designation of certain waters, and the provisions set in order to establish new parameters in accordance with Regulation 9.

295. A person shall be guilty of an offence under these Regulations if he: fails to comply with any provisions of these Regulations or with any order lawfully given in terms of those provisions; acts in contravention of any restriction, prohibition, requirement, or any other provision of these Regulations; and conspires or attempts, aids, or abets another person by any means to act in contravention or to fail to comply with any provisions under the Regulations. A first conviction entails a fine (*multa*) of not less than EUR 23,290 but not exceeding EUR 232,900. A second or subsequent conviction entails a fine (*multa*) of not less than EUR 116,450 but not exceeding EUR 465,800, imprisonment for a term not exceeding two years, or both. A person who is found guilty of an offence shall be ordered by the Court to pay for the expenses incurred by the Competent Authority, public entity, or anyone acting on behalf of the implementation of these Regulations. The offender has to pay for the restitution of the environment as a result of the offence, as well as the confiscation of the *corpus delicti*. Moreover, upon conviction, such a person shall be disqualified from holding or obtaining a licence, permit, or authority and in no case shall this be for less than a year. Proceedings for an offence against these Regulations shall be carried out before the Court of Magistrates of Malta (or Gozo) as courts of criminal judicature. The Attorney General shall always have a right of appeal to the Court of Criminal Appeal from any judgment given by the mentioned courts in respect of proceedings for any offence falling under these Regulations.

296. The Industrial Emissions (Titanium Dioxide) Regulations[435] partly implement the Recast IPPC Directive and fully implement the Maltese IPPC Framework Regulations as regards installations producing titanium dioxide. Emissions from these installations into water must not exceed the limit values laid down in Schedule I, which vary depending on whether the installation uses the sulphate or the chloride process. The operator must monitor these emissions in accordance with Schedule III to ensure compliance with both the permit conditions and the Regulations. A person shall be guilty of an offence under these Regulations if he: fails to

435. L.N. 13/2013 (S.L. 549.80).

comply with any provisions of these Regulations or with any order lawfully given in terms of those provisions; acts in contravention of any restriction, prohibition, requirement, or any other provision of these Regulations; and conspires or attempts, aids, or abets another person by any means to act in contravention or to fail to comply with any provisions under the Regulations. Where the offence occurs by means of a vehicle, its owner will, where applicable, be held liable in the same manner and degree. A first conviction entails a fine (*multa*) of not less than EUR 23,000 but not exceeding EUR 233,000. A second or subsequent conviction entails a fine (*multa*) of not less than EUR 46,000 but not exceeding EUR 466,000, imprisonment for a term not exceeding two years, or both. A person so found guilty may be ordered by the court[436] to pay for the expenses incurred by the Competent Authority as a result of the offence. The court may also order the revocation of the permit and the confiscation of the *corpus delicti*.

436. The Court of Magistrates (Malta or Gozo) as courts of criminal judicature. The Attorney General always has a right of appeal to the Court of Criminal Appeal.

Chapter 4. Noise Pollution

297. One of the first pieces of legislation which dealt with noise was the Criminal Code, which contains a contravention for any person to disturb, during the night-time, the repose of the inhabitants by rowdiness or bawling or in any other manner.[437]

298. The 1991 EPA included noise under the definition of 'energy', which included all types of radiation forming part of the electromagnetic energy spectrum or resulting from a nuclear source, as well as all vibrations and noise. A number of regulations related to noise pollution were adopted under this Act and are being implemented by ERA. However, the 2016 EPA does not contain a definition of 'energy', nor does it refer to 'noise' or 'vibrations' in its definitions section, though it does refer to 'energy', such as in defining 'pollution'.

Two other important Acts under which regulations were adopted in order to control noise pollution are the Product Safety Act[438] and the Malta Standards Authority Act.[439] Under these Acts, the Malta Standards Authority (MSA) may prescribe standards[440] in relation to any class, category, or type of products which are in accordance with regionally or internationally recognised standards, and which any product falling within that class, category, or type is to satisfy. This enables the MSA to set standards on noise and energy pollution with respect to a number of goods or activities. Regulations under this Act were mainly adopted as transposing EU Directives.

299. One of these Directives is Directive 2002/49/EC of 25 June 2002,[441] which aims to provide a common basis for tackling the noise problem across the EU. The underlying principles of this text are similar to those of other overarching environmental policy Directives:

– *Monitoring the environmental problem* by requiring the Competent Authorities in Member States to draw up 'strategic noise maps' for major roads, railways, airports and agglomerations, using harmonised noise indicators L_{den} (day-evening-night equivalent level) and L_{night} (night equivalent level). These maps will be used to assess the number of people annoyed and sleep-disturbed, respectively, throughout Europe.

437. Article 338(m) of the Criminal Code, Ch. 9 of the Laws of Malta.
438. Chapter 427 of the Laws of Malta.
439. Chapter 419 of the Laws of Malta, now repealed.
440. Which means the definition, classification, specification, or description of a product or process including wherever possible reference to its procedure, safety requirement, mode of manufacture, nature, material, methods of test or measurement, weight, grade, purity, origin, age, composition, quantity, dimensions, properties, labelling, packaging, performance in respect of availability, or other characteristics or any combination of the same.
441. Directive 2002/49/EC of the European Parliament and of the Council of 25 June 2002 relating to the assessment and management of environmental noise-Declaration by the Commission in the Conciliation Committee on the Directive relating to the assessment and management of environmental noise.

- *Informing and consulting the public* about noise exposure, its effects, and the measures considered to address noise in line with the principles of the Aarhus Convention.
- *Addressing local noise issues* by requiring Competent Authorities to draw up action plans to reduce noise where necessary and maintain environmental noise quality where it is good. The Directive does not set any limit value, nor does it prescribe the measures to be used in the action plans, which remain at the discretion of the Competent Authorities.
- *Developing a long-term EU strategy*, which includes objectives to reduce the number of people affected by noise in the longer term, and provides a framework for developing existing Community policy on noise reduction from the source.

This Directive was amended by Commission Directive (EU) 2015/996, which established common noise assessment methods as of 31 December 2018. The Directive was again amended in 2020 with regard to the assessment methods.[442]

300. This Directive, as amended, has been adopted under Maltese law by means of L.N. 193/2004, the Assessment and Management of Environment Noise Regulations.[443] The aim of these Regulations is to define a common approach to avoid, prevent, or reduce on a prioritised basis the harmful effects, including annoyance, due to exposure to environmental noise. This aim can be achieved through noise mapping, the adoption of action plans, and adequate information to the public on environmental noise and its effects. These Regulations apply to environmental noise to which humans are exposed, in particular in built-up areas, in public parks or other quiet areas in an agglomeration, in quiet areas in open country, near schools, hospitals, and other noise-sensitive buildings and areas.

301. The implementation of these Regulations falls under the responsibility of ERA. In fact, the Competent Authority is to make and, where relevant, approve noise maps[444] and action plans, together with strategic road maps for agglomerations, major roads, major railways, and major airports, and it must also collect noise maps and action plans. Furthermore, it is duty-bound to inform the general public about its noise maps and action plans. Of particular relevance to Malta are the roads since Malta International Airport does not qualify as a major airport under the Directive. In its work, the Competent Authority has to follow the noise indicators[445] as referred to in Schedule I, but for acoustical planning and noise zoning, the Competent Authority may use other indicators. The values of such indicators shall be determined by means of the assessment methods in Schedule II. Together with this, harmful effects may be assessed by means of the dose-effect relations referred to in

442. Through Commission Directive (EU) 2020/367 of 4 Mar. 2020 and Commission Delegated Directive (EU) 2021/1226 of 21 Dec. 2020.

443. S.L. 549.37.

444. 'Noise mapping' means the presentation of data on an existing or predicted noise situation in terms of a noise indicator, indicating breaches of any relevant limit value in force, the number of people affected in a certain area, or the number of dwellings exposed to certain values of a noise indicator in a certain area.

445. L_{den} which is a day-evening-night indicator and L_{night} which is a night-time noise indicator.

Schedule III. Furthermore, the strategic noise maps shall satisfy the minimum requirements laid down in Schedule IV, and ERA has to cooperate with other Member States while preparing strategic noise mapping and action plans near borders.

Another important obligation that the Authority has to follow under these Regulations is that of constantly informing and consulting with the public. In fact, ERA is to ensure that the strategic noise maps it has made, and, where appropriate, adopted, and the action plans it has drawn up are made available and disseminated to the public. It is important that this information is clear, comprehensible, and accessible, and it must provide a summary of the most important points. Apart from the dissemination of information, the Competent Authority shall set up a database of information on strategic noise maps in order to facilitate the compilation of a report as required under these Regulations and also for the compilation of other technical and informative work. In fact, such report shall, in particular, assess the need for further actions on environmental noise and, where appropriate, propose implementing strategies on various aspects, such as long-term and medium-term goals for the reduction of the number of persons harmfully affected by environmental noise and the protection of quiet areas in open country.[446] This report shall be reviewed every five years, and it shall contain an assessment of the implementation of these Regulations and proposed strategies and measures taking into account the reduction of harmful effects and the cost-effectiveness ratio for the selection of the strategies and measures proposed. ERA also has reporting obligations: the information in the Sixth Schedule,[447] strategic noise maps and action plans are to be submitted to the European Commission.

302. The following are offences under the Regulations: failure to comply with any provision of the Regulations; failure to comply with the permit conditions or with any order lawfully given in terms of any provision of the same. Contravening any restriction, prohibition, or requirement imposed by or under the same; and to conspire, attempt, aid, abet, advertise, counsel, or procure in order to contravene the provisions of these Regulations, together with failure to comply with the Regulations. Any person who commits an offence against these Regulations shall, on a first conviction, be liable to a fine (*multa*) of not less than EUR 1,164.69 but not exceeding EUR 2,329.37. If there is a second or subsequent conviction, he shall be liable to a fine (*multa*) of not less than EUR 2,329.37, but not exceeding EUR 4,658.75 or imprisonment for a term not exceeding two years, or both such fine and imprisonment. Furthermore, the Court may also order any person who has been found guilty of committing an offence which is mentioned above to pay for the expenses incurred by the Competent Authority as a result of the said offence and also to revoke the permit issued by the Competent Authority and confiscate the *corpus delicti*. Proceedings for such criminal offences shall be held before the Court of Magistrates of Malta (or Gozo) as courts of criminal judicature. The Attorney General shall always have a right of appeal to the Court of Criminal Appeal from any judgment given by the Court of Magistrates in respect of proceedings for any offence against these Regulations.

---

446. *See* Art. 12 of L.N. 193/2004.
447. Specific details relating to agglomerations, roads, major railways, and major airports.

303. Another Directive related to noise is Directive 2000/14/EC of 8 May 2000 on the approximation of the laws of the Member States relating to the noise emission in the environment by equipment for use outdoors. The aim of this Directive is to harmonise the national laws of Member States regarding noise emission limits and labelling requirements at the manufacturing stage. The regulation applies to a wide range of product types, from gardening equipment to construction and waste management equipment. Such products must bear a *Conformité Européenne* (European Conformity) (hereinafter, 'CE') mark and the indication of their guaranteed sound-power level and be accompanied by an EC declaration of conformity before they can be placed on the market. The Directive also places sound-power limits on twenty-two of the fifty-seven types of equipment for use outdoors. Of these twenty-two, eleven were already subject to noise limits laid down in seven older Directives which are now withdrawn and replaced by the new Directive. The other eleven types are subject to noise limits for the first time. All manufacturers of products subject to noise limits must follow conformity assessment procedures under the supervision of notified bodies which are appointed by the EU Member States. Failure to comply with these Regulations may result in products being prohibited from being placed on the EU market.

304. This Directive has been transposed under Maltese law by means of L.N. 64/2002[448] and has been adopted under the Product Safety Act. The scope of this Legal Notice is to cover equipment for use outdoors[449] that is placed on the market or put into service as an entire unit suitable for the intended use. Furthermore, the provisions of these Regulations are intended to cover noise emission standards, conformity assessment procedures,[450] marking, technical documentation, and collection of data concerning the noise emission in the environment of equipment for use outdoors, be it imported equipment as well as equipment manufactured for the local market.

305. The Legal Notice makes a distinction between equipment subject to noise limits and that which is subject to noise marking only. The equipment listed in Schedule XI (based on Article 12 of the Directive; for example, builder's hoists for transports of goods, compressors, excavators, lawnmowers, power generators and tower cranes) is subject to noise limits. In fact, no person may construct, import, or place on the market any equipment which is not in compliance with the provisions of L.N. 64/2002. It must be ensured that equipment subject to this legislation is not put on the market or into service unless:

448. S.L. 427.19, Noise Emission in the Environment by Equipment for Use Outdoors Regulations.
449. Equipment for use outdoors includes self-propelled machinery, or machinery which can be moved, which is intended to be used in open air; the term 'open air' including also including tents, roofs for protection against rain, or shell of houses, as well as non-powered equipment for industrial or environmental applications which is intended to be used outdoors.
450. Conformity Assessment Procedures are laid down in Annexes V, VI, VII, and VIII, which deal with the internal control of production, internal control of production with assessment of technical documentation and periodical checking, unit verification, and full quality assurance, respectively. These annexes lay down the procedure to which the manufacturer or authorised representative must adhere in order to respect the obligations laid down under these Regulations.

(1) it specifies the requirements concerning noise emission in the environment;
(2) it has completed the conformity assessments; and
(3) it bears the CE marking and is accompanied by an EC declaration of conformity.

The manufacturer or his representative is bound to draw up an EC declaration in order to certify that the equipment is in conformity with these provisions. The minimum content of this declaration is laid down in Schedule II and includes name and address of manufacturer or his authorised representative, name and address of the person who keeps the equipment, description of the equipment, measured sound-power level, and guaranteed sound-power level for the equipment. The specimen of the EC declaration should be kept for a minimum of ten years from the date on which the equipment was last manufactured.

The manufacturer or his representative shall also subject such equipment to one of the mentioned conformity assessment procedures, namely:

- the internal control of production with assessment of technical documentation and periodical checking procedure (a notified body evaluates the equipment prior to placing it on the market and during production; the frequency of checks, which control continuing compliance with technical documentation, is defined by the notified body according to the results of previous evaluations and the need to monitor corrective actions);
- the unit verification procedure (notified body carries out necessary noise tests and issues a certificate of conformity; if the latter is refused, reasons must be given); and
- the full quality assurance procedure (must ensure compliance of the product with the requirements of the regulations that apply to it).

As for equipment subject to noise marking only, this is listed in Schedule XII, based on Article 13 of the Directive, and includes brush cutters, chain saws, concrete or mortar mixers, drill rigs, and suction vehicles. This equipment should be subject to internal control of production defined in Schedule V, whereby it is ensured and declared that the equipment concerned satisfies the requirements set out by the regulations in this Legal Notice. For both types of equipment, the manufacturer or his representative is allowed to show a product which falls under these Regulations in a trade fair, exhibition, demonstration, or similar events, even if the product does not conform with the regulations stipulated by the L.N. 64/2002, as long as the demonstrator provides a visible sign that clearly indicates that such equipment does not conform and therefore will not be placed in the market or put into service until it conforms.

306. The responsible entities under these Regulations are mainly the manufacturer and the Competent Authority. The manufacturer is the person who is primarily responsible for the design and construction of the equipment so that it complies with the requirements of these Regulations. He is also responsible for the re building or modification of existing equipment, who, in so doing, is creating an 'as-new' equipment, and the person who takes responsibility for the appraisal of the design, construction, and modification of used imported equipment. An authorised representative established in Malta (i.e., any person or organisation) may be appointed to act and be responsible for these tasks on his behalf. Together with the manufacturer and his representative, one must also include the importer, who is the person who places equipment from abroad onto the Maltese market and also the wholesalers, distributors, and retailers. According to Regulation 3(1)(19), the manufacturer and his local authorised representative are the primary persons responsible for such equipment, but if these are not established in Malta, then the importer or the persons who supply such equipment are obliged to follow these Regulations and to adhere to all the responsibilities established thereunder. This means that if a person obtains equipment listed in Regulation 2(1) of these Regulations directly from a company abroad, he himself must check and confirm whether it is in conformity with the standards required by law under this Act and perform the obligations mentioned above. No person may import or put into service any equipment which does not comply with the provisions of these Regulations.

307. The Competent Authority was originally the MSA, and indeed the Regulations still refer to the responsible figures under the MSA Act since the MSA was responsible for the Product Safety Act. Since the former Act's repeal, the MSA's functions, and those of its Directors and Directorates (such as Director of Consumer Affairs), in relation to these Regulations have been vested in the Director General (Technical Regulations) of the MCCAA. Any reference to the former here should be construed as a reference to the latter. The Director of Consumer Affairs shall take appropriate measures to ensure that the equipment relating to this Legal Notice may be placed in the market or put into service if it conforms with the Regulations, bears the CE marking[451] and the indication of the guaranteed sound-power level and is accompanied by an EC declaration of conformity. When a manufacturer or his representative does not abide by the regulations of this Legal Notice, the Director of Consumer Affairs has an obligation to take all the appropriate measures to restrict the placing on the market of the equipment or put into service or withdraw the said equipment. Also, he has an obligation to advise so that the manufacturer or his representative shall bring his equipment in conformity with these Regulations and also to inform the Consumer and Industrial Goods Directorate of the MSA. On any decision taken in pursuance of these Regulations, the Director has an obligation to notify as soon as possible, explain the grounds upon which the decision was taken to the injured party, and advise on any legal remedies.

308. As for offences and penalties, the general offences provisions of the Product Safety Act are applicable. Under Article 12 of this Act, it is laid down that any

451. Decision 93/465/EEC defined marking; the visible, legible, and indelible affixing on the equipment of the CE accompanied by the indication of the guaranteed sound-power level. The CE marking affixed to industrial products symbolises the fact that the natural or legal person having affixed or been responsible for the affixing of the said marking has verified that the product conforms to all the EC total harmonisation provisions which apply to it and has been the subject of the appropriate conformity evaluation procedures.

person who sells, hires, exposes, or offers for sale or hire or has in his possession any product which does not comply with the provisions of this Act or of any regulation made under this Act, deposits with, or otherwise supplies to any other person any such product, shall be guilty of an offence. It shall also be an offence for a producer to fail to give any information as may be required by the Director General (Technical Regulations) in the exercise of his functions. In fact, the Director Generals, apart from the functions highlighted above under L.N. 64/2002, also has other functions under the general provisions of this Act, which he may apply for the best surveillance of such products. Apart from prohibiting the placing on the market, he may, among other things, also prohibit the supply, offering, or otherwise exposing any product if he has reasonable grounds to believe a product to be unsafe and if tests need to be carried out, or he may order in writing the immediate withdrawal of any unsafe product from the market.[452] The Director also has the power of enforcement, a power which may be delegated to any public officer. Furthermore, this Act gives the power of inspection, a power which may be granted by any Magistrate by means of a warrant issued upon an application confirmed on oath by the Director or by any public officer duly authorised in writing by the Director.[453]

The Director is duty-bound to inform any operator who has failed to comply with any provision of the Act or of any regulation made under it. In such written notification, the Director will indicate the provisions of the law which are being infringed and specify remedial measures which need to be taken and order the proprietor to implement such measures within a stipulated period of time.[454] If such person duly notified fails to comply with the notice, he shall be guilty of an offence. Proceedings in relation to any offence under this Act may only be instituted at the instance of the Director, who may conduct the prosecution before the Court.[455] There is a prescriptive period of two years whereby criminal actions for offences under this Act may be presented. A person who obstructs or gives false information shall, on conviction, be liable to a fine (*multa*) of not less than EUR 465.87 and not exceeding EUR 2,329.37 or imprisonment for a term not exceeding six months or both such fine and imprisonment. Any other offence is punishable by a fine (*multa*) of not less than EUR 1,164.69 but not exceeding EUR 11,646.87 or imprisonment for a term not exceeding three years or both such fine and imprisonment. Being found guilty of a second or subsequent offence means being liable to a fine (*multa*) of not less than EUR 1,747.03 but not exceeding EUR 23,293.73 or imprisonment not exceeding four years or both such fine and imprisonment. The person found guilty may also be liable to the additional fine (*multa*) of not more than EUR 465.87 for each day that a notice or undertaking has not been complied with.

The court[456] may also order the suspension or cancellation of any licence or licences issued in favour of the person charged or in respect of the premises

452. Article 15 of the Product Safety Act.
453. Articles 17 and 18 of the Product Safety Act.
454. Article 26 of the Product Safety Act.
455. Article 30 of the Product Safety Act.
456. The Court of Magistrates (Malta or Gozo).

involved in the proceedings. Additionally, the court shall order such person to reimburse the Director within such period as it shall stipulate any costs incurred in connection with the proceedings instituted against him. Such costs shall include expenses incurred in the seizure, lifting, detention, testing, analysis, and examination of products, or samples thereof, involved in the said proceedings. The Attorney General shall have the right to appeal from any judgment given in proceedings instituted under the Act or in connection with regulations made thereunder.

Chapter 5. Pollution from Other Sources

§1. Hazardous Substances

I. General

309. Under the 2016 EPA, the word 'chemicals' is not used, but one will find a definition of 'substances', which means any matter, chemical, mixture, compound, or product and includes fuels, combinations of elements, mixtures, or compounds of a chemical reaction, as well as the mixture of substances of different molecular identities. Under this same Act, it is the duty of the government to take such preventive and remedial measures as may be necessary to address and abate the problem of pollution and any other form of environmental degradation in Malta and beyond, in accordance with the polluter-pays principle and the precautionary principle. Furthermore, the Competent Authority, apart from issuing the required licenses and permits to better control any dangerous substances on the market, must seek to cooperate or to make arrangements with other entities or persons to enable it to better monitor the implementation of and compliance with the provisions of the EPA. In fact, another valid primary law under this chapter is the Product Safety Act,[457] which tries to safeguard the interests of the consumer and ensures that only healthy and environmental-friendly products are put on the market. The Director General (Technical Regulations)[458] is the person responsible for this objective to be attained, and this person works together with the Authority responsible for the protection of the environment in order to protect both sectors.

310. The MSA, established under the Malta Standards Authority Act,[459] was formerly responsible for the Product Safety Act. The former Act was repealed by Act VI of 2011, which brought the Malta Competition and Consumer Affairs Authority Act into force, and with it, established the aforementioned Director General. The MCCAA is the legal successor to the functions of the MSA, which, among other things, was obliged to make, adopt, and publish standards in relation to any class, category, or type of products and/or services. This Act has to be read together with the Product Safety Act under which the Minister may, under the advice of the aforementioned Director General, issue regulations, among other things, prescribing mandatory requirements with respect to the design, methods of manufacture, construction, safety, finishing, testing, quality control, labelling, classification, packaging, grading, storage, transportation, and environmental impact of any class, category, or type of goods, materials, substances, plant, installations, or structures.

311. The Director General may authorise in writing any person, either generally or for specific cases, to, *inter alia*, examine samples and conduct inspections or

457. Chapter 427 of the Laws of Malta.
458. Head of the Technical Regulations Division within the Malta Competition and Consumer Affairs Authority. *See* Ch. 510 of the Laws of Malta, Art. 19.
459. Chapter 419 of the Laws of Malta.

investigations[460] to ensure that orders made under this Act are being implemented. Being found guilty of an offence under the Act warrants liability, on conviction by the Court of Magistrates, to a fine (*multa*) of not less than EUR 1,164.69 and not exceeding EUR 11,646.87 or imprisonment for a term not exceeding three years or both such fine and imprisonment. And when the offence is that of obstructing or giving false information as provided under Article 23, the offender shall be liable to a fine (*multa*) of not less than EUR 465.87 and not exceeding EUR 2,329.37, or imprisonment for a term not exceeding six months or both such fine and imprisonment. Furthermore, a person found guilty of a second or subsequent offence shall, on conviction, be liable to a fine (*multa*) of not less than EUR 1,747.03 but not exceeding EUR 23,293.73 or imprisonment not exceeding four years or both such fine and imprisonment. Moreover, the court may, upon conviction for any offence committed under this Act, with the exception of offences committed under Article 23, if it feels that circumstances so warrant, additionally order the suspension or cancellation of any licence or licences issued in favour of the person charged or in respect of the premises involved in the proceedings. And any person convicted in relation to an offence under Articles 26[461] or 29[462] shall additionally be liable to the additional fine (*multa*) of not more than EUR 465.87 for each day that a notice or undertaking has not been complied with.

Furthermore, where a person has been convicted of an offence under this Act, the Court shall order that person to reimburse to the Director, within such period as it shall stipulate, any costs incurred in connection with the proceedings instituted against him. Such costs include expenses incurred in the seizure, lifting, detention, testing, analysis, inspection, and examination of products, or samples thereof, involved in the said proceedings. The Attorney General has a right to appeal from any judgment given in proceedings instituted under this Act or in connection with Regulations made thereunder.

II. Shipping, Carriage, and Storage of Hazardous and Controlled Substances

312. The Code of Police Laws[463] contained rules relating to dangerous substances on board ships and the duties of the shipmaster in this regard. However, these were repealed by Act XVII of 1991 and Act XV of 2009. Act XVII of 1991 was the Malta Maritime Authority Act,[464] which also repealed the Ports Ordinance.[465] It established the Malta Maritime Authority, which assumed the power vested by law in the Director of Ports and the exercise and performance by or on behalf of such Authority of functions relating to ports and relevant shipping in

460. When in possession of a warrant duly issued by a Magistrate and confirmed on oath by the Director General.
461. Article 26 is about failure of operator to comply with the provisions of the Act.
462. Article 29 is about undertakings in respect of contraventions against this Act.
463. Chapter 10 of the Laws of Malta.
464. Chapter 352 of the Laws of Malta.
465. Chapter 170 of the Laws of Malta.

Malta. It thus had authority with regard to the shipping, etc., of dangerous substances. This Act is now no longer relevant in this regard and has been renamed the Ports and Shipping Act by Act XV of 2009, the Authority for Transport in Malta Act,[466] which established the Authority for Transport in Malta as the legal successor to, *inter alia*, the Malta Maritime Authority. However, it is worth noting two saving clauses. Article 45 to the Ports and Shipping Act saves anything done, including the issuing of orders, subsidiary legislation, etc., by the Ports Ordinance before its repeal by the Malta Maritime Authority Act and by the latter Act before it was amended by the Authority for Transport in Malta Act. Likewise, the last mentioned Act, in Article 49, provides that any subsidiary legislation, licences, etc., issued under the enactments listed in the Second Schedule[467] shall remain in force and continue to have effect as though made or done under the same Act.

313. The Merchant Shipping Act[468] regulates the carriage of dangerous goods.[469] Rules as to the carriage of dangerous goods issued under this Act may be applicable to Maltese ships or other ships while they are within any port in Malta. Failure to comply with any rules issued accordingly shall constitute an offence, and the owner or the master of the ship concerned shall be liable, upon conviction, to a fine not exceeding 300 units,[470] and the ship shall be deemed unsafe for the purposes of this Act. The carriage of dangerous goods can only be effected if these goods are distinctly marked as being dangerous on the outside of the packaging and a written notice is given regarding the nature of these goods. The name and address of the sender or carrier must also be supplied to the master or owner of the vessel at or before the time of sending the goods to be shipped or taking the goods on board the vessel. Failure to do so is also an offence, subject to a fine (*multa*) not exceeding 100 units.[471]

314. The giving of a false description of the goods or of false information regarding the sender and carrier is prohibited under the Act.[472] The master or owner of any vessel, whether Maltese or foreign, may refuse to take on board any package or parcel he suspects to contain any dangerous goods and may require it to be opened to ascertain the contents. The Act provides that the master or owner may throw overboard any dangerous goods which were not properly marked without incurring civil or criminal liability. This provision is to be qualified vis-à-vis Malta's international obligations regarding dumping at sea, which may only be allowed to ensure safety aboard the ship. Dangerous goods which were improperly sent, as

466. Chapter 499 of the Laws of Malta.
467. Which includes the Malta Maritime Authority Act, as renamed.
468. Chapter 234 of the Laws of Malta.
469. Which for the purpose of this Act includes aqua fortis, vitriol, naphtha, benzine, gunpowder, lucifer matches, nitroglycerine, petroleum, explosives, and any goods declared to be dangerous by rules made under the next following section, this being Art. 285.
470. Under the Act, 1 unit is equivalent to EUR 2.33 at the time of writing. *See* Art. 372C.
471. Exemption: if the offender is the agent who had no reason to suspect that the goods shipped were of a dangerous nature, the fine is of ten units.
472. This offence is punishable by a fine (*multa*) not exceeding 500 units.

above-mentioned, may be forfeited[473] and disposed of, notwithstanding that court proceedings have not been initiated against the owner and there is no notice of proceedings or disposed evidence to whom these goods belong. The court may, however, in its discretion, require such notice as it may direct to be given to the owner or shipper of the goods before they are forfeited. The concluding provision regarding the shipping of dangerous goods under this Act declares that the Merchant Shipping Act, by virtue of these provisions, is additional to and does not substitute or restrain any similar provisions in other legal instruments.

315. The Authority for Transport in Malta Act[474] provides for the establishment of a body corporate, namely the Authority for Transport in Malta. One of the Authority's functions is to 'prevent and control the pollution of any port or the approaches thereto by oil or any other substances', without prejudice to the EPA. The Minister responsible for transport, after consultation with the Authority for Transport, has the power to make regulations defining dangerous, hazardous, inflammable, explosive, or offensive goods, regulating the movements and berthing of ships carrying such goods, and prescribing the duties of masters of any such ship and of persons engaged in or supervising the loading, unloading, landing, and transport of any such goods. Likewise, the Minister may issue regulations prescribing penalties for criminal offences against any regulations under the Act, which may prescribe various fines (*multi*) and terms of imprisonment for different offences as well as prescribe fines (*multi*) calculated in accordance with the duration of the offence, so long as they shall not provide for imprisonment for more than eighteen months, or a fine (*multa*) of more than EUR 100,000, or EUR 1,500 each day during which the offence persists.

316. The 1966 Ports Regulations[475] were issued under the Ports Ordinance and deal, *inter alia*, with signals and ship behaviour to be observed when a ship is carrying dangerous or inflammable goods.[476] By virtue of these Regulations, the Authority for Transport may deal with dangerous goods at the expense of the owner or agent. A whole section (Part VIII) deals with explosives and inflammable or dangerous goods. This section excludes naval ships and small craft. Radioactive materials and fissile materials are both defined as radioactive materials.[477] Ships having any dangerous, inflammable, or radioactive materials on board shall be berthed only in specific ports and places, and any movement therefrom requires the written permission of the Authority. The Authority may set standards regarding the quantity of

473. Their packing included.
474. Chapter 499 of the Laws of Malta.
475. L.N. 43/1966 (S.L. 499.01).
476. Article 2 defines these as 'any goods included in any of the classes specified in Part IV of the First Schedule'.
477. Defined as any material which spontaneously emits ionising radiation and of which the radioactivity per gram is greater than 0.002 microcurie or any radioactive material the packing or transportation whereof is regulated by any provisions made by the International Atomic Energy Agency or any national atomic energy agency or authority and in respect of fissile materials plutonium 239, plutonium 241, uranium 233, or any material containing any of the foregoing that falls within the definition of radioactive materials.

such materials and has the discretion to refuse entry into or to order the ship to leave from any port. The master of the ship must notify and confirm in writing that there are explosives or inflammable and dangerous goods (including radioactive and fissile materials) on board.

317. Explosives are not to be conveyed in any craft conveying other explosives, and explosives are not to be conveyed with any other goods whatsoever. Explosives do not include distress signals that are kept in safe storage and custody and mean any of the goods listed in Parts I and II of the First Schedule to the Regulations, divided into divisions as provided by Part III of the same Schedule. Ships carrying only certain classes of explosives are exempt from the provisions of Part VIII of the Regulations, such as explosives falling within the 'Safety Class' and within Division 1 of Class 6.[478]

The Regulations impose strict requirements to prevent accidents by fire or explosion and prevent unauthorised persons from obtaining access to explosives. These include proper procedures for berthing, landing, and loading or unloading explosives from a ship, the ship to be in a state of readiness to move, the prohibition of repairs in or about any ship carrying explosives, and the prohibition of any smoking, fire or lights of any description (save those lights allowed by law) in any craft being used to carry explosives or flammable goods. Rules regulating proper traffic signals relating to explosive or dangerous materials are to be found in the Third Schedule to the Regulations. It is unlawful for dangerous goods to be carried in any ship except in ships involved in the carriage of goods which comply with laws regulating such carriage of the Member State where the ship is registered or when the 1960 International Convention for the Safety of Life at Sea applies or in the case of any other ship which has complied with these rules when taking dangerous goods on board in Malta. In the latter case, the Minister may also exempt any ship from these 1974 rules if the ship is not registered in Malta and it has complied with the rules of the flag State, which are not less effective than these rules.

318. Nuclear-powered ships and ships carrying nuclear substances or other substances which are hazardous in nature may be required to seek prior informed consent (PIC) and authorisation from the authority stipulated in regulations which can be issued under the Territorial Sea and Contiguous Zone Act[479] before passing through the territorial waters of Malta.[480]

319. The Dangerous Cargo Ships, Marine Terminals and Facilities and Bunkering Regulations[481] were issued under the Petroleum (Importation, Storage and Sale) Ordinance,[482] the Malta Maritime Authority Act 1991,[483] and the Bunkering (Fuels)

478. These are safety cartridges, safety fuses for blasting, railway fog signals, and percussion caps.
479. Chapter 226 of the Laws of Malta.
480. Ships having nuclear and hazardous substances as cargo have to follow the same procedure, as is the case with warships, when affecting passage through Malta's territorial waters, that is, the ship must inform the stipulated Authorities when effecting passage through Maltese territorial waters.
481. L.N. 1/1996 (S.L. 499.12), now under the Authority for Transport in Malta Act.
482. Chapter 25 of the Laws of Malta.
483. Chapter 352 of the Laws of Malta.

Tax Act 1995.[484] These Regulations regulate the movement, transfer, storage, and handling of dangerous cargoes, bunkers, ballast, and tank-cleaning operations on all ships and at all marine terminals and facilities within or connected to the internal and territorial waters of Malta. These Regulations declare that the primary obligation, responsibility and consideration of any cargo, ship and bunker barge master and owner, marine terminal or facility operator and cargo interests shall be the safety of life, the prevention and effective and efficient control of pollution of the marine environment, and the protection of the property of others. These persons, as well as the master of any vessel, are responsible for ensuring that no substance is discharged or allowed to escape into the ports or internal or territorial waters of Malta. Non-compliance is an offence, and upon conviction, the offender is liable to a fine (*multa*) not exceeding EUR 11,646.87 for each offence. The Regulations specify who the person responsible for reporting is in each different situation or incident. The reporting must be made to the Authority for Transport in Malta. The Regulations, however, declare that 'this shall not exclude any other person from reporting such matters to the Authority'. Liability for non-compliance, in this case, is an offence punished with a fine (*multa*) of EUR 2,329.37.

320. The Authority may appoint inspectors to monitor and ensure compliance with the said Regulations. Inspectors may take samples and have access to inspect relevant documents. Non-compliance gives rise to an offence punishable upon conviction by means of a fine (*multa*) not exceeding EUR 1,164.69. Construction, operations, equipment, and practices of all ships, bunker barges, marine terminals, and facilities must comply with multilateral legal instruments and standards.[485] Ships entering the internal and territorial waters of Malta must conform to Regulations laid down for tankers if they carry a full cargo of dangerous substances in containers. If the ship carries a partial cargo of dangerous packaged substances, it must comply with all the requirements laid down in the International Maritime Dangerous Goods (IMDG) Code of the International Maritime Organization and other relevant multilateral instruments of law or standards. An advance notice of seventy-two hours prior to arrival is to be made by the master, owner, or agent of any ship specifying the ship's status. Non-compliance is an offence punishable upon conviction by a fine (*multa*) not exceeding EUR 174.70 for each offence.

321. In the case of ships carrying dangerous packaged cargoes,[486] the master of such a ship must provide the clearing inwards officer with full details regarding the

484. Chapter 381 of the Laws of Malta.

485. For example, IMPO Conventions and Codes of Practice.

486. Dangerous cargoes 'in the absence of a specified description means any and all or any combination of volatile substances as described in the definitions of petroleum, volatile petroleum, solid bulk dangerous cargoes, oil, liquefied gas, LNG, LPG or chemicals, carried in bulk and any non-volatile petroleum, solid bulk dangerous cargoes, oil, liquefied gas or chemicals, carried in bulk which may constitute a hazard to human life of to the marine environment in the event of contact or spillage'. Dangerous packaged cargoes means 'any dangerous cargoes or cargoes covered by the IMDG Code carried in containers on ships other than tankers. It includes any empty uncleaned packages (such as tanker containers, intermediate bulk containers, bulk packaging, portable tanks or tank vehicles) which previously contained dangerous cargoes, unless the packaging have been sufficiently cleaned

confirmation of its status and its certificate of compliance with the IMDG Code or the rules of the loading port, otherwise, the cargo cannot be handled. Any master making a false statement in this regard, whether knowingly or recklessly, shall be guilty of an offence and liable to a fine (*multa*) not exceeding EUR 6,988.12 for each such false declaration. Dangerous packaged cargoes shall not be loaded, discharged, handled, or transferred on board any ship in the Grand Harbour or Marsamxett Harbour from sunset to sunrise, and no lighters may remain near the ship during the period.[487]

322. Handling and stowing procedures and operations on dangerous packaged cargoes are to be in strict accordance with the IMDG Code and any relevant instrument. Dangerous packaged cargoes on board a ship being carried in transit for discharge in any subsequent foreign port shall be stowed in compartments or areas which do not contain goods for discharge in Malta. Compartments containing dangerous packaged cargoes in transit shall remain closed and secured throughout the whole of the ship's stay in the waters of Malta. No person may accept, for loading or discharging, any container containing dangerous cargoes which is leaking or materially damaged. The Regulations lay down the procedure for dealing with such a situation.[488] No person shall discharge or deposit any dangerous packed cargoes within any port area until the transport or carriage by which it is to be removed is ready to receive it, and all dangerous packaged cargoes, landed or deposited, shall forthwith be removed from the quay to the ship or from the quay to the duly appointed place of storage. The Authority has the prerogative to determine berthing conditions for ships carrying substances in bulk.

323. Tankers and ships carrying dangerous cargoes have restricted access to the Grand Harbour. Tankers may proceed directly and with all cargo tanks securely closed to a tank-cleaning berth for the purpose of tank cleaning and/or gas-freeing only with the express written permission of the Authority. The Authority may prohibit the entry or stay of any ship to which these Regulations are applicable[489] in the territorial or internal waters of Malta. Under the general operational requirements, the regulations lay down that all external openings in a ship's superstructures leading to any potential hazardous zone on shore[490] must remain closed when: loading or handling dangerous cargoes, in the case of ballasting non-gas-free tanks,

---

of all the residues of the dangerous cargoes and purged of vapours so as to nullify any hazard or has been filled with a non-dangerous substance'.

487. Without prejudice to the Director's express orders in writing.

488. *See* Regs 16(10)–(13).

489. That is, (a) any ship carrying dangerous cargoes, or the residues or slops of such cargoes; (b) any ship having previously carried such cargoes and which has not been certified gas-free; (c) any ship engaging in cargo handling operations, or handling of slops or residues of such cargoes; (d) any ship undergoing inerting, tank cleaning, gas-freeing, or purging operations; (e) any bunker barge and bunker-receiving ship; (f) any road tanker being within any port area for the purpose of supplying bunkers to ships; (g) any terminal and marine facility engaged in the handling or storage of dangerous cargoes; (h) any ship carrying or engaging in cargo handling operations on dangerous cargoes in packaged form; (i) any ship carrying or engaging in cargo handling operations on solid bulk dangerous cargoes; (j) all cargo interests.

490. Exception: the pump room.

ballasting into tanks which have contained dangerous cargoes, as well as in the case of tank cleaning, crude oil washing, tank venting, and gas-freeing.

324. The Regulations restrict the movement of tankers that are not certified gas-free or inert, such that they may enter the Grand Harbour only to proceed directly, with all tanks closed, to a tank-cleaning berth and in accordance with relevant international instruments of law and practice. Tankers which are certified as partly gas-free and inert may, with the express written permission of the Authority, enter the Grand Harbour for repairs. Tankers certified as fully gas-free and/or inert may enter the Grand Harbour for repairs following safety checks. The Regulations lay down conditions of stay in the Grand Harbour and checklists for a tanker certified as gas-free and/or inert. The transportation of dangerous cargoes between the islands of Malta and Gozo is allowed, provided that all safety precautions relating to carriage and handling of such cargo are complied with. No passengers are to be on board such ships, and no smoking is allowed.

III. Fuels

325. The Petroleum (Importation, Storage and Sale) Ordinance[491] was enacted in 1889.[492] This is one of the oldest pieces of national legislation aiming at environmental protection. This Ordinance is a source of environmental legislation aiming at the prevention of marine pollution and the regulation of chemicals or dangerous goods or fuels, and it must be assessed in light of the Oil Pollution (Civil Liability and Compensation) Act.[493]

The Minister responsible for ports is empowered to issue regulations concerning the importation, storage, and hawking of any 'explosive or inflammable substance'. However, this power does not extend to making regulations of the same nature in relation to which the power to make regulations is vested in the Regulator for Energy and Water Services under the Regulator for Energy and Water Services Act.[494] This means this power may be used but only to a very limited extent. Obviously, the regulations made under the Ordinance can refer to waste products, but the other sections of the Ordinance mainly deal with the regulation of ships carrying a 'cargo any part of which consists of petroleum'.

Petroleum is defined in the Ordinance as all-natural hydrocarbons, whether in liquid or gaseous form, including crude oil and natural gas, and whether in a crude or natural state or in a processed or refined form.

Owners or masters of ships carrying petroleum shall report to the Authority for Transport in Malta regarding the nature of the cargo and give three days' prior notice of the arrival of the ship. The Authority is to give orders itself as to which

491. *See also* the Oil Pollution (Liability and Compensation) Act, Ch. 412 of the Laws of Malta.
492. Ordinance IX of 1889, Ch. 25 of the Laws of Malta.
493. Chapter 412 of the Laws of Malta, which repealed Ch. 351 of the same name.
494. Chapter 545 of the Laws of Malta.

port or bay the ship may enter and where it may discharge its cargo. The Comptroller of Customs, in turn, has the authority to extract a sample of the petroleum on board the ship to certify the flashing point of the petroleum so tested.

326. Wilful obstruction on the part of any person while the above-mentioned officers execute their duties is punishable by imprisonment for a term not exceeding three months and a fine. The Minister responsible for ports has the power to make regulations regarding the entry, mooring, and landing of cargo of ships carrying petroleum. The regulations may also prescribe any precautions that must be taken. Upon the failure on the part of the master to abide by the provisions of the Ordinance or any regulations issued under it, the Director of Ports may act in his stead at the expense of the owner. The expenses incurred are recoverable by an action to be made by the Attorney General on behalf of the government before the competent Civil Court. The ship and the master, in his personal capacity, are liable for the payment of any fines and expenses incurred by the government.

327. The Petroleum Ships (Entry and Discharge of Petroleum in Harbours) Regulations,[495] issued under the Petroleum (Importation, Storage and Sale) Ordinance, laid down definitions and conditions for the entry, loading, and unloading of petroleum from merchant ships. The Regulations contained a schedule which provided rules that had to be observed during the time that the vessel had petroleum as cargo. These Regulations are now repealed; however, their function has been taken up by the Merchants Shipping Act as 'petroleum' is included in the definition of 'dangerous goods' in Part VIII of the Act, mentioned in the last Section.

IV. Explosives

328. The Explosives Ordinance,[496] as subsequently amended, regulates and controls the use of explosives in Malta. The term 'explosives' is defined in such a manner as to refer to chemicals.[497] Waste which has explosive properties is not included unless it happens to be specifically mentioned in the definition as one of the chemicals listed therein. The importation, establishment, and keeping of explosives require a licence from the Commissioner of Police.[498] The preparation and manufacturing of explosives can only be carried out at a licensed gunpowder factory.[499]

495. L.N. 53 of 1965.
496. Chapter 33 of the Laws of Malta.
497. The word 'explosive' means 'gunpowder, nitroglycerine, dynamite, gun-cotton, blasting powders, fulminate of mercury or of other metals, coloured fibres, chlorate of potash, chlorate of barium and every other substance whether similar to those above-mentioned or not, used or manufactured with a view to producing a practical effect by explosion or a pyrotechnic effect; and includes fog signals, fireworks, fuses, rockets, percussion caps for mines, detonators, cartridges, ammunition of all descriptions and every adaptation or preparation of an explosive as above defined'.
498. The licence is granted only when necessary precautions for protecting life and property have been taken.
499. Exception: when it is for scientific use and if used in small quantities.

Conditions are laid down which must be complied with for the operation of a gunpowder factory. These include distance limits from any inhabited areas and streets and the need to have an efficient lightning conductor and a magazine for the storage of explosives. The use, sending, delivery, and purchase of certain types of explosives[500] is only allowed if done by manufacturers or retailers to public authorities or persons so authorised and who are in possession of a permit to that effect, signed by the Commissioner of Police.

329. Persons who hold a licence to carry a shotgun for pursuing or killing a game are required only to present this licence[501] when purchasing sporting cartridges or powder to fill cartridges for the said shotgun. The granting of the permit requires the applicant to show that he is required to use explosives to exercise his profession, art, or trade. The obligation of due diligence is incumbent upon the person to whom the explosives are sold or delivered. A register open to inspection by the police is to be kept, which would keep an account of the quantity and nature of the explosives manufactured, acquired, or sold and the particulars of the persons to whom such explosives were sold or delivered.

330. Similarly, the keeping for sale or storage of gunpowder or explosives requires a police licence issued by the Commissioner of Police. Such a licence is not transferable, and the seller must inform the police of any sale he makes, providing the name and address of the purchaser. The licence would also specify the amount of and nature of explosives that may be kept. Shops licensed for the retail of explosives are still not allowed to keep certain types of explosives.[502]

331. Shops in inhabited areas licensed for the sale of gunpowder shall not be allowed by the Commissioner of Police to keep more than 7 kg of gunpowder unless the gunpowder is kept completely closed in suitable containers and appropriately stored, in which case the Commissioner of Police has the discretion to grant a licence for the keeping of up to 23 kg of gunpowder. Shops not situated in inhabited areas may be granted a licence for keeping double these quantities. The Ordinance also determines the manner in which explosives and gunpowder should be kept. This provision[503] is the only provision which also includes 'very inflammable substances', thus possibly including waste which has inflammable properties. The packaging of gunpowder is also regulated and varies according to the quantity.[504]

500. Dynamite, gun-cotton, fulminates, picrates and substances containing nitroglycerine or substances which when mixed produce the same effects produced by dynamite or the substances mentioned in the definition. *See supra* note 487.

501. Issued under Art. 205, Code of Police Laws, Ch. 10 of the Laws of Malta.

502. Namely nitroglycerine, picrates, fulminates, chlorate of potash or explosives the composition of which is unknown or not clearly determined.

503. Chapter 33 of the Laws of Malta, Art. 17.

504. For example, gunpowder in quantities not exceeding 2 kg shall be kept in a receptacle made and closed to exclude leaks, while if the quantity of gunpowder exceeds 2 kg, it shall be conveyed in a single or double package and the amount of gunpowder shall not exceed 45 kg in any single package, which shall be well labelled.

332. The Minister responsible for the police may issue regulations for the control, restriction, or prohibition of the importation, manufacture, preparation, storage, keeping, conveyance, handling, distribution, and use of explosives. The same Minister may also make regulations for the construction of gunpowder and fireworks factories and premises where explosives are prepared, kept, or sold and for precautions that need to be taken in such premises. These Regulations may also stipulate qualifications relating to age, health, ability or any other essential qualities deemed necessary for persons who own or who are employed in, or have access to such premises.[505] Punishment for the transgression of the Ordinance's provisions varies according to the offence committed. It may be a fine or imprisonment, or both a fine and imprisonment.[506] Punishments prescribed by the Ordinance, or any regulations made under it, shall only apply in the absence of an offence punishable by higher punishments under other laws.

333. The Minister has the power to include by order any substance as an 'explosive substance' if it appears to him that although this substance does not fit within the definition of explosive substance in the Ordinance, its properties are such that it can be deemed to be an explosive within the meaning of this Ordinance.[507] Persons carrying out certain processes like dividing into component parts, unmarking, remarking, altering, or repairing an explosive shall be subject to the provisions of the Ordinance as if he has manufactured the explosive. Furthermore, also by order, the Minister may define the composition, quality, and character of any explosive and classify explosives for the purpose of the Ordinance.

334. Regulations and orders issued by virtue of this Ordinance shall be published by notice in the Government Gazette.[508] Similarly, any offence committed against this Ordinance or any regulations made thereunder shall give rise to the forfeiture of the *corpus delicti*.[509]

335. Proceedings for offences against regulations made under this Ordinance are to be instituted by the executive police before the Court of Magistrates, acting as a court of criminal judicature. The court shall proceed to order the destruction of any explosive when the explosive cannot be preserved without danger to persons and property. Damages are recoverable by the injured party as a civil debt. If the offence is committed by a person who has already been convicted under the provisions of the Ordinance or its regulations, he shall, on a second conviction, be liable to the

505. This is to include that the granting of a licence for the keeping of an explosives factory shall be subject to the taking out of an insurance policy at the expense of the licensee.
506. Fines may vary from not less than EUR 150 to not more than EUR 80,000, while imprisonment may range from not more than one month to the highest punishment awarded in case of Art. 26, Ch. 34 of the Laws of Malta, regarding the use of explosives for fishing, which may range from one year to nine years imprisonment.
507. The order may specify exceptions, limitations, and restrictions.
508. They come into operation either upon an appointed date specified therein or in the absence of such specification, upon publication.
509. Mandatory, unless a person who has not taken part in an offence has a lawful claim to any of the objects forfeited. In such case, a claim must be made within four working days from the date when the judgment becomes definitive.

punishment for the offence increased by two degrees, and on a third or subsequent offence to the punishment increased by three degrees. The Ordinance also makes provisions for reductions in punishments, compensations, and the applicability of the Probation Act and other like provisions relating to convictions under it.

Any nuisance arising from the contravention must be removed by the offender within a stipulated time limit. Failure to comply would lead to liability to pay a fine at a daily rate until the nuisance is removed, and the court may ultimately order the police to remove the nuisance at the expense of the offender. The provisions of this Ordinance shall not apply to the Armed Forces of Malta.

336. The White Phosphorus Matches (Prohibition) Ordinance of 1910[510] prohibits the manufacture, sale, and importation of matches made with white phosphorus.[511] Infringement of the provisions of the said Ordinance is tantamount to contravention and liable to a fine.

V. The Use of Hazardous and Dangerous Substances in Industry

337. The 1986 Work Places (Health, Prevention, General Welfare) Regulations (today renamed Work Places (Health, Safety and Welfare) Regulations) were issued by the Minister responsible for labour in consultation with the Health Council.[512] These Regulations mainly relate to industrial health provisions, but they are relevant to be addressed in this context because they control the use and importation of hazardous substances, air quality controls, and the disposal of industrial waste.

Any exposed structure or hole which contains hazardous substances must be covered or shielded, and where possible, all necessary safety measures must be taken to ensure no accidents may happen at the workplace. The Regulations provide that entry in confined spaces, which may be subject to the presence of hazardous substances or smoke such that suffocation may occur, must only be allowed if special breathing apparatus is worn and if time is kept by someone else. The Regulations provide for safety measures which must be adopted when explosive and inflammable substances are in use. Any plant, tank, or container where such substances are present cannot be used for welding, braising, soldering, or other means of cutting with heat, cutting, dismantling or removal of any part of the said plant, tank, or container unless all the necessary practical measures are taken to ensure that the explosive and inflammable substances have been removed or neutralised.

338. The Superintendent of Public Health's approval is necessary for any person to be able to import any chemical or toxic substance and to use or permit the use of such substances at the workplace. Where possible, these substances must be substituted with substances which are less harmful. Any employer must make

510. Chapter 38 of the Laws of Malta.
511. No scientific list/name or definition, but Art. 2, Ch. 38 states that white phosphorus means white or yellow phosphorus.
512. Issued as L.N. 52/86 (S.L. 424.09) under the Factories Ordinance. The Ordinance was abrogated but the regulations issued by virtue of Art. 3 of the same Ordinance remain in force under the Occupational Health and Safety Authority Act, Ch. 424 of the Laws of Malta.

arrangements to conduct examinations by the Sanitary Authority to ensure that air quality is safe in workplaces where potentially hazardous or noxious substances are manufactured or used. It is prohibited to allow work to be carried out in places which have not been subjected to such examinations.

339. The Occupational Health and Safety Act contains other subsidiary legislation intended at workplace safety that touch upon environmental law. These include regulations relating to protection against exposure to carcinogens,[513] biological agents,[514] chemical agents[515] and others.

§2. PESTICIDES

340. The Pesticides Control Act[516] provides for the control of pesticides and for other purposes connected therewith or incidental thereto. The Act defines a number of technical terms.[517] An interesting definition in this Act is that of the term 'owner', which includes any person who may dispose of or who is interested in any capacity with the disposal of any consumable produce or pesticide.

341. The Minister responsible for the execution of the Act is the Minister responsible for agriculture, in consultation with the Minister responsible for Health and the Environment. The said Minister may, by regulations, prescribe the manner in which authorised pesticides are to be registered and the time limit for the expiry of such registration. Once this expiration occurs, the applicant is to re-submit the relevant application together with the then current toxicological data for the pesticide in question. Furthermore, the Minister may make regulations for regulating, prohibiting, or restricting the importation, sale, or use of any pesticide.

342. The practical implementation of the provisions of the Act and its Regulations is vested in the Director General (Technical Regulations),[518] as appointed under the MCCAA Act. He is advised on any matter related to pesticides by the Pesticides Control Board,[519] which, *inter alia*, also reports to him on matters related to the regulation, enforcement, and monitoring of all legislation or matter related to pesticides.

If the Director has reason to believe that any product has been treated with a pesticide and consequently may present hazards to the consumers, he is empowered by the Act to require any owner by means of a notice to ensure that no part of such

513. L.N. 122/2003.
514. L.N. 228/2003.
515. L.N. 227/2003.
516. Chapter 430 of the Laws of Malta.
517. For the purpose of the Act and its Regulations, 'pesticide' includes all plant protection and biocidal products.
518. The definition includes, to the extent of the authority given, any officer authorised by him, in writing, to act in that behalf for any of the purposes of this Act.
519. Composed of ministerial appointees, the Director and a number of representatives of various sectors and government Departments.

produce may be picked, gathered, or disposed of. This notice is valid for ten working days from the day it is served unless criminal proceedings are taken, in which case the notice shall continue in force until such proceedings are finally determined.

The Director may authorise any officer to enter and inspect any land, site, building, and even any means of transport in order to ascertain that the provisions of any regulations made under this Act are being complied with. The authorised officer may take any sample for the purposes of analysis. If, after the analysis, the Director deems that such produce presents a hazard to consumers of such produce or to anyone coming in contact with it, he is responsible for taking all the necessary measures in order to ensure that such produce is withheld from consumption or use or that such brand of pesticide is withheld from importation, manufacture, packing, sale, or use.

Furthermore, transgression of the provisions of the Act or of any regulations or order made thereunder constitutes an offence punishable by a fine or imprisonment, or both.[520]

A number of subsidiary pieces of legislation were issued under the Act and are tackled below.

343. The Act repealed the Pesticides (Control of Importation, Sale and Use) Act[521] but saved the Importation, Sale and Use of Pesticides Regulations[522] issued under it, which regulated the importation, sale, use, and disposal of pesticides. These were repealed by the Plant Protection Products Regulations,[523] which provided exhaustively for the authorisation and control of the dealing, advertising, and use of any plant protection product or any other active substances intended for use in any plant protection product. These were revoked by eponymous Regulations in 2009,[524] which transposed Commission Directive 1991/414/EC of 15 July 1991 concerning the placing of plant protection products on the market and Council Directive 79/117/EEC of 21 December 1978 prohibiting the placing on the market and use of plant protection products containing certain active substances. These were, in turn, revoked by separate legal notice in 2018[525] once the relevant EU legislation was repealed.

344. The current legislation in force governing plant protection products are the Plant Protection Products (Implementation) Regulations,[526] which implement the provisions of Regulation (EC) No. 1107/2009 of the European Parliament and of the Council of 21 October 2009 concerning the placing of plant protection products on the market and repealing the EU legislation transposed under the 2009 Plant Protection Regulations.

520. Fine not exceeding EUR 1,164.69 and/or imprisonment not exceeding three months upon the first conviction. In the case of any subsequent conviction, a fine not exceeding EUR 2,329.37 and/or imprisonment not exceeding six months.
521. Chapter 192 of the Laws of Malta.
522. L.N. 22/1967, as amended.
523. L.N. 115/2004.
524. L.N. 358/2009.
525. L.N. 330/2018.
526. L.N. 284 of 2011 (S.L. 430.07).

The competent authority, within the meaning of Article 75 of Regulations (EC) No. 1107/2009, under the Regulations, is the Technical Regulations Division under the MCCAA Act. Any person aggrieved by a decision of the Director of the Division may either appeal the decision before the Civil Court, First Hall, or commence arbitration proceedings.[527]

The sanctions applicable for infringement of the provision of the mentioned EU Regulation are those provided in Article 9 of the parent Act mentioned above.

345. The Biocidal Products (Implementation of Regulation (EU) No. 528/2012) Regulations[528] implement the provisions of Regulation (EU) No. 528/2012 of the European Parliament and of the Council of 22 May 2012 concerning the making available on the market and use, of biocidal products. They were preceded by, and revoked, the more voluminous Biocides Regulations,[529] which adopted the now-repealed Biocides Directive (98/8/EC). The competent authority is the same as in the previously mentioned Regulations, and so are the penalties.

It is prohibited to deal in any active substance or biocidal product unless authorised in accordance with the Regulations and in biocidal products containing active ingredients that are under evaluation unless there is notification of these products. Furthermore, dealing in any active substance or biocidal product requires possession of an authorisation to so deal issued by the Director.

Biocidal products containing active ingredients or active substances not included in the approved list under Article 9.2 of the EU Regulation and undergoing evaluation are to be notified to the Division before being placed on the market.

Furthermore, the language used on labels shall be as indicated in the Schedule to the Regulations.

346. The Sustainable Use of Pesticides Regulations[530] concern the authorisation, placing on the market, use and control of plant protection products in commercial form and the placing on the market and control of active substances intended for particular uses, and complement the two aforementioned Regulations. The scope of these Regulations is to transpose Directive 2009/128/EC of the European Parliament and of the Council of 21 October 2009, establishing a framework for Community action to achieve the sustainable use of pesticides and Commission Directive (EU) 2019/782 of 15 May 2019 amending Directive 2009/128/EC of the European Parliament and of the Council as regards the establishment of harmonised risk indicators. They apply to plant protection products as defined in the EU legislation implemented by the Plant Protection Products (Implementation) Regulations and to biocides as defined in the Biocides Regulations.

The aforementioned Director is to adopt a National Action Plan to set up the necessary framework to reduce the risks and impacts of pesticide use on human health

527. In accordance with the Malta Arbitration Act (Ch. 387) and the Arbitration Rules of the Malta Arbitration Centre.
528. L.N. 348/2013 (S.L. 430.09).
529. L.N. 525/2010, which revoked the Biocides Regulations, L.N. 294/2004, that adopted the same Directive.
530. L.N. 489/2011 (S.L. 430.08).

and the environment and to encourage the development and introduction of integrated pest management and alternative approaches or techniques to reduce dependency on the use of pesticides.

The Regulations require a certification system for professional users,[531] distributors[532] and advisors[533] to provide, as a minimum, evidence of sufficient knowledge of the subjects in Schedule I[534] either by undergoing training or by other means. Valid certificates are a prerequisite to perform the roles mentioned, and obligations are imposed upon them in the exercise of those roles to attain the objectives of the Regulations. These mainly relate to customer awareness of the hazards, etc., of pesticide use. Pesticide application equipment must be subjected to inspection at regular intervals and meet specific standards aimed at achieving a high level of protection for human health and the environment.

The Director must adopt the necessary measures to ensure that handling and storage of pesticides and treatment of their packaging and remnants by professional users, and where applicable by distributors, do not endanger human health or the environment. In the case of non-professional operators, the Director is to take the necessary measures to avoid dangerous handling operations, such as ready-to-use formulations.

347. The Regulations make provisions for specific situations. Aerial spraying is prohibited and may only be allowed in specific cases on the advice of the Pesticides Control Board, provided a number of stringent conditions are met, one of which is the absence of any other viable alternative.

The Director is to ensure that appropriate measures to protect the aquatic environment and drinking water supplies from the impact of pesticides are adopted. These include giving preference to pesticides not classified as dangerous for the aquatic environment pursuant to the Dangerous Substances and Preparations Regulations nor containing priority hazardous substances under the Water Policy Framework Regulations.

Furthermore, pesticide use is to be minimised or prohibited in specific areas[535] due to necessary hygiene and public health requirements and biodiversity. However, the Director, on the advice of the Board, may authorise the controlled use of herbicides for the removal of invasive species subject to the relevant legislation.

531. Defined as any person who uses pesticides in the course of their professional activities, including operators, technicians, employers, and self-employed people, both in the farming and other sectors.
532. Defined as any natural or legal person who makes a pesticide available on the market, including wholesalers, retailers, vendors, and suppliers.
533. Defined as any person who has acquired adequate knowledge and advises on pest management and the safe use of pesticides, in the context of a professional capacity or commercial service, including private self-employed and public advisory services, commercial agents, food producers and retailers where applicable.
534. These include the hazards and risks associated with pesticides and how to identify and control them.
535. These include public parks and gardens, child care centres, conservation areas under the relevant legislation, and roundabouts and central strips.

348. The penalties for infringement of the provisions of all three Regulations are those found in Article 9 of the parent Act. However, the Director may recover all the costs incurred by the MCCAA in case of such violations as a civil debt due to the same Authority.

349. The Activities concerning the Professional Rules of Toxic Products Regulations[536] implement the rules found under EU Council Directive 74/556/EEC to attain freedom of establishment and freedom to provide services in respect of activities of self-employed persons and of intermediaries engaging in the trade and distribution of toxic products. It lays down the criteria required for these freedoms to be granted.

350. The maximum level of pesticide residues in produce is regulated by the Maximum Residue Levels of Pesticides in Produce of Plant and Animal Origin (Implementation of EC Regulation) Regulations.[537] These Regulations implement the provisions of Articles 30, 31, 34, and 38 of Regulation (EC) No. 396/2005 of the European Parliament and of the Council of 23 February 2005 on maximum residue levels of pesticides in or on food and feed of plant and animal origin and amending Council Directive 91/414/EEC. The competent authority within the meaning of the EU legislation is the MSA, with penalties for infringement being those in Article 9 of the parent Act.

The sampling techniques to assess these residue levels are found in the European Community Methods of Sampling for Official Control of Pesticide Residues in and on Products of Plant and Animal Origins Regulations,[538] which implement the relevant EU legislation on the matter. The sampling for the checks provided for in Article 6 of Directive 76/895/EEC, Article 8 of Directive 86/362/EEC, Article 8 of Directive 86/363/EEC and Article 6 of Directive 90/642/EEC are to be carried out in accordance with the methods described in the Schedule.

Prior to these Regulations, the subjects were tackled in separate legal notices,[539] which were revoked to bring the existing Regulations into force.

§3. Ozone-Depleting Substances

351. The Environment Protection (Control of Substances Depleting the Ozone Layer) Regulations[540] aim at regulating ODS as controlled substances,[541] listed in Schedules A, B, C, and D to these Regulations, and which, for the purposes of the

536. L.N. 350/2005 (S.L. 430.06).
537. L.N. 14/2009 (S.L. 430.02).
538. L.N. 479/2004 (S.L. 430.04).
539. L.N. 199/2004, the Maximum Residue Levels of Pesticides in Produce of Plant Origin Regulations, revoked by L.N. 13/2009, and L.N. 117/2005, the Maximum Residue Levels of Pesticides in Produce of Animal Origin Regulations, revoked by L.N. 12/2009.
540. L.N. 133/95 (S.L. 549.06) was issued by virtue of Arts 13 and 16 of the EPA, Ch. 348 of the Laws of Malta empowering the Minister to: publish a list of substances which in his discretion he deems to be potentially toxic and make regulations concerning their use; and make regulations to prohibit or impose conditions on their importation, impose conditions on their carriage and storage, and how

EPA are deemed to be 'potentially toxic substances'. The Regulations are intended to control the import and export, use, carriage, storage, destruction, or disposal of these ODS to limit and phase-out these substances in accordance with Malta's international obligations. The handling of any of the above-mentioned operations is subject to prior approval by the Minister for the Environment to act in such a manner.

Prior to the importation of a controlled substance, the importer shall request and obtain this permit after giving the following information on the controlled substances: the country of origin, the brand name and trademark, the correct chemical name, the internationally recognised chemical formula, the net weight in kilograms or metric tonnes, and the name and address of the manufacturer. If the controlled substance forms a mixture, each substance should be identified with its chemical name and formula, and the weight of each controlled substance making up the mixture should be stated.

352. The Regulations also require that the final destination of the controlled substances shall be given, stating the user's name and address together with the weight of each controlled substance. If the final destination is still unknown when the application for permission is made, the address of the place where the controlled substance shall be stored or kept is to be provided. Similarly, the end use of the controlled substances listed in the Schedules also must be stated in the application. Failure to provide the information requested would prevent the customs department from releasing the controlled substances unless the EPD approves in writing their release.[542]

The EPD may inspect the place where the controlled substances are being kept or stored and may specify which records are to be kept regarding the stocks of controlled substances. The importer's liability under other laws subsists, even with the written approval issued by the Minister. The Regulations are applicable to other government departments, State or parastatal organisations, industries, and Corporations, even if these controlled substances are directly imported by them.

353. Due to Malta's EU membership, the Ozone-Depleting Substances Regulation (EC No. 1005/2009)[543] is applicable to Malta. This is the EU's legislative instrument to phase-out ODS. Substances covered by the Regulation are identified as controlled substances in line with the definitions of the Montreal Protocol. The Regulation includes controls for the production, importation, exportation, supply, use, leakage, and recovery of controlled substances. It also establishes a licensing procedure for all imports of ODS. This Regulation was adopted by the EU in order

---

these substances or their residues may be destroyed or disposed of. The Minister may even demand the giving of any guarantee in connection with any of the above-mentioned operations. Now under the 2016 EPA.

541. Defined as any substance whether existing alone or in a mixture, including the isomers of any such substance but excluding any controlled substance or mixture which is in a manufactured product other than a container used for the transportation or storage of that substance.

542. No controlled substance is to be released out of the place of temporary storage without the prior written approval of the Department.

543. This Regulation repealed Regulation (EC) No. 2037/2000.

to take the necessary action at the Community level in order to carry out the Community's obligations under the Vienna Convention and the latest amendments and adjustments to the Montreal Protocol,[544] even though the provisions of the EC Regulation are stricter than the Montreal Protocol.

354. Since Malta's accession to the EU, it had to set targets to reduce and eventually eliminate consumption and production of a range of ODS. It has also adopted L.N. 280/2010 – Substances Depleting the Ozone Layer Regulations[545] – in order to implement the provisions of the EC Regulation. As this legal instrument controls the ODS, it sets out controls for the production, trade, use, and recovery of ODS. They include detailed requirements for these substances and a legal basis for inspections and penalties while also foreseeing the inclusion of new substances into the control scheme.

355. The Competent Authority is vested in the ERA and also in any other body or person as may be ordered by the Minister responsible for the environment. The Competent Authority may be designated as the authority for different provisions and different purposes of these Regulations.

The ERA shall issue a licence and permit for the purposes of these Regulations under any conditions which it may deem fit. Also, the ERA may, in carrying out the tasks assigned to it by these Regulations, request all relevant information from the personnel involved and from undertakings concerned. It is its duty to carry out any investigations necessary under these Regulations; moreover, it may conduct random checks and audits on imports, exports, shipments, storage facilities, users, and disposal facilities of substances. The ERA's officials shall label any containers filled with substances prior to their release from Customs. The ERA may develop as appropriate and ensure the dissemination of guidance notes and documents for the purpose of ensuring the proper implementation of these Regulations and of the EC Regulation.

356. The operating personnel involved is listed under Regulation 5 of L.N. 280/2010. This includes all producers, importers, shippers, exporters, technicians, users (including retailers), and also any persons involved in the destruction, recovery, reclamation, and recycling of the substances covered by the EC Regulation. The personnel shall possess the minimum qualification requirements, which take the form of a course with a duration and curriculum as defined and approved by the ERA. On successful completion of this course, the licence and permit (valid for ten years) are issued by such authority. These licenses and permits may be reviewed, renewed, or terminated at any time by the ERA. Such personnel may also be subject to random audits by officials of the authority. The operators involved who may only handle, use, or trade in substances falling within the scope of the EC Regulation have to be registered with the Competent Authority.

544. The Montreal Protocol (amended in 1990) on Substances that Deplete the Ozone Layer is an international treaty designed to protect the ozone layer.
545. S.L. 549.58. It revoked L.N. 145/2007, the Substances Depleting the Ozone Layer Regulations.

Moreover, they are to duly fill out a logbook stating all amounts of controlled substances recovered, recycled, reclaimed, or destroyed during their day-to-day operations. For this purpose, each user and shipper of substances, every year before 31 January, shall communicate to the Competent Authority the data as specified in the Act for each controlled substance for the period 1 January to 31 December of the preceding year.[546]

357. All owners or refrigeration technicians of fixed equipment with a refrigerating fluid charge of more than 3 kg and all entities involved in the recovery, recycling, reclamation, and destruction of controlled substances shall communicate to the ERA, before 31 January of each year, in a hard copy and in electronic version, for each specifically identified piece of equipment, all the amounts of leakages detected, the actions taken to eliminate such leakages for each specifically identified piece of equipment, the quantity and nature of substances involved, and so forth,[547] for the period from 1 January to 31 December of the previous year. They shall send copies of their logbooks to the Competent Authority for review. These copies shall be signed off by the official person in whose name the logbook was issued as a true copy of the original logbook in their possession.

All shippers (including both importers and exporters) shall inform the ERA about any upcoming shipment (import or export) at least fifteen working days in advance of the actual shipment. All details shall be submitted according to the requirements of the format established for this purpose by such authority. In addition, the shipper, exporter, or importer shall be responsible, as stipulated in Regulation 9 thereof, for keeping and reporting information related to any sales and/or transfer by whatever means of these substances until the point of sale, when this responsibility will devolve to the new natural or legal persons involved.

358. If a person fails to comply with any provision stated by the EC Regulation or the above Regulations, he is guilty of an offence of infringing these Regulations. Failing to comply with the permit conditions or with any order lawfully given in terms of any provision of the latter Regulations will also render a person guilty of an offence. He will also be liable for an offence if he contravenes any restriction, prohibition, or requirement imposed by or under the EC Regulation or the local Regulations. The acts in contravention of these Regulations are to conspire, to attempt, to aid, to abet, to advertise, to counsel, or to procure in order to contravene the provisions of these Regulations, together with failure to comply with the Regulations.

359. The penalties and enforcement provisions are laid down under Regulation 18, whereby any person who commits an offence against the EC Regulation or these Regulations shall, on a first conviction, be liable to a fine (*multa*) of not less than EUR 1,200 but not exceeding EUR 2,300 and where applicable, there can also be the revocation of such person's licence and confiscation of *corpus delicti*. If there is a second or subsequent conviction, he shall be liable to a fine (*multa*) of not less

546. *See* Reg. 13.
547. *See* Reg. 12.

than EUR 2,300, but not exceeding EUR 4,700 or imprisonment for a term not exceeding two years, or both such fine and imprisonment.

Furthermore, this Regulation also provides that the court may also order any person who has been found guilty of committing an offence which is mentioned above to pay for the expenses incurred by the Competent Authority as a result of the said offence and also to revoke the permit issued by the Competent Authority and confiscate the *corpus delicti*. The court shall also order to bear all or part of the costs incurred due to any relevant infringement action brought against Malta by the European Commission under the provisions of the EC Regulation or of the Treaty establishing the EC. It is further known that such offence is a criminal offence; thus, proceedings shall be held before the Court of Magistrates as courts of criminal judicature. The Attorney General shall always have a right of appeal to the Court of Criminal Appeal from any judgment given by the Court of Magistrates in respect of proceedings for any offence against the EC Regulation or these Regulations.

§4. Chemicals

360. Regulations on this topic are mainly targeted to protect the environment and to create common standards to protect consumers in order to ensure the free circulation of goods among the EU Member States without there being any damage to the environment or to human health. As discussed in the general section above, the word 'chemicals' is not used in the EPA, but the government still has obligations to address and abate the problem of pollution, and the competent authority must seek to cooperate with other entities to better monitor the implementation of, and compliance with, the provisions of the Act. The Product Safety Act, as also discussed, is very important in this regard due to its focus on safeguarding the health of both consumers and the environment. It will be recalled that the competent authority under this Act is the Director General (Technical Regulations) under the MCCAA Act, who works hand-in-hand with the ERA to attain the objectives of both Acts.

361. A European law covering dangerous substances was introduced in 1967 to protect public health, in particular, the health of workers handling dangerous substances. The law, known as the Directive on Dangerous Substances (67/548/EEC), introduced EU-wide provisions on the classification, packaging, and labelling of dangerous substances.

The classification of dangerous substances places a substance into one of several defined classes of danger and characterises the type and severity of the adverse effects that the substance can cause. The packaging of dangerous substances protects individuals from the known risks of a substance, and the labelling of dangerous substances provides information about the nature of the substance's risks and about the safety measures to apply during handling and use.

Since it was adopted in 1967, the Directive has regularly been updated to take into account the latest scientific and technical progress so as to ensure the highest level of protection for individuals and the environment. This also ensures that the internal market functions most efficiently. The amendments to the Directive enable newly identified hazardous materials to be added to the list of dangerous substances.

This Directive applies in parallel with the Registration, Evaluation, Authorisation and Restriction of Chemicals (REACH) Regulation. Under this Regulation, substances classified as carcinogenic, mutagenic, or having reproductive toxic effects may need authorisation to be used or placed on the market.

362. Under Maltese law, the Dangerous Substances Directive, as further amended, has been adopted by the Dangerous Substances Regulations,[548] issued under the Product Safety Act.[549] The Director General aforementioned, together with his officials, are responsible for doing the required surveillance with regard to the classification, packaging, and labelling of substances dangerous to man or the environment where such substances are placed on the market. These Regulations do not apply to medicinal products for human or veterinary use, cosmetic products, and mixtures of substances which in the form of waste are covered by Directives 75/442/EEC and 78/319/EEC, foodstuffs, animal feeding stuffs, pesticides, radioactive substances, and any other substances or preparations for which an EC notification or approval procedures exist or which require the same requirements established under these Regulations. Also, these Regulations are not applicable to the carriage of dangerous substances by rail, road, inland waterway, sea, or air; and to substances in transit which are under customs supervision, provided they do not undergo any treatment or processing. The Directorate-General is compelled to see that substances cannot be placed on the market on their own or in preparations unless they have been packed and labelled in accordance with the Regulations and with criteria in Annex VI of the Directive. As for registered substances, these have to be in accordance with the information obtained through the application of Articles 12 and 13 of Regulation (EC) No. 1907/2006 (the REACH Regulation), save in the case of preparations where provisions exist in other Directives. Furthermore, where, in the light of new information, the Competent Authority has justifiable reasons to consider that a substance which has been accepted as satisfying the requirements of these Regulations nevertheless constitutes a danger for man or the environment by reason of classification, packaging, or labelling which is no longer appropriate, it may temporarily reclassify or, if necessary, prohibit the placing on the market of that substance or subject it to special conditions.[550]

363. Under these Regulations, the main obligations of the required labelling and packaging have to be observed mainly by the producer and importer, and the distributor has to guarantee compliance with the general safety requirement. Under the Product Safety Act, 'producer' means the manufacturer of the product, when this is established in Malta, and any other person presenting himself as the manufacturer by affixing to the product his name, trade mark or other distinctive mark, or the person who reconditions the product, or the manufacturer's representative, and on the

548. L.N. 306/2008 (S.L. 427.14).
549. Chapter 427 of the Laws of Malta.
550. Regulation 14 of L.N. 306/2008.

absence of this person, the importer of the product and others in the supply chain, insofar as their activities may affect the safety aspects of a product placed on the market. The distributor includes any person in the supply chain whose activity does not affect the safety properties of a product and shall include wholesalers, retailers, commission agents, and other intermediaries. Under the Product Safety Act, the producer and importer have to provide consumers with the relevant information to enable them to assess the risks inherent in a product, must take the necessary precautions to prevent or minimise risks, and adopt measures such as marking products or product batches in such a way that they can be identified, sample testing of marketed products, investigate complaints, and keep distributors informed of such monitoring.[551]

364. Under Regulation 4, it is stipulated that tests on substances carried out within the framework of these Regulations shall be conducted according to the requirements of Article 13 of the REACH Regulation and according to the requirements set in Regulation (EC) No. 440/2008 of 30 May 2008 laying down test methods pursuant to the REACH Regulation. Furthermore, substances shall be classified on the basis of their intrinsic properties according to the categories laid down in these Regulations. And in the classification of substances, impurities shall be taken into account as far as any concentration of the latter exceeds the concentration limits specified in these Regulations or the regulations laid down under the Dangerous Substances and Preparations Regulations.[552] Any advertisement for a substance which belongs to one or more of the categories referred here shall be prohibited if no mention is made therein of the category or categories concerned.[553] The general principles of the classification and labelling of substances and preparations shall be applied according to the criteria in Annex VI of the Directive, save where contrary requirements for dangerous preparations are specified in separate provisions. Whereas the dangerous substances listed in Annex I of the Directive shall, where appropriate, be characterised by concentration limits or any other parameter enabling an assessment to be made of the health or environmental hazard of preparations containing the said dangerous substances or substances containing other dangerous substances as impurities. Furthermore, manufacturers, distributors and importers of dangerous substances which appear in the European Inventory of Existing Commercial Chemical Substances but which have not yet been introduced into Annex I of the Directive shall be obliged to carry out an investigation to make themselves aware of the relevant and accessible data which exist concerning the properties of such substances. Then, on the basis of this information, they shall package and provisionally label these substances according to the rules laid down in these Regulations and the criteria in Annex VI of the Directive.

365. According to these Regulations, 'substances' means chemical elements and their compounds in the natural state or obtained by any production process, including any additive necessary to preserve the stability of the products and any impurity

551. Article 6.
552. L.N. 10/2007 (S.L. 427.28).
553. Regulation 12 of L.N. 306/2008.

deriving from the process used, but excluding any solvent which may be separated without affecting the stability of the substance or changing its composition. Furthermore, the Regulations list a number of substances which are considered to be 'dangerous' such as explosive substances and preparations, oxidising substances and preparations, extremely or highly flammable substances and preparations, toxic, harmful, or corrosive substances, and so forth. Dangerous substances cannot be placed on the market unless certain requirements laid down in these Regulations related to packaging and labelling are satisfied.[554]

As to packaging, some of the requirements are that this has to be so designed and constructed that its contents cannot escape, and the materials constituting the packaging and fastenings must not be susceptible to adverse attack by the contents or liable to form dangerous compounds with the contents, and these must be strong and solid throughout to ensure that they will not loosen and will safely meet the normal stresses and strains of handling.

As to labelling, every package shall show clearly and indelibly: the name of the substances under one of the designations given in Annex I of the Directive, and if this is not listed there, the name shall be given using an internationally recognised designation; the full particulars of the person established in the EC who is responsible for placing the substance on the market; and the danger symbols, when laid down, together with an indication of the danger involved in the use of the substance. Together with these, there shall also be included standard phrases (R-phrases) indicating the special risks arising from the dangers involved in using the substance or S-phrases relating to the safe use of the substance and the EC number when allocated. These Regulations also provide for the dimensions of the label.[555] Furthermore, dangerous substances may only be placed on the market if they are labelled in at least one of the official languages of Malta.[556] Finally, it is good to note that where dangerous substances do not leave the territory of Malta, labelling which complies with national rules instead of with international rules on the transport of dangerous substances may be permitted.

366. As for offences and penalties, the general offences provisions of the Product Safety Act are applicable. Under Article 12 of this Act, it is laid down that any person who sells, hires, exposes, or offers for sale or hire or has in his possession any product which does not comply with the provisions of this Act or of any regulation made under this Act, deposits with, or otherwise supplies to any other person any such product, shall be guilty of an offence. It shall also be an offence for a producer to fail to give any information as may be required by the Director in the exercise of his functions.

In fact, the Director General, apart from the functions highlighted above under L.N. 306/2008, also has other functions under the general provisions of this Act, which he may apply for the best surveillance of such substance. Apart from prohibiting the placing on the market, he may, among other things, also prohibit the supply, offering, or otherwise exposing any product if he has reasonable grounds to

---

554. Regulations 8 and 9 of L.N. 306/2008.
555. Regulation 10 of L.N. 306/2008.
556. Regulation 10(5) of L.N. 306/2008. The official languages are Maltese and English.

believe a product to be unsafe and tests need to be carried out, or he may order in writing the immediate withdrawal of any unsafe product from the market.[557] The Director General also has the power of enforcement, which power may be delegated to any public officer. Furthermore, this Act also gives the power of inspection, which power may be granted by any Magistrate by means of a warrant issued upon an application confirmed on oath by the Director or by any public officer duly authorised in writing by the Director.[558]

367. The Director is duty-bound to inform any operator who has failed to comply with any provision of the Act or of any regulation made under it. In such written notification, the Director will indicate the provisions of the law which are being infringed and specify remedial measures which need to be taken and order the proprietor to implement such measures within a stipulated period of time.[559] If such person duly notified fails to comply with the notice, he shall be guilty of an offence.

368. Proceedings in relation to any offence under this Act may only be instituted at the instance of the Director, who may conduct the prosecution before the court.[560] There is a prescriptive period of two years whereby criminal actions for offences under this Act may be presented. The penalties for infringing the various provisions of the Act or any Regulations issued under it have been tackled in preceding sections.

369. As already highlighted, the REACH Regulation[561] apply in parallel with the Dangerous Substances Directive (67/548/EEC). This Regulation is designed to manage and control the potential hazards and risks to human health and the environment from the manufacture, import, and use of chemicals within the EU and, at the same time, enhance the competitiveness of European industry by fostering innovation. A fourth stage of REACH is restriction.

The REACH Regulation gives greater responsibility to industry to manage the risks from chemicals and to provide safety information on the substances. Enterprises that manufacture or import more than one tonne of a chemical substance per year will be required to register it in a central database administered by the new European Chemicals Agency (ECHA). The Agency, which is located in Helsinki, will act as the central point in the REACH system: it will run the databases necessary to operate the system, coordinate the in-depth evaluation of suspicious chemicals, and run a public database in which consumers and professionals can find hazard information. The Agency will therefore manage and, in some cases, carry out the technical, scientific, and administrative aspects of REACH so as to ensure consistency at the Community level in relation to these aspects. The Agency shall provide the Member States and the institutions of the Community with the best possible scientific and technical advice on questions relating to chemicals covered by the

557. Article 15 of the Product Safety Act.
558. Articles 17 and 18 of the Product Safety Act.
559. Article 26 of the Product Safety Act.
560. Article 30 of the Product Safety Act.
561. Regulation (EC) No. 1907/2006.

Regulation. The Regulation also calls for the progressive substitution of the most dangerous chemicals when suitable alternatives have been identified.

370. REACH came into force on 1 June 2007; however, the main titles of REACH became enforceable as of 1 June 2008 so as to allow a one-year period for the establishment of ECHA. The Regulation is directly applicable in Malta as a result of its EU membership. Nevertheless, certain Legal Notices have been adopted in order to indicate which authority will be responsible for the implementation of the Regulation and also to establish the penalties applicable for its breach. The following Legal Notices implement the requirements of this Regulation:

- Registration, Evaluation, Authorisation and Restriction of Chemicals (REACH) (Implementation) Regulations, 2008 (L.N. 61/2008): Under these Regulations, the MSA has been appointed as the Competent Authority for the implementation and surveillance of the obligations arising from this Regulation. Interestingly, this has not been amended at the time of writing, even though the MSA is now defunct.
- Registration, Evaluation, Authorisation and Restriction of Chemicals Enforcement (E-REACH) Committee Regulations, 2008 (L.N. 207/2008): The objectives of these Regulations is to set up a committee to assist the MSA, with the aim to achieve a holistic multi-partite approach for the implementation and management of the enforcement of Regulation (EC) No. 1907/2006 of the European Parliament and of the Council of 18 December 2006 concerning REACH, establishing a ECHA.
- Chemicals Co-ordinating Committee Regulations, 2002 (L.N. 328/2002).

371. The EU has also adopted legislation to control the importation and exportation of dangerous chemicals. This was done by means of Regulation (EC) 304/2003,[562] which was replaced by Regulation (EC) 689/2008 of the European Parliament and the Council of 17 June 2008. This has, in turn, been replaced by Regulation (EU) No. 649/2012. This Regulation is the latest in a series of measures over the years that seek to address international trade with dangerous chemicals. It implements, within the Community, the Rotterdam Convention on the PIC Procedure for certain hazardous chemicals and pesticides in international trade, with a view to protecting human health and the environment from potential harm and contributing to the environmentally sound use of such chemicals.

The Regulation reaffirms the Community's commitment towards ensuring proper control in the trade and use of dangerous chemicals at the global level, based on the principle that it should help to protect human health and the environment beyond its borders as well as within. The Regulation (EU) 649/2012 includes a number of provisions that go beyond the Convention. In fact, under the EU Regulation, requirements for export notification and for explicit consent extend to all countries and not only to Parties of the Convention.

---

562. This was annulled by the Court of Justice of the European Union, ruling that there should have been a dual legal basis including both Arts 133 and 175 first paragraph of the Treaty.

Furthermore, the scope of the EU Regulation is not limited to chemicals that are banned or severely restricted under the Convention but also covers chemicals that are banned or severely restricted at the EU level, irrespective of the requirements of the Convention. Some chemicals might not qualify for PIC notification pursuant to Article 5 of the Convention, but the restrictions are such that the EU would like to alert importing countries so as to ensure a higher level of protection.

In order to increase the number of dangerous chemicals that are subject to export notification from the EU, the two Conventions-use categories have been divided into two further subcategories: pesticides are divided into plant protection products and other pesticides, including biocides, and industrial chemicals are separated into chemicals for professional use and chemicals for public use. Therefore, under the EU Regulation, the ban or severe restriction of a chemical at the subcategory level but not at the Convention-use level can trigger an export notification.

Furthermore, the EU makes export notifications irrespective of the intended use and whether or not that use is banned or severely restricted within the EU. This is because it cannot be guaranteed that the intended use is identical to the final use in the importing country.

Lastly, it should be emphasised that, unless specified to the contrary, the Regulation's obligations extend to exports to all countries, irrespective of whether or not they eventually are Parties to the Convention.

372. As a Member State of the EU, this Regulation is directly applicable to Malta. L.N. 327/2002, the Export and Imports of Certain Dangerous Chemicals Regulations,[563] was adopted to crystallise the obligations under Regulation (EC) 689/2008, as well as the Rotterdam Convention. This was revoked by the Export and Import of Hazardous Chemicals Regulations,[564] which implement the provisions of Regulation (EU) 649/2012. The Competent Authority for the implementation of these Regulations is the Technical Regulatory Directorate (TDA) within the MCCAA.[565]

The penalties applicable for a violation of the Regulations are those contemplated under Part IV of the Products Safety Act, discussed previously.

373. The role of the Chemicals Coordinating Committee shall be reviewed for historical reasons, as it is no longer the competent authority under the new Regulations on exporting and importing hazardous chemicals. This notwithstanding, the relevant Legal Notice is still in force and provides that the Committee is the national competent authority on the subject. Of course, *lex posteriori derogat priori*, and this law can indeed be said to be a living fossil.

Any person requiring a permit for the import and export of dangerous chemicals was to submit his notification for the permit to the Committee. The Committee was

563. S.L. 549.33. These Regulations provided for the establishment of a local system of notification and information for imports from and exports to third countries of certain chemicals which were banned or severely restricted due to their effects on human health and the environment and also to apply the PIC procedure established under international law.

564. L.N. 27/2017 (S.L. 427.92).

565. For the former Regulations, this was the Chemicals Coordinating Committee established under L.N. 327/2002.

to authorise the granting of such permits and the registration of such chemicals through the ERA. The members of the Committee are appointed for a period of three years, with the Committee's composition being determined by schedules attached to the Regulations. The members are mainly public officers from the various authorities and ministries relevant to the subject matter, such as the OHSA, ERA, MSA (even though defunct), Regulator for Energy and Water Services and others.

§5. Specific Sources of Pollution

I. Genetically Modified Organisms

374. Genetically Modified Organisms (GMOs) are similar in effect to invasive and alien species because they are also introduced in areas where they do not occur naturally. However, there are also other environmental risks associated with GMOs which are not necessarily exhibited by alien species. The principal concerns relating to GMOs are their potential adverse impacts on the environment and human health. From an environmental standpoint, their release into the wild threatens local biodiversity on two fronts. First, GMOs may copulate with local wild or cultivated relatives, leading to an abnormal hybridisation of the species. Second, they pose a threat to ecosystems at large as their artificially mutated genes may give them advantages over local species, particularly through potential invasive behaviour that allows them to outcompete indigenous and endemic species.

375. One of the EU Directives concerning this issue is Directive 2001/18/EC, which repealed Council Directive 90/220/EEC on the deliberate release into the environment of GMOs. The main aim of this Directive is to make the procedure for granting consent for the deliberate release and placing on the market of GMOs more efficient and more transparent, to limit such consent to a period of ten years (renewable) and to introduce compulsory monitoring after GMOs have been placed on the market. It also provides for a common methodology to assess the risks associated with the release of GMOs (the principles applying to environmental risk assessments are set out in Annex II to the Directive) and a mechanism allowing the release of the GMOs to be modified, suspended, or terminated where new information becomes available on the risks of such release. Furthermore, public consultation and GMO labelling are made compulsory under the new Directive. The system of exchange of information contained in notifications, set up under Directive 90/220/EEC, is maintained. The Commission is obliged to consult the competent scientific committees on any question which may affect human health and/or the environment. It may also consult ethical committees. The Directive requires registers to be established for the purpose of recording information on genetic modifications in GMOs and on the location of GMOs. Rules on the operation of these registers are laid down in Decision 2004/204/EC. Every three years, the Commission must publish a summary of the measures taken in the Member States to implement the Directive and a report on experience with GMOs placed on the market (the first report was due to be published in 2003). An annual report on ethical issues will also be published. The Directive invited the Commission to present a proposal for implementing the Cartagena Protocol on bio-safety, which led to the adoption of Regulation (EC) No. 1946/2003 of the European Parliament and of the Council on transboundary movements of GMOs.

376. The provisions of this Directive have been adopted by L.N. 170/2002, the Deliberate Release into the Environment of Genetically Modified Organisms Regulations, which were revoked and replaced by eponymous Regulations in 2010.[566] These Regulations aim to provide for the protection of human health and the environment in the same way as L.N. 290/2002[567] and L.N. 127/2008[568] aim to do (both discussed below). L.N. 485/2010 provides such protection when carrying out the deliberate release into the environment of GMOs for any other purpose than placing them on the market within Malta and when placing GMOs on the market as or in products within Malta. This objective trusts that the deliberate release into the environment of GMOs will be well controlled and will safeguard both human health and the environment from potential damaging effects.

377. The user who plans to release or place GMOs on the market must follow the regulations set out in Parts B and C of the Legal Notice. Part B tackles the deliberate release of GMOs for any other purpose than for placing on the market, which means that such release is usually intended to take place in the natural environment. In fact, Part B obliges the user in Article 5(1) to certify that such release is authorised by any relevant legislation. Moreover, it is the duty of the user to issue a specific EIA[569] in accordance with the provisions of this Legal Notice, to have the 'explicit consent prior to release' from the Competent Authority, to document a monitoring plan which aims to detect the effects of such GMOs on human health and the environment, and finally giving a detailed evaluation on the results of releases and the measures taken, all of which will be made available to the public. Prior to undertaking a deliberate release of a GMO, the user must present a notification to the ERA. The information and specifics of what is required in the notification referred to in Regulation 6(1) are given in detail in Article 6(2). An EIA is also to be conducted by the user and given to the ERA.

378. The Competent Authority must ensure the observance of the requirements of the Regulations, evaluate the assessment provided by the user, and guarantee that

566. L.N. 485/2010 (S.L. 549.60).
567. The Bio-safety Coordinating Committee Regulations (S.L. 549.31).
568. Contained Use of Genetically Modified Micro-Organisms Regulations (S.L. 549.49).
569. The objective of an EIA is to identify and evaluate potential adverse effects of the GMO on human health and the environment, which the deliberate release or the placing on the market of GMOs may have. When performing an EIA, one must keep in mind the precautionary principle. Thus, one should compare the GMO, which has potential to cause adverse effects to the non-modified organism from which it is derived. Furthermore, the EIA should be carried out in a scientifically sound and transparent manner. If new information on the effects of the GMO on human health or the environment become available, the EIA may need to be readdressed to determine whether the risk has changed and thus whether there is need to amend the risk management.

it is appropriate according to the instructions of the legislation.[570] ERA must also organise inspections and other control measures to ensure compliance with these Regulations. In the event that no authorisation is given to the release of a GMO or its placing on the market, ERA, by Regulation 4(5), must ensure that the required measures are taken to cease the said release and to notify the general public and other States which may possibly be negatively affected.

Part C of the Legal Notice tackles the placing on the market of GMOs as or in products within Malta. Before a GMO is placed on the market for the first time, a notification is submitted to the Competent Authority, which examines that notification to make sure it contains the necessary information. Regulation 12(2) gives the intricate details of what the notification entails from both the Competent Authority and the user. The Competent Authority must prepare an assessment report which indicates whether GMOs should or should not be placed on the market. If the Competent Authority decides that the product should be placed on the market, it gives its consent in writing. If the Competent Authority decides that the product should not be placed on the market, the notification is rejected, and reasons will be given for this decision. The consent is given for a maximum of ten years starting from the date on which the consent was issued.

After the GMO is placed on the market, the notifier ensures that monitoring and reporting on it are carried out according to the conditions specified in the consent of the Competent Authority. If new information becomes available from the users or other sources with regard to risks of GMOs to human health or the environment after the written consent has been given, the notifier informs the Competent Authority about these risks and takes the measures necessary to protect human health and the environment.

Although the Competent Authority may not prohibit, restrict, or impede placing on the market of GMOs when they comply with the regulations of L.N. 170/2002, if, as a result of new information, the Competent Authority considers such GMOs to constitute a risk to human health or the environment, the Competent Authority may restrict or prohibit the use and/or sale of such GMOs as or in a product.

379. Any person is guilty of an offence if he fails to comply with any of the regulations, orders, or permits which are stated in L.N. 485/2010. Other offences include contravening any restriction, prohibition, or requirement imposed by the regulations of L.N. 485/2010.

Any person who commits an offence against the provisions concerning the deliberate release of GMOs into the environment for purposes other than placing on the market is liable on a first conviction to a fine (*multa*) of not less than EUR 50,000 but not exceeding EUR 75,000. Subsequent convictions entail liability to a fine (*multa*) of not less than EUR 65,000 but not exceeding EUR 100,000 and/or imprisonment for a term not exceeding two years.

Any person who commits an offence against the provisions concerning the placing on the market of GMOs is liable on a first conviction to a fine (*multa*) of not less than EUR 60,000 but not exceeding EUR 90,000. Subsequent convictions entail

570. Regulation 4(4) of L.N. 485/2010.

liability to a fine (*multa*) of not less than EUR 75,000 but not exceeding EUR 120,000 and/or imprisonment for a term not exceeding two years.

These punishments include payment of any expenses incurred by ERA as a result of the offence, the revocation of the permit issued, and the confiscation of the *corpus delicti*.

Articles 23 and 30 of the Criminal Code apply to proceedings regarding offences against the regulations of L.N. 485/2010. The disqualification from holding or obtaining a license, permit, or authority shall never be less than one year.

380. Another Directive related to GMOs is the Contained Use of Genetically Modified Micro-organisms (Recast) Directive.[571] The aim of this Directive is practically the same as the one mentioned above; that is, to try to minimise the potential negative effects on human health and the environment, as micro-organisms released in the environment of one Member State in the course of their contained use may spread into other Member States. The Directive classifies genetically modified micro-organisms (GMMs) into two groups according to the level of hazard. In order to minimise the risk to human health and the environment, the user must adhere to certain principles of safety and health. In addition, before undertaking for the first time in a particular installation the use of GMMs, the user must submit to the authorities a notification enabling them to ensure that the proposed installation can be used for this activity without danger. The notification will contain different information depending on the level of risk involved. Furthermore, Member States may, if they wish, make provision for consulting groups or the public on any aspect of the proposed contained use.

Member States must ensure that an emergency plan is drawn up to ensure an effective response in the event of an accident and that the persons likely to be affected by an accident are informed about all matters relating to their safety. In the event of an accident, the user must immediately inform the Competent Authority and communicate all the information required to assess its impact and enable the appropriate measures to be adopted. In addition, the Member State must inform the Commission and any other Member State liable to be affected by the accident. The Commission must set up a register of the accidents which have occurred, including an analysis of their causes, the experience gained, and the measures taken to avoid similar accidents. And in order to enable the contained use of genetically modified micro-organisms to be monitored throughout the Community, Member States have to provide the Commission with certain information.

381. This Directive has been adopted under Maltese Law by means of L.N. 127/2008, the Contained Use of Genetically Modified Micro-Organisms Regulations.[572] The objectives of this L.N. are laid down in Regulation 2(1), which states that the objective is to lay down measures for the contained use of genetically modified micro-organisms with a view to protecting human health and the environment. Both the EU Directive and L.N. 127/2008 provide a detailed approval process which is

571. Directive 2009/41/EC, which repealed Directive 90/219/EEC.

572. S.L. 549.49. This L.N. repeals L.N. 169/2002.

applied on a case-by-case basis, and through this process, an assessment is made of the risks to human health and the environment.[573]

An exemption from such assessments is granted where the genetic modification is obtained through the use of techniques or methods listed in Schedule II, Part A or for contained uses involving only types of GMMs as listed in Schedule II Part C meeting the criteria listed in Schedule II Part B, which establish their safety to human health and the environment. Assessment exemptions are also granted in case of the transportation of GMMs by road, sea, or air. Moreover, these exemptions are extended to the 'storage, culture, transport, destruction, disposal, or use of GMMs', which have been made in accordance with the Deliberate Release into the Environment of GMO Regulations.[574]

382. The Legal Notice requires from the user specific obligations which must be carried out. Primarily an assessment is to be carried out in order to ensure that the contained use of GMMs does not produce detrimental effects on human health and the environment as set out by Regulation 4(1). The legislation presents the user in Regulation 4(2) with a detailed account of how the assessment is to be carried out and the specifics expected within the said assessment. In fact, it requests that the assessment shall result in the final classification of the contained uses in four classes applying the procedure set out in Schedule III. These four classes are set out by the same Regulation giving the user the necessary guidelines as to how to classify the contained use of the GMMs. This classification into four classes results in the assignment of containment levels as per sub-Regulations (6) and (7), which state that the user must apply the general principle and the appropriate containment and other protective measures so as to keep the workplace and environment exposure to any GMMs to the lowest reasonably practicable level[575] and that the assessment and the containment and other protective measures applied shall be reviewed periodically.[576] These obligations must be met by the users, ensuring that a high level of safety is maintained. The user, according to Regulation 6, is also required to submit to ERA a notification when premises for the contained uses are to be used for the first time prior to being used. Furthermore, Regulations 7, 8 and 9 list how and when the notifications to ERA on different classes of contained use should be carried out depending on the class of contained use.

383. The obligations of the Competent Authority, that is, ERA, are detailed in Regulation 10. Regulation 10(3) expressly states that it is the duty of the Authority to examine the conformity of the notifications with the requirement of this L.N. ERA must also ensure that the information given is accurate, complete, and in conformity with all the regulations included in the Directive. Regulation 10(4)(a) gives ERA the power to ask the user to provide further information or modify the conditions of the proposed contained use or amend the class to any contained use. When

573. *See* Reg. 4.
574. L.N. 170/2002, Deliberate Release into the Environment of Genetically Modified Organisms Regulations.
575. Regulation 4(6) of L.N. 127/2008.
576. Regulation 4(7) of L.N. 127/2008.

this decision is taken, the Authority may instruct that the contained use does not begin or, if in progress, is suspended or terminated until it gives its full approval following the gaining of further information or of the modified conditions.[577] It is also in the Authority's power to regulate and control the time for which the contained use should be permitted or subject to certain specific conditions according to Regulation 10(4)(b).

ERA is given the authority to hold public consultations on aspects of the proposed contained use according to Regulation 15. Among ERA's duties, it must also certify that prior to the commencement of a contained use, an emergency plan is drawn up in case of a failure[578] and that information on such emergency plans are supplied well to bodies and authorities likely to be affected by the accident while also being made public.[579] ERA, according to Regulations 17(3)(a) and 18, must alert foreign countries likely to be affected in the event of an accident and consult with them on the proposed implementation of emergency plans. If it considers that it is necessary, the Competent Authority may carry out additional investigations and other control measures as per Regulation 19(2).

384. People deemed to be guilty of an offence under these Regulations are listed in Regulation 12. A user is deemed to be guilty of an offence under these Regulations if he: fails to act in accordance with these Regulations; contravenes any restriction, prohibition, or requirement imposed; acts in contravention of any of the provisions of these Regulations; makes a statement or presents information or documentation, which is false in order to obtain the approval or continuation of a permit; or conspires or attempts, or aids, or abets, any other person by whatever means, including advertising, counselling, or procurement to contravene the provisions of these Regulations or to fail to comply with any such provisions.

The penalties awarded on conviction of any of these offences include being liable to a fine (*multa*) of an amount not less than EUR 500 and not more than EUR 35,000. The penalties are differently awarded depending under which class the offence has been committed.[580] Apart from such fines for second or subsequent convictions, even imprisonment for a term not exceeding two years may be awarded.

Furthermore, the court shall order the offender to pay for the expenses incurred by the Competent Authority as a result of the said offence, including any remedying action for any damage caused by the said offence, the revocation of the permit issued by the Competent Authority,[581] and the confiscation of the *corpus delicti*, including any expenses incurred for the keeping and transport of the said *corpus delicti*. Furthermore, the court shall order the offender to remove the causes of the offence and to undo anything which was done without a permit within a time sufficient for the purpose to be fixed by the court, and if the offender fails to comply with any such order within the time so fixed, he shall be liable to a fine (*multa*) of

577. Proviso of Reg. 10(4)(a) of L.N. 127/2008.
578. Regulation 16(1)(a) of L.N. 127/2008.
579. Regulation 16(1)(b) of L.N. 127/2008.
580. Regulation 12(2)(a–d) of L.N. 127/2008.
581. The disqualification from holding or obtaining a licence or permit from the Competent Authority shall in no case be for less than one year.

not less than EUR 60 and not more than EUR 500, as the court may fix, for every day that the default continues after the expiration of the said time.

Articles 23 and 30 of the Criminal Code apply to the proceedings in respect of offences against these Regulations, and the Court of Magistrates has the competence to decide on these offences, and the Attorney General shall always have a right of appeal to the Court of Criminal Appeal.

385. These Regulations are to be read and construed with the Protection of Workers from Risks Related to Exposure to Biological Agents at Work Regulations.[582] The scope of these Regulations is to protect workers against risks to their health and safety, including the prevention of such risks arising or likely to arise from exposure to biological agents at work.

These Regulations lay a number of obligations which an employer has to respect, and he must also ensure that his employees are not exposed to any risk to health or safety, and any worker's exposure must be prevented. Assessments of risks must be carried out, and the Competent Authority, which in this case is the OHSA, has to be informed where the results of the assessment reveal risks to workers' health and safety. Employers are also obliged to inform the Competent Authority in case of any accident or incident which may have resulted in the release of a biological agent and which could cause severe human infection and or illness. Furthermore, workers have to be informed and trained on the potential risks to health, hygiene requirements, and the steps to be taken in case of incidents and their prevention, etc. The employers must keep a list of workers exposed to group 3 or group 4 biological agents, indicating the type of work done and, whenever possible, the biological agent to which they have been exposed, as well as records of exposures, accidents, and incidents, as appropriate. The Competent Authority has to be notified when group 2, 3, and 4 agents are to be used for the first time, and also a re-notification is required when there are substantial changes of importance to safety or health at work to processes and, or procedures which render the notification out of date.

Any person who knowingly or recklessly interferes with the process of providing a safe and healthy place of work shall be guilty of an offence.

386. Another Legal Notice, which must be read and construed both with L.N. 485/2010 on the deliberate release into the environment of GMOs and L.N. 127/2008 on the contained use of GMMs, is L.N. 290/2002.[583] The objective of this Legal Notice is the setting up of a committee with the aim of achieving an integrated approach to bio-safety, the contained use of GMMs, the deliberate release into the environment of GMMs and the placing of the market of GMMs in order to achieve a high level of protection of human health and the environment taken as a whole without prejudice to other relevant Regulations. Under these Regulations, this Committee is referred to as the Bio-Safety Coordinating Committee (also referred to as the BCC or the Committee), whose composition is stated in Schedule I of the Legal Notice, and together with it, there is the setting up of the Scientific Support and Advisory Subcommittee.

582. L.N. 228/2003 (S.L. 424.25).

583. Bio-safety Coordinating Committee Regulations (S.L. 549.31).

The BCC is responsible for giving recommendations to the Competent Authority, which is ERA, on permit applications which are sent to the Competent Authority by any person. The Committee may decide to forward such notifications to the Scientific Support and Advisory Subcommittee or to any other public entity for consultation before finalising its recommendations. The Committee must forward its recommendations to ERA within a period stipulated in the main regulations.[584] Then, after forwarding notifications to the BCC and receiving feedback from the BCC, the Competent Authority shall assess the feedback/recommendations and notifications of the BCC and shall forward its decision to the notifier or user on the legal basis set in the main regulations. The individual institutions represented in the Committee shall undertake any monitoring compliance and enforcement activities of relevance to the main regulations or the BCC. The Committee shall act in terms of the legal remits and requirements of the institutions and report back to the BCC.

387. The Access to Genetic Resources and the Fair and Equitable Sharing of Benefits arising from their Utilisation Regulations[585] aim at ensuring the fair and equitable sharing of the benefits for genetic resources for which Malta has sovereign rights,[586] as well as the same sharing of benefits arising from local traditional knowledge associated with genetic resources.[587] They establish the framework required for these purposes by and implement three important pieces of international legislation: Article 15 of the Convention on Biological Diversity, the Nagoya Protocol[588] to the Convention, and Regulation (EU) No. 511/2014 on compliance measures for users from the Protocol in the Union. In fact, the Regulations are to be read and construed as one with these instruments. The provisions are furthermore not to prejudice specialised international access and sharing-instruments consistent with the Nagoya Protocol.

There are a number of competent authorities depending on the organisms at hand. The overarching authority responsible for the implementation of the Regulations and their associated instruments is the Director for Plant Health, and thus one of its responsibilities is the granting of access to genetic resources through PIC. However, for this particular responsibility, the authority is to be assisted by assistant authorities, which themselves are responsible for granting such access. Thus, the ERA is responsible as regards wildlife (except birds) as laid down under the EPA, the WBRU is responsible for birds as laid down under the Conservation of Wild Birds Regulations, and the Department of Fisheries and Aquaculture as laid down

584. 'Main regulations' mean the Contained use of Genetically Modified Micro-Organisms Regulations (L.N. 127/2008) and the Deliberate Release into the Environment of GMO Regulations (L.N. 170/2002).
585. L.N. 379/2016 (S.L. 549.111).
586. These are genetic resources originating in Malta or acquired in accordance with the Convention after entry into force of the Protocol for the Union.
587. This is traditional knowledge held by an indigenous or local community relevant for the utilisation of genetic resources, that is described as such in the mutually agreed terms applying to the utilisation of genetic resources.
588. Protocol on Access to Genetic Resources and the Fair and Equitable Sharing of Benefits arising from their Utilisation.

in the Fisheries Conservation and Management Act.[589] These assistant authorities are also to aid the Director in ensuring that the implementation of the Regulations and their associated instruments is in line with other sectorial legislation, and together they are to compile an annual report on such implementation.

The Regulations also establish an advisory committee, the Access to Benefit Sharing Advisory Committee, to advise the competent authority in the implementation of the provisions of due diligence as laid down in the Council Regulation. It is also to provide technical, scientific and other relevant advice on request. The Committee is composed of eleven members from various departments and authorities relevant to the Regulations. Without prejudice to the Regulations, it may regulate its own procedures and meetings.

388. The competent authority, or any authorised officer or person, has a number of powers to ensure compliance with the relevant pieces of legislation. These include the power of inspection of premises and of entry when authorised and, if necessary, with the aid of the police force. These powers also apply to vehicles, vessels, aircraft, or hovercraft reasonably suspected to be transporting evidence. An inspector who has entered premises in exercise of these powers may, *inter alia*, search the premises, have access to inspect and copy any documents, records or other information, and do the same for any computer data. However, documents, etc., subject to legal professional privilege are excluded from the purview of any inspector.

389. The access to genetic resources for which Malta has sovereign rights to other countries requires the PIC from the competent or assistant authorities, as stipulated. Once granted, the access is to be on mutually agreed terms between the concerned user of genetic resources and Malta, and the drafting and negotiation process of such terms is to be undertaken by the competent authority. The access should guarantee that the benefits arising from the utilisation of genetic resources, as well as any subsequent application and commercialisation, shall be shared in a fair and equitable way with Malta. A certificate of compliance[590] is to be issued to the user of genetic resources upon establishment of the mutually agreed terms as evidence of such and the decision to grant PIC. The utilisation of traditional knowledge associated with genetic resources held by local communities requires a joint PIC or approval from the competent authority following consultation with the relevant assistant authority and the community concerned where applicable. No person is to utilise such knowledge unless mutually agreed terms have been established. The power to draft and negotiate and the guarantees are the same as in the genetic resources for which Malta has sovereign rights. The user requesting PIC for the utilisation of genetic resources must submit an application in writing to the Director or the concerned assistant authority at least six months prior to utilisation, together with the relevant documents and other requisite information specified by the authorities. The authorities are not to divulge any information contained in the application to third parties. However, the applicant's name and address, the species

589. Chapter 425 of the Laws of Malta.

590. Under the Nagoya Protocol this constitutes an internationally recognised certificate of compliance.

involved, the aim and purpose of the application, and the possible impacts on local biodiversity, *inter alia*, are not to be kept confidential.

The Director is to facilitate the registration of collections in the register to be established and maintained by the European Commission under the Regulation, and the relevant assistant authority has the right to review the records and any specimens held in a collection registered accordingly. The outcome of the review is to be communicated to the competent authority within thirty days from the date of inspection. The competent or assistant authorities may promote additional measures and provisions which in general protect human and plant health and may adopt interim measures in case of imminent threats to human, animal or plant health.

390. The Director may serve a remedial notice on a person he believes has contravened any of the provisions of the Regulations or following the detection of shortcomings from an inspection, which would contain certain requirements. It may also issue an administrative penalty for non-compliance. Some of the due diligence obligations of the Council Regulation are also subject to administrative fines. Administrative fines may also be issued when the authority has reasonable cause to believe that an offence against the Regulations has been committed by any person, where having regard to that person's previous conduct, such a penalty would be appropriate. The person may, however, request that proceedings in respect of the alleged offence be dealt with by the court.

391. It is an offence to obstruct an inspector exercising a power under the Regulations. It is also an offence to fail to observe the provisions of the Regulations or the Council Regulation, infringe any restriction, prohibition or need imposed in their virtue, and fail to observe any condition of mutually agreed terms, PIC or permit granted under any of their provisions, among other offences. Committing or attempting to commit an offence against the Regulations entails liability for a first conviction to a fine (*multa*) of not less than EUR 800 but not exceeding EUR 4,658.75 and for a subsequent conviction to a fine (*multa*) of not less than EUR 6,000 but not exceeding EUR 10,000 and/or imprisonment for a term not exceeding two years. Where the convict is a director, secretary, or manager for a body corporate for the economic benefit of which the offence was committed, this body corporate is liable *in solidum* with the offender for the payment of the fine as a civil debt due to the government. Conviction also entails payment of any expenses incurred as a result of the offence. Articles 23 and 30(1) of the Criminal Code apply to the provisions of the Regulations; however, the disqualification from holding a licence, etc., shall never be for less than one year. The competent Court for such offences is the Court of Magistrates as a Court of Criminal Judicature, from which decision the Attorney General shall always have a right of appeal.

II. Animal Experiments

392. Council Directive 86/609/EC was adopted to ensure the approximation of laws, regulations, and administrative provisions of Member States (MS) regarding the protection of animals used for experimental and other scientific purposes. However, due to new scientific knowledge in respect of factors influencing animal welfare and the capacity of animals to sense and express pain and distress, even at the foetal stage, this Directive was replaced by the new Directive 2010/63/EU of the European Parliament and the Council. The first Directive was transposed locally under the Animal Experimentation Regulations,[591] now revoked. The new Directive has been transposed twice, a few years apart, with minor changes from the first to the second. The laws are the Protection of Animals for Scientific Purposes Regulations[592] and the Protection of Animals Used for Scientific Purposes Regulations,[593] both under the Animal Welfare Act.[594] Both Regulations are currently in force. Since both reproduce the same basic text verbatim with only minor changes from one to the other, the most recent Regulations will be used for reference (*lex posteriori derogat priori*). Any differences between the two will be highlighted where necessary.

393. The Regulations establish measures for the protection of animals used for scientific and educational purposes. They focus on replacing, reducing, and refining such use of animals, and actions ancillary thereto, laying down certain minimum standards. There is ample reference to the notion of 'procedures', which is defined as 'any use, invasive or non-invasive, of an animal for experimental or other scientific purposes, with known or unknown outcome, or educational purposes, which may cause the animal a level of pain, suffering, distress or lasting harm equivalent to, or higher than, that caused by the introduction of a needle in accordance with good veterinary practice, provided that this includes any course of action intended, or liable, to result in the birth or hatching of an animal or the creation and maintenance of a genetically modified animal line in any such condition, but excludes the killing of animals solely for the use of their organs or tissues'. Nevertheless, where appropriate, Malta may, together with other MS, facilitate the establishment of programmes for the sharing of organs and tissues of animals killed.[595]

394. The Regulations apply to live non-human vertebrates, including independently feeding larval forms and foetal forms of mammals from the last third of their normal development, and to living cephalopods, as well as to animals at an earlier stage of development used in procedures where the animal is to be allowed to live beyond that developmental stage and is likely to experience pain, suffering, distress or lasting harm after it has reached such stage as a result of the procedures. Furthermore, they apply where such animals are used, or intended to be used, for procedures or bred specifically to use their organs or tissues for scientific purposes and until those animals have been killed, rehomed or returned to a suitable habitat or husbandry system. The use of animals in procedures is not excluded from the scope

591. L.N. 263/2003 (S.L. 439.06), revoked by L.N. 419/2014.
592. L.N. 124/2013 (S.L. 439.13).
593. L.N. 161/2017 (S.L. 439.20).
594. Chapter 439 of the Laws of Malta.
595. Regulation 18.

of the Regulations if the pain, suffering, etc., is eliminated by anaesthesia or other methods. The procedures may only be carried out for the following purposes:

(1) basic research;
(2) applied/translational research with any of the following aims:
  (a) avoidance, prevention, diagnosis or treatment of disease, ill-health or other abnormality or their effects on human beings, animals or plants;
  (b) assessment, detection, regulation or modification of physiological conditions in the same; and
  (c) the welfare of animals and the improvement of the production conditions for animals reared for agricultural purposes;
(3) for any of the three mentioned aims in the development, manufacture or testing of the quality, effectiveness and safety of drugs, foodstuffs and feed-stuffs and other substances or products;
(4) protection of the natural environment in the interests of the health or welfare of humans and animals;
(5) research aimed at the preservation of the species;
(6) higher education or training for the acquisition, maintenance or improvement of vocational skills; and
(7) forensic inquiries.

The competent authority is also to ensure that animals are killed with minimum pain, suffering or distress in the establishment of a breeder, supplier, or user[596] by a competent person. Certain requirements are laid down in Annex IV for specific species.

395. Endangered species listed in Annex A to Council Regulation (EC) No. 338/97 on the regulation of trade in wild fauna and flora are not to be used in procedures unless they have specific purposes (bullets (2)(a), (3) or (5) above) and that purpose is unattainable without the use of those species. The same prohibition applies to the use of non-human primates, with the added requirement that when used, this be with a view to the avoidance, prevention, diagnosis or treatment of debilitating[597] or potentially life-threatening clinical conditions in humans. Further provision is made for the use of non-human primates covered by Annex A of Directive 338/97. It is forbidden to use animals taken from the wild in procedures, with the exception of when the purpose is unattainable by an animal bred for procedures. Nevertheless, the capture of wild animals is to be performed by competent persons using methods that do not cause pain, suffering, etc. If a captured animal is found to be injured or in poor health, it is to be examined by a veterinarian, and action is to be taken to minimise its suffering. Animals listed in Annex I to the Regulations can only be used in procedures when bred for that purpose, with added provision for non-human primates. Strays and feral animals cannot be used in procedures unless there is an essential need for studies concerning the health and welfare of

596. Any person, natural or legal, using animals in procedures, whether for profit or not.
597. This means a reduction in a person's normal physical or psychological ability to function.

such animals or serious threats to the environment or human/animal health, and there is scientific justification ensuring that the procedure's purpose is unattainable without those animals.

396. It is the responsibility of the competent authority to ensure that procedures are carried out in a user's establishment within the framework of a project.[598] It must furthermore ensure that procedures are not performed if an alternative methodology not involving the use of live animals is recognised under EU law. If this is not the case, a procedure using the minimum number of animals possible, which animals have the lowest capacity to experience pain, suffering, etc., and which procedure causes the least pain, suffering, etc., to provide satisfactory results, is to be chosen. The procedures are to be individually classified in order of severity. Death is never to be the endpoint of a procedure, and when this is unavoidable, it is to be as painless as possible and involve a minimal number of animals. Anaesthesia, whether general or local and other pain-relievers are to be used during procedures except in specific circumstances, such as the anaesthesia causing more distress, etc., than the procedure itself. An animal is only to be reused in procedures when specific criteria are met.[599] An animal used or intended to be used in procedures may be rehomed or set free on the satisfaction of particular conditions, such as there being no danger to the public or animal health or to the environment.[600] Each facility is to have a scheme for rehoming animals or setting wild animals free. In the latter case, this is to include a rehabilitation programme where appropriate.

397. All breeders, suppliers and users are to be authorised by and registered with the competent authority, provided the person's establishment is in compliance with the requirements of the Regulations. The authorisation may be granted for a limited period. It shall specify the person responsible for ensuring such compliance, the designated veterinarian and other personnel with specific requirements, such as those responsible for ensuring the staff are adequately educated and trained for overseeing the welfare and care of the animals in the establishment. Any change of these persons is to be notified to the competent authority, which must also ensure itself that it is so authorised. It is also to ensure itself of the presence of the suitable and necessary installations and equipment suited to the species housed in the establishment and to the procedures it performs and the competence of the personnel. Any significant change to the structure or function of the establishment that could negatively affect animal welfare requires a renewal of the authorisation. Non-compliance with the Regulations empowers the authority to take remedial action and, where necessary, suspend or withdraw the authorisation, such that the welfare of the animals housed in the establishment.

All projects are to be carried out by authorisation from the competent authority, which requires a favourable project evaluation. The specifics for the application, evaluation and authorisation are laid down in Regulations 36 to 41.

598. A programme of work having a defined scientific objective, involving one or more procedures.
599. Regulation 16.
600. Regulation 19.

398. All breeders, suppliers, and users are to keep animal records, detailing, *inter alia*, the number and species of animals bred, acquired, etc., their origin, and the number and species of animals that died or were killed. Specific identification information is to be kept for all dogs, cats and non-human primates, each individual having its own history file. These specific animals are to be marked to facilitate individual identification. All animals are to be provided with adequate care and accommodation, and these conditions are to be checked daily. Transportation of animals is also to occur under appropriate conditions. Each breeder, supplier and user is to have an animal welfare body, including, at a minimum, the persons responsible for the welfare and care of the animals and, in the case of a user, a scientific member. The body is tasked with, *inter alia*, advising the staff dealing with animals on matters of animal welfare, establishing and reviewing internal operational processes, and advising on rehoming schemes.

399. The competent authority is the Department responsible for the Veterinary Services of Malta. However, it may designate bodies other than public authorities for the implementation of specific tasks laid down in the Regulations. This delegation requires proof that the body has the necessary infrastructure and expertise to perform such tasks and is free of any conflict of interest regarding the performance of its tasks. These designated bodies are to be considered competent authorities for the purposes of the Regulations as well. The Animal Welfare Council[601] and the Director for Veterinary Services are to advise the animal welfare bodies of the establishments on matters dealing with the acquisition, breeding, accommodation, care, and use of animals in procedures and ensure sharing of best practice. The Council is also to exchange information on the operation of such bodies and project evaluation and share best practice within the EU. Regular inspections must be carried out by the competent authority of all breeders, suppliers and users and their establishments to verify compliance with the Regulations. The frequency of the inspections is to be adjusted based on a risk analysis of each establishment. An appropriate number of inspections are also to be performed without prior notice. The authority is also to offer all necessary assistance to the experts of the EU Commission, whose duty it is to undertake controls of the infrastructure and operation of national inspections in Malta.

400. Failure to abide by the provisions of the Regulations amounts to an offence, liable to all such administrative measures deemed necessary by the authority to ensure no further breaches and to reduce the risk for final consumers and any additional risk to the animals or the environment. These include: direct confiscation of the product; suspension of the activities carried out by the breeder, supplier or user; and the withdrawal, forfeiture or suspension of the authorisation, licence or permit regarding such activities when these create a risk to final consumers and the environment. Administrative fines[602] and effective and dissuasive penalties as stipulated in the parent Act may also be applied. The penalties are a fine (*multa*) of not less than EUR 2,000 but not exceeding EUR 65,000 on a first conviction and a fine

601. Established under Art. 4 of the Animal Welfare Act.
602. Under Art. 47 of the Animal Welfare Act.

(*multa*) of not less than EUR 6,000 but not exceeding EUR 80,000 and/or imprisonment for a term not exceeding three years on a subsequent conviction.

401. The main differences between the two Regulations are the following. The 2013 Regulations do not make provision for the delegation of tasks by the competent authorities to further competent authorities. The 2017 Regulations include safeguard clauses[603] when the use of non-human primates in procedures is required without any of the aims mentioned earlier. The 2013 Regulations refer to the Union Reference Laboratory in the Regulations with details in Schedule VII.[604] The 2017 Regulations retain the Schedule (restyled Annex VII) but make no reference to the Laboratory in the Regulation provisions proper. Finally, the 2013 Regulations give the Director discretion to adopt national legislation offering more extensive protection of animals falling within the scope of the Regulations, with certain qualifications,[605] while the 2017 Regulations provide that the competent authority may not maintain such legislation in force.[606] For all intents and purposes, it is the later Regulations that should be followed insofar as they have altered the earlier ones.

III. Asbestos

402. The Prevention and Reduction of Environmental Pollution by Asbestos Regulations[607] adopt the provisions of Council Directive 87/217/EEC of 19 March 1987 on the prevention and reduction of environmental pollution by asbestos. It is important to note that the Directive was part of the then-EEC's aim (now the EU) to approximate the Member State's legislation in this field in order to prevent the creation of unequal conditions of competition, which would have a direct effect on the functioning of the common market. However, the motivation behind the endorsement of such a Directive is not just economic; it is also aimed at reducing pollution by asbestos in order to protect and improve the environment, which is also on the EU's agenda.[608] Therefore, as stated in Article 1 of the same Directive, the objective is to lay down measures and to supplement provisions already in force, with a view to preventing and reducing pollution by asbestos in the interests of the protection of human health and the environment.

403. The object of the Regulations is construed as one with the Directives. The Regulations give power to a Competent Authority and assign to it several functions, which it must carry out in order to pursue such an aim. Regulation 2 establishes the Competent Authority as the Department for Environmental Protection. The Department has to ensure that emissions of asbestos into the environment and solid asbestos waste are reduced at, and prevented from, their source point as practicably as

603. Regulation 50 of L.N. 161/2017.
604. Regulation 49 of L.N. 124/2013.
605. Regulation 4 of L.N. 124/2013.
606. Regulation 2 of L.N. 161/2017.
607. L.N. 228/2001 (S.L. 549.18).
608. Council Directive 87/217/EEC.

possible, and it must ensure the use of the best available technology without incurring extensive costs in order to reduce and eliminate emissions of asbestos into the air when dealing with existing and new plants. As to the concentration of asbestos emitted into the air during the use of asbestos, it must ensure that this does not exceed the limit value of 0.1 milligrams of asbestos per m^3 of air discharged, as set out in the Directive. An exemption on this can be given by the Competent Authority to plants emitting less than 5,000 m^3/hour total gaseous discharges, where the discharge of asbestos into the air is not more than 0.5 grams per hour at any time under normal operating conditions. When such exemption is granted, the Competent Authority is to ensure that such limit value is not exceeded. The Competent Authority must also ensure that the aqueous effluent arising in the manufacture of asbestos cement is recycled unless the plant operator proves that it is not economically viable to do so. In such case, the Authority is required to take the necessary measures to ensure that the disposal of liquid waste containing asbestos does not pollute the environment. Moreover, when disposing of the waste, the Authority must apply the limit value set out in the Directive of 30 grams of total suspended matter per m^3 of aqueous effluent discharged. And it must also ensure that all aqueous effluent arising in the manufacture of asbestos paper or board is recycled.

The Competent Authority has to take account of the volume of the total quantity of suspended matter discharged per tonne of product for each plant concerned. The quoted measurements have to be taken at routine intervals of asbestos emissions, and the Competent Authority has to adopt the sampling and analysis procedures and methods that conform to or are similar to those described in the Annex as long as they provide equivalent results in order to examine compliance with the limit values. Furthermore, it must also ensure that activities involving the working of products containing asbestos do not result in significant environmental pollution by asbestos fibres or dust; and that the demolition of buildings, structures, and installations that contain asbestos and the removal of asbestos from such fixtures or materials that contain asbestos, does not have adverse effects on the environment. While waste containing asbestos fibres or dust is being transported or deposited in licensed landfills, the Competent Authority must ensure there are no spillages during transportation, and such waste which is going to be landfilled has to be adequately treated, packaged, or covered in order to prevent the release of asbestos particles into the environment.

404. Finally, the Competent Authority has to ensure that all materials containing asbestos are adequately maintained by the user or operator. And according to Article 3(1), the general rule is that no person may make use of asbestos.

405. Regulations 9, 10, and 11 of the Regulations deal with liability and penalties. Failing to comply with or violating a provision of the Regulations is considered an offence. Furthermore, one is also guilty of an offence if one contravenes a restriction, prohibition, or requirement imposed by the Regulations. Conspiring or attempting, aiding, or assisting other persons in committing the aforementioned offences also gives rise to liability under the Regulations. A direct application of the polluter-pays principle can be observed in Regulation 10, where the punishment for committing an offence under the Regulations is largely manifested in the payment of fines. The offender could also be imprisoned for a term not exceeding two years on a second conviction and may additionally have to suffer both the term of imprisonment and the fine. The punishments laid out in Regulation 10 also apply, in the same manner, and degree, to a person who has committed an offence under the Regulations by means of a vehicle. Furthermore, in the second proviso to Regulation 10, the offender is also obliged to pay any damages caused by his actions to cover the costs incurred by the public entities involved in the implementation of the Regulations and to repair the damage made to the environment. This provision also provides for the revocation of the permit issued by the police and for the confiscation of the *corpus delicti*.

In Regulation 11, the legislator makes use of the Criminal Code to apply criminal sanctions to offences under the Regulations. This is done by means of the provisions of Articles 23[609] and 30(1)[610] of the Criminal Code, which apply *mutatis mutandis* to offences under the Legal Notice. However, in cases of disqualification from holding or obtaining a license, permit, or authority, regulation 11 makes it clear that such disqualification must not be for less than one year. Moreover, the legislator appoints the Court of Magistrates (Malta and Gozo) as the competent court that has jurisdiction over proceedings in respect of offences under the Regulations. Furthermore, the Attorney General is granted a right of appeal before the Court of Criminal Appeal from judgments handed down by the Court of Magistrates in relation to proceedings for offences under the Regulations.

406. There are two other Regulations relating to asbestos. The Prohibition of Importation of Asbestos Fibres Regulations[611] predates the aforementioned Regulations and complements them. The only provision they contain prohibits the importation into Malta and the taking out of the bond of any asbestos fibres in loose form. The Protection of Workers from the Risks Related to Exposure to Asbestos at Work Regulations[612] is a second complementary law of a more industrial nature that regulates the use of asbestos in workplace environments. The aim is to protect workers, with environmental protection being a necessary by-product of this.

609. Forfeiture of *corpus delicti*.
610. Disqualifications in case of convictions.
611. L.N. 129/1994 (S.L. 37.11), issued under the Customs Ordinance (Ch. 37 of the Laws of Malta).
612. L.N. 323/2006 (S.L. 424.23), issued under the Occupational Health and Safety Authority Act (Ch. 424 of the Laws of Malta).

Part III. Waste Management

Chapter 1. Solid Wastes

§1. Littering and Public Cleanliness

407. The Code of Police Laws[613] provides that the owner or occupier[614] of any house is to keep clean the internal and external parts of the house. Furthermore:

> no person may throw or dump in any place any refuse or rubbish or may keep or suffer to be kept in any place any accumulation of refuse, of rubbish, of dirty, polluted or stagnant water, or of sewage, dung or other foul matter.

The dumping of material in any open space is permitted only in spaces which are surrounded by a wall at least 2.5 m high and if a licence to that effect is issued by the Commissioner of Police, who may impose any conditions he deems fit. Nevertheless, the granting of a licence for the dumping of material is limited to dumping of matter forming part of, or which is ancillary to, the business of the applicant. The Superintendent of Public Health may order the removal or destruction of any such accumulation of refuse if it becomes a threat to public health or to abate the nuisance. If the occupier or owner fails to comply with any order issued by the said Superintendent, he shall be guilty of a contravention, and the court shall order the Superintendent to intervene without any right to compensation on the part of the owner or occupier. The Minister for Public Health may make regulations, among other things, for the removal from any house or other place of refuse and rubbish or of any dirty, stagnant, or polluted water or of sewage, dung, or other foul matter or for anything connected with the keeping, removal, and disposal of any such matter or liquid. Regulations may also be made, generally, for the proper working of any service that may be established for any of the above purposes.

408. By virtue of the above-mentioned enabling provisions, the 1899 Regulations on Scavengers and the Removal of Refuse were issued. These Regulations provided that scavengers licensed by the Chief of the Public Health Department were to collect house refuse and other refuse. Collection of refuse had to be granted to licensed 'scavengers' who, in turn, were to remove the refuse from the houses.

613. Chapter 10 of Laws of Malta, Art. 121.
614. It is the occupier who is primarily responsible. The owner is responsible when the occupier is not found.

The occupier of any house, in turn, was bound to 'once at least in every day, excepting Sundays and other holidays, cause the house refuse to be removed therefrom, in a suitable receptacle'. Refuse had to be placed in suitable receptacles and could not at any time be left strewn on pavements or lying around elsewhere. Similarly, it was prohibited to shake or beat clothes, carpets, mats, or other articles in or over any street except at times and places fixed by the police. Dead animals were to be delivered to the said scavengers within twenty-four hours after their death. The unloading of any article producing dust or dirt had to be done before 8 o'clock in the morning, and the ground was to be swept by the person causing such dust and dirt, according to the provisions of these Regulations. When removing refuse from any premises, scavengers or any other persons could not deposit or cause to be deposited refuse upon any footway, pavement, or carriageway. If any refuse was spilt during removal, the scavenger was obliged to sweep or otherwise cleanse the place thoroughly and immediately. Nowadays, various contracts exist between local councils and waste collectors that operate more or less according to these same rules.

409. Enacted on 27 February 1968, the Litter Act used to fall under the responsibility of the Minister responsible for public health. Before the setting up of an Environment Ministry, it was the Ministry for Public Health which had environmental protection as part of its portfolio. The Litter Act was repealed[615] and replaced by the Littering Regulations,[616] which adopted many of its provisions.

410. The Littering Regulations, under the EPA, are concerned with the overall cleanliness of streets and public places. Therefore, it is prohibited to litter, dump, or deposit material, in any manner, in any public place, street, sea, or open space to which the public has access unless lawfully authorised.

The Minister responsible for the environment may establish an Advisory Committee for the control and monitoring of littering under these Regulations, which members are nominated by a variety of stakeholders such as the Department for Local Government, the Commissioner of Police, and ERA. The Committee's function is to advise the Minister on any matter relating to public cleansing in general and any matter within the scope of the Regulations, but it may be delegated other duties by the Minister after consultation with ERA. It also has the function of coordinating with all competent authorities and NGOs engaged in public cleansing and may recommend to such authorities good practice in the field of public cleaning and for controlling the disposal of litter in streets and public places. The Regulations establish waste collection schemes for the collection of commercial and domestic waste from the various localities on the Islands, which must be adhered to. It is unlawful to leave such waste for collection in any street or public place unless at a time reasonably approximate to the time at which refuse collection occurs at that specific locality – the general rule is not more than one hour before the scheduled

615. By the Public Health Act (Ch. 465).
616. L.N. 344/2005, Abandonment, Dumping and Disposal of Waste in Streets and Public Places or Areas Regulations (S.L. 549.40).

time. Furthermore, it is unlawful to leave the wrong refuse for collection on a specific day. Where bins are provided, all litter must be placed inside the bin and not near it. Finally, the collection and sorting of waste must be performed by duly authorised persons.

The Regulations burden hawkers and street sellers operating in a public place with the responsibility of keeping the place they are operating in clean and sanitary, with a government-approved bin by them during operating hours. The owner or occupier of commercial premises may also be required to provide bins within the premises for the deposit of litter at his expense. Event organisers also have a duty to ensure no litter is created through advertising. Contravening these provisions leads to a fine (*ammenda*) upon conviction, with the amounts varying depending on the specifics of the offence. The more serious unlawful dumping, such as that of construction waste and electronic material, is subject to heavy fines (*multi*). The *ammendi* are converted to *multi*, and in any case, the amount of the fine (*multa*) is increased, due to aggravating circumstances, such as littering and dumping in the immediate vicinity of a school, museum, or public monument or in the immediate vicinity of or within UNESCO World Heritage Site or any protected area by the EPA. Second or subsequent offences are also liable to a higher fine (*multa*). Administrative fines may also be imposed by ERA on any contravener. Depending on the nature of the offence, they may be triable either before a Commissioner for Justice or the Court of Magistrates.

411. There is a general duty to separate waste, in line with Regulation 4B of the Waste Regulations, described below. Every person must separate recyclable waste in a phased approach set out by separate Government Notice in the *Government Gazette*, starting from the year 2023. Hawkers, street sellers, or stalls operating in a specific context (such as open-air markets or public events) must be accompanied by bins, provided by the appropriate Local Council at the expense of the Local Council or vendor concerned, for the separate collection of organic waste, glass, mixed waste, and metal, plastic, cardboard, and paper. Specific rules govern specific operational contexts. Offences and corresponding punishments are established for the contravention of these rules.

412. Littering and public cleansing from a sanitary perspective and for the purposes of good order are regulated by the laws mentioned above, but these are now superseded by a much more adequate body of rules addressing waste management that is discussed below.

§2. Waste Management

413. Whereas the 1991 EPA did not include waste management anywhere in its provisions, although its Part 5 was dedicated to 'Disposal and Dumping on Land', the 2001 EPA provided that the Minister had the power to make regulations in relation to waste management. Such provision was needed because, at that time, Malta was negotiating with the EU to become a full Member State of the Union, and hence, new environmental laws had to be introduced in the Maltese legal system, among which those related to waste management and control. Furthermore, the 2001 EPA provided that licences had to be issued by the Competent Authority in order for any person to carry out activities related to waste management. The required laws in order to adopt this licensing system have been adopted. These powers have now been transferred under the new 2016 EPA.[617] Those provisions of the 2016 EPA grant the Minister the power to make regulations in relation to waste management. Aside from licensing mentioned above, regulations may be made: in order to classify waste and prescribe rules in relation thereto in accordance with the type and category thereof; to regulate the management, recycling and disposal of waste; and to establish quotas (in quantitative and qualitative terms) of permitted generation of waste as well as to otherwise provide for the prevention and reduction of waste.

The EPA also empowers the Minister to issue regulations[618] which formulate objectives in qualitative and quantitative terms, to control the quality of the environment, give directives with regard to particular uses of the environment, and establish the maximum quantities or concentrations of discharge or emission, or use of such substances as may be prescribed during works, undertakings, or activities of any nature and ensure the enforcement and monitoring of these standards. Furthermore, the Minister may, by regulations, establish codes of practice to determine procedures, methods, and limits of discharge applicable to works or activities at the time of execution of the works, as well as after their completion. These general provisions have empowered the Minister to issue a number of regulations which could not have been issued under the individual chapters on the subject. Cases in point are the Sewer Discharge Control Regulations and the Deposit of Wastes and Rubble (Fees) Regulations.

414. Following Malta's accession to the EU, waste-related policy and legislation are primarily based on EU policies. To this effect, any future legislation will be dictated, although not exclusively, by EU Directives and Regulations. The EU has experience of at least thirty years in waste policy. Waste legislation in Member States and at the EU level covers the major issues on waste disposal, controlling the point sources of pollution and regulating industrial waste. To this effect, several new laws have been introduced in the sector of the environment.

I. Waste Deposit

415. The Deposit of Wastes and Rubble (Fees) Regulations[619] were issued by virtue of the EPA,[620] the Fees Ordinance,[621] and the Water Services Corporation Act.[622] They regulate the deposit of waste and rubble and establish fees for their

617. Article 54(2)(l).
618. The wording here is a bit ambiguous in the sense that directives are by their very nature directory, not mandatory, while regulations can only be mandatory.
619. L.N. 128/1997 (S.L. 459.07).
620. Under Arts 6(b)(2), 30, 47 and 48 of the first EPA (Ch. 348 of the Laws of Malta).
621. *See* Art. 2 of the Fees Ordinance (Ch. 35 of the Laws of Malta).
622. *See* Art. 45 of the Water Services Corporation Act (Ch. 355 of the Laws of Malta).

deposit. Schedule A to the Regulations lists hazardous wastes, namely toxic and potentially toxic substances originating from industrial and non-industrial services containing chemicals listed in this schedule. Schedule B lists Waste Deposit Sites. Schedule C lists the fees due for the deposit of waste in public waste management facilities. Schedule D lists rules for the treatment of hazardous waste at the Thermal Treatment Facility.

416. These Regulations prohibit the deposit of any rubble,[623] waste,[624] or hazardous waste[625] unless this is done in a waste deposit site.[626] The owners of a site to be used for the depositing of rubble, waste, or hazardous waste must be in possession of a licence which is issued by ERA for that purpose. The site is subject to inspection[627] at any time, and any tests, samples, or other evidence may be gathered to ascertain that the deposit of rubble, waste, or hazardous waste is in no way prejudicial to the environment or to the integrity of the water resources. The owner or the person responsible for the site must provide access, assistance, and the information requested. Any person who deposits rubble, waste, or hazardous waste must register every vehicle with the Department for Waste Strategy Implementation. Such registration must be renewed annually. However, the Director of the said Department can cancel it before it expires. No person may transport rubble, waste, or hazardous waste by means of a vehicle which is not registered as mentioned above after 31 October 1997. The vehicle is subject to inspection at any time.[628]

The deposit of rubble in a public waste deposit site carries a fee of EUR 3.21, excluding VAT, for every metric tonne deposited. An exemption applies to the deposit of domestic rubble in the public waste deposit sites indicated in Schedule B. The deposit of waste which is not hazardous waste in a public waste deposit site is subject to the fees established by Schedule C. The fee is not chargeable against deposits of domestic waste in certain sites by the householder generating that waste. A person cannot deposit hazardous waste in a waste deposit site unless he is in possession of a permit in writing to this effect issued by ERA. Furthermore, if hazardous waste or other waste is deposited in a public facility, the person who deposits such waste shall pay a fee in accordance with Schedule D to the government entity entrusted with the responsibility for waste management strategy implementation for

623. Defined as, 'rubble originating in Malta, and which is not soil and includes such materials as dust, limestone, or other kinds of stone, concrete, floor tiles, ground stone, sand, gravel and rubble which results from excavations, ground preparation, demolition of buildings, road works and other similar works'.
624. Defined as, 'all types of wastes originating in Malta which are transported by a vehicle, but does not include hazardous waste'.
625. Means 'any waste included in Schedule A and any other type of waste which [ERA] has reason to believe is hazardous'.
626. Defined as 'any site on land or at sea, which is licensed by [ERA] for the deposit of rubble, waste or hazardous waste and which is included from time to time in Schedule B'.
627. By ERA, the Director for Waste Strategy Implementation, and the Chief Executive of the Water Services Corporation, or anyone authorised on their behalf.
628. By ERA and the Director for Waste Strategy Implementation.

every metric tonne of such waste to be deposited. These rates may be adjusted periodically to reflect changes to the Retail Price Index. The deposit of domestic hazardous waste by the householder generating that waste is exempt from the fee if the deposit is made in certain specified sites.

417. Although the Regulations allow for wastes and hazardous wastes to be deposited at waste deposit sites at sea, a permit to that effect has to be issued by ERA. Malta has international obligations[629] which prohibit the deposit of wastes, whether hazardous or otherwise, at sea unless such wastes are inert, as in the case of rubble. Furthermore, it is the government's strict policy not to allow the deposit of hazardous wastes and wastes at sea unless allowed under international law. The fee for the deposit of rubble, wastes, and hazardous wastes at sea is now at the discretion of ERA. The Minister responsible for the environment, jointly with the Minister for Finance, may exempt any person from the payment of such fees, in full or in part, if the project in question is declared to have any strategic or national significance. The fee for registering the vehicle to transport rubble, waste, or hazardous waste is EUR 23.29, and the same amount is due upon renewal of the registration of the vehicle.

418. The applicant for the registration of a waste deposit site is to have an insurance policy for environmental damages that may result from the deposit of rubble, waste, or hazardous waste. The Chief Executive for the Water Service Corporation is to decide upon the sum to be covered by the insurance policy, which may not be less than EUR 582,343.35, depending on the site's location vis-à-vis the vulnerability area of the aquifer. If, in such cases, the aquifer suffers damage which exceeds the amount covered by the insurance policy, the owner of the registered waste deposit site is liable for the additional costs.[630] To permit registered vehicles exclusive entry at waste deposit sites, a means of identification is to be provided by the Director for Waste Strategy Implementation, which must be portrayed by the vehicle at all times. The Director for Waste Strategy Implementation and ERA may refuse to permit the deposit of rubble, waste, and hazardous waste until the fees due are paid after the expiry of a reasonable time limit, which shall not be more than sixty days from the day the first request was made.

419. The contamination of rubble with waste or hazardous waste is an offence under these Regulations. The Regulations are applicable to both private and public entities. Any person who fails to comply with or contravenes the provisions of these Regulations or any order, restriction, prohibition, or requirement given in terms of the provisions of the Regulations is guilty of an offence. Furthermore, any person who conspires, attempts, aids or abets another, by whatever means, to contravene

629. Malta is a Party to both the London Dumping Convention and the Protocol to the Barcelona Convention on the Dumping of Wastes, as amended.

630. Damages would be estimated also on the loss of water production and all remedial works to reverse the damage.

the provisions of these Regulations or any order restriction, prohibition, or requirement given in terms of these Regulations is also guilty of an offence. Upon conviction, the offender is liable to a fine of not less than EUR 1,164.69 but not exceeding EUR 2,329.37, imprisonment for a term not exceeding two years, or both such fine and imprisonment.[631] Furthermore, the court shall order the revocation of the permit issued by the police and the confiscation of the *corpus delicti*.[632] Proceedings for an offence against these Regulations are taken before the Court of Magistrates of Malta (or Gozo).[633] The Attorney General shall always have a right of appeal to the Court of Criminal Appeal from any judgment given by the Court of Magistrates of Malta (or Gozo) in respect of proceedings for any offence against these Regulations.

II. The Waste Regulations

420. The Waste Regulations,[634] issued under the EPA, is a general piece of legislation providing for the permit and control system needed for waste management in Malta. Its objective is to protect the environment and human health through appropriate waste reduction and management techniques, particularly to transition to a circular economy. The permit and control system was previously regulated by the Waste Management (Permit and Control) Regulations,[635] which also transposed the general EU Directive on waste and the hazardous waste Directive, both repealed.[636] The Waste Regulations transpose the provisions of Directive 2008/98/EC, as amended (most recently by Directive (EU) 2018/851), and Article 35 of Directive 2009/31/EC.

421. The Competent Authority is ERA. It is responsible for issuing permits and doing the necessary controls in order to ensure that the operator (permit holder), that is, the person who is involved in waste management, is carrying out such activity without endangering human health or harming the environment. In fact, the Authority, apart from issuing permits, must also plan for the type and quantity of waste to be disposed of, the general technical requirements to do this, the suitable disposal sites to do this in, and arrange for any special arrangements for particular wastes. The Competent Authority is exempt from civil liability under these Regulations. The privilege is limited, however: immunity subsists only in relation to things done reasonably and in good faith in the execution of its duties under the Regulations, as per Regulation 25.

631. If any person found guilty of committing an offence under these Regulations by means of a vehicle, the owner of the said vehicle, where applicable, is held liable in the same manner and degree.
632. Articles 23 and 30(1) of the Criminal Code, Ch. 9 of the Laws of Malta, are to apply; disqualification from holding or obtaining a license, permit, or authority shall in no case be for less than one year.
633. Notwithstanding *ibid.*, Art. 370.
634. L.N. 184/2011 (S.L. 549.63).
635. L.N. 337/2001.
636. Directive 2006/12/EC and Directive 91/689/EEC, respectively.

Furthermore, the Minister responsible for the environment, together with Circular Economy Malta (a government agency) and the Authority, is to establish a number of plans, programmes and registers:

- waste management plans; and
- waste prevention programmes.

These are to be made available to the public electronically. The previous Regulations also provided for a national waste registry, where the public could have access to permit holders (and suspensions and revocations of permits), convictions under the Regulations and authorised officials, among others. However, this system was not carried over to the new Waste Regulations.

Finally, the Regulations set up a Waste Management Fund, composed of funds listed in Schedule 11 (essentially revenue through fines, fees and out-of-court settlements), which are to be used for waste management purposes.

422. The Regulations provide for a hierarchy of waste to be enforced in all waste management legislation and policy. The order of priority, in descending order, is: prevention, preparing for reuse, recycling, other recovery, and disposal. In applying the hierarchy, the Minister, in consultation with ERA and the Agency, must take measures to encourage the options that deliver the best overall environmental outcome. He must also take into account the general environmental protection principles of precaution and sustainability, technical feasibility and economic viability, protection of resources, and the overall impacts on the environment, human health, the economy and society. The Regulations also contemplate and require the application of the principles of self-sufficiency and proximity in terms of waste disposal and recovery systems, taking BAT into account. The aim is to make the EU as a whole self-sufficient in waste management and to enable Malta to move towards that aim individually – this does not mean, however, that the full range of recovery facilities are located in Malta.

423. The waste management control system is divided into two depending on the activity performed: collection and transport of waste and waste treatment (which includes storage pending recovery or disposal operations). The latter requires a permit to be issued by the Authority, which, *inter alia*, is to specify the type and quantity of waste to be treated, methodology of the operation, precautions, monitoring and closure and after-care provisions. Permits may be refused, varied, suspended, or terminated, as detailed in the Regulations. The permit holder is legally responsible for ensuring that his waste management activity is carried out in accordance with the Regulations and the permit provisions. Employees of the permit holder can also perform the permitted activities, provided they act on his behalf and within the remit of his own duties and obligations. Furthermore, they must be duly qualified following a course with a duration and curriculum approved by the Authority.

The former activities require no permit so long as they are performed on a professional basis, but a registry of persons performing them is to be held. The same applies to dealers, brokers and waste treatment operations. All these persons must be duly qualified, as explained above.

424. All persons involved in the waste management system mentioned above are subject to periodical inspections by the Authority. In relation to waste collection and transport operations, inspections cover the origin, nature, quantity and destination of the relevant waste. Waste treatment operators must also keep a chronological record of the quantity, nature and origin of the waste, and the quantity of materials and products resulting from preparing for reuse, recycling or other recovery operations, as well as the destination, frequency, mode of transport and treatment method foreseen where necessary. All this data is to be made available to the Authority through an established electronic registry. Furthermore, waste treatment operators, and dealers and brokers of waste must submit annual audit reports to the Authority.

425. The Regulations place a duty on every person to separate their recyclable waste at source prior to their separate collection. The applicable waste streams are paper, metal, plastic, glass, bio-waste, and any other waste stream determined by the Minister. If the waste is generated in public places, this obligation subsists only insofar as bins for the separate collection of the waste in question are available. The relevant legal provision, Regulation 12A, was added in 2023, and so the enforcement of its provisions will be introduced in a phased approach by means of a Government Notice in the Government Gazette.

426. These Regulations also pay special attention to hazardous waste. In fact, producers, dealers and brokers of hazardous waste and professional collectors and transporters of hazardous waste must keep the same records as waste treatment operators in relation to that waste. These records are to be preserved for at least three years, and an electronic registry is to be set up by the Authority to record that data for the entire geographical territory of Malta. Producers of hazardous waste are also to be subject to periodic inspections. Holders of hazardous waste must also keep a precise plan of where they are storing the different kinds of waste and identify them appropriately. Furthermore, hazardous waste and non-hazardous waste are not to be mixed unless the mixture does not increase the harm or if such a mixture would improve the safety during disposal or recovery or if such mixing was approved prior to the mixing of the waste. Hazardous waste is to be securely packaged and labelled in accordance with national and international standards. In addition, hazardous waste being transferred within Maltese territory or waters must be accompanied by a consignment note issued by the Competent Authority, which note may also be required for non-hazardous waste. The Competent Authority will charge a processing fee to cover expenses incurred in assessing and processing applications, the issue of permits, processing coded consignments notes, and any other services.

427. The Waste Regulations mostly deal with the permits required for disposing of waste, hazardous or otherwise (as laid down in the schedules), as well as the controls needed to ensure that the conditions of the permits and the regulations are being respected. Consequently, they also include the punishments and penalties applicable for the infringement of such regulations. The punishments and penalties laid down in the regulations can be divided into those which are of an administrative nature and those which are of a criminal nature. Punishments of an administrative nature include all those measures taken by the Competent Authority when the conditions of a permit or the regulations are not observed. Such administrative sanctions include the refusal to grant (or renew) a permit in the cases where an applicant fails to provide the necessary information required for the Authority's inquiries. Nevertheless, we find that the Regulations provide the permit holder with an opportunity to remedy any infringement of the conditions of his permit or of the Waste Regulations in general. This is provided through an Order specified within Regulation 23(3), which may be issued by the Competent Authority. However, sub-Regulation (4) of this Regulation provides that if the permit holder fails to adhere to the enforcement or remedial notice, the Competent Authority may revoke the permit, wholly or in part, as well as take the remedial action required itself, putting the burden of all expenses incurred on the permit holder's financial assurance. This is a very relevant step in conformity with the 'polluter-pays principle'. It is also very important to note that sub-Regulation (5) of this same regulation allows the Competent Authority to bring into effect any punitive measures specified therein, including confiscation of all or part of the financial assurance.

The Regulations consider certain infringements of the Regulations to be criminal offences subject to criminal proceedings. A person shall be guilty of an offence under these Regulations in the cases mentioned in Regulation 34. Sub-regulation (e) of this Regulation also specifies that even conspiring, attempting, aiding, or abetting any other person to infringe these Regulations makes one guilty of an offence. The punishments and penalties applicable on conviction are specified under Regulation 35 and consist, on a first conviction, of a fine (*multa*) of not less than EUR 1,165.00 but not exceeding EUR 2,330.00 and, in the case of a second or subsequent conviction, of a higher fine (*multa*) of not less than EUR 2,330.00 but not exceeding EUR 4,660.00 or imprisonment not exceeding two years, or both such fine and imprisonment. Other penalties comprise paying for the expenses incurred by the Competent Authority, revocation of the permit and confiscation of the *corpus delicti*, including the vehicle if it was used to commit the offence. Articles 23 (forfeiture of *corpus delicti*) and 30 (disqualification in case of conviction) of the Criminal Code are applicable to proceedings for offences under the Regulations. The court may decide to order a person who has committed an offence to be disqualified from holding or obtaining a license, warrant, permit, or authority for a certain period of time as decided by the same court. Additionally, the court may, on application by such person, either remove the suspension or disqualification or refuse the application. Proceedings for such offences are to be held before the Court of Magistrates of Malta (or Gozo), although the punishment applicable would otherwise exceed the competence of that court in terms of Article 370 of the Criminal Code (offences recognisable by the Court of Magistrates as a court of criminal judicature). The Attorney General is given the right of appeal from all judgments by the competent court under the Regulations to the Court of Criminal Appeal.

428. L.N. 106/2007, the Waste Management (Activity Registration) Regulations,[637] provides additional measures, procedures, and guidance to those regulations in the Waste Regulations. L.N. 106/2007 was brought into force by means of L.N. 230/2007 in August of 2007.[638] It tackles a number of specific waste streams, which are mainly contained in Schedule I of these Regulations. The permission granted under these Regulations shall only be granted for the specified activity, and this shall not include any other indirect activity related or ancillary thereto. Moreover, such permission shall only be executed by the specified parties; if executed by third parties, the law shall not exempt liability or responsibility, especially when contravening any provision of law.[639] This permission shall be granted in conjunction with any other permit or licence specified in Regulation 3(3). However, such permission 'shall not apply if it runs counter to policies or plans or legislation or policy guidance approved according to the [Environment Protection] Act' 'or the DPA'.[640]

429. The Competent Authority for the adoption and implementation of these Regulations is ERA. The Authority must be notified prior to the commencement of any work in an application form provided by the Authority itself. This form shall be accompanied by a description of the proposed activity, the established fee, if any, two good-quality colour photographs representative of the site on which the activity is to be carried out, if any, and other relevant documentation as provided in the Regulations or as the Authority may deem necessary.[641] Moreover, it shall also include the full nature and extent of the activity, the class of Schedule I permitting such activity, all previous permits, applications and notifications affecting the activity, and all the information as requested in Schedule II of the same Legal Notice.[642] As stipulated in Regulation 5(2), a notification to the Authority 'may cover activities which fall into more than one class or paragraph within a class where these are to be carried out on the same site, or are consequential to each other'.[643] In addition, such activities may only be carried out by the same applicant.

After such application being received from the applicant and where it is provided in the regulations set out in this Legal Notice, the Authority shall respond in writing to this notification, also sending a copy of the document on which the proposed activity is described. Regulation 5(3)(b) states that if an activity is not permitted, the Authority shall give detailed reasons for such a decision, while if the activity is permitted, it shall be valid for a period of one calendar year commencing on the date on which the official endorsement by the Authority is issued. Besides having a valid permit, a waste producer must have a consignment note (during transfer) in order to

637. S.L. 549.45.
638. L.N. 230/2007 – Commencement Notice of the Waste Management (Activity Registration) Regulations.
639. L.N. 106/2007, Waste Management (Activity Registration) Regulations, Reg. 3(2).
640. *Ibid.*, Reg. 3(5).
641. *Ibid*, Reg. 5(1).
642. *Ibid.*
643. *Ibid.*, Reg. 5(2).

dispose of/transport his waste. These notes must accompany waste, which consists of hazardous, biodegradable, or non-hazardous waste. The consignment note procedure is divided into two stages:

(1) Stage One: Waste Consignment Permit Application (CP); and
(2) Stage Two: Waste Consignment Note (CN).

All Waste Consignment Permit Applications (CP) and Waste Consignment Notes (CN) have a unique number (code) allocated by the Competent Authority. The Waste Consignment Permit Application (CP) is used in order to obtain a permit for the disposal of waste, while the Waste Consignment Notes (CN) must be used for the transfer of waste.

The provision found in Regulation 5(5) tackles situations where an activity has been carried out without notification required in accordance with sub-regulation (1). In such an instance, if the activity 'complies fully with the relevant exceptions, limitations and conditions specified in these Regulations',[644] it shall be treated as though ERA was notified of it prior to its commencement as indicated in sub-Regulation (1). However, the following subsection provides situations where the Authority shall have the right to stop any activity or work or to take enforcement or other action in accordance with the EPA. Moreover, the Authority has the power to stop the activity or take enforcement action if the permit validity has expired; that is, one calendar year has passed or after the regulations which permit such execution have been repealed. This L.N. is an extension to the provisions laid down under the Waste Regulations. In fact, it is completely focused on the details and requirements needed in order to obtain a permit or consignment note. No penalty sections are present because the aim of these Regulations is to start the setup for the adoption and implementation of the permit and control system needed for waste management.

III. Specific Sectors of Waste

430. Other specific laws regulate specific sectors of waste. These will be reviewed in this subsection. The laws tend to make additional provision to the Waste Regulations, which, as noted in the previous subsection, are a general piece of legislation.

431. L.N. 311/2007, the Batteries and Accumulators Regulations,[645] adopted under the Product Safety Act,[646] implements the provisions of Directive 2006/66/EC, as amended. This Directive repeals Directive 91/157/EEC duly adopted under Maltese law by means of L.N. 158/2002, Waste Management (Batteries and Accumulators) Regulations.[647] The aim of the new Batteries Directive is to promote a less polluted environment by minimising harmful substances in batteries. In fact, it

644. *Ibid.*, Reg. 5(5).
645. S.L. 427.08.
646. Chapter 427 of the Laws of Malta.
647. Revoked by L.N. 55/2010, Waste Management (Batteries and Accumulators) Regulations.

covers a wider range of products than Directive 91/157/EEC, which applied only to batteries containing mercury, lead or cadmium and excluded 'button cells', but otherwise, the waste management provisions existent in the previous Directive have been restated. L.N. 311/2007 prohibits from the market:

- batteries and accumulators, whether or not incorporated in appliances, containing more than 0.0005% by weight of mercury (except for button cells, which must have a mercury content of less than 2% by weight until 1 October 2015);
- portable batteries and accumulators, including those incorporated in appliances, with a cadmium content by weight of more than 0.002% of weight by cadmium (except for portable batteries and accumulators for use in emergency and alarm systems, medical equipment). Until 31 December 2016, cordless power tools using such devices were also exempted.

Regulation 6 lays down the labelling requirements and provides that all batteries, accumulators, and battery packs shall be appropriately marked with a symbol shown in the First Schedule attached to these Regulations. The Competent Authority responsible for such labelling is the Director General (Technical Regulations) as detailed in the Product Safety Act. The Regulations require manufacturers to promote and improve the overall environmental performance of batteries and accumulators, as well as develop ones with smaller quantities of dangerous or polluting substances. Furthermore, they are to develop appliances in a manner that allows waste batteries and accumulators to be readily removed by the end user. Where this is not possible, they are to be at least readily removable by qualified professionals independent of the manufacturer. In any case, the appliance must be accompanied by instructions on how to remove the batteries or accumulators. The only exception is where continuity of power supply is necessary, and a permanent connection between battery/accumulator and appliance is required on the grounds of safety, performance, medical or integrity reasons. All products meeting the requirements of the Regulations are allowed to be placed on the market, except those which were lawfully there prior to the respective prohibitive provisions until stocks are exhausted.

432. The control and disposal of batteries and accumulators are regulated by L.N. 55/2010, the Waste Management (Waste Batteries and Accumulators) Regulations.[648] This Legal Notice has been adopted under the EPA and is ancillary to L.N. 337/2001 (Waste Regulations) in that it provides additional measures, procedures, and guidance relating to the recovery, control and disposal of spent batteries and accumulators.

433. The Competent Authority responsible for the implementation of these Regulations is ERA. It must monitor compliance with established collection targets on a yearly basis as set out in Schedule 1 to these Regulations. It is responsible for registration of producers and for the upkeep of the register of producers, and it shall process the necessary permits for the operation of a waste batteries and accumulators collection, treatment, and recycling scheme. Together with this, the producers

648. S.L. 549.54.

are obliged to provide the Authority with the required information and reporting. The Competent Authority shall make this information available in accordance with the Freedom of Access to Information on the Environment Regulations. For the purpose of achieving the objectives and satisfying the provisions of these Regulations, economic operators may be parties to agreements with the Competent Authority, which agreements shall specify the detailed rules of implementation of these Regulations.

434. Otherwise, most of the obligations enlisted under these Regulations have to be followed by:

- The producers of portable batteries and accumulators, who are obliged to use existing collection systems or set up collection systems in order to provide for the collection of such portable batteries and accumulators, and they shall finance any net costs arising from the collection, treatment and recycling of all waste portable batteries and accumulators, industrial and automotive batteries and accumulators collected in accordance with these Regulations. They must also use the services of an independent auditor, approved by the Authority, to certify all information they report.
- The manufacturers who are obliged to design appliances in such a way that waste batteries and accumulators can be readily removed.

Furthermore, these economic operators must ensure that end-users are fully informed, among other things, about the potential effects on the environment and human health of the substances used in batteries and accumulators and about the collection systems and treatment and recycling systems available to them. Additionally, these Regulations encourage the development of new recycling and treatment technologies for waste batteries and accumulators and research into environmentally friendly and cost-effective recycling methods for all types of waste batteries and accumulators shall be promoted. Economic instruments may be used to promote the use of batteries and accumulators containing less polluting substances or promote the collection of waste batteries and accumulators, for instance, by adopting differential tax rates. These Regulations prohibit the disposal in landfills or by incineration of waste industrial and automotive batteries and accumulators unless such residues of waste batteries and accumulators have undergone both treatment and recycling in accordance with the Regulations. The treatment and recycling may be undertaken outside Malta or outside the Community, provided that the shipment of waste batteries and accumulators must comply with Regulation (EC) No. 1013/2006.[649]

435. Sanctions in cases of offences against the provisions of this Legal Notice are laid down under Regulation 26. These offences are the following:

649. Regulation (EC) No. 1013/2006 of the European Parliament and the Council of 14 Jun. 2006 on shipments of waste.

- failing to comply with any of the Regulations laid down, with permit conditions, or with any lawful order under these Regulations;
- contravening any restriction, prohibition, or requirement of these Regulations;
- acting in contravention of the provisions of these Regulations; and
- planning, attempting or helping any other person to commit any breaches as set out above.

Whenever a person is guilty of any of the above Regulations, Regulation 27 prescribes various sanctions:

- on a first conviction, a fine (*multa*) of between EUR 1,164.69 and EUR 2,329.37; and
- on a second or subsequent conviction, a fine of between EUR 2,329.37 and EUR 4,658.75, or imprisonment not exceeding two years, or both.

The Regulations also provide that vehicles used while contravening these Regulations shall be confiscated; the owner of the vehicle is to be held responsible as much as the person guilty of contravention; permits issued may be revoked; and the guilty persons shall be required to pay the cost of any expenses incurred by the Competent Authorities as a result of their offence. Furthermore, the provisions of Articles 23 and 30 of the Criminal Code shall regulate the proceedings in cases of offences against the Regulations.

436. Another type of waste being regulated is that of polychlorinated biphenyls (PCBs) and polychlorinated terphenyls (PCTs). The PCB and PCT Directive (96/59/EC) has been adopted under Maltese law, mainly under the EPA, by means of L.N. 166/2002, the Waste Management (Polychlorinated Biphenyls and Polychlorinated Terphenyls) Regulations.[650] These Regulations also provide additional measures, procedures, and guidance to those in the Waste Regulations on the controlled disposal of PCBs and PCTs, the decontamination or disposal of equipment containing PCBs, and/or the disposal of used PCBs in order to eliminate them completely.

437. The Competent Authority for the monitoring of this type of waste is ERA. This must ensure that holders of used PCBs and/or equipment containing PCBs decontaminate or dispose of them as soon as possible but not later than 31 December 2010. For this purpose, the Competent Authority has to establish an inventory and all holders of equipment containing PCB volumes greater than 5 dm^3 shall submit to the Competent Authority all the relevant information as stipulated under these same Regulations. Furthermore, the holder of such equipment must inform the Competent Authority of any changes, and the latter shall update this inventory on a regular basis. Apart from the inventory, the Competent Authority is also responsible for issuing permits to all undertakings engaged in the decontamination and, or disposal of PCBs, used PCBs and/or equipment containing PCBs in accordance with the Waste Regulations. Together with the permit, the person who undertakes to carry out disposal of PCBs shall keep registers of the quantity, origin, nature, and PCB

---

650. S.L. 549.28.

content of used PCBs delivered to him and make available this information to the Competent Authority, the Local Authorities, and the general public, upon request. Finally, the Authority is to draw up plans for the decontamination and/or disposal of inventoried equipment and PCBs contained in them, as well as outlines for the collection and subsequent disposal of equipment not subject to inventory.

438. The separation of PCBs from other substances for the purpose of reusing the PCBs, the topping up of transformers with PCBs, the incineration of PCBs and/or used PCBs on ships, the landfilling of PCBs, and equipment containing PCBs are all prohibited. Apart from these prohibitions, other obligations have to be observed, such as continued maintenance of transformers containing PCBs until they are decontaminated, and decontamination conditions have to be followed when the transformers contain more than 0.05% by weight of PCBs. If all these obligations are not followed, then the person concerned shall be guilty of an offence under these Regulations. Such person shall, upon conviction, be liable on a first conviction to a fine (*multa*) between EUR 1,164.69 and EUR 2,329.37; and on a second or subsequent conviction to a fine of between EUR 2,329.37 and EUR 4,658.75 or imprisonment not exceeding two years, or both. Moreover, vehicles used while contravening these Regulations shall be confiscated; the owner of the vehicle to be held responsible as much as the person guilty of contravention; permits issued may be revoked; and the guilty persons shall be required to pay the cost of any expenses incurred by the Competent Authorities as a result of their offence, the revocation of the permit and the confiscation of the *corpus delicti*. The provisions of Articles 23 and 30 of the Criminal Code shall regulate the proceedings in cases of offences against the regulations.

439. Waste management for end-of-life vehicles is regulated by L.N. 99/2004, the Waste Management (End of Life Vehicles) Regulations.[651] This Legal Notice fully adopts the provisions of EU Directive 2000/53/EC of 18 September 2000, relating to the Waste Management of the End of Life Vehicles, as amended. The primary aim of these Regulations is to prevent waste from vehicles by reusing, recycling, and recovering (usually referred to as the '3 Rs') in order to minimise the discard of waste. In addition, this law seeks to improve the performance of such economic operators involved with the life cycle of the vehicles, as well as the operators charged with the disposal and treatment of end-of-life vehicles in an environmentally friendly way. Thus, this Regulation tackles both the periodic lifetime of the vehicle regardless of its date of being put into the market while taking into consideration the safety standards, air emissions, and noise controls, together with the protection of soil and water on the eventual disposal of the vehicle. One must keep in mind that this law addresses those motor vehicles which hold a maximum of eight passengers besides the driver and those used in the transportation of goods. However, the regulation specifically excludes vintage cars, bearing in mind these are rarely discarded. Nonetheless, when they are discarded, they would then fall under this law.

651. S.L. 549.36.

440. The Regulations are directed at the economic operators, which include various entities involved in the whole process from production to disposal of the vehicle. The law requires such entities to hold a permit in line with the Waste Regulations, in conformity with Schedule 3 of L.N. 99/2004. It highlights a minimum technical requirement for the treatment of such vehicles, which includes the dismantling and separating of components and materials which are hazardous from those which are not. This is done in view of the latter being reused, recovered, and recycled. Moreover, such establishments and undertakings shall make use of Certified Environmental Management Systems when implementing treatment operations. The law stresses the '3 Rs' in the economic operators' performance, but this should not be done to the detriment of the environment. The specific goals to be reached by these economic operators go up in stages from a minimum of 85% reused and recovered vehicles by 1 January 2006, reaching 95% by the end of 2014. Furthermore, lower targets have been set out for the reuse and recycling of vehicles and even lower targets for vehicles produced before 1980.

The economic operators referred to above include the producers as well as the material and equipment manufacturers specifically mentioned in Regulation 8. The said provision points out that such operators must use coding standards to easily identify the components suitable for their reuse and recovery. Such relevant information must be available to the public within six months of the model being introduced on the market. In addition, potential buyers must have access to information on the design and components of vehicles, their environmentally sound treatment of dismantling, and the best way of reusing, recovering, and recycling the components. The public shall also be informed of any progress reached in methods of treatment. All of this must be made available in all marketing strategies used to promote the vehicles. The economic operators are given the opportunity, through Regulation 10, to form part of any agreements, objectives, and deadlines implemented in the regulations enforceable at law. The agreement must be published in the Government Gazette, and any results achieved shall be monitored regularly, reported to the competent authorities, and made available to the public.

441. The role of official regulator is divided between three Authorities, depending on their designated responsibilities. These are ERA, the MCCAA and the Authority for Transport in Malta. They are to encourage manufacturers to limit and decrease the use of harmful substances which would have a negative impact on the environment and stress the use of recycled material. Thus, they specifically take into consideration the important principles of implementing the '3 Rs'. Specific substances, including lead, mercury, cadmium, and hexavalent chromium, are the hazardous substances listed which must not be used except in certain unavoidable instances provided for in the law. They should also make sure that the economic operators use any system available for the collection of these vehicles' waste, and as Authorities, they must provide for the availability of such collection facilities. The responsible Authority may exempt any economic operator from part or all of these Regulations, provided he presents a signed agreement with an authorised operator for the collection and treatment of the vehicle. The latter operator must hold a valid permit issued in accordance with a number of formalities stated in the law. The Competent Authority has the duty to make the information about the environment public in accordance with the Freedom of Access to Information on the Environment Regulations.

442. The law also addresses the owner/holder of the vehicle whereby, in order to strike off a vehicle from the register, he must present a certificate of destruction issued by an authorised treatment facility on transfer of the vehicle. The holder does not have any compensation in performing such a duty, except when specifically provided for by the Authority; however, any costs incurred during the delivery of such vehicle will not be suffered by the owner/holder. Furthermore, a proviso states that if a vehicle does not contain the essentials, the responsible Authority may issue a charge on the owner/holder.

443. The law concludes with a number of penalties for failing to comply with this Regulation, with the necessary permit requirements, as well as if any one contravenes any condition imposed. Punishment stands for anyone who conspires, attempts, aids, or abets any other person to contravene these Regulations. On a first conviction, the person is liable to a fine (*multa*) ranging from EUR 1,164.69 to EUR 2,329.37. On any following convictions, the fine (*multa*) would be between EUR 2,329.37 and EUR 4,658.75 and/or imprisonment for less than two years. Moreover, any expenses suffered by the Competent Authority as a result of the offence may also be imposed on the offender. The permit may be revoked, and any *corpus delicti* confiscated. The Regulations conclude with the applicability of the Criminal Code, as per Articles 30 and 23, respectively, and Regulation 16 specifies that any disqualification of a license, permit, or authority shall be for at least one year.

444. If the electrical and electronic waste is not landfilled nor incinerated or not even recovered without any pre-treatment, the pollutants could be released into the environment and contaminate air, water, and soil. This issue is tackled by the Waste Management (Electrical and Electronic Equipment) Regulations,[652] which revoked and replaced previous eponymous Regulations on the matter.[653] The older Regulations transposed the provisions of Directive 2002/96/EC of 27 January 2003 on waste electrical and electronic equipment (WEEE) into Maltese law, which itself was repealed by Directive 2012/19/EC of 4 July 2012 on the same subject, now transposed under the new operative Maltese Regulations. The Regulations have applied to all WEEE as of 15 August 2015, as per the transitory provision on its application to specific types of WEEE. Schedule 3 provides for the categories of classification of WEEE, with Schedule 4 providing a non-exhaustive list of electrical and electronic equipment (EEE) encompassed within Schedule 3.

The Competent Authority is ERA, which has the general duty of overseeing the proper implementation of the Regulations and adopting measures to minimise the disposal of WEEE, properly treat collected WEEE and achieve high levels of separate collection of WEEE. It must also ensure the availability of necessary collection

652. L.N. 204/2014 (S.L. 549.89).
653. L.N. 63/2007, Waste Management (Electrical and Electronic Equipment) Regulations.

facilities. Additionally, it is to conduct inspections and monitoring to ensure implementation of the Regulations, and all information required to be submitted to it must be certified by an auditor approved by it. Finally, it is under a duty to cooperate and facilitate the flow of information between Member States in order to implement the Directive. The fulfilment of ERA's obligations allows it to conclude agreements with economic operators in order to achieve the objectives of the Regulations. The form, content and duties tied to these agreements are detailed in the Regulations and are enforceable at law, allowing the Authority to examine their progress directly. One should also note that the responsible Minister may provide economic incentives for the application of the waste hierarchy in order to contribute to the objectives of these Regulations pursuant to the Waste Regulations.

445. The main obligations have to be followed by producers, authorised representatives, and third parties acting on behalf of producers. Under the Regulations, producers include importers of EEE as well as manufacturers.[654] In fact, collection targets are established under the Regulations according to the producer responsibility principle, which must be met by producers or third parties. These take the form of percentages calculated as stipulated, provided for each year. Furthermore, minimum recovery targets are laid down in Schedule 5, calculated as stipulated, and all information required for the calculation must be kept by the producers or third parties acting on behalf of producers or authorised representatives. If the WEEE is from private households, those three types of persons must ensure: systems to return waste free of charge; and that distributors are responsible for the return of waste to the distributor free of charge on a one-to-one basis when supplying a new product so long as the equipment is of equivalent type and fulfils the same functions as the supplied equipment. They are allowed to set up and operate individual and/or collective take-back systems so long as these are in line with the objectives of the Regulations. Furthermore, if the WEEE presents a health and safety risk to personnel due to contamination, it can be refused for return. ERA can designate which operators can collect WEEE from private households. If the WEEE is not from private households, the producers or third parties acting on their behalf are to provide for the collection of the waste.

The disposal of WEEE is prohibited if it has not undergone treatment. As a minimum, where preparation for reuse is not required, treatment is to include the removal of all fluids and a selective treatment according to Schedule 7. ERA is to ensure that producers or third parties set up systems for recovery using the best available technologies, individually or collectively. The technical requirements are laid down in Schedule 8, and the Authority can establish minimum quality standards for environmental protection as well as encourage certified environmental management systems according to Regulation (EC) No. 1221/2009 on the voluntary participation by organisations in a Community eco-management and audit scheme. It is possible to ship WEEE for treatment outside Malta, so long as this is in accordance with Regulation (EC) No. 1013/2006 and Commission Regulation

654. In Malta, these Regulations are more applicable to importers of electrical and electronic equipment since actual manufacturers do not exist.

(EC) No. 1418/2007. Producers or authorised representatives must finance the collection, treatment, recovery and environmentally sound disposal of WEEE from private households. Where the waste is from other sources, the obligation remains the same. However, WEEE resulting from products placed on the market before 13 August 2005: if the waste was replaced by new equivalent products or products fulfilling the same function, the burden is to be borne by the producers or authorised representatives; if not, the financing falls to the users themselves. The producers or authorised representatives must provide a guarantee, when placing products on the market, for the financing of the management of all WEEE related to his product. The guarantee is to take the form of either a recycling insurance or a blocked bank account submitted to the Authority upon registration or renewal. Persons are exempt from the guarantee requirement if they are members of waste electrical and electronic compliance schemes. The producer or authorised representative is to provide all information related to WEEE to users of EEE in private households supplied by them. Furthermore, when placing new products (EEE) on the market, information regarding preparation for reuse and treatment must be provided by the producer. Finally, the transfer of a producer's business to another does not obviate his responsibilities under the Regulations for EEE in respect of which he has made an application to register unless he can prove, to ERA's satisfaction, that the transferee has agreed to meet the producer's responsibilities in relation to those products.

446. Permits must be acquired according to Regulations 19–24 of the Waste Regulations by any establishment or undertaking carrying out treatment operations. The permit is to include all conditions necessary for compliance with the proper treatment requirements and the achievement of the recovery targets. ERA is to keep a general register of producers, including substantiated estimates on an annual basis of EEE placed on their markets and other information to monitor compliance with the requirements of the Regulations. It is the duty of the producer or authorised representative to register upon placing EEE on the market for the first time and to renew his permit annually. Part A of Schedule 9 details the information to be supplied upon application for registration, while Part B of the same contains the information required for renewal. Furthermore, those persons are to apply for deregistration when they cease to place products on the market. Failure to register or renew is a criminal offence entailing fines (multi) calculated per tonne of EEE placed on the market. In the case of failure to register, the time runs from the date of the first placement of the product on the market until he applies for registration. In the case of failure to renew, this runs from the beginning of the year, when he should have renewed, until he applies for renewal.

447. Reference was made above to the possibility of producers, etc., establishing collective organisations. These WEEE collective organisations require a separate permit to operate and, therefore, to collect, store, sort, treat, export and recycle WEEE. The application requires certain specific information, such as the Memorandum and Articles of Association, the financial plan and annual stipulated targets. The collective organisations also have certain specified duties in terms of reporting and compliance. A producer opting to participate in such an organisation is to submit a copy of the agreement with the organisation upon ERA's request. Such a producer will then be exempt from part of these Regulations.

448. Offences under these Regulations are the following: failure to comply with the Regulations, the permit conditions, or lawfully given orders; when any conditions, limitations, or prohibitions are contravened; acting in contravention to any provision of the Regulations; when there is a conspiracy to contravene the provisions of these Regulations; or, aiding or abetting another to contravene the Regulations or fail to comply with them or any lawful order given under them. A first conviction for an offence under the Regulations entails a fine (*multa*) between EUR 1,164.69 and EUR 2,329.37. A second conviction entails a higher fine (*multa*) of between EUR 2,329.37 and EUR 4,658.75 or imprisonment for a term not exceeding two years, or both fine and imprisonment. The person committing an offence by making use of a vehicle shall also be liable in the same way. As a result, the *corpus delicti*, including the vehicle, can be seized. Since permits in such offences can also be classified as *corpus delicti*, they can also be subjected to confiscation. Furthermore, the convicted person can be ordered to pay for the expenses incurred by ERA as a result of the offence.

Reference is also made to Articles 23 and 30 of the Criminal Code. Article 23 refers to the *corpus delicti*. It states that if the instrument of the crime is co-owned, then it is possible that this is not confiscated. Furthermore, it makes a distinction between contraventions and offences. This is so because, in case of offences, the instrument can be seized, even though it is not expressly laid down in the law. This is in opposition to contraventions since it is necessary that this should be provided for in the law. This similarly applies to these Regulations. On the other hand, Article 30, among other things, deals with the prohibition of permits and licenses. The government or a Competent Authority may cancel a permit when an offence has been committed. This offence can be committed either when one is exercising his profession or else by making use of transport or materials in order to carry around equipment, in this case, EEE. In such cases, apart from being charged with a punishment, there will also be the suspension of their permits or licenses and so on, which enabled them to carry out their work for a period of time. But due attention is given to the offender's behaviour after having committed the offence, together with the nature of the offence committed and any other circumstances. After hearing either the police or the Attorney General, the court may decide to remove the suspension of the said permit or license. However, if the court refuses, one is to attempt this again after three months and not before. The court hearing is to take place either in front of the Court of Magistrates of Malta (or Gozo). These are to comply with the provisions of the Criminal Code. The Attorney General shall always have a right to appeal with respect to these Regulations.

449. Another piece of subsidiary legislation which must be read together with L.N. 204/2014 is L.N. 84/2013, the Restriction of Use of Hazardous Substances in

Electrical and Electronic Equipment Regulations,[655] which revoked the eponymous Regulations of 2004.[656] These Regulations transpose Directive 2011/65/EU of the European Parliament and of the Council of 8 June 2011 on the restriction of the use of certain hazardous substances in electrical equipment (recast), as amended. These Regulations were issued under the Product Safety Act and provide that new electrical and electronic equipment put on the market shall not contain lead, mercury, cadmium, hexavalent chromium, polybrominated biphenyls (PBB), polybrominated diphenyl ethers (PBDE), bis(2-ethylhexyl) phthalate (DEHP), benzyl butyl phthalate (BBP), dibutyl phthalate (DBP) and diisobutyl phthalate (DIBP) in excess of the levels which are deemed hazardous for the purpose of these Regulations.[657] However, these exemptions are being gradually phased out. Certain electrical and electronic devices placed on the market before specific dates are exempt from these restrictions.

450. The Competent Authority is the Technical Regulations Division within the MCCAA, which is to ensure that EEE is placed on the market with the symbol shown in Schedule 7 in order to minimise the disposal of WEEE as unsorted municipal waste and to facilitate its separate collection. The symbol is referred to as a CE marking, which indicates the product's conformity with the applicable requirements in the European harmonising legislation providing for its affixing. The CE marking is subject to the general principles set out in Article 30 of Regulation (EC) No. 765/2008. It must be affixed legibly, visibly and indelibly to the finished EEE or its data plate, though it may be so affixed to the packaging and accompanying documents if this is not possible or not warranted due to the nature of the EEE. In any case, it must be duly affixed before the EEE is placed on the market. There is a presumption of conformity with the Regulations if an EEE bears a CE marking. As part of its role in ensuring compliance with the Regulations, the Division is to perform market surveillance in accordance with Articles 15–29 of Regulation (EC) No. 765/2008.

451. Obligations are imposed on manufacturers, authorised representatives, importers, and distributors of EEE, with the Division responsible for ensuring compliance with those obligations. Manufacturers must ensure, among other things, that EEE placed on the market are designed and manufactured according to the Regulations, draw up the required technical documentation and carry out the internal production control procedure in line with module A of Annex II to Decision No. 768/2008/EC; draw up an EU declaration of conformity[658] and affix the CE marking on the product; ensure their EEE is identifiable (such as through a serial number); ensure their information and contact details are on the EEE; and take correctional measures if they suspect non-compliance of their products with the Regulations.

655. S.L. 427.57.

656. L.N. 396/2004, Restriction of Use of Hazardous Substances in Electrical and Electronic Equipment Regulations.

657. Regulation 4 on Prevention. The list of substances and their maximum allowed concentrations is found in Sch. 2.

658. This is to declare that the substance restrictions have been observed and is to be made in the form and manner provided in Sch. 6.

Authorised representatives can be appointed by a mandate by the manufacturer and are subject to the same obligations as their principal, being required to comply with the Regulations in the same manner.

Importers must, *inter alia*, only place compliant EEE on the EU market after having undergone the appropriate conformity assessment procedure by the manufacturer and the latter has complied with all his obligations; ensure his contact details and information are on the EEE; and ensure corrective measures as explained. Distributors must generally verify compliance with the EEE and only place compliant products on the market, as well as ensure correctional measures in case of suspected non-compliance. Importers and distributors are considered manufacturers, with all the obligations this entails, if they place EEE on the market under their names or trademarks or if they modify any EEE already on the market in a way that may affect compliance. Furthermore, all economic operators must indicate any operator who has supplied them with EEE and any operator to whom they have supplied EEE to the Division for ten years following the placing of the EEE on the market.

452. According to the Product Safety Act, the power of enforcement of the provisions of the Act or of the Regulations made thereunder shall vest in the Director General (Technical Regulations), provided that the Director may delegate in writing any of the powers vested in him by virtue of this Act to any public officer, or, with the consent of the Minister, to any other person being a person employed by a body corporate established by law or a person falling within such category. Furthermore, officers who are in possession of a warrant from the Magistrate's Court may enter and search premises and carry out therein any inspection as may be necessary and seize any unsafe products found therein. And if the Director suspects that such unsafe products are likely to be removed, destroyed, or the evidence of the commission of any offence under this Act may be otherwise suppressed, he may himself, in writing, authorise any public officer to carry out such inspection on the premises and if need be seize the unsafe products.

453. The provisions on general offences laid down mainly under Article 12 of the Act[659] are also applicable to these Regulations, as well as the offences referred to under Article 23.[660] Part IV of the Act lays down the proceedings which have to be followed once an offence under the Article or of the regulations issued under it is being alleged by the Director or any one of his duly authorised officers. In case where a person is found guilty of an offence under Article 23, the penalty varies from a fine (*multa*) of not less than EUR 465.87 and not exceeding EUR 2,329.37 or imprisonment for a term not exceeding six months or both such fine and imprisonment. A person found guilty of any other offence under this Act shall be liable,

659. These general offences are related to the selling, hiring, exposure, or being in possession for the purpose of such sale and so forth of any product which does not comply with the provisions of the Act or of any regulation made under it.

660. Article 23 stipulates that: 'Whosoever shall wilfully obstruct, resist, threaten or otherwise give misleading or false information to the Director or to an authorized officer in the exercise of any of the functions mentioned in Art. 15, or wilfully fails to assist or comply with any requirement lawfully made by such officer, shall be guilty of an offence under this Act.'

on conviction, to a fine (*multa*) of not less than EUR 1,164.69 but not exceeding 11,646.87 or imprisonment for a term not exceeding three years or both such fine and imprisonment. Any second or subsequent offences shall entail a penalty of a fine (*multa*) of not less than EUR 1,747.03 but not exceeding EUR 23,293.73 or imprisonment not exceeding four years, or both such fine and imprisonment.

454. L.N. 161/2002, the Waste Management (Waste Oils) Regulations, transposed the Waste Oils Directive 75/439/EEC, as amended. The Directive was repealed and replaced by Directive 2008/98/EC, incorporated locally under the Waste Regulations, which also revoked and replaced the Waste Oils Regulations. The waste stream of waste oils is addressed through the Waste Regulations as part of the movement aimed at protecting the environment and human health in as much of a holistic manner as possible. Waste oil refers to any mineral or synthetic lubrication or industrial oil which has become unfit for the use for which it was originally intended – a trite example would be used combustion engine oils. It should be borne in mind that the specific provisions on waste oils are without prejudice to the other provisions in the Regulations related to hazardous waste. Waste oils are to be collected separately where this is technically feasible and not be used as fuel in engines of road vehicles, aircraft, or sea vessels. Furthermore, they must be treated as provided in Regulation 18(1)(a). Waste oils of different characteristics are not to be mixed, and waste oils are not to be mixed with other waste where this is economically feasible if such mixing impedes treatment. Shipment of waste oils to incineration or co-incineration facilities outside Malta can be restricted in order to give priority to the regeneration of waste oils. This is so where Regulation (EC) No. 1013/2006 applies and is in accordance with Schedule 4 to the Regulations.

455. The waste management plans required to be set up by ERA under the Waste Regulations are to contain existing waste collection schemes and major disposal and recovery installations, including special arrangements for waste oils already existing. In fact, the old Waste Oils Regulations required ERA to set up a waste oils collection scheme. The plans must also assess the need for new waste collection schemes and any changes required to waste installation infrastructure. The regeneration of waste oils, in particular, is to be encouraged through appropriate measures where this is technically feasible.

456. Aside from these specificities, the general provisions on waste management in the Waste Regulations apply to waste oils insofar as applicable. This includes the provisions on criminal offences, penalties, and ancillary measures such as the forfeiture of the *corpus delicti*.

457. L.N. 205/2000, Environment Protection (Control of Transboundary Movement of Toxic and Other Substances) Regulations, was adopted under the first EPA in order to implement the obligations of the Basel Convention. This Convention was the first global attempt to regulate and monitor the international transport of hazardous waste. In fact, the objective of the local regulations was to control all operations relating to the transit, export, and import of toxic substances and to promote their environmentally sound management. These Regulations have now been revoked and replaced by the Waste Management (Shipments of Waste) Regulations.[661] The Shipments of Waste Regulations also transpose the provisions of Council Regulation (EC) No. 1013/2006 on shipments of waste, which itself is modelled on the Basel Convention. This was predated by EC Regulation 259/93/EC. The Regulations establish a system of supervision and control of shipments of waste to guarantee the protection of human health and the environment, and they stipulate that the provisions of Regulation 1013/2006 *mutatis mutandis* apply.

458. The Regulations aim to reduce the amount of waste circulating within the Union, both from its own sources and from third countries. To this end, all shipments of waste destined for Malta are prohibited, and any application for such shipment is to be refused *ipso iure* by ERA. Nevertheless, this is without prejudice to rights and obligations under international law, and so imports from parties to the Basel Convention are allowed. It is also without prejudice to applicable provisions in other national legislation, such as the Waste Regulations. Transhipment of waste, that is, the shipping of waste into, out of, or within the EU, is allowed subject to a permit and a fee set out in the Schedule to the Regulations. This rule applies without prejudice to the rights and obligations of the competent authorities of destination and transit.

459. The following are offences under the Regulations: failure to comply with, or breaching, any provision of the Regulations, permit condition or lawfully issued order; contravention of any restriction or prohibition imposed by or issued under the Regulations; failure to abide by any requirement so imposed or issued; and unlawfully conspiring, aiding or abetting, or attempting to so act, the performance of the offences just listed. A first conviction is liable to a fine (*multa*) between EUR 1,170 and EUR 2,330. A second conviction is liable to a fine (*multa*) between EUR 2,330 and EUR 4,660, or imprisonment for a term not exceeding two years, or both such fine and imprisonment. The owner of a vehicle used for the commission of the offence is also liable in the same manner and degree as the perpetrator. Furthermore, the court may order the person guilty to pay for the expenses incurred by the competent authorities in terms of the Regulations as a result of the offence. It may also order the revocation of the permit and the confiscation of the *corpus delicti*. Furthermore, Articles 23 and 30 of the Criminal Code apply *mutatis mutandis* to proceedings in respect of these offences. The competent court is the Court of Magistrates of Malta or Gozo, as a court of criminal judicature. The Attorney General always has a right to appeal to the Court of Criminal Appeal.

460. A common, compulsory notification system has been introduced together with a standard consignment note for shipments of waste under the EU Regulation. The notifier (the original producer, the holder, or the person designated by the laws of the State of dispatch in the case of waste imported into or in transit within or through the Community) must apply for authorisation to the Competent Authorities

661. L.N. 285/2011 (S.L. 549.65).

of destination and send a copy of the application to the authorities of dispatch, transit, or destination. The notifier must make a contract with the consignee for the disposal of the waste. The contract must oblige:

- the notifier to take the waste back if the shipment has not been completed or if it has been effected in violation of this Regulation; and
- the consignee to provide a certificate to the notifier that the waste has been disposed of in an environmentally sound manner.

The shipment may not be made until the Competent Authority of destination has granted authorisation to the notifier. Furthermore, where waste is exported from a Member State to a third State, the notifier must apply for authorisation to the Competent Authority of dispatch. Waste may not be shipped to a third State until the Competent Authorities of destination or dispatch have acknowledged receipt of the application for authorisation of the shipment. Also, waste which does not comply with the provisions of the current measures regarding its shipment must be returnable to the notifier or, if this is not possible, otherwise disposed of or recovered in an environmentally sound manner.

461. Exports of waste intended for disposal are prohibited, except to EFTA (European Free Trade Association) countries which are parties to the Basel Convention. Exports of hazardous waste intended for recovery are prohibited, except those directed to OECD (Organisation for Economic Cooperation and Development) countries, third countries which are party to the Basel Convention, or countries which have concluded a bilateral agreement with the Community (or, before 6 May 1994, with a Member State). All exports of waste covered by the measures to ACP (African, Caribbean, and Pacific) States are prohibited. Imports into the Community of waste for disposal are prohibited except imports from countries which are parties to the Basel Convention or countries with which the Community (or a Member State) has concluded bilateral agreements. Imports from a non-EFTA country are permitted only on the basis of an application from the exporting country stating that it does not have the capacity to dispose of the waste in an environmentally sound manner. Imports of waste for recovery into the Community are prohibited except those from countries to which the OECD decision applies, countries which are parties to the Basel Convention, or countries with which the Community (or a Member State) has concluded bilateral agreements. In the case of transit of waste through the Community originating outside the Community and for disposal or recovery outside the Community, the transit must be notified to the last Competent Authority of transit within the Community. In the case of transit of waste for recovery from a country to which the OECD decision applies and to such a country, the notification must be sent to all of the Competent Authorities of transit in the Member State(s) concerned.

462. The Waste Management (Ship Recycling) Regulations[662] are sister Regulations to the Shipments of Waste Regulations, and indeed they provide for a

662. L.N. 84/2019 (S.L. 549.131).

system of penalties for failure by an operator of a ship recycling facility to comply with the requirements set out in Regulation (EU) No. 1257/2013, which amended Regulation 1013/2006. It is the operator's obligation to ensure the facility is duly authorised by the ERA, as well as compliant with the relevant EU Regulation and the EPA. A person committing or attempting to commit an offence against these Regulations is liable on a first conviction to a fine (*multa*) between EUR 10,000 and EUR 50,000. A second or subsequent conviction entails a fine (*multa*) between EUR 20,000 and EUR 100,000 or a term of imprisonment not exceeding two years, or both such fine and imprisonment. The court is bound to order the guilty person to pay for the expenses incurred by ERA as a result of the offence and undertake mitigation or prevention measures to address offence-related damages. It must also order the revocation of the issued authorisation and the confiscation of the *corpus delicti*, where applicable.

463. Another complimentary piece of legislation is the Waste Management (Supervision and Control of Shipments of Radioactive Waste and Spent Fuel) Regulations,[663] which bring the provisions of Council Directive 2006/117/EURATOM and Commission Decision 2008/312/EURATOM into effect. They lay down a system of supervision and control of transboundary shipments of radioactive waste and spent fuel to guarantee adequate protection of the population so as to supplement the Nuclear Safety and Radiation Protection Regulations.[664]

Much like Council Regulation (EC) No. 1013/2006 on shipments of waste, the Regulations provide for various types of shipments, either within the Community itself or from outside it, which originate from, are destined to, or transit through Malta. Each type of shipment is regulated in its own right, leading to a total of six different types of shipment for the purposes of the Regulations. All forms of shipment require authorisation from ERA, as the competent authority, to enter, leave or transit through Malta. Specific rules then apply for each form of shipping, with certain types of export and import being prohibited. Where various Member States are involved, the competent authorities of each must cooperate among themselves pursuant to the Union legislation on the matter, following strict procedures laid down therein and also detailed in the local Regulations. The offences are: failure to comply with the Regulations, permit conditions or lawfully issued orders; contravention of any restriction, prohibition or requirement imposed by or under the Regulations; acting in contravention of any provision of the same; and conspiring, aiding or abetting any person to contravene the same or fail to comply with the same or any lawfully issued order, or to contravene any restriction, prohibition or requirement imposed by or under the Regulations. A first conviction entails a fine (*multa*) between EUR 1,164.69 and EUR 2,329.37. A second or subsequent conviction entails a fine (*multa*) between EUR 2,329.37 and EUR 4,658.75 or imprisonment for a term not exceeding two years or both fine and imprisonment. Commission of the offence through a vehicle will entail the same liability on the vehicle owner. Furthermore, the confiscation of the *corpus delicti* and the revocation of the permit may be ordered by the court, along with an order to pay for the expenses incurred by

663. L.N. 48/2009 (S.L. 549.51).
664. L.N. 44/2003 (S.L. 365.15).

ERA due to the offence. Furthermore, Articles 23 and 30 of the Criminal Code apply. The competent court is the Court of Magistrates, Malta or Gozo, as a court of criminal judicature, and the Attorney General always has a right of appeal to the Court of Criminal Appeal.

464. Council Directive 1993/31/EC on the Landfill of Waste, as amended, was adopted under Maltese Law by means of L.N. 168/2002, the Waste Management (Landfill) Regulations.[665] Under the Directive, landfills are divided into three classes, depending on the waste which is permitted in them: landfills for hazardous waste, landfills for non-hazardous waste, and landfills for inert waste. In Malta, one doesn't find landfills for hazardous waste, as this type of waste is exported. Inert landfills require a permit under the Waste Regulations. The Regulations aim, pursuant to the Waste Regulations and the EU legislation they implement, to ensure a progressive reduction of landfilling waste, particularly waste suitable for recycling or other recovery. This is through stringent operational and technical requirements on waste and landfills and through providing measures, procedures and guidance to prevent or reduce, as far as possible, negative effects on the environment, particularly the pollution of surface water, groundwater, soil and air, and the global environment, including the greenhouse effect, as well as any resulting risk to human health, from the landfilling of waste, during the whole life cycle of the landfill. The Regulations also elaborate the technical requirements for landfills falling under the general terms of the Integrated Pollution Prevention and Control Regulations. The requirements of the latter are to be deemed fulfilled if those of the former are complied with.

465. The Competent Authority is ERA. Hence, the Minister responsible for the environment may also designate other different bodies and persons, such as WasteServ, as competent authorities by order in the Gazette. WasteServ is responsible for managing, monitoring, and operating all government-owned waste management facilities that include the composting plant, the material recovery facility, the engineered landfill, and the Gozo waste transfer station. It also monitors the transport of all non-inert waste from Gozo to Malta for recovery, treatment, and final disposal. The company operates integrated systems for waste management in accordance with the Law of Malta. It is responsible for the waste management policy and plan of the Government of Malta while observing internationally recognised waste management principles.

On the other hand, ERA is obliged through Regulation 5 to create national strategy to reduce biodegradable waste ending up in landfills. This strategy shall seek to adopt the targets and levels set out in paragraph 2 of the same Regulation [666] and to come up with alternative ways of reducing waste and coming up with alternative forms of energy. The final target of a reduction to 10% or less of the total municipal waste generated being landfilled must be reached by the year 2035. However, by

665. S.L. 549.29.

666. Under this paragraph, time limits are stipulated within which the Authority has to reach certain fixed percentages of the total amount by weight of biodegradable municipal waste produced in 1995. New targets and calculations have been set starting from the year 2021.

2030 the Minister may consider postponing this deadline by up to five years, provided he notifies this decision to the Commission of the EU at least twenty-four months beforehand and submits to it an implementation plan duly prepared according to Schedule IV.[667] The postponement is, in any case, contingent upon the attainment of the landfill of at least 60% of municipal waste generated in 2013. If the deadline is postponed, a new target of reduction to 25% must be reached by the year 2035 instead.

Together with the strategy mentioned, the Competent Authority may issue new declarations on objects which are not permissible in the landfills. It is also obliged to ensure that by 2030 all waste suitable for recycling or other recovery, particularly municipal waste, is not accepted in a landfill, with the exception of such waste for which landfilling delivers the best environmental outcome as per the Waste Regulations. Certain types of waste, such as liquid waste, are prohibited from being landfilled since they are hazardous to the public in general. In order to curb abuse, Regulation 7 was included to prohibit diluted or mixed waste, as this would still be hazardous. Going a step further, Regulation 8 declares that only waste which has been treated can be dumped. This does not apply to inert waste for which treatment is not possible or not in conformity with the criteria of Schedule 2. Additionally, before starting discarding operations, the Competent Authority is obliged to examine the site and make sure that it complies with the conditions set out in the permit. This, however, still poses an obligation on the operator to comply with the conditions laid down in his permit. Apart from this, ERA is obliged to be transparent and accessible in its work regarding the collection and use of information in conformity with the Regulations on the Access to Information on the Environment. Furthermore, at the closing of a landfill, ERA or any adjudicating body has to carry out on-site inspections and assess the reports submitted by the operator before giving its go-ahead for the closure.

466. The operator is any natural or legal person responsible for a landfill, and this person may change from the preparation to the after-care phase. The operator shall, after having been issued a permit, report to the Competent Authority at least once a year regarding monitoring results in the landfill, and for this purpose, the regulations set out control and monitoring procedures both at the operational stage as well as at the closure of the landfill, respectively, which are also outlined in Schedule 3. Furthermore, the operator has the duty to alert the Competent Authority in the case of any major unfavourable effects on the environment detected by the aforementioned procedures. It is then the obligation of the operator to comply with the decision taken on the corrective measures to be followed at his own expense. Due to hazards that could still be present at the landfill, the operator is still responsible for the maintenance, monitoring, and control in the after-care phase for the period requested by the Authority. This also includes the monitoring of toxic gases and leachate from the site and the water regime. The operator has to give financial security to ensure that the obligations imposed on him are followed. Permits are issued according to the class of the landfill and include the description of the types and total quantity of waste to be deposited, the capacity and description of the site,

667. The Commission can request the plan's revision.

the monitoring and control procedures, and provisions for the closure, which imply after-care operations. The permit also includes the obligation for the operator to report annually on quantities and types of waste.

467. Offences and their correlated punishments are set down in Regulations 18, 19, and 20 of the Waste Management (Landfill) Regulations. Under Regulation 18, a person is guilty of an offence if he fails to comply with any provision of the Regulations, if he contravenes any imposed restrictions or provisions of the Regulations, or if he conspires or helps another person to do so. Any person found guilty of such an offence is liable to a fine (*multa*) of between EUR 1,164.69 and EUR 2,329.37 on a first conviction or a fine of EUR 2,329.37 to EUR 4,658.75 or imprisonment not exceeding two years on a second or subsequent conviction. This person is also liable to the revocation of the permit issued by ERA and, where applicable, to the confiscation of the *corpus delicti*. The proceedings for the offences mentioned above will be held before the Court of Magistrates (of either Malta or Gozo) in accordance with the provisions of the Criminal Code regulating the procedure as a court of criminal judicature.

468. The Waste Management (Management of Waste from Extractive Industries and Backfilling) Regulations[668] is a piece of legislation complementary to both the Landfill Regulations and the Waste Regulations. They implement the provisions of Directive 2006/21/EC on the management of waste from extractive industries. The aim is to provide measures, procedures, and guidelines to prevent or reduce, as far as possible, any adverse impacts on the environment and any resultant risks to human health via management of waste from extractive industries or of the backfilling of waste into excavation voids. Extraction waste is that waste resulting from the prospecting, extraction, treatment and storage of mineral resources and the workings of quarries. When this waste is used for backfilling, it is referred to as 'backfill', with backfilling itself being the refilling of the excavation void for rehabilitation or construction purposes relative to the mineral extraction process. These Regulations apply only to those wastes resulting directly from extractive industries; hence, waste such as end-of-life vehicles from quarries are excluded. They also do not apply to offshore waste extraction. Waste to which these Regulations apply is not subject to the Landfill Regulations. Under these Regulations, the abandonment, dumping, uncontrolled deposit of extraction waste or uncontrolled backfilling into an excavation void are prohibited. Extractive waste is to be managed without endangering human health and without processes or methods which could harm the environment, without causing a nuisance through noise or odours and without adversely affecting the landscape or places of special interest. The same rule applies to the backfilling of excavation voids. The operator is to take all measures necessary to prevent or reduce these adverse effects using the best available technologies, which may include managing a waste facility after its closure.

668. L.N.. 22/2009 (S.L. 549.50).

469. There are three types of waste facilities for extractive waste for the purposes of the Regulations. Category A facilities containing hazardous waste[669] above a certain threshold, containing substances or preparations classified as dangerous,[670] or being subject to a potential major accident (after an appropriate risk assessment of the facility) for more than six months. Category B facilities are for the accumulation or deposit of non-hazardous non-inert waste for more than one year. Category C facilities accumulate and deposit unpolluted soil, non-hazardous prospecting waste[671] or waste from the extraction, treatment and storage of peat and inert waste for more than three years.

All these facilities require a permit issued by ERA, as competent authority, to operate. The application details are highly detailed and specific to ensure maximum accountability and include a suitable financial guarantee as laid down in the Regulations themselves. There must be a waste management plan appropriately drawn up and submitted to ERA for approval. ERA is under a duty to monitor the facility in relation to the plan, and it must also conduct periodical inspections of permitted facilities. The plan is to pay particular attention to the prevention and information related to major accidents within the facility since these can have excruciatingly adverse impacts on human health and the environment. The management of the facility itself must be in the hands of a competent person. Any modification of a facility, and the construction of new facilities, is subject to voluminous precautions and considerations to ensure minimum impact in line with the aims of the Regulations. The Regulations also deal with closure and after-closure procedures to fulfil the same aims.[672] Finally, facilities must take all necessary measures to meet national and EU environmental standards, such as those relating to water pollution and gas and dust emissions, which is a duty falling on the operator.

If a Category A facility is likely to have significant transboundary effects, the Minister responsible for the environment must forward all relevant information to the other State in order to collaborate to deal with the matter.

The public is to be informed of permit applications and related details. The management plan itself is to be made available to the public.

470. The rules on backfilling are generally similar to those of waste facilities above. Particularly, the construction and management of excavation voids must follow the analogous rules applicable to the construction and management of waste facilities. Backfilling can only occur through a permit, which requires the operator's backfilling plan to be in accordance with national and EU environmental standards, as explained. Likewise, all information must be made available, and ERA has monitoring and inspecting powers to ensure compliance.

---

669. According to the Waste Regulations, or if ERA so deems it to be.
670. Within the meaning of the Dangerous Substances and Preparations Regulations (S.L. 427.28).
671. Prospecting waste is that arising from the search for mineral deposits of economic value, such as drilling and trenching.
672. All closure procedures can only commence upon either meeting the permit requirements for the closure or upon ERA's decision to that effect.

471. It as an offence under the Regulations to: fail to comply with any of their provisions, permit conditions or an order lawfully issued in terms of the Regulations; contravene any restriction, prohibition or requirement imposed by or under the Regulations; act in contravention of any of their provisions; or conspire, aid or abet another, by whatever means, to perform any of the above acts or omissions. A first conviction is liable to a fine (*multa*) of between EUR 1,164.69 and EUR 2,329.37. A second or subsequent conviction is liable to a fine (*multa*) of between EUR 2,329.37 and EUR 4,658.75, or imprisonment for a term not exceeding two years, or both. The owner of a vehicle used to commit the offence is also liable, where applicable, in the same manner and degree. The court[673] is empowered to order the convict to pay for the expenses incurred by ERA as a result of the offence, as well as the revocation of the permit issued by ERA and the confiscation of the *corpus delicti*. To this end, Articles 23 and 30 of the Criminal Code apply, but the disqualification from holding a licence, etc., is not to be for more than one year.

472. Incineration of waste generates its own pollutants, posing potential threats via emissions into the air, soil, surface water and groundwater, as well as risks to human health. This was originally covered by the Waste Management (Incineration) Regulations,[674] revoked and replaced by the Industrial Emissions (Waste Incineration) Regulations.[675] These partly implement Directive 2010/75/EU on Industrial Emissions (Integrated Pollution Prevention and Control) (Recast) and fully implement the Industrial Emissions (Framework) Regulations.[676] The Waste Incineration Regulations ensure that Malta meets its international commitments to reduce pollution, particularly by introducing limits on certain emissions arising from waste incineration.[677] The Regulations apply to waste incineration plants and waste co-incineration plants of both solid and liquid waste, hazardous and non-hazardous.[678] Waste incineration plants are 'dedicated' incineration plants, while co-incineration plants are facilities whose main purpose is to produce energy or material products and which use waste as a regular or additional fuel (which waste is thermally treated prior to disposal).

However, they do not apply to experimental plants intended to improve the incineration process, which treats less than 50 tonnes of waste per year, and to plants treating only:

673. The Court of Magistrates (Malta or Gozo, respectively) as a court of criminal judicature, subject to the right of appeal of the Attorney General to the Court of Criminal Appeal.
674. L.N. 336/2001.
675. L.N. 14/2013 (S.L. 549.81).
676. L.N. 9/2013 (S.L. 549.76).
677. Protocols signed in 1998 under the aegis of the United Nations Economic Commission Convention on long-distance cross-border atmospheric pollution.
678. By 2003 Malta had to close down all non-conforming incineration plants; however, it did not meet this target, notably in the case of the St Luke's Hospital incinerator. But now even this incinerator has been closed and the new incineration facility has been installed at the Civil Abattoir in Marsa. This incineration facility had originally been intended for the treatment of animal and animal by-products; however, after the completion of the necessary modifications the facility can treat other waste streams, including clinical and other hazardous wastes, up to a capacity of 12,900 tonnes per year.

- vegetable waste from agriculture, forestry, the food-processing industry or paper production;
- wood waste, except if containing heavy metals or halogenated organic compounds;
- cork waste;
- radioactive waste;
- animal carcasses, according to Regulation (EC) No. 1774/2002; and
- waste from the exploration for, or exploitation of, oil and gas from offshore installations incinerated on board the installation.

473. All incineration or co-incineration plants must be authorised. Permits will be issued by ERA, which is the Competent Authority under these Regulations, and such permits will list the categories and quantities of hazardous and non-hazardous waste which may be treated, the plant's incineration or co-incineration capacity, and the sampling and measurement procedures which are to be used. Furthermore, a new permit is needed when the operator of an incinerator or co-incinerator plant for non-hazardous waste is envisaging a substantial change in the operation of the installation, such as the incineration or co-incineration of hazardous waste. Permit applications must detail specific information, and each permit must contain conditions addressing various aspects of the plant's operations. In order to guarantee complete waste combustion, ERA has to ensure that all plants keep the incineration or co-incineration gases at a temperature of at least 850°C for at least two seconds. If hazardous waste with a content of more than 1% of halogenated organic substances, expressed as chlorine, is incinerated, the temperature has to be raised to 1,100°C for at least two seconds. The heat generated by the incineration process has to be put to good use as far as possible. Plants must be operated and designed in a manner to prevent the unauthorised and accidental release of pollutants into the soil, surface water and groundwater. Emissions of waste gases must be controlled during their discharge to safeguard human health and the environment, respecting the limit values in Schedules 2 and 3 and the limit values determined in accordance with Schedule 4. The discharge of wastewater from the cleaning of waste gases into the aquatic environment must likewise be limited as much as practicable, not exceeding the limit values in Schedule 4. All emissions are to be monitored in accordance with Schedules 5 and 6[679] using automatic measurement systems subject to annual surveillance tests. The results of the emissions monitoring are to be sent to ERA in such a manner as to enable verification of the plant's compliance with its operating conditions and ELVs. Compliance with the latter will be deemed if the conditions in Schedule 7 are fulfilled.

679. Schedule 6 details the formula to calculate the emission concentration at the standard percentage oxygen concentration. Schedule 5 regulates the monitoring of emissions, detailing the maximum percentages for the following: carbon monoxide, sulphur dioxide, nitrogen dioxide, total dust, total organic carbon, hydrogen chloride, hydrogen fluoride.

474. Before accepting hazardous waste, operators of incineration or co-incineration plants must have available the prescribed administrative information on the generating processes, information on the physical and chemical composition of hazardous waste, and information on the hazardous characteristics of the waste. Rain or firefighting water will be collected and analysed before being discharged from any plant. Furthermore, operators have to ensure that incineration residues must be reduced to a minimum and, as far as possible, recycled. When dry residues are transported, precautions must be taken to prevent their dispersal in the environment. Tests must be carried out to establish the physical and chemical characteristics and polluting potential of residues. Also, they must make proposals for the equipment, location of sampling, and measurement points and techniques in order to monitor the parameters, conditions, and mass concentrations relevant to the incineration or co-incineration process, which is subject to approval by ERA. The operator has to ensure that all necessary precautions are taken regarding the delivery and acceptance of waste in order to limit pollution of air, soil, surface water, groundwater, as well as other negative effects on the environment, odour, noise and direct risks to human health. Special procedures and requirements apply to those operators receiving hazardous waste in order to ensure the maximum possible protection of the environment and human health.

475. Under Regulation 17, a person is guilty of an offence if he fails to comply with any provision of the Regulations, if he contravenes any imposed restrictions or provisions of the Regulations, or if he conspires or helps another person to do so. Any person found guilty of such an offence is liable to a fine (*multa*) of between EUR 23,000 and EUR 233,000 on a first conviction or a fine of EUR 46,000 to EUR 466,000. Both first-time offenders of the Regulations and recidivists may also suffer a term of imprisonment not exceeding two years, to be subject to both their respective fines and imprisonment. The owner of a vehicle used to commit the offence is also liable to criminal proceedings in the same manner and degree as the actual offender(s). The person is also liable to the revocation of the permit issued by MEPA and to the confiscation of the *corpus delicti*, as well as the payment of expenses incurred by ERA as a result of the offence. The proceedings for the abovementioned offences will be held before the Court of Magistrates (of either Malta or Gozo) in accordance with the provisions of the Criminal Code regulating the procedure as courts of criminal judicature.[680]

476. L.N. 212/2001, the Sludge (Use in Agriculture) Regulations,[681] transposes the provisions of EU Council Directive 86/278/EEC. The aim of this Directive is to regulate the use of sewage sludge in agriculture in such a way as to prevent harmful effects on soil, vegetation, animals, and man while encouraging its correct use. Sludge has valuable agronomic properties, and it is therefore justified to encourage its application in agriculture, provided it is used correctly, whereas the use of sludge

680. The provisions of Arts 23 and 30 of the Criminal Code also apply, and the Attorney General has a right of appeal from the decision to the Court of Criminal Appeal.
681. S.L. 549.09.

sewage must not impair the quality of the soil and of agricultural products. According to these Regulations, the sludge, which must be controlled, is: the residual sludge from sewage plants treating domestic or urban waste waters and from other sewage plants treating waste waters of a composition similar to domestic and urban waste waters; residual sludge from septic tanks and other similar installations for the treatment of sewage; and residual sludge from any other sewage plant.

477. There are a variety of obligations listed in this piece of legislation for the different authoritative figures as well as for the producers of sludge and any other persons who use sludge. The Competent Authority under these Regulations is ERA, and such other body or person as the Minister responsible for the environment may, by order in the Government Gazette, prescribe. Different bodies or persons may be designated as a Competent Authority for different provisions and different purposes of these Regulations. The Competent Authority shall ensure that the sludge be tested in accordance with Schedule 1. The Director of Agriculture and any officer in such department who acts on his behalf shall ensure that agricultural soil is tested or assessed in accordance with Schedule 2.

478. Persons who use sludge shall not use sludge on agricultural land unless it is treated in accordance with these Regulations. Furthermore, when such sludge is used on agricultural land, it must be done in such a way that account is taken of the nutrient needs of the plants and that the quality of the soil and of the surface and groundwater is not impaired. Such person must also inform the sludge producer of the following information:

(1) the address and area of the agricultural land concerned;
(2) the date on which the sludge was used;
(3) the quantity of sludge so used; and
(4) where he has used sludge not supplied by the sludge producer, the name and address of the person who supplied that sludge, and the quantity of sludge so used which was supplied by that person.

479. Every sludge producer shall ensure that sludge produced by him and supplied for the purpose of use in agriculture is tested in accordance with Schedule 1 at intervals of not more than six months and in any event where changes occur in the characteristics of the wastewater being treated. Together with such testing, the sludge producer shall prepare and maintain a register containing the following particulars:

(1) the total quantity of sludge produced within a year from when these Regulations come into force and subsequently, for each year thereafter;
(2) in relation to sludge supplied for the purpose of use in agriculture within a year from when these Regulations come into force and subsequently, for each year thereafter:
    (a) the total quantity of sludge supplied;
    (b) the composition and properties of that sludge as determined in accordance with Schedule 1;

(c) the quantities of treated sludge supplied and the type of treatment carried out;
(d) the names and addresses of the persons to whom the sludge was supplied; and
(e) the address and area of each agricultural land on which sludge has been used, the quantity of sludge used thereon, and the amount of each of the elements listed in the sludge table in Schedule 1, which have been added thereto.

(3) a copy of every analysis or assessment made under Schedule 2(6).

Such register shall be maintained for inspection by the Competent Authority or the Director of Agriculture in order to obtain further information on the matter. Moreover, as soon as reasonably practicable after testing sludge in accordance with Schedule 1, the sludge producer shall provide details of the analysis made under that schedule to all persons to whom the sludge producer supplies sludge.

480. The final provisions of these Regulations stipulate the related offences and penalties. In fact, a person is deemed to be guilty of an offence if he:

- fails to comply with any provision of the Regulations;
- breaches any restriction, prohibition or requirement;
- he conspires or attempts, or aids, or abets, any other person by whatever means (including advertising, counselling or procurement to contravene the provisions of the Regulations);
- fails to comply with any such provisions (including any order lawfully given in terms of any of the provisions of the Regulations);
- contravenes any restriction, prohibition or requirement imposed by or under the Regulations.

As to the award of penalties, there is a distinction between first-time offenders and repeat offenders. The fine (*multa*) bracket here is EUR 1,164.69 to EUR 2,329.37 for a first conviction. A second or subsequent conviction is punishable by a fine (*multa*) between EUR 2,329.37 to EUR 4,658.75, or imprisonment for a term not exceeding two years, or both such fine and imprisonment. The punishments are extended in the same manner to an owner of a vehicle with which the offence would have been carried out. Furthermore, the court is given the authority to order any person who would have been found guilty to pay for the expenses incurred by the public entities and/or other persons acting on their behalf involved in the implementation of these Regulations and restitution of the environment, the revocation of the permit issued by the police, and the confiscation of the *corpus delicti*. Judgments are decided by the Court of Magistrates, and the Attorney General always has a right of appeal to the Court of Criminal Appeal from any judgment given by the Court of Magistrates of Malta (or Gozo) in respect of proceedings for any offence against these Regulations.

§3. Extended Producer Responsibility and Eco-Contributions

I. Extended Producer Responsibility

481. The Extended Producer Responsibility Framework Regulations[682] provide a framework for extended producer responsibility schemes. These consist of a set of measures, including legislative measures promulgated under the Act, or other national or EU legislation, to ensure that producers of products bear financial responsibility or financial and organisational responsibility for the management of the waste stage of a product's life cycle. The Regulations also apply to such schemes established under other laws under the EPA. The competent authority is ERA, but it must cooperate with Circular Economy Malta (the Agency) and the Department for Local Government in carrying out its responsibilities. It may also seek the advice of the Office of Competition. Furthermore, the Minister responsible for the environment must set up an Extended Producer Responsibility Consultative Committee to act as an advisor to ERA.

482. The Minister is empowered to take either legislative or non-legislative measures to ensure that producers of products have extended producer responsibility, and this is to strengthen the reuse and prevention, recycling, and other recovery of waste. Such a producer is identified as any natural or legal person who professionally develops, manufactures, processes, treats, sells, or imports specific products.

When applying extended producer responsibility, the Minister must take into account the technical feasibility and economic viability and the overall environmental, human health, and social impacts, respecting the need to ensure the proper functioning of the EU's internal market. It must also be applied without prejudice to the responsibility for waste management under the Waste Regulations and without prejudice to any applicable waste-specific legislation. Pursuant to the measures taken by the Minister, producers are to wholly bear the costs of waste management of the product from which the waste came. Distributors of such products can share these costs.

483. Where the measures include the establishment of extended producer responsibility schemes, the Minister must, in consultation with ERA and the Agency, ensure that a number of things are regulated. First, he must define in a clear way the roles and responsibilities of all relevant actors involved, including producers placing products on the national market, producer responsibility organisations, private or public waste operators, local authorities and, where appropriate, reuse and preparing for reuse operators and social economy enterprises. Second, he must set waste management targets in line with the waste hierarchy aiming to attain, as a minimum, the quantitative targets relevant to extended producer responsibility under specific laws as well as set other such targets considered relevant. Third, he must ensure that a reporting system is in place to gather data on the products placed on the national market by the producers subject to extended producer responsibility

682. L.N. 151/2021 (S.L. 549.141).

and data on the collection and treatment of waste resulting from those products specifying, where appropriate, the waste material flows, as well as other data relevant for the purposes of monitoring the targets set. Finally, he must ensure equal treatment of producers regardless of their origin or size without placing a disproportionate regulatory burden on producers, including small- and medium-sized enterprises, of small quantities of product. It should be noted that producers established in other EU Member States and placing products on the Maltese market can appoint a natural or legal person established in Malta as their authorised representative for the purposes of fulfilling their obligations pursuant to such schemes.

484. Producers and producer responsibility organisations must fulfil a number of requirements, such as: having a clearly defined geographical, product and material coverage (without limiting those areas to those where the collection and management of waste are the most profitable); providing an appropriate availability of waste collection systems within those areas; and have the necessary financial means or financial and organisational means to meet its extended producer responsibility obligations. They are also under specific financial and auditing responsibilities and responsibilities relative to certain information that must be publicly available (such as membership and the financial contributions paid by its members).

485. ERA can conduct investigations into particular producers or producer responsibility organisations in collaboration with the Consultative Committee. This extends to investigations into particular types of agreements. It can investigate either of its own motion, upon request by the Minister, or upon reasoned allegation in writing of a breach of the provisions of the Regulations by a complainant. It can collect information from other authorities and request information from the entity being investigated. Failure to submit the requested information is subject to daily penalties established by law. Any entity being investigated must clearly identify any material which it deems confidential (with reasons) from any documents it submits to ERA and, where applicable, must also provide a separate non-confidential version of the document. It is in ERA's discretion to accept the material as confidential, and if it does not and thus intends to disclose it, it must inform the entity being investigated in writing of this, providing time for the entity to reply. If the disagreement as to the confidential nature of the material persists, ERA must take a decision on the matter, which is appealable to the Environment and Planning Review Tribunal.

486. It is an offence under these Regulations to: fail to comply with any provision of the Regulations, or with any order lawfully given in terms of any provision thereof; contravene any restriction, prohibition, order, or requirement arising from the Regulations, or imposed by ERA in accordance with the same; act in contravention of any provision of the Regulations; conspire with, aid, abet, counsel, instigate, procure, or knowingly allow any other person to contravene or fail to comply with the provisions of the Regulations or of any restriction, order, prohibition, or requirement imposed by or under the same; or attempt to commit any of the breaches just mentioned.

A first conviction is liable to a fine (*multa*) of not less than EUR 1,165 but not exceeding EUR 2,330. A second or subsequent conviction is liable to a fine (*multa*) of not less than 2,330 but not exceeding EUR 4,666, imprisonment for a term not exceeding two years, or both. The court must also order the person found guilty to pay for the expenses incurred by any of the authorities as a result of the offence and order the revocation of the permit issued by ERA and of the *corpus delicti*.

II. The Eco-Contribution Act

487. In order to encourage the recovery of waste, the Eco-Contribution Act, Chapter 473 of the Laws of Malta, makes provision for the imposition of an eco-contribution on products which result in waste and to provide for matters ancillary or incidental thereto. Under Article 3 of this Act, the Competent Authority shall charge, on account of the government, an eco-contribution at the rates shown in the third column of the First Schedule payable on products described in the first and second columns of the said Schedule, which are placed on the market, and in the fourth column of the Second Schedule payable on services described in the first, second, and third columns of the said Schedule.

488. The Minister responsible for waste management may, with the concurrence of the Minister responsible for finance, exempt any producer from the payment of the eco-contribution, in whole or in part, which would otherwise have been payable on products produced by him, or grant any producer a credit of the contribution paid on such products, in whole or in part, against eco-contributions, which may fall due in future, if the producer provides or participates in a scheme, approved as provided in the specified Regulations, for the recovery of waste from those products. Producers of bags of plastics falling under the first schedule and producers of services falling under the second schedule shall not qualify for the purpose of this exemption. The Minister shall, by not later than the second week of each month, publish in the Government Gazette a list of the exemptions which may have been allowed in this respect. The Act is also an enabling act delegating power to the Minister responsible for waste management and the Minister responsible for finance to issue subsidiary legislation to supplement the obligations under the Act and provide for procedural details.

489. The Competent Authority is responsible for the administration of this Act and for any regulations made under it. It also has the function of advising the Minister on: the products on which an eco-contribution should be charged and the applicable rate of contribution, the issue of any regulations under this Act, and any matter as may be necessary for the better carrying out of the provisions of this Act or of any regulations made under it. The Authority is a person or body designated as such by the Minister by order in the Gazette.

490. In cases of recovery of waste from products on which eco-contribution is paid in terms of this Act, the producers of those products may be granted a credit of the contribution paid, or part thereof, against eco-contributions which may fall due in future. Under Article 7 of the Act, it is stipulated that the liability for the payment of the eco-contribution rests with the producer. Where two or more persons are liable for the payment of the contribution, their liability under the Act shall be joint and several. The eco-contribution shall be payable on a quarterly basis in arrears on submission of the return relative to the preceding quarter. The Third Schedule establishes the registration and reporting procedure to be adhered to by all producers liable to the payment of an eco-contribution.

491. Where any person liable for the payment of eco-contribution fails to furnish a return when due or furnishes a return with an understatement of the eco-contribution due for that period, or an incomplete or incorrect return, the competent authority may issue an assessment on that person indicating the amount of eco-contribution due and shall serve such assessment at any time after the expiration of the time allowed in terms of this Act for the furnishing of the return and by not later than six years from the end of the period to which the return relates. Such an assessment shall not relieve the person who has not furnished a return or the corrected return, as the case may be, from his obligation to furnish the return and from his liability to any or to further administrative penalties due in terms of this Act. The power of the Competent Authority to issue an assessment includes the power to issue an additional or revised assessment within the same time limits and to cancel an assessment so issued. Such an assessment shall be made in such form and contain such particulars as the Competent Authority may deem appropriate. An assessment may be issued by reference to such information, estimates or criteria as the Competent Authority may, in its judgment, deem appropriate. Where an assessment is issued, any amount of eco-contribution indicated in such assessment shall, except if and to the extent that the assessment is cancelled or revised, be deemed as the eco-contribution properly due and chargeable with respect to the period to which the return relates. Any statement issued by the Competent Authority and any assessment issued showing any amount of eco-contribution due by a person shall, unless the contrary is proved, be sufficient evidence that the amount is due to the Competent Authority by that person and shall constitute an executive title within the meaning and for the purposes of Title VII of Part I of Book Second of the COCP. Any statement, assessment, warrant or other proceeding purporting to be made in accordance with the provisions of the Act shall not be deemed to be void or voidable for want of form or be affected by reason of a mistake, defect or omission therein if the same is in substance and effect in conformity with or according to the intent and meaning of the Act.

492. Any person who contravenes or fails to comply with any of the provisions of this Act or of regulations made thereunder shall be guilty of an offence and shall be liable, on conviction, to a fine (*multa*) not exceeding EUR 23,290.00 or an amount equal to three times the amount of the eco-contribution payable on the products in respect of which the offence is committed, whichever shall be higher. Specific criminal sanctions are imposed on persons in the course of economic activity found to be in breach of the provisions of the Act in relation to plastic bags. Administrative penalties may be imposed by the Authority for infringement of, or failure to comply with, the Act or regulations made under it, which is not to exceed EUR

11,645.00 for each shortcoming. Where the Authority imposes such a penalty and the same fact constitutes a criminal offence, no criminal proceedings are to be taken against the contravener. The Act provides for an appeals system for these administrative penalties.

Chapter 2. Liquid Wastes

493. The provisions of the Code of Police Laws and the EPA that address waste[683] also apply to the regulation of pollution from sewage and wastewater.

494. The Water Services Corporation Act[684] establishes the Water Services Corporation (WSC), and this Act, among other things, lists the duties of the WSC in relation to the provision of sewage services. It is the duty of the WSC, insofar as it is able to do so, to provide a public sewer system to be used for the drainage of domestic sewage and to take such steps which may be necessary from time to time to ascertain the cleanliness, safety, and efficiency of the public sewers. It is up to the WSC to take all necessary action for augmenting and improving the means of disposal and the ways of treating the contents of the public sewers and the necessary steps to ensure the safe discharge, reception, treatment, and disposal of trade effluent. The WSC can also take all actions it considers necessary to encourage the reuse of treated effluent, to carry out tests, and to make regulations relating to waste and sewage connections so as to ensure the proper and fit disposal of wastewater and sewage, as well as to reuse storm water run-off, as appropriate. The WSC is not liable for any nuisance from drainage caused by flooding arising from the action of naturally occurring storms, groundwater, or the action of the sea.

495. The WSC acts under the regulation of the Regulator for Energy and Water Services (REWS).[685] REWS is the entity responsible for regulating, monitoring, and supervising all activities relating to energy and water services, which include, by definition, all the activities of the WSC in relation to sewage, wastewater, and stormwater run-off. Indeed, REWS's functions under its constitutive Act are to secure and regulate what are materially the same functions as the WSC under its own constitutive Act.

496. The WSC's power to grant licences, etc., for the disposal of sewage or wastewater, the treatment of trade effluent, and the disposal of stormwater run-off are now vested in REWS. Indeed, under the Regulator for Energy and Water Services Act, no person can carry out activities or operations related to water services or be engaged in them without a licence, permit, or authorisation by REWS. Breaching this is an offence subject to the penalties laid down in Article 10(2). Furthermore, authorisation by REWS does not exempt the person so authorised from fulfilling other requirements necessary to obtain any other authorisation, etc.,

683. *See*, Art. 121 of the Code of the Police Laws, Ch. 10 of the Laws of Malta, and Art. 54 of the EPA, Ch. 549 of the Laws of Malta.
684. Chapter 355 of the Laws of Malta.
685. Established under Act XXV of 2015, the Regulator for Energy and Water Services Act, Ch. 545 of the Laws of Malta.

required under any other law. The legal provisions regulating licences, the conditions that may be imposed, fees, and other relevant matters are found in subsidiary legislation.[686]

497. It was previously the power of the WSC, with the Minister's approval, to make regulations not inconsistent with the provisions of the Act regarding the quality, design, and workmanship standards required in connection to sewers and waste waters owned by the WSC, as well as regulations setting punishments for any infringements committed under the Act. These powers have now been vested in the Minister after consultation with REWS.

498. L.N. 139/2002, entitled the Sewage Discharge Control Regulations,[687] was issued under the Malta Resources Authority Act.[688] That Act is now partly repealed and replaced by the Regulator for Energy and Water Services Act, and the Regulations in question are to be deemed as if made under the latter Act, along with any licence, etc., issued under them, and may therefore be dealt with according to the same Act.[689] These Regulations prohibit any person from discharging any prohibited effluent from any trade premises[690] into the public sewerage system.

The effluents that are prohibited are those discharges which contain any of the group of substances listed in Schedule A to the Regulations in concentrations which are significantly higher than those existing upstream of the discharge point in the receiving sewer. There is no definition in the Regulations, however, as to what 'significantly higher' means, but Schedule C lists guideline maximum discharge concentration values for selected substances. Anything else is left to the discretion of the Chief Executive of the WSC.

499. Discharges of any trade effluent into the public sewerage system are only allowed when the person involved holds a Public Sewer Discharge Permit issued by the Chief Executive. The Regulations, however, do not only cover 'trade premises' but 'any premises', including, therefore, domestic premises. In fact, no person may discharge from any premises into the public sewer any effluent containing any material which alone or in combination with the contents of the sewer is likely to cause damage to the sewerage system, block it, or cause overflows or interfere with the free flow of the contents of the sewer. It is also prohibited to discharge from any

686. L.N. 525/2004, Water Supply and Sewerage Services Regulations (S.L. 545.14); L.N. 195/2008, the Authorisations (Suspension, Refusal and Revocation) Regulations (S.L. 545.19).

687. S.L. 545.08.

688. Chapter 423 of the Laws of Malta.

689. Regulator for Energy and Water Services Act, Ch. 545 of the Laws of Malta, Art. 41.

690. 'Trade premises' in turn is defined as 'any land or building, used partly or in whole for the purposes of undertaking any commercial or industrial activity and any premises wholly or mainly used (whether for profit or not) for agriculture, or animal husbandry, or horticultural purposes or for scientific research or experiment'.

premises any effluent which constitutes a health hazard to sewer maintenance personnel,[691] which interferes with the treatment and recovery of liquid and solid wastes, and which brings about adverse aesthetic or other objectionable effects upon discharge into the marine environment.

500. The maximum discharge concentration values of any substance, including substances listed in Schedule B,[692] shall be restricted accordingly. One must apply for a Public Sewer Discharge Permit as soon as there is the intention to start operations in trade premises which would lead to the discharge of trade effluents into the public sewer. Once an application is submitted, the applicant is deemed to be in conformity with these Regulations until the permit is either issued or refused by the Chief Executive. Similarly, when a person who has been granted a permit intends to perform a change in activities in his trade premises, which may alter the nature of the effluent to be discharged, he has to apply for the modification of the permit conditions prior to the expiry date indicated on the same permit.[693]

Schedule D to the Regulations provides a copy in the prescribed form of the application for the issue of a Public Sewer Discharge Permit.[694] The permit may be issued subject to a number of conditions as the Chief Executive may deem fit to impose. The conditions may include the establishment of a convenient point for inspecting and sampling the effluent before discharge into the receiving sewer at an indicated point on the sewer line at which the effluent may be discharged. The applicant may also be asked to record discharge parameters and to make available the records to the Chief Executive from time to time. Specific discharge regimes may be imposed, which may dictate the maximum component discharge concentrations which shall not be reached by dilution of the effluent by tap waters, groundwater, storm water, or sewage, and the maximum amount of components discharged, which amount shall not be exceeded over a stipulated period of time.

501. Any person who discharges effluent into the public sewerage system shall give the Chief Executive or his representative all the access and information that may be required to ascertain that these Regulations are being complied with. The Chief Executive has the right to conduct inspections, examine and investigate, direct that the premises subject to investigations remain undisturbed for a stipulated time limit, take measurements, as well as to take photographs and samples. The Chief Executive may also question any person whom he has reasonable cause to believe is able to give any information relevant to any examination or investigation. The Chief Executive in these cases may also ask such person to sign a declaration of truth of his answers.

502. The Chief Executive may require the production and inspection of, and the making of copies of, any entry in documentation kept by virtue of these regulations

691. By emission of flammable, explosive, toxic, irritating or asphyxiating gases or vapours.
692. Of a less significant hazardous nature than those listed in Sch. A.
693. This must be done prior to the expiry date indicated on the same permit.
694. Information submitted is confidential and the Director may demand additional information.

or any other relevant documentation. A blanket clause stating that the Chief Executive may exercise 'any another power which is necessary for that purpose' allows the Chief Executive leeway for securing all the evidence necessary in such cases. The Chief Executive has the power to delegate any of his duties under these Regulations to any officer in the Water Services Corporation whom he may wish to appoint or authorise. An officer so appointed shall be prohibited from disclosing confidential information submitted to him and shall be guilty of an offence if he transgresses this obligation.

503. Any person found guilty of an offence against the provisions of these Regulations shall be liable to a fine (*multa*) of not less than EUR 232.94 and to an additional penalty of not less than EUR 232.94 per day from the date of conviction to the date on which such person complies with the said provisions.[695] If a person is convicted for any subsequent offence under these Regulations and that person is exercising any Act, trade, or any other calling in virtue of a licence from the Competent Authority, the court may, at its discretion, cancel the licence or suspend the same, for any period of time. Apart from awarding punishment, the court may also order the offender, where the occasion so requires, to abate the nuisance arising from the offence within a stipulated time limit, and in case of default, the offender would be liable to a fine (*multa*) of not less than EUR 232.93 for every day the default continues, until the expiration of the time limit. The court may also order that the nuisance be abated or that the provisions of the regulations be observed by the police at the offender's expense.[696] The burden of proof in any proceedings for an offence under these Regulations for failing to comply to act according to the principles of the best available technology[697] shall lie with the accused; that is, he must show that it was not possible for him to do more than was in fact done to satisfy these principles.

504. When an offence against these Regulations is committed by a body of persons, any person who was a director, manager, secretary, or other similar officer of such body or association shall be deemed to be guilty of an offence unless he proves that the offence was committed without his knowledge and that he exercised due diligence to prevent the offence from being committed. The owner or person in whose name the trade is carried on, as the case may be, shall not be guilty of an offence unless it is proved that he failed to take all the reasonable steps to prevent the offence. Any damages suffered shall be recoverable by the Chief Executive or by an injured party as a civil debt.

695. Provided that such fine and penalty together shall not in any case exceed the amount of EUR 23,293.73.
696. *See* Art. 15 of L.N. 139/02. The offender would be made to refund the expense under a warrant issued by the court.
697. Defined as those measures which are generally and authoritatively practised and accepted, as complying with established standards of performance.

Chapter 3. Packaging Waste

§1. General Regulations on Packaging Waste

505. L.N. 277/2006, the Waste Management (Packaging and Packaging Waste) Regulations,[698] brings into effect the provisions of European Parliament and Council Directive 94/62/EC of 20 December 1994, as further amended. These Regulations provide additional measures, procedures, and guidelines to those in the Waste Regulations. The aim of these Regulations is, on the one hand, to prevent and reduce the impact of the management of packaging and packaging waste on the environment, thus providing a high level of environmental protection, and on the other hand, to avoid obstacles to trade and distortion and restriction of competition. To this end, these Regulations lay down measures aimed, as a first priority, at preventing the production of packaging waste and, additionally, at promoting the reuse of packaging, its recycling, and other forms of recovery, thereby reducing the final disposal of such waste. Under these Regulations, packaging should be marked to facilitate identification and classification in order to facilitate the collection, reuse, and recovery, including recycling, of packaging waste. Also, the users and consumers of packaging and the holders of packaging waste shall cooperate with and participate in any system set up for the reuse, recovery, and recycling of packaging waste. Accordingly, they shall segregate, deposit, and return packaging as required by the system.

506. The Competent Authority under these Regulations is ERA. It must maintain a database with annual records of packaging and packaging waste in the format specified in Schedule 4 and shall provide in particular information on the magnitude, characteristics, and evolution of the packaging and packaging waste flows at the national level, including information on the toxicity or danger of packaging materials and components used for their manufacture. It must also include a chapter on the management of packaging and packaging waste in the waste management plans required under the Waste Regulations,[699] with specific details.

Furthermore, the responsible Minister must, in consultation with ERA and Circular Economy Malta (a government agency), take measures to promote the increase in the share of reusable packaging placed on the market and of systems to reuse packaging in an environmentally sound manner. This must occur in line with the waste hierarchy established under the Waste Regulations.

507. The Authority, together with producers, may implement systems and programs intended for the recovery, reuse, or recycling of packaging and packaging waste and in order to reduce the formation of packaging waste; together, they can also conduct information campaigns for users or consumers and producers. The Competent Authority may charge producers such fees as may be necessary to cover the costs of administration of these Regulations, but it shall not impede the placing on the market of packaging that satisfies the provisions of the same. Furthermore,

698. S.L. 549.43.
699. S.L. 549.63 (*see* above).

the Competent Authority, among other things, may require producers to provide adequate facilities at their premises or at other designated areas or premises for the deposition of packaging by customers at no net cost to the latter and for the reception, segregation, and storage of packaging waste. A notice on such areas or premises has to be displayed indicating that packaging waste of the type placed on the market by the producer will be accepted free of charge.[700]

Together with this, the Competent Authority shall maintain and make available a register of producers. In fact, producers were required to register with the Competent Authority by 31 January 2006, and new producers putting packaging or packaging material on the market for the first time must apply to be registered. Registered producers must renew their registration on an annual basis, containing all required information, including reporting information set out in Part B of Schedule 5. All information reported must be certified by a duly approved independent auditor and submit that report as well. Furthermore, the Competent Authority is to be informed if a business is transferred from one person to another. Proof is to be provided that the new owner of the business has entered into an agreement with the previous owner on issues related to the recycling and recovery targets to be achieved and so forth.

Special provision is made on the Authority's power to achieve a sustained reduction in the consumption of lightweight plastic carrier bags. This aim can be achieved through one or both of two routes. The first is limiting the annual consumption of such bags per person by set dates. The second is by adopting instruments ensuring the bags are not provided free of charge at the point of sale of goods or products. These aims can be arrived at through a variety of suitable methods, as appropriate. Specific Regulations have been issued on these matters, tackled below.

508. Producers can import, manufacture, supply, or use packaging material and packaging only if it complies with the Regulations. Producers shall not import, manufacture, supply, or use packaging material if the aggregate concentration of lead, cadmium, mercury, and hexavalent chromium present in each packaging material or packaging exceeds 100 ppm by weight. The 100-ppm limit could have been exceeded in plastic crates and pallets until 8 February 2009, subject to certain conditions. The 100-ppm limit may also be exceeded for glass packaging, subject to conditions. Furthermore, producers and industry organisations are required to meet recycling and recovery targets established under Schedule 3. Producers shall not dispose of collected packaging waste without first making it available for reuse or recovery. In fact, packaging should be marked to facilitate identification and classification in order to facilitate the collection, reuse, and recovery, including recycling of packaging waste. Furthermore, these producers are obliged to keep records and are required to submit reports as explained. A producer may be exempted from the obligations under these Regulations if he gives proof that he is participating in an authorised recovery scheme. If a producer chooses to make use of an existing authorised waste recovery scheme, he shall be required to submit to the Competent Authority a signed agreement with the operator of the authorised waste recovery scheme to prove that the scheme complies with the provisions of these Regulations.

700. *Ibid.*, 13(2)(a–d).

509. The users and consumers of packaging and the holders of packaging waste shall cooperate with and participate in any system set up for the reuse, recovery, and recycling of packaging waste. Accordingly, they shall segregate, deposit, and return packaging as required by the system. In fact, the Regulations place an obligation on the Regional Councils to take the necessary measures to attain the recovery and recycling targets laid down in Schedule 3 within their respective territories. The targets are expressed as a percentage by weight of all packaging waste, to be reached by specific dates (subject to postponement under certain conditions).

510. Persons who intend to operate a packaging waste recovery scheme as required under these Regulations, including the collection, sorting, storage, export, recovery, and recycling of packaging waste on behalf of producers, shall require and obtain a valid permit from the Competent Authority. The Regulations specify the procedure to be followed and the information to be submitted when applying for such a permit. The services offered by operators of packaging waste recovery schemes shall:

(1) be available to all producers under non-discriminatory conditions[701] and shall be designed so as to avoid any barriers to trade or distortions of competition in conformity with the relevant regulations; and
(2) take into account, generally, requirements regarding the protection of environmental and consumer health, safety and hygiene, the protection of the quality, the authenticity and the technical characteristics of the packed goods and materials used and the protection of industrial and commercial property rights.

511. The final provisions of this Regulation stipulate the related offences and penalties. In fact, a person is deemed to be guilty of an offence if he:

- contravenes any restriction, prohibition, or requirement imposed by or under the Regulations;
- conspires or attempts, or aids, or abets, any other person by whatever means (including advertising, counselling or procurement to contravene the provisions of the Regulations); and
- fails to comply with any such provisions, including any order lawfully given in terms of any of the provisions of the Regulations.

A first conviction is liable to a fine (*multa*) of between EUR 1,164.69 and EUR 2,329.37. A second or subsequent conviction is punishable by a fine (*multa*) between EUR 2,329.37 and EUR 4,658.75, or imprisonment for a term not exceeding two years, or both such fine and imprisonment. Furthermore, whenever a person is found guilty of committing an offence under these Regulations by means of a vehicle, the owner of the said vehicle, where applicable, is held liable in the same manner and degree. The court is given the authority to order any person who would have been found guilty to pay for the expenses incurred by the public entities and/or other persons acting on their behalf as a result of the offence, as well as order the revocation of the permit issued by the Authority and the confiscation of the *corpus delicti*.

701. Participation is not to be refused or revoked without reasonable justification.

Judgments are delivered by the Court of Magistrates, and the Attorney General always has a right of appeal to the Court of Criminal Appeal from any judgment given by the Court of Magistrates of Malta (or Gozo) in respect of proceedings for any offence against these Regulations.

§2. Specific Regulations on Plastic Waste

I. Beverage Containers

512. The Non-Alcoholic Beverages (Containers) Notice[702] were promulgated by the Minister responsible for the environment and provides that the composition of containers for non-alcoholic beverages, which are not refillable glass containers, is harmful to the environment.

513. The Packaging Regulations are inapplicable to those beverage containers covered by the Beverage Containers Recycling Regulations.[703] These implement the provisions of Directive 94/62/EC, and Article 8(2) and (4) and Article 9 of Directive (EU) 2019/904 on the reduction of the impact of certain plastic products on the environment, with respect to beverage containers. The aim is to enhance the circular economy by making provision for the establishment and operation of a beverage container refund scheme, enhancing the collection and recycling of beverage containers, increasing national recycling efforts, and reducing litter. The beverages covered are those listed in Schedule 1, such as water, flavoured water, malt beverages and ready-to-drink coffee. Beverage containers covered are those of the type listed in Schedule 2. These must be bottles or cans with a capacity of between 0.1L and 3L made out of steel, aluminium, and glass polyethylene terephthalate. Cartons, foil pouches and high-density polyethylene, as well as composite materials, are explicitly excluded. The scheme is coupled with collection targets laid down in the Fifth Schedule.

514. The scheme is operated by Circular Economy Malta (the Agency). The details of the scheme are set out exhaustively in the Regulations. It hinges on a deposit paid along the entire supply chain and by consumers on all applicable beverage containers. The persons involved in the supply chain can reclaim their deposit from the next person on the chain. Consumers and other persons can reclaim their deposit by returning the container to the licensed operator(s) of beverage container refund systems. These operators require a licence from the Agency to be able to set up, establish, and operate a beverage container refund system. They must keep the Agency informed on all information relevant to the scheme, including their annual accounts and audited statements. The operators have a number of responsibilities in operating their refund systems. First, the system must be run on a 'not-for-profit' basis or on a basis where profit is not intended for distribution since the ultimate

702. L.N. 103/1994 (S.L. 549.05).
703. L.N. 311/2020 (S.L. 549.134).

aim is not profit-making. Second, it must have an independent management, operating at arm's length from shareholders, partners, members or founders (as the case may be). Third, it must assume extended producer responsibility on behalf of producers and retailers of single-use containers. Finally, it must allow the participation of all producers and retailers in a non-discriminatory manner. Any producer, distributor, retailer or catering undertaking must register with the operator if intending to make any beverage container available on the market, as well as provide information on the container itself and register it. Furthermore, producers placing or intending to place beverages in a refillable container on the market must be registered with the Agency. These latter persons can be subject to exemptions from the scheme by the Agency.

515. It is an offence to place beverages in beverage containers on the market or make these available unless he complies with the Regulations. More broadly, the contravention of any of the provisions of the Regulations is an offence subject to a fine (*multa*) of between EUR 5,000 and EUR 50,000 or imprisonment not exceeding six years, or both fine and imprisonment, irrespective of whether the offender is a first-time offender or not. Making a declaration which is false, misleading or incorrect is an offence punishable with a fine (*multa*) of between EUR 2,500 and EUR 20,000, or imprisonment for a term not exceeding three months, or both. Refusing or failing, without sufficient cause, to provide information or documentation required by the Agency is also an offence, as is the general breach of the Regulations beyond the breach of an obligation as just described. The court[704] has a number of additional powers to make orders, such as for the person convicted to make restitution to the injured party of any property or proceeds knowingly obtained by fraud or other unlawful gain to his detriment by or through the offence. The Regulations provide for the power of investigation of the Chief Executive of the Agency to ensure compliance with the same, as well as the power to request specific information and documentation to that end. The Chief Executive, or any of his officers, with the assistance of the police (by warrant of a magistrate), can enter into premises, inspect, and seize objects, etc., for the purposes of investigation or to ensure compliance with the Regulations. The Chief Executive may also assist the prosecution in criminal proceedings under the Regulations.

516. Specific types of beverage containers are also regulated under the Single-Use Plastics Framework Regulations, discussed in the next subsection.

II. Plastic Bags and Single-Use Plastics

517. The Restrictions on Placing on the Market of Lightweight Plastic Carrier Bags Regulations[705] bring into effect the provisions of Directive (EU) 2015/720, amending Directive 94/62/EC as regards reducing the consumption of lightweight plastic carrier bags. They only apply to lightweight plastic carrier bags intended for

704. The Court of Magistrates (Malta or Gozo, as appropriate).
705. L.N. 480/2020 (S.L. 549.139).

placing on the market in Malta, and ERA and the Customs Department must collaborate and cooperate in their enforcement. These bags are supplied to consumers at the point of sale of goods or products and have a wall thickness of less than 50 microns. The phasing out of plastic bags is in two stages. From 1 January 2021, the importation, intra-Community acquisition, and manufacturing of such bags for circulation on the market in Malta in the course of a commercial activity was prohibited. From 1 January 2022, any supply of the same for distribution, consumption or use on the market in Malta in the course of a commercial activity, whether in return for payment or free of charge, shall be prohibited. However, very lightweight bags,[706] biodegradable and compostable bags,[707] and reusable bags[708] are exempt from these prohibitions. Producers of the second must submit the certificates indicating conformity to the harmonised standard upon renewing their registration in accordance with the Packaging Regulations. It is an offence against the Regulations to contravene or fail to comply with the mentioned prohibitions. On a first conviction, this entails a fine (*multa*) not exceeding EUR 1,500. A second conviction entails a fine (*multa*) not exceeding EUR 2,500. The Court must order any person so found guilty to pay for the expenses incurred by any of the competent authorities as a result of the offence and must moreover order the confiscation of the products to which the offence relates, even though their owner may not be a party to the proceedings.[709]

518. Single-use plastic products are in the process of being phased out in an EU-wide initiative under Directive (EU) 2019/904. Consequently, Malta promulgated the Single-Use Plastics Framework Regulations and the Restrictions on the Placing on the Market of Single-Use Plastics Regulations to transpose the relevant provisions of this Directive.

519. The Single-Use Plastics Framework Regulations[710] provide a framework for single-use plastic products listed in Schedule 1 and for fishing gear containing plastic. It should be noted that these Regulations prevail in cases of conflict with the provisions of other applicable subsidiary legislation. The competent authority is ERA, but Circular Economy Malta (the Agency) is also entrusted with responsibilities under the Regulations.

520. The main aim of these Regulations is consumption reduction in single-use plastic products. The Minister responsible for the environment, in consultation with ERA and the Agency, must take the necessary measures to achieve an ambitious and

706. Bags with a wall thickness below 15 microns which are required for hygiene purposes or provided as primary packaging for loose food when this helps to prevent food wastage.
707. Bags certified by an accredited conformity assessment body to comply with harmonised standard EN 13432:2000 on requirements for packaging recoverable through composting and biodegradation.
708. Bags which have been conceived, designed and placed on the market to accomplish within their life cycle multiple trips or rotations by being reused for the same purpose for which they were conceived.
709. Articles 23 and 30(1) of the Criminal Code apply *mutatis mutandis* to such proceedings.
710. L.N. 237/2022 (S.L. 549.149).

sustained reduction in the consumption of the single-use plastic products listed in Part A of Schedule 1, in line with the overall objectives of the EU's waste policy, in particular waste prevention, leading to a substantial reversal of increasing consumption trends. Those measures shall achieve a measurable quantitative reduction in the consumption of the single-use plastic products listed in Part A of Schedule 1 by the year 2026 compared to the year 2022. The measures may include national consumption reduction targets and reusable alternatives to single-use plastics being made available at the point of sale to consumers. The description of any measures adopted must be informed to the European Commission and made publicly available. Such description must also form part of key plans under other laws, such as waste management plans under the Waste Regulations and programmes of measures under the Water Framework Regulations.

The same entities must take measures to inform consumers and to incentivise responsible consumer behaviour in order to reduce litter from products covered by these regulations and shall take measures to inform consumers of the single-use plastic products listed in Part E of Schedule 1 and users of fishing gear containing plastic about three things. First is the availability of reusable alternatives, reuse systems, and waste management options for those items as well as best practices in sound waste management carried out in accordance with the Waste Regulations. Second is the impact on the environment, in particular on the marine environment, of littering and other inappropriate waste disposal of those items. Third is the impact on the sewage network of inappropriate means of waste disposal of those items.

521. Each single-use plastic product listed in Part B of Schedule 1 placed on the market must bear a conspicuous, clearly legible, and indelible marking on its packaging or on the product itself on the basis of Commission Implementing Regulation (EU) 2020/2151 of 17 December 2020, informing consumers of appropriate waste management options for the product (or waste disposal means to be avoided for it) and of the presence of plastics in the product and the resulting negative impact of littering or other inappropriate means of waste disposal of the product on the environment. It is prohibited to place incompliant products in the market.

522. Beverage containers are particularly regulated under the Regulations. Beverage bottles listed in Part D of Schedule 1 placed on the market on the territory of Malta, which are manufactured from polyethylene terephthalate as the major component ('PET bottles'), must contain a minimum percentage content of recycled plastic, calculated as an average for all PET bottles placed on the market on the territory of Malta, by specific dates. The minimum targets are 25% by 2025 and 30% by 2030.

523. A catering establishment[711] is prohibited from providing the single-use plastics listed in Part A of Schedule 1 free of charge to final consumers if provided empty or filled at the point of sale. The fee charged for such products must be

711. Understood as 'any building, premises, or other establishment, including kiosks, howsoever described, purveying for reward food and, or, beverages including wines and spirits, for consumption', but excluding nightclubs and discotheques.

informed to consumers. Furthermore, as of 1 January 2023, catering establishments must provide an adequate number of reusable alternatives to the listed single-use plastic at the point of sale as long as practically feasible, informing consumers of these alternatives and that the fee applicable to the single-use plastic products is inapplicable to the alternatives.

524. Producers[712] must reach the targets for PET bottles previously mentioned, either individually or collectively. To this end, an annual report must be submitted to ERA containing information on the recycled content of bottles they place on the market, as well as whether the targets are being achieved individually or collectively within four months from the previous year's end. Defaulting producers are subject to an administrative penalty imposed by ERA, calculated according to a mechanism laid down in Schedule 2. Producers of the products listed in Part D of Schedule 1 must comply with the Beverage Containers Recycling Regulations in order to ensure that specific minimum targets for separate collection for recycling are attained. The targets are expressed as a percentage of those products placed on the market in a given year by weight. Furthermore, the Minister, in consultation with ERA and the Agency, must ensure that producers of the products listed in Section III of Part C of Schedule 1 cover certain minimum costs, such as awareness and litter clean-up.

The Minister, in consultation with ERA and the Agency, must also establish extended producer responsibility schemes for the single-use plastic products listed in Section III of Part C of Schedule 1 and fishing gear containing plastic which are placed on the market of Malta, in accordance with the Extended Producer Responsibility Framework Regulations.[713] Extended producer responsibility is also applicable to producers of those products listed in sections I and II of Part C of Schedule 1, who are bound to participate in a packaging waste recovery organisation. Acting on behalf of producers, such an organisation must also cover certain costs associated with the mentioned plastics. Producer responsibility organisations must be authorised to operate under these Regulations by ERA.

525. It is a criminal offence under these Regulations to: fail to comply with any of their provisions or fail to comply with permit conditions or with any order lawfully given in terms of any provision of the same; contravene any restriction, prohibition, or requirement imposed by or under the same; act in contravention of any of the provisions of the Regulations; or conspire or attempt, or aid, or abet, any other person by whatever means, including advertising, counselling, or procurement to

---

712. A producer may be either: (a) any natural or legal person established in Malta that professionally manufactures, fills, sells, or imports, irrespective of the selling technique used (including by means of distance contracts) and places on the market of Malta single-use plastic products, filled single-use plastic products, or fishing gear containing plastic, other than persons carrying out fishing activities as defined in point (28) of Art. 4 of Regulation (EU) No. 1380/2013 or (b) any natural or legal person established in one Member State or in a third-country that professionally sells in Malta directly to private households or to users other than private households, by means of distance contracts, single-use plastic products, filled single-use plastic products, or fishing gear containing plastic, other than persons carrying out fishing activities as defined in the same Regulation.

713. These Regulations are discussed in Ch. 1.

contravene the provisions of the regulations or to fail to comply with any such provisions, including any order lawfully given in terms of any of the provisions of the same, or to contravene any restriction, prohibition, or requirement imposed by or under the said Regulations.

A first conviction entails liability to a fine (*multa*) not exceeding EUR 2,330. A second or subsequent conviction is liable to a fine (*multa*) not exceeding EUR 4,660. The owner of a vehicle used to commit any mentioned offence, if applicable, is also criminally responsible in the same manner and degree. The court[714] may also make additional orders, and the Attorney General always has a right to appeal any such judgment.

526. The Restrictions on the Placing on the Market of Single-Use Plastic Products Regulations[715] phases out the placing on the market of specific single-use plastic products mentioned in the Schedule to the Regulations. The Regulations must be implemented by ERA and the Customs Department.

527. Those products listed in Part A of the Schedule are prohibited as of 1 January 2021, along with products made from oxo-degradable plastic.[716] The distribution, consumption, or use in the course of a commercial activity, whether in return for payment or free of charge, of these items is also prohibited. Those products listed in Part B of the Schedule are absolutely prohibited (but this provision is yet to enter into force). Finally, those products listed in Part C having caps and lids made of plastic will be prohibited from 3 July 2024. However, the latter are exempt if the caps or lids remain attached to the products during their intended use stage. Furthermore, metal caps and lids with plastic seals are not considered to be made of plastic and are thus exempt from prohibition.

528. It is a criminal offence to contravene or fail to comply with the provisions of these Regulations. A first conviction entails liability to a fine (*multa*) not exceeding EUR 1,500, while a second or subsequent conviction entails liability to a fine (*multa*) not exceeding EUR 2,500. The court must also order the person convicted to pay for the expenses incurred by any of the competent authorities as a result of the offence and order the confiscation of the product to which the offence relates, even though the owner may not be the person convicted. It may also make additional orders.

714. The competent court is the Court of Magistrates (Malta or Gozo).
715. L.N. 481/2020 (S.L. 549.140).
716. Plastic materials that include additives which through oxidation lead to the fragmentation of the plastic material into micro-fragments or to chemical decomposition.

Part IV. Nature Conservation and Management

529. About 34.5% of mainland Malta supports no vegetation cover, while 44.1% is cultivated. Natural vegetation covers only 21.3% of the land surface. Human presence on the islands since prehistory has cleared whole forests of Aleppo pines and evergreen oaks, which once covered the islands. Malta's vegetation is a consequence of the climate, the soil, and human intervention. The typical vegetation found is indicative of the various ecosystems, some of which are widespread and some of which are rare. The most typical vegetation of the Mediterranean is woodlands dominated by hard-leafed evergreen trees and shrubs, but in Malta, only remnants of this type of ecosystem exist, and the mature woodland ecosystem is semi-natural. The maquis is more common, and it is characterised by small trees and large shrubs. Maquis occurs on the sides and bottoms of valleys and at the base of cliffs. Maquis and forested areas, however, cover only about 4% of the islands' surface area. The most widespread type of natural ecosystem on the islands is the garigue, of which there are several types, characterised by different dominant plant species. Garigue areas provide an important habitat for dense, low-lying growing shrubs.

530. Steppes, which are dominated by herbaceous plants, are also widespread, and although some steppes have been formed naturally, others are mainly derived from degraded maquis and garigue areas. Cliffs provide a habitat for many species of flora and fauna, among them endemic species of plants which occur only on the Maltese Islands. Saline marshlands are not only rare but may also dry up completely as a result of evaporation during the dry season. Nevertheless, some species of plants and animals are found only in these marshlands. The last remaining sand dunes harbour specialised plants and animals.

531. Freshwater habitats such as rock pools and springs are very scarce. They are found in certain valleys where one finds a number of rare species and in deep caves, which are important habitats not only for bats but also for other cave-dwelling invertebrate species, some of which are endemic. As with other sectors of Maltese environmental law, legal sources addressing nature conservation are rather fragmented. It is only recently, with the publication of the various regulations issued under the EPA, that one finds legal sources which are conservationist in their objective, as many of the older sources were motivated by other reasons, namely, the regulation of the commercial exploitation of these species.

Chapter 1. Nature Reserves

532. The Filfla Nature Reserve Act[717] provides for the establishment of the Filfla Natural Reserve, whereby all the terrestrial area of the Island of Filfla is protected as a nature reserve. Consequently, it is prohibited to kill, capture, collect, trap, maintain in captivity or taxidermy, commercially exploit, pick, or hunt any species of flora and fauna in or from the reserve. The Minister may waive such prohibition for scientific purposes in particular cases. Access to the nature reserve shall be by permission, which is to be granted by the Minister for the Environment for educational and scientific purposes only.[718] The police and the Armed Forces of Malta have access to the Filfla Nature Reserve for the purposes of defence, security, rescue operations, the control of smuggling, and the investigation of crime. Any person who contravenes the provisions of this Act or any condition of a permission granted under it is liable on conviction to imprisonment for a term not exceeding three months or to a fine (*multa*) not exceeding EUR 164.69 or both such imprisonment and fine.

533. The Fungus Rock (*Il-Ġebla tal-Ġeneral*) Nature Reserve Regulations[719] establishes all the surface of fungus rock (*Il-Ġebla tal-Ġeneral*) as a nature reserve. It is prohibited to kill, capture, collect, trap, maintain in captivity or taxidermy, commercially exploit, pick, or hunt any species of flora and fauna in or from the Fungus Rock Nature Reserve. It is also prohibited to climb and accede to the plateau surface of the reserve. The Minister may choose to waive the above-mentioned prohibitions for the purpose of scientific and educational studies in particular cases.[720] A person who contravenes any of the provisions of these Regulations or any condition of a permission granted in relation to these Regulations is guilty of a criminal offence and is liable on conviction to imprisonment for a term not exceeding three months or to a fine (*multa*) not exceeding EUR 1,164.69 or both imprisonment and a fine.

534. The Selmunett Islands (St. Paul Islands) Nature Reserves Regulations[721] were issued to declare as a nature reserve all the surface area of Selmunett Islands, more commonly known as Saint Paul Islands. It is prohibited to kill, capture, collect, trap, keep in captivity or taxidermy, exploit commercially, and pick and hunt any species of flora and fauna[722] from the Selmunett Islands. The Minister may waive such prohibition under these Regulations for the purpose of scientific studies in particular cases. Access to Selmunett Islands is only permissible between sunrise and sunset and only for swimming, berthing of seacraft, and walking along designated footpaths. Other activities are prohibited. Any person who contravenes any of the provisions of these Regulations is guilty of an offence and, upon conviction, is

717. Chapter 323 of the Laws of Malta.
718. The Minister may impose any conditions he may deem appropriate in such a permit.
719. L.N. 22/1992 (S.L. 549.01).
720. The Minister may impose the conditions he deems appropriate, upon effecting such a waiver.
721. L.N. 25/1993 (S.L.549.03).
722. In these Regulations, construed as meaning all plants and animals, resident or migratory, species of which exist in the wild state on Selmunett Islands.

liable to a fine (*multa*) not exceeding EUR 1,164.69, imprisonment for a term not exceeding three months, or both such fine and imprisonment.

535. The *Majjistral* Nature and History Park[723] was established in 2007 by virtue of the powers conferred by Article 9 of the second EPA[724] by the Minister for Rural Affairs and the Environment. The protected area is in the northwest of Malta, as delineated in the site map found in Annex I attached to the Regulations. The various levels of protection within the park shall be determined, from time to time, by the relevant Competent Authorities. There is a management structure for the management of the Park, made up of a management board known as the *Majjistral*, Nature and History Park Management Board and the managing organisations. The Board has the responsibility to develop a plan for the management of the park, which is to be submitted to the Competent Authority for approval, and to carry out regular updating and review of the said management plan. The Board is also to supervise the implementation of the management plan, which shall be implemented by the managing organisations. It shall also act as a contact point between the government, stakeholders, and the managing organisations for the implementation of the management plan. The Board shall regulate its own procedure, with the Chairperson having a casting vote.

The Board is composed of not less than five members and not more than eight members who shall be appointed by the Minister for a term of five years, renewable for further periods. The members are a chairperson; three members representing the Government of Malta after consultation with the Director General of Lands and the Director of Environment; three members to be nominated respectively from each of the three NGOs listed in Annex II[725] to the Regulations; and one member representing the Mellieħa Local Council. The Minister is also to appoint managing organisations from time to time by written agreements between the Minister, or his representative, and the Competent Authority on the one hand, and the managing organisations on the other, for periods of five years, renewable for further periods, so that these can implement the management plan according to the Regulations. The rights and duties of the managing organisations shall be laid out in the said written agreements. The Park Manager is required to abide by any law, regulation or other official order given by the management board and shall not carry out or appoint any person to carry out any work in the Park without the prior approval of the Board. In cases of emergency, he can take any action as necessary but must immediately inform the Board of it. The Minister or his representative can also enter into an agreement with any NGO working in the fields of heritage or environmental management to carry out specific tasks related to the *Majjistral*, Nature and History Park.

723. L.N. 251/2007 (S.L. 549.48), Establishment of the *Majjistral*, Nature and History Park Regulations.
724. Environment Protection Act, Act XX of 2001 (Ch. 435 of the Laws of Malta).
725. NGOs empowered to nominate one member each on the Board: Nature Trust; *Din l-Art Ħelwa*; Gaia Foundation.

536. Subsequent to the above, the *Majjistral* Nature and History Park Site Regulations were issued[726] to establish prohibited activities and restrictions within the Majjistral Park and related offences and penalties. The prohibitions and restrictions concern: the possession of hunting and trapping equipment for wild birds and wild rabbits; the time limits and rules for such hunting and trapping; the storage of the mentioned equipment within Park boundaries and the necessary equipment husbandry; the possession of wild birds or wild rabbits within Park boundaries; the presence of vehicles; camping and the kindling, or attempts to kindle, a fire for entertainment purposes including fireworks; organised operations, activities or work; organised filming activities or similar events; the removal of any stones, pebbles or sand from the beach or sand dunes; and the movement, removal or damage of equipment used for the Park management. It is absolutely forbidden to damage the Park or its biodiversity. These prohibitions and restrictions apply without prejudice to the provisions of any other relevant Regulations. Falconry may be practised within the Park in line with the applicable Regulations, but no person may be in possession of any wild bird or rabbit, dead or alive, within the Park outside of the permitted falconry hours. The Park Manager is the designated person responsible for ensuring that any applicable regulations and requirements are duly complied with at all times to the satisfaction of the competent authorities. He may also issue a permit prior to the performance of any activity prohibited in the Regulations, provided it does not prejudice any related regulations and other permits, authorisations, licences, or clearances required by law. It is important to note that the provisions of these Regulations are inapplicable in cases of defence and national security, public safety and health, salvage operations and the investigation of offences, provided that all reasonable measures are taken to avoid unnecessary environmental damage.

537. It is an offence for any person to fail to observe the provisions of the Regulations or of any other lawful order given by virtue of any provision under those Regulations; infringe any restriction, prohibition, or need imposed by the Regulations or by their virtue; fail to observe any condition of a permit or consent granted under the provisions of the Regulations; make a statement or present information or documentation which he knows to be false for the purpose of obtaining the approval of a permit or derogation in line with the Regulations; conspire or attempt to conspire, aid or attempt to aid, abet or attempt to abet, counsel or attempt to counsel, procure or attempt to procure any other person to contravene any of the provisions in the Regulations; or to fail from complying with any one of the provisions, including any lawful order given by virtue of the same provisions; or to infringe any restriction, prohibition or need imposed by the Regulations or by their virtue. Any person who commits an offence against Regulations 3(1)–3(8) shall be subject to the punishments contained in the Conservation of Wild Birds Regulations.[727] Any person who commits, or attempts to commit, an offence against any regulation other than Regulations 3(1) –3(8) is liable to a fine (*multa*) of not less than EUR 400 and not exceeding EUR 50,000 on a first conviction, and to a fine (*multa*) of not less

726. L.N. 217/2013 (S.L. 549.83).

727. The provisions of the Conservation of Wild Birds Regulations (S.L. 549.42) apply *mutatis mutandis* to any person who commits an offence against Reg. 3(1)–3(8).

than EUR 600 and not more than EUR 60,000, or imprisonment for a term not exceeding two years, or both fine and imprisonment, on a second or subsequent conviction.

Any person found guilty of committing an offence under the Regulations shall, in addition to the mentioned penalties, be liable to all applicable penalties and measures by way of civil liability. In this regard, the court shall order: the payment of the full expenses incurred by the public entities and/or other persons acting on their behalf in the implementation of the regulations for remedying the damage caused to the Park as a result of the offence, to the satisfaction of the Park Manager; the payment of any other expenses incurred and/or the implementation of any mitigation measures that may be reasonably required to contain or prevent the impact of the offence; the payment of the value, liquidated by the court, of any irreparable and irrevocable loss or damage to the environment, biological diversity, landscape, natural heritage or cultural heritage, as may be relevant to the regulations. These penalties, however, must not exceed the limits imposed by the parent EPA when added together.

The Court shall also order a person found guilty of an offence under the Regulations to remove the causes of the offence and to undo anything that was committed without the necessary permits within a sufficient time to be fixed by the Court, that in any case does not exceed three months from the date of the judgment. Failure to comply within the times fixed renders the person liable to a fine (*multa*) of not less than EUR 50 and not more than EUR 150 for every day that the default continues. The provisions of Articles 23 and 30(1) of the Criminal Code apply *mutatis mutandis* to offences committed against these Regulations; however, the disqualification from holding a licence, permit, clearance, or authority shall in no case be for more than one year. Proceedings for offences under these Regulations shall be taken before the Court of Magistrates (Malta) or the Court of Magistrates (Gozo), as the case may be,[728] and shall be in accordance with the provisions of the Code regulating the procedure before the mentioned Courts as courts of criminal judicature.[729]

538. The Park Nazzjonali tal-Inwadar was established in 2016[730] as another national park in the Southeast of Malta, as delineated in the site map in Schedule I to the Regulations. The Minister may extend the boundaries of the Park by notice in the *Gazette*. It is intended to promote and conserve the ecological, geological, cultural, and national features within its borders, balanced against the sustainable use of the Park's resources for recreation and other appropriate activities, and indeed is both designated as a special area of conservation of national importance[731] and declared as part of the National Ecological Network.[732] The Minister may declare additional levels of protection for the Park by notice in the Gazette. Furthermore,

728. Notwithstanding the provisions of Art. 370 of the Criminal Code.
729. Notwithstanding the provisions of the Criminal Code, the Attorney General always has a right of appeal to the Court of Criminal Appeal from any such judgment.
730. L.N. 343/2016 (S.L. 549.109), Establishment of the *Park Nazzjonali tal-Inwadar* Regulations.
731. In line with Art. 9 of S.L. 549.44.
732. Under and in line with Art. 5 of S.L. 549.44.

any action undertaken under these Regulations shall ensure the sustainable management and use of the biodiversity and natural resources of the Park. The management structure of the Park is composed of the Park Nazzjonali tal-Inwadar Management Board and an Implementation Body where applicable. The Management Board is appointed by the Minister responsible for the Environment for a term of three years that is renewable for further periods. The seven members of the Board are a Chairperson and six persons appointed on the basis of their knowledge and experience in relevant sectors. One of these six is to be appointed vice-chairman. The Board is to regulate its own procedure, and the Chairperson has the casting vote. The Board has an executive role and is responsible for the development, regular monitoring, updating and review of a management plan for the Park, which is to be submitted to the Competent Authority (ERA) for approval. It is also to prepare and monitor a business plan and oversee the Implementation Body. The implementation of the management plan is to be administered by the Board and implemented by the Implementation Body. To ensure proper implementation, this is to be done through networking and coordination with the government, including government departments, entities and local councils, rights holders and stakeholders. The Minister is empowered to assign the overall responsibility for the management of the Park to any other legal person, which shall report to the Board.

The Implementation Body is to be appointed by the same Minister, or his representative, by written agreements between himself and the Competent Authority on the one hand, and Implementation Body on the other, for five-year periods that are renewable for further periods.[733] The rights and duties of the implementing organisations are to be set out in the same written agreements. The Body shall execute the work contained in the management plan in line with the Board's direction and shall abide by any law, regulation, or other official order given by the Board and not carry out, or appoint any person to carry out, works in the Park without the prior approval of the Board. However, the Body may take any action as necessary and immediately inform the Board of it in times of emergency. The functions of the Body are to: ascertain that any works and initiatives carried out within the Park are in line with the approved management plan and follow best practice; implement the approved management plan and business plan; coordinate actions with implementation partners, government departments and agencies, and it may involve individual volunteers and registered voluntary organisations to assist in the management plan's implementation; and being responsible for operating and maintaining the Park's assets which are within its remit and monitor, progress and recommend changes and improvements to the management plan and business plan.

The overall strategic direction for the Park is to be provided by the Minister or any other legal or administrative person identified by him. Nevertheless, the Board shall be allocated its own budget for it to conduct its business, subject to the

733. The Minister or his representative is empowered to enter into an agreement with any NGO working in the fields of heritage or environmental management to carry out specific tasks related to the Park. The Competent Authority may also enter into a management agreement to carry out specific tasks related to the Park for the purpose of the implementation of the management plan, in accordance with Art. 15 of S.L. 549.44.

approved business plan, and is free to engage in initiatives to secure funds from third-party organisations to supplement its budget.

539. The site of Il-Ponta tal-Qawra was designated as a nature reserve in 2022,[734] with the site of the reserve delineated in Schedule I to the relevant Regulations. The competent authority is ERA, and the reserve is to remain protected notwithstanding any deliberate or accidental cause whereby it or its surroundings, or part thereof, is destroyed or damaged unless otherwise published by the competent authority.

Vehicular access to the reserve is prohibited without prior authorisation by ERA. It is also prohibited to conduct a number of activities, listed in Regulation 5(2), which tend to damage or harm the biodiversity of the reserve, including being in possession of any equipment that may be used for hunting within the reserve and within a 200 m radius of the reserve's borders. Permits, however, may be granted by ERA for individuals to perform certain activities that would otherwise be prohibited. However, permits for the exploitation of flora and fauna may only be granted either for bona fide scientific studies or for the management and monitoring operations of the reserve in accordance with the provisions of the Flora, Fauna and Natural Habitats Protection Regulations and other operations indicated as essential by ERA for the management of the site.

Permits are subject to application criteria and cannot exceed one calendar year when granted (subject to renewal). If the results of any research or investigations are published, a copy must reach ERA within three months from the date of publication. Persons must be in possession of a copy of their permit while on site.

540. There are two brackets of offences associated with violations against these Regulations.

In the first bracket are offences against Regulation 5(2)(a), which prohibits the capturing, hunting, collecting, trapping, picking, uprooting, cutting, killing, destroying, damaging, creating any adverse conditions, disturbing, keeping, selling, and the offering for sale or exchange of any species or specimens of flora or fauna from the reserve. This is punishable, on a first conviction, with a fine (*multa*) of not less than EUR 750 for each specimen but not exceeding EUR 5,000 for each specimen. A second or subsequent conviction is liable to a fine (*multa*) of not less than EUR 1,500 for each specimen but not exceeding EUR 10,000 for each specimen, imprisonment for a term not exceeding two years, or both.

In the second bracket, it is an offence to wilfully, or through negligence, imprudence, or incompetence: fail to observe any condition of a permit granted under the provisions of these Regulations; fail to comply with any provision of the Regulations or, with any order lawfully given in accordance with any provision of the same; infringe any restriction, prohibition, order, or requirement arising from the same; act in contravention of any provision of the same; conspire with, aid, abet, counsel, instigate, procure, or knowingly allow any other person to contravene or fail to comply with the provisions of these Regulations or of any restriction, order, prohibition, or requirement imposed by or in accordance with the same; attempt to

734. L.N. 240/2022 (S.L. 549.150), Il-Ponta tal-Qawra Nature Reserve Regulations.

do any of the aforementioned actions; or make a statement or submit information or documentation, knowing it to be false, for the purpose of obtaining the approval of a permit in accordance with these Regulations. Where these violations do not fall within the first bracket of offences, they are punishable on a first conviction to a fine (*multa*) as established in Schedule II and on a second or subsequent conviction to the same or imprisonment not exceeding two years or both. The Schedule establishes maximum and minimum amounts for the *multa* depending on the provision being breached.

In determining the gravity of the offence under the second bracket, the court may consider a number of considerations, including the public interest and the intrinsic value or socioeconomic benefit of any habitat or wildlife within the reserve. The court may also, for any conviction, take a number of other measures, such as the revocation of permits.

Chapter 2. Wildlife Protection

541. Various laws are in force in order to protect the wildlife of the Maltese Islands. From an international perspective, Malta has ratified and incorporated the Rio de Janeiro Convention on Biological Diversity, done on 5 June 1992, through L.N. 160/2002,[735] and as such, this forms part of the Laws of Malta. The Competent Authority here is ERA. The objectives of the Convention, set out in Article 1, which Malta must follow, are: the conservation of biological diversity, the sustainable use of its components and the fair and equitable sharing of the benefits arising out of the utilisation of genetic resources. These are largely reflected in the local legislation set out in this chapter.

542. The current DPA and EPA in force provide for Scheduling Orders and Conservation Orders to be made to protect natural heritage. Under the DPA,[736] the Executive Council of the PA is obliged to maintain a list of scheduled property consisting, *inter alia*, of areas of natural beauty or of ecological or scientific value. It can also make conservation orders with respect to the same to regulate their conservation. The Council can also issue emergency conservation orders if areas which would qualify to benefit from a scheduling order are at risk of damage or destruction, and in case of urgency, the Chairperson can issue such an order without consulting the Council. Under the EPA,[737] ERA is obliged to prepare and, from time to time, review a list of protected areas, habitats, and species which are to be protected for conservation and may, in respect of all or any one or more of these, make protection and conservation orders to regulate their protection, conservation, and management. Ministerial endorsement is required to downgrade or remove any protection afforded in this manner. ERA can also make emergency conservation orders, and in urgent cases, the Chairperson can issue them alone. The relevant lists and orders under both Acts are to be published in the *Gazette* and made available online.

543. Following accession to the EU, the fragmented regulations for the protection of flora and fauna were amended and consolidated, updated, and brought in line with those of the EU. The present regulations in force are the Flora, Fauna and Natural Habitats Protection Regulations.[738] These repealed the previous Legal Notices on this subject, namely, L.N. 49/1993,[739] L.N. 167/2002,[740] and L.N. 257/2003.[741] These Regulations (L.N. 311/2006) are divided into twelve parts with twelve schedules attached:

---

735. Convention on Biological Diversity (Incorporation) Regulations (S.L. 549.27).
736. Development Planning Act, Ch. 552 of the Laws of Malta. The regime of scheduling orders and conservation orders is regulated by Art. 57 and 58.
737. Environment Protection Act, Ch. 549 of the Laws of Malta. The regime of protection orders and conservation orders is regulated by Art. 69.
738. L.N. 311/2006 (S.L. 549.44).
739. Flora and Fauna Protection Regulations.
740. Capture and Killing Methods (Prohibition) Regulations.
741. Flora, Fauna and Natural Habitats Protection Regulations.

(1) Part I of these Regulations deals with the interpretation of certain words in the Regulations.

(2) Part II deals with ecological networks. The Competent Authority shall set up a coherent ecological network of protected areas under the title of the National Ecological Network, outlining the criteria for their selection. The Competent Authority shall also contribute to the setting up of a coherent European ecological network of special areas of conservation, established under the title of Natura 2000 by way of Article 3 of the European Council Directive 92/43/EEC of 21 May 1992 on the Conservation of Natural Habitats and of Wild Fauna and Flora.

(3) Part III deals with protected sites. The Competent Authority shall, from time to time, propose a list of sites indicating with respect to each site which natural habitat types in Schedule I to the Regulations and which species in Schedules II and III to the regulations that are native to Malta are hosted by the sites in question. These have to be declared according to the basis of the criteria set out in Schedule IV (Stage 1) to the same Regulations and relevant scientific information, with the aim of designating that site as a Special Area of Conservation as soon as possible. The Competent Authority is to furthermore distinguish between those special areas of conservation, which, in the opinion of the Competent Authority, are of National Importance or of International Importance. Once a site is a Special Area of Conservation or Specially Protected Area, the Competent Authority is to publish details of such site or sites in the Government Gazette, as well as extensions of existing areas. Guidelines are also to be issued by the Competent Authorities for the management and conservation of protected sites, as well as for the conservation measures and management agreement required for the protected sites.

(4) Part IV deals with the protection of species. Species of flora, in all stages of their biological cycle, listed in Schedules V(b) and VI(b) attached to the Regulations, shall not be deliberately picked, collected, cut, uprooted, destroyed, or damaged in any way.

With regard to fauna, no person can pursue, take or attempt to take, deliberately capture or kill or attempt to kill, deliberately destroy, keep, transport, by any method sell, buy, exchange, offer for sale or for exchange, import, or export any specimen of species listed in the Schedules V(a) and VI(a) to these Regulations, except for those taken legally before the Regulations came into force, and unless he is in possession of a prior official permit from the Competent Authority or Director as appropriate. Furthermore, no person shall deliberately disturb any species listed in Schedules V(a) and VI(a) to these Regulations, particularly during periods of breeding, rearing, hibernation and migration, The fauna species, in all stages of life, listed in Schedules V(a) and VI(a), are protected against the destruction and deterioration of their breeding sites or resting places. Furthermore, the deliberate destruction or taking of eggs from the wild is also prohibited. Besides, all endemic species are protected, except for those endemic species listed in Schedule X to the Regulations. However, the Competent Authority or the Director, as appropriate, can issue a prior official permit for the exploitation of endemic species or specimens of species not listed in Schedule X to the Regulations. The Competent

Authority can take any measures it deems necessary to ensure that the taking in the wild of specimens of species of wild fauna and flora listed in Schedules VII and VIII, as well as their exploitation, is compatible with their being maintained at a favourable conservation status. Such measures may also include, in particular, the temporary or local prohibition of the taking of specimens in the wild and exploitation of certain populations; the regulation of the periods and, or methods of taking specimens; the application, when specimens are taken, of hunting and fishing rules which take account of the conservation of such populations; the establishment of a system of licenses for taking specimen or of quotas; the regulation of the purchase, sale, offering for sale, keeping for sale or transport for sale of specimen; the breeding in captivity of animal species as well as artificial propagation of plant species, under strictly controlled conditions, with a view to reducing the taking of specimen of the wild; any other measure deemed necessary and an assessment of the effect of the measures adopted.

(5) Part V regards the introduction and re-introduction of species. This part outlines measures which can be taken by the Competent Authority regarding the control of alien species and the re-introduction of species.

(6) Part VI regards capture and killing methods regarding the prohibited use of means of capture and killing and modes of transport.

(7) Part VII, Conservation and Sustainable Use, outlines the obligations of the Competent Authority to develop a national strategy and other relevant policies and plans, action plans and related programmes aimed at the conservation and sustainable use of biodiversity; the integration of the conservation and sustainable use of biodiversity into relevant sectoral or cross-sectoral plans, programmes and policies, and the promotion and the integration of conservation policies and sustainable use of biodiversity in plans, programmes and policies prepared by other Authorities. It also provides for in situ and *ex situ* conservation measures.

(8) Part VIII regards access to genetic resources and conservation measures, in accordance with the United Nations Convention on Biological Diversity, done at Rio de Janeiro on 5 June 1992.

(9) Part IX threats the surveillance and monitoring obligations of the Competent Authority, such as the setting up of national inventories aimed at the conservation and sustainable use of biodiversity, and as far as practically possible, to have these inventories digitised and made freely available to the public, subject to the provisions of the Freedom of Access to Information on the Environment Regulations, 2005.

(10) Part X deals with communications and research, communication education and public awareness, research and scientific cooperation, and the establishment of a clearinghouse mechanism.

(11) Part XI deals with permitting and penalties regarding the issue of permits, derogations, applications, and other supplementary provisions, keeping of a register with regards to such permits, and confidentiality. It also outlines the offences and penalties with regard to the various infringements regarding the different schedules.

(12) Part XII deals with other provisions, among them the repealing of the previous Regulations, as indicated above.

With regard to the different schedules of the flora and fauna protection Regulations, these are:

- Schedule I – Natural habitat types whose conservation requires the designation of Special Areas of Conservation;
- Schedule II – Animal and plant species of Community interest whose conservation requires the designation of special areas of conservation;
- Schedule III – Animal and plant species of national interest whose conservation requires the designation of special areas of conservation;
- Schedule IV – Criteria for selecting sites eligible for identification as sites of national importance or of international importance and designation as special areas of conservation;
- Schedule V – Animal and plant species of Community interest in need of strict protection;
- Schedule VI – Animal and plant species of national interest and in need of protection;
- Schedule VII – Animal and plant species of Community interest whose taking in the wild and exploitation may be subject to management measures;
- Schedule VIII – Animal and plant species of national interest whose taking in the wild and exploitation may be subject to management measures;
- Schedule IX – Identification and monitoring;
- Schedule X – Endemic species not covered by regulation;
- Schedule XI – Animal species of Community interest whose capture and killing, and transport are regulated; and
- Schedule XII – Prohibited methods and means of capture and killing and modes of transport.

§1. Protection of Flora

I. Trees

544. Government Notice 269 of 1933,[742] issued under the Antiquities (Protection) Act,[743] lists trees which are of antiquarian importance. This Government Notice, in fact, considers all those trees which are at least 200 years of age to be of antiquarian importance, in the sense of Article 3 of the Antiquities (Protection) Act. It also affords protection to historical trees. It lists what it identifies as the 'more important trees protected by law' while the Appendices list 'Memorial trees planted in the Gardens of Verdala and San Anton'.

742. List of Historical Trees having an Antiquarian Importance Order (S.L. 445.02).

743. Chapter 54 of the Laws of Malta, which provided: 'The provisions of this Act shall apply to monuments and other objects whether movable or immovable, having a geological, archaeological, antiquarian or artistic importance.'

The Act has now been repealed and replaced by the Cultural Heritage Act,[744] and the Government Notice has been transposed under this new Act.

545. For the purpose of the Conifer Trees (Preservation) Regulations,[745] 'conifer trees' means cypress (*Cupressus sempervirens*) and pine trees (*Pinus* spp.). These Regulations prohibit the destruction, cutting down, and uprooting of conifer trees wherever they are situated unless a written permission from the Director of Agriculture provides otherwise.

The Director of Agriculture, in fact, may give permission in writing for the cutting down, uprooting, and removal of any conifer trees where he is satisfied that the land is required for building purposes or for other reasons sufficient in his discretion. These Regulations are to have effect notwithstanding anything contained in any other law, and no claim for compensation or damage or any other remedy whatsoever shall arise out of the prohibition or out of the refusal of the Director of Agriculture to grant a permit, as provided for under these Regulations.

546. The old DPA[746] provided for the possibility of the publication of a list of scheduled trees. The PA, in fact, should have prepared and, from time to time, renewed a list of individual trees, groups of trees, or woodlands which it would refer to as 'scheduled trees'. These trees were to be considered protected, and in respect of any of them, tree preservation orders could be made to regulate such protection. No list of scheduled trees had ever been issued under the Act until its repeal. The list of scheduled trees was to be published in the Government Gazette. The Authority was to notify any one of the known owners of any scheduled tree that had been included in the list and of any tree preservation order made with respect to it.

No scheduled tree was to be cut down, lopped, topped, or wilfully damaged or destroyed except with the permission of the PA on an application made to it or as may have been allowed under a tree preservation order.[747] The PA could also issue an Emergency Conservation Order to protect trees which were not scheduled but which the Authority believed could have an importance or value sufficient to have it listed. The Authority could impose any conditions it deemed necessary, and a tree preservation order could regulate any matter affecting scheduled trees. If the case arose when trees which were not scheduled had to be urgently protected, the Authority could issue an emergency conservation order with respect to these trees, as in the case of buildings and sites. The Emergency Conservation Order was valid for six months from the date of its publication in the Government Gazette, and until that time, the trees protected by it were deemed to be 'scheduled' for all intents and purposes. The Act has been repealed, and while the scheduling and emergency conservation order systems have been retained, there is no express provision under the new

744. Chapter 445 of the Laws of Malta.
745. G.N. 328/1949 (S.L. 10.22).
746. Chapter 356 of the Laws of Malta, now repealed.
747. The Authority's permit and a tree preservation order granted or made under this piece of legislation may have contained such conditions and other provisions as the Planning Authority deemed necessary. A Tree Preservation Order may have regulated any matter affecting scheduled trees.

Act[748] allowing trees to benefit under them. However, trees may be protected under the EPA instead through a similar regime, as explained in the introduction to this chapter above.

547. The Trees and Woodland Protection Regulations were published by L.N. 12/2001 by virtue of the second EPA. The Regulations contained five schedules detailing strictly protected trees, protected trees, protected areas and invasive or damaging species, and set up a framework controlling or prohibiting specific activities in relation to the said trees and areas, with penalties for any breach. These Regulations were replaced by eponymous regulations in 2011,[749] which were in turn replaced by the latest Trees and Woodlands Protection Regulations in 2018[750] under the new EPA.[751] The aim of all three was to protect trees and woodlands in the Maltese Islands, safeguard them and regulate activities that may have an effect on them. The Competent Authority under the latest version is ERA.

548. Trees, woodlands, and sites listed in the First Schedule to the latest Regulations are protected. Table 1 to Part A of Schedule I lists trees protected in all locations in Malta, while Table 2 lists trees protected within protected areas, in ODZs, green areas, natural or rural/green enclaves in an urban area (development zone), or in urban public open spaces. Some species in Table 2 are exempted from protection if horticulturally grown or if planted for agricultural purposes for fruit or oil production in a field registered for agricultural use with the Agriculture Directorate and used by a registered farmer. Part B protects certain trees without prejudice to Tables 1 and 2. These are: all trees visible on 1967 aerial photos or that are more than 50 years of age if found within protected areas, ODZs, urban conservation areas or in an urban public open space; trees, woodlands and sites of historic or antiquarian importance under the aforementioned G.N. 269/1933; trees, woodlands and sites or their biological diversity protected under Article 7[752] or any other protected area; trees woodlands and sites protected by a Tree Preservation Order or by an approved management plan for a protected area;[753] the Indian fig (*Ficus microcarpa*) in urban public open spaces, so long as in the competent authority's opinion they are not causing any damage or adverse effect to the environment or to features of natural or cultural heritage value; provided that the protection shall not apply to trees listed in the Second Schedule unless otherwise specified in the relevant notice, order or plan.

549. ERA can designate specific areas as Tree Protection Areas, details of which are to be published in the Gazette, including a clearly delineated map of the site

748. Development Planning Act, Ch. 552 of the Laws of Malta. The relevant provisions are Arts 57 and 58.
749. L.N. 200/2011 (S.L. 549.64).
750. L.N. 258/2018 (S.L. 549.123).
751. Chapter 549 of the Laws of Malta.
752. As directed by the relevant notice issued under it.
753. As directed by such order or plan.

boundaries. These areas automatically form part of the National Ecological Network[754] and are to be registered in an index held by the Authority. The establishment of Tree Protection Areas is to be based on criteria which include: Maltese characteristic woodland communities; trees or woodland communities which are rare, threatened, or endangered or that have a reduced or restricted distribution in Malta; trees and woodland habitats critical to the survival, reproduction and recovery of endangered, threatened, vulnerable, endemic or otherwise important flora and fauna species; trees or woodland communities of scientific, ecological, aesthetic, historical, cultural, arboricultural, silvicultural, agricultural, educational, or landscape interest; prominent landmark trees; historical trees listed in G.N. 269/1933; *ex situ* live collections of rare, threatened, or endangered specimens. ERA may also establish an important site for any other specimen meriting protection.

550. Trees listed in the Second Schedule are deemed detrimental to the natural environment at all stages of their growth, and indeed the Schedule lists alien, invasive, or environmentally incompatible species. However, certain species are protected in urban public open spaces. No person shall propagate, sow, plant, import, export, transport, sell, exchange, or donate any specimen of species listed unless duly permitted. The Authority can issue removal orders obliging the owner or occupier[755] of a site to remove, uproot, kill, or destroy any tree listed in Schedule II on his property where such removal would constitute an environmental improvement. It may also issue a works method statement to ensure the order is executed with minimal damage to biodiversity, any building/structure worthy of retention, or the surrounding environment. The Authority can implement the required intervention, in whole or in part, as it deems most appropriate, at the expense of any person failing to comply with the Order issued. The Authority can also implement, finance, or commission eradication, control, or relocation programmes on a national or localised level in relation to any species listed in Schedule II or any other trees adversely impacting their surrounding environment. These programmes are to take into account the wider environmental considerations pertinent to the site in question and may include additional measures for the prevention, remediation, mitigation or containment of the adverse environmental effects associated with such trees. In these endeavours, the Authority may seek or require the participation or collaboration of other persons or institutions as it deems reasonable or necessary. Finally, without prejudice to the powers and obligations vested in the Director responsible for Plant Health, the Authority may stop or restrict the transportation, importation, possession, discarding, or disposal of trees it deems may endanger the biological diversity of trees or woodlands in Malta or may be detrimental to the environment in any way.

551. The Regulations regulate specific activities. No person may carry out, or be permitted to carry out, any activity which, in the Authority's opinion, may be

754. Without prejudice to the Flora, Fauna and Natural Habitats Protection Regulations.

755. If the person is unknown, it may publish the order in the Gazette and may implement it at its own expense after ninety days from its publication. However, it may implement the order, in whole or in part as it deems most appropriate, where immediate action is required. In any case, the Authority's right to indemnification once the person is identified is not prejudiced.

damaging to any specimen covered by Schedule I unless permitted by the Authority. It is prohibited, without the Authority's prior permission, to fell, cut, remove the bark or leaves of, uproot, remove timber from, hard prune, poison, burn, affix anything to, pierce, saw, or in any way destroy, kill, mutilate, destabilise, or significantly damage any tree or part thereof if the specimen is listed in the First Schedule. These prohibitions are inapplicable[756] to the pruning of horticulturally grown trees for the purpose of: reviving already diseased or damaged trees, preventing their further deterioration or improving their health; preserving their strength, enhancing their overall health, removing water sprouts or suckers, grafting, improving their fruit productivity or avoiding likely injury to persons or likely damage to property; controlling growth to avoid the entry of mice or rats within a building, provided that any branch or offshoot to be pruned must lie within not more than 1.5 m from such building and the main trunk of the tree is left unaffected. These apply provided the actions are carried out in line with good practice, at the appropriate time of the year and as long as all necessary measures and precautions are taken to minimise any adverse effects, provided further that the intervention does not mutilate, deform, destabilise, kill, weaken or otherwise significantly affect the tree. Nevertheless, the exceptions do not apply to trees in Table 1 of Part A of Schedule I and to trees falling under G.N. 269/1933.

Nevertheless, if, in the Authority's opinion, the works may have had unreasonable, unavoidable, or unacceptable environmental impacts, or if it has reasonable doubts as to whether the criteria laid down have been duly satisfied, it may intervene to: prevent, restrict, or stop works; impose limitations, specifications, or conditions as necessary; request further information, clarifications, or evidence about the situation; request clarifications about or amend the methodologies to be used; require that the works be submitted for prior authorisation by the Authority;[757] impose any remedial measures to prevent, limit, mitigate, reverse or offset any damage inflicted by works which are in progress or have already been carried out; adopt a combination of these actions.

The aforementioned prohibitions are likewise inapplicable to activities related to pruning, cutting, felling, treatment, and/or destruction of any tree harbouring quarantine pests and diseases[758] after written approval by the Director responsible for Plant Health, provided the tree does not fall under Table 1 of Part A of Schedule I. Finally, the prohibitions are inapplicable to the pruning of trees planted in private dwellings in urban areas, excluding trees in protected areas. It is forbidden to dump, throw, pour, place, bury in the ground, or deposit any dangerous, harmful, combustible, or explosive substances, waste, or scrap near any protected tree[759] or protected area unless the activity is duly authorised. The Authority may authorise the

756. The onus to prove that the action meets the criteria laid down lies with the person/entity carrying out, or intending to carry out, the action in case of any doubt, disagreement, claim or contestation on the matter.

757. Without prejudice to its eventual decision.

758. As listed in Schedules I and II of the Plant Quarantine (Harmful Organisms) Regulations (L.N. 97/2004, S.L. 433.03).

759. Any area within a distance of 5 m away from the circumference of the tree canopy or within the distance of 10 m away from the tree trunk, whichever is the larger.

use of specific substances[760] or any other treatment for weeding or surgical interventions which, in its opinion, may be reasonably required. This prohibition shall not apply to the use of substances for the treatment of trees for the purpose of preserving their strength, improving their overall health, improving their fruit productivity or preventing their deterioration. However, the Authority may still prohibit such use, irrigation, or treatment if it is of the opinion that the conservation of the specimen in question would be in conflict with the conservation of the trees, woodland, the ecosystem or any relevant management plan.

No person shall: set fire to any protected tree; generate a fire within a Tree Protection Area or near any tree covered in the First Schedule; let off fireworks within 20 m of a tree covered by the First Schedule. These prohibitions do not apply to: a fire directly connected with, or necessary for, the management of a protected area with the prior approval of, or upon a request by, the Authority; or a confined fire within the confines of a private dwelling. Without prejudice to any related environmental regulations,[761] no person shall sell, trade in or otherwise commercially exploit any products derived from activities prohibited by the Regulations, except with the prior written authorisation of the Authority.

552. A permit issued by the Authority is required before any intervention on any tree listed in Schedule I, with the exception of the Director responsible for Plant Health for any interventions related to phytosanitary purposes except for specimens falling under Table 1 of Part A of Schedule I. The Authority is not to issue the permit if it is of the opinion that the activity is not sufficiently justified or that the adverse impacts, implications, or risks of the activity outweigh any possible benefits. In issuing the permit, the Authority shall consider the impacts, implications, risks and benefits on: the existing trees and woodland per se; the species, habitats and ecosystems associated with the trees, as may be relevant; the structural integrity of buildings, structures and infrastructure or natural physical features located in the vicinity and meriting retention; the landscape, general character and environmental characteristics of the site and its surroundings; the integrity of any protected area, and the continued effectiveness of any protection, as may be relevant; any other material considerations as deemed relevant by the authority. The Authority may also issue a permit prior to the carrying out of any activity under the Regulations, provided it may not issue such a permit if, after considering the proposed activity, it is of the opinion that it is unjustified or that its adverse impacts outweigh any possible benefits.

An application in writing is to be submitted to the Authority at least three weeks before carrying out the activity, together with any relevant documents and requisite information by the Authority[762] and a permitting fee. The application is to be processed without undue delay; however, the Authority may request an independent assessment of the risks, impacts and implications on the area's environment, be it

---

760. Namely, any biocide, defoliant, acid, alkali, saline water or any poisonous, corrosive or growth-inhibiting chemical substance.
761. L.N. 79/2015 and L.N. 115/2015, discussed hereunder.
762. Including but not limited to a site plan marking the positions of all the relevant trees and photos of the trees for identification purposes.

rural or urban, to be financed by applicant. Furthermore, the Authority may impose any conditions it deems appropriate in the permit, and the period of validity is to be clearly indicated in the permit. The Authority's refusal of the application shall be accompanied by reasons therefor. The Authority may not issue or renew a permit if applicant has defaulted on the terms and conditions, etc., of any other permit issued by the Authority in relation to the site in question or otherwise affecting it, whether under the Regulations or not. Any permit issued does not exonerate applicant from obtaining all other permits required by law, nor is not to be construed as an in-principle commitment or agreement towards the issue of any other permit, etc., or intervention beyond the scope of the Regulations. A permit issued can be revoked, varied or suspended, and the Authority can order that the tree or site affected be restored to its condition preceding the permit, giving reasons for such decision. Where applicant is not at fault or responsible for the revocation, etc.,[763] he shall be entitled to any reasonable claims for the recovery of material costs and remediation of any physical damage consequent to the Authority's decision. Without prejudice to the above, the Authority may apply one or more listed measures to avoid, mitigate or offset the adverse impacts of any activity or intervention. The holder of a bona fide scientific or educational studies permit is to submit, *inter alia*, a detailed report of the activities undertaken, the outcome and the results to the Authority within a month of the permit's expiration, without prejudice to any other condition or obligation laid down by the Authority. A copy of the published results is to reach the Authority within three months of their publication. The Director may issue an emergency permit in cases of emergency or grave danger for the carrying out of any activity regulated by these Regulations, together with any directives, terms and conditions, and decisions he deems appropriate. An electronic public register shall be kept containing the details of applications submitted for a permit and of the decision taken thereupon. A person is to hold a copy of the permit on-site during the execution of the permitted activity or operation.

553. The Authority may establish, publish and, from time to time, update a Register of Licensed Tree Specialists and may delegate this function to any other public entity or committee. The Regulations provide for the licensing and qualifications of the Tree Specialists and their special privileges in carrying out interventions on specific important trees. However, this part of the Regulations is not yet in force at the time of writing.

554. The Authority has the power to impose an administrative fine[764] upon any person infringing any provision of the Regulations or failing to comply with any directive or decision taken by it in ensuring compliance with the same Regulations. It is an offence for any person to, wilfully or through imprudence, negligence or incompetence: fail to comply with any provision of the Regulations or with any order lawfully given in terms of those provisions; contravene any restriction, prohibition, order or requirement arising from the Regulations or imposed by the

763. For example, if the permit was issued on the basis of misleading or fraudulent information, Reg. 22(4).

764. In line with Arts 80 and 81 of the EPA.

Authority in accordance with them; act in contravention of any of those provisions; conspire with, aid, abet, counsel, instigate, procure or knowingly allow any other person to contravene or fail to comply with any such provision or any restriction, order, prohibition or requirement issued under the Regulations; attempt to do any of the above. These also apply in cases of negligence and voluntary damage by means of a vehicle. The penalties are consolidated in the Fourth Schedule depending on the character of the tree or area involved and the extent of damage inflicted. Apart from any fines (*multi*) or imprisonment term due under the Schedule, the court[765] may also order the offender to pay for any direct, indirect or consequential damage caused[766] and may order him to remove the cause of the offence and to undo any anything done without a permit within a time fixed by it sufficient for the purpose but not exceeding three months from the date of judgment. Failure to comply merits a fine (*multa*) of not more than EUR 150 for each day of default.

555. L.N. 79/2015[767] and L.N. 115/2015[768] implement the provisions of Regulation (EU) No. 995/2010 of the European Parliament and of the Council of 20 October 2010,[769] and Council Regulation (EC) No. 2173/2005 of 20 December 2005[770] and Commission Regulation (EC) No. 1024/2008[771] (the Implementing Regulation), respectively. The Competent Authority for both Regulations is the Director for Agriculture, as well as for Commission Implementing Regulation (EU) No. 607/2012[772] and Commission Delegated Regulation (EU) No. 363/2012.[773] The Director may request the assistance of members of the police force and of the Comptroller of Customs to enforce the provisions of both Regulations. Any person seeking to import timber from a partner country[774] is obliged to submit a FLEGT licence in the English language, covering the shipment, to the Director prior to the arrival of the shipment and in sufficient time to allow for its validation.

556. The Regulations provide for inspections. Under L.N. 79/2015, an operator[775] shall permit any authorised officer, at all reasonable times, for the purpose of

765. The provisions of Arts 23(1) and 30 of the Criminal Code apply *mutatis mutandis* to these proceedings. The disqualification from holding or obtaining a licence, permit, authorisation or clearance shall in no case be for less than one year.
766. Regulation 29(3) on remediation and mitigation expenses.
767. Timber and Timber Products (Placing on the Market) Regulations (S.L. 549.94).
768. Forest Law Enforcement, Governance and Trade Licencing Scheme Regulations (S.L. 549.95).
769. Laying down the obligations of operators who place timber and timber products on the market as set out in the Annex thereof.
770. On the establishment of a FLEGT licensing scheme for imports of timber into the European Community, as amended.
771. For the implementation of Council Regulation (EC) No. 2173/2005.
772. On detailed rules concerning the due diligence system and the frequency and nature of the checks on monitoring organisations as provided for in Regulation (EU) No. 995/2010 of the European Parliament and of the Council.
773. On the procedural rules for the recognition and withdrawal of recognition of monitoring organisations as provided for in Regulation (EU) No. 995/2010.
774. Listed in Annex I of Regulation (EC) No. 2173/2005, as may be subsequently amended.
775. Any natural or legal person that places timber or timber products on the EU market for the first time.

carrying out his functions under the Regulations and upon production of identification, to perform the listed inspections. Under L.N. 115/2015, the Director may, for the purposes of the regulations, appoint officers who will have such functions as the Director may deem necessary for the enforcement and implementation of the regulations, the Regulation (EC) No. 2173/2005 and the Implementing Regulation, and shall have the right to conduct the inspections listed. The inspections are to: enter into premises after giving prior notice, provided that the requirement of prior notice does not apply in cases where efforts to arrange an appointment have failed or when such notice would defeat the purpose of the entry, or where there is reasonable suspicion that an offence against the regulations has been committed; stop and/or board any vehicle, vessel, aircraft or other means of transport that the officer has reasonable grounds to believe is transporting timber; inspect the premises, any plant, machinery or equipment, containers and timber found on the premises; have access to, examine and copy any documentation, records or other information to which the regulations may apply, in whatever form they are held, and remove them to enable them to be copied or require computer records to be produced in a form in which they may easily be accessed and taken away by the officer; take samples of any timber; carry out any examination, investigation or test; take photographs, measurements or recordings. An operator or economic regulator, depending on the Regulations, shall provide all reasonable assistance to any authorised officer performing the above-mentioned actions, particularly: providing for inspection such document or record as may be required by the officer; making any timber available for examination, as may be required.

557. L.N. 79/2015 empowers the Director to serve, in writing, a notice of remedial actions[776] on any person he has reasonable cause to believe has contravened or failed to comply with any provision of Articles 4 and 5 of Regulation (EU) No. 995/2010 and Article 5 of the Implementing Regulation. The notice must specify the nature of the offence, the facts upon which the allegation that an offence has been committed is based, the measures that, in the Director's opinion, must be taken to in order to ensure compliance, and the period within which any such measures must be taken as is reasonable in the circumstances. In addition, the Director may prohibit the placing on the market of the timber as an interim measure until the remedial actions specified are carried out, provided the grounds for taking such measures are specified in the notice, and the authorised officer can mark the timber in question for identification. Failure to comply with the notice within the specified time allows the Director to serve the person with a notice specifying: the date and nature of the offence; a summary of the facts upon which the allegation that an offence has been committed is based; any other matter (not being previous convictions) that the Director considers relevant to the imposition of a penalty; the amount of the penalty due and, where the penalty due depends on a previous conviction, the date of such previous conviction. It shall be endorsed on a statement setting out the provisions of the regulation. The person then has two alternative routes to tackle this administrative penalty. First, he may, within thirty days, by notice served on the Director,

776. This is deemed to have been delivered and duly notified if it is physically delivered or sent by registered post to the person at his place of residence or business or place of work or postal address.

require that proceedings regarding the alleged offence be dealt with by the court. In this case, the following apply: the Director shall take no further proceedings under the regulation; and the institution of any proceedings in respect of the alleged offence or the person's conviction of it by the court, or the imposition of any penalty or forfeiture under the regulations upon such conviction, is not prevented.

Second, if he does not wish that the proceedings be dealt with by the court, the person may, within thirty days by notice in writing served on the Director, admit the offence,[777] pay the amount of the penalty to the Director within the same timeframe or after such subsequent period as the Director may determine, and take the necessary remedial actions to ensure conformity with the Regulations. Where a person admits an offence, the Director shall impose a monetary penalty on that person in respect of the offence amounting to one-third of the maximum penalty to which the person would be liable if he were convicted of the offence by the court. The penalty is due as a civil debt enforceable by the competent court of civil jurisdiction in favour of the government. The declaration by the person that he admits the charge constitutes an executive title[778] as though it were a judgment of the same competent court.

Where a person does not within thirty days admit the offence, the Director shall institute proceedings, or cause them to be instituted, before the court in respect of the alleged offence.

558. It is an offence[779] under L.N. 79/2015 to: fail to comply with the prohibition on placing illegally harvested timber on the market in accordance with Article 4(1) of Regulation (EU) No. 995/2010; fail to comply with the obligation to exercise due diligence and maintain and regularly evaluate the due diligence system in accordance with Articles 4(2) and (3) of the same Regulation; fail to comply with the obligation of traceability in accordance with the same Regulation; fail to comply with the record-keeping obligation in accordance with Article 5 of the Implementing Regulation; fail to comply or contravene any provision of the L.N. or fail to comply with any order lawfully given in terms of any provision of Regulation (EU) No. 995/2010, the Implementing Regulation, or the L.N.; conspire or attempt, or aid, or abet, any other person by whatever means, including advertisement, counselling or procurement to contravene the provisions of the L.N. or to fail to comply with the said provisions, or to contravene any restriction, prohibition or requirement imposed by or under the L.N.; intentionally obstruct or cause the obstruction of any person acting in the proper exercise of his functions under the L.N. and/or fail to allow an inspection authorised under it; without reasonable excuse, fail to give any person acting as mentioned any assistance or information which he may be required to give under the L.N. or any other law, or give false or misleading information; alter, forge, counterfeit or destroy any document presented to or issued by the Director under the L.N.

777. Admittance of the offence allows no charge to be laid in respect of the offence against the person admitting it.
778. Under Art. 253 of the COCP, Ch. 9 of the Laws of Malta.
779. The provisions of Arts 23(1) and 30 of the Criminal Code apply *mutatis mutandis* to these proceedings. The disqualification from holding or obtaining a licence, permit, authorisation or clearance shall in no case be for less than one year.

The punishment on a first conviction relating to the first, second, seventh, eighth and ninth offences is a fine (*multa*) between EUR 2,500 and EUR 25,000, while in relation to the rest, it is a fine (*multa*) between EUR 1,500 and EUR 5,000. A second or subsequent conviction is liable to a fine (*multa*) between EUR 2,500 and EUR 50,000. The court may, in addition: order that the timber, etc., be forfeited to the government, and if so, it shall be disposed of in such a manner as the court may determine on the Director's advice; suspend any licence or permit held by the offender and related to any business or trade to which the offence relates for a period the court deems proper but not less than one month; impose an additional fine equivalent to the estimated economic benefit which the convict derived, or would have derived if the offence remained undetected, from the commission of the offence; sentence the offender to imprisonment for a term not less than thirty days and not more than two years. The proceedings shall be held by the Court of Magistrates (Malta) or the Court of Magistrates (Gozo) as the case may be and shall be in accordance with the provisions of the Criminal Code regulating the procedure before the said courts as courts of criminal judicature. In respect of proceedings for any offence charged against the Regulations, the court may award in favour of the government such costs and expenses incurred in relation to the proceedings as it deems proper. In respect of proceedings for an offence consisting of a failure to comply with Articles 4 and 5 of Regulation (EU) No. 995/2010 and Article 5 of the Implementing Regulation, the onus of proof that all necessary due diligence was done to satisfy the duty or requirement, or that there were no better practicable means than was used to satisfy the same, is on the accused.

559. It is an offence[780] under L.N. 115/2015 to: fail to comply with the prohibition on timber imports from partner countries unless covered by a FLEGT licence accordingly; use a false, falsified, invalid or expired licence or one altered without authorisation for any purpose connected with the regulations; make no import notification or a false one; make use of a licence for any other timber shipments other than the one for which it was issued; fail to submit the FLEGT licence to the Director; fail to comply with or contravene any provision of the regulations, the Regulation (EC) No. 2173/2005 or the Implementing Regulation, or fail to comply with any order lawfully given in terms of the same; alter, forge, counterfeit, or destroy any licence or document presented to or issued by the Director under the regulations; conspire or attempt, or aid, or abet, any other person by whatever means, including advertisement, counselling or procurement to contravene the provisions of the L.N. or to fail to comply with the said provisions, or to contravene any restriction, prohibition or requirement imposed by or under the L.N.; intentionally obstruct or cause the obstruction of any person acting in the proper exercise of his functions under the L.N. and/or fail to allow an inspection authorised under it; without reasonable excuse, fail to give any person acting as mentioned any assistance or information which he may be required to give under the L.N. or any other law, or give false or misleading information. The punishment on first conviction is a fine

780. The provisions of Arts 23(1) and 30 of the Criminal Code apply *mutatis mutandis* to these proceedings. The disqualification from holding or obtaining a licence, permit, authorisation, or clearance shall in no case be for less than one year.

(*multa*) between EUR 1,500 and EUR 25,000, and on the second or subsequent convictions, it is a fine (*multa*) between EUR 2,500 and EUR 50,000. The court may also impose the additional penalties mentioned in the previous legal notice and order the convict to pay for any expenses incurred for the storage, removal, transport and disposal of the imported goods and any other expenses incurred in relation to the proceedings. The competent court is the Court of Magistrates, as mentioned in the previous L.N.

II. Other Protected Flora

560. The Protection of Wild Thyme Regulations[781] were published by virtue of the Code of Police Laws. These Regulations prohibit any person from destroying, cutting down, or uprooting the shrubs of wild thyme (*Thymus capitatus*) or selling, purchasing, using, or keeping such shrubs for any purpose. The Superintendent of Agriculture (today taken to mean the Director of Agriculture) may, however, give permission in writing for the cutting, uprooting, and removal of wild thyme 'whenever the land is required for reclamation or to be otherwise industrially exploited or in order to reduce the number of the shrub where it becomes overgrown'. These old Regulations are still valid today, although responsibility for the protection of wild thyme, an important component of the garigue habitat typical to the islands, lies nowadays with the EPD. Furthermore, it is unlikely that land reclamation would constitute a valid reason to allow for the uprooting of wild thyme, as this is contrary to the policy of the EPD. Nevertheless, since this piece of legislation has not been abrogated or replaced, it still has the force of law.

561. The Plant Quarantine Act[782] aims at preventing the introduction into Malta of plant pests and diseases and at controlling and checking their spread. The Act also provides for other matters incidental and ancillary thereto. Its main aim, however, pertains to the protection of the agro-industry rather than the environment. Consequently, although it does control the introduction of alien species, it does so incidentally because its primary purpose is the control of plant pests and diseases, and hence it does not constitute an appropriate legal framework to safeguard Malta's biological diversity in this sense. Furthermore, the new Act also adopts EU internal market measures since the terms 'import' and 'export' do not include the introduction of a thing into Malta or the taking out of a thing from Malta, from or to, respectively, a Member State of the EU. In this case, the principle of free movement has to be respected, and all border checks have to be abolished. 'Owner' is defined by the regulations as either the direct owner or any person who holds a title of lease, emphyteusis, or any other right of possession, or both owners of property and title together, jointly or separately.

562. The administration and implementation of this Act fall under the authority of the Director responsible for the Department of Plant Health. This Department is

781. G.N. 85/1932 (S.L. 10.10).
782. Chapter 433 of the Laws of Malta, repealing the Agriculture (Plant Protection) Act.

duty-bound to inspect growing plants, areas under cultivation, and plants and plant products in storage or locally in transit in order to report the existence, outbreak, and spread of plant pests and to control such plant pests. They are also responsible for consignments of plant materials moving in international traffic and for issuing phytosanitary certificates or plant passports, and they must periodically update and disseminate lists of plant material, plant pests, and beneficial organisms the importation of which into Malta is prohibited or restricted, and they must also disseminate information within Malta about pests of plant and plant products and how to prevent and control them. Research and surveys in the field of plant protection and the administration and enforcement of these provisions also fall under the responsibility of this Department.

Under this Act, there is also the setting up of a Plant Protection Board, which shall regularly review the state of plant quarantine in Malta on the formulation of policies in this regard and advise the Minister on any matters with which this Act is concerned.

563. The functional part is on imports and exports. In fact, no person shall import into Malta any plant material, plant pest, beneficial organism, soil, or packaging material except in accordance with this Act. Also, any person intending to export a consignment of plants or plant products to another country shall submit the consignment to the Plant Health Service for pre-export examination. Any importation of any plant material, plant pest, and so forth has to be accompanied by the required permits and certificates, which shall be examined by an inspector at the designated point of entry. Furthermore, any person in Malta who receives any plant material, plant pest, and so forth from outside Malta shall immediately notify an inspector and carry out the inspector's instructions regarding its destruction, disposal, or treatment to the satisfaction of the inspector. If these provisions are not respected, the police have the power to seize such products, and they will follow the inspector's instructions on their treatment or destruction or their disposal. Moreover, the issuance of such a permit may be prohibited or restricted by the Director after consultation with the Board. Also, the Minister for Agriculture may, acting on the advice of the Board, make regulations establishing rules for the marketing of vegetative propagating and planting material and may, by such regulations, establish the conditions for the grant of permits for the importation and transport of any plant material, plant pest, or other organisms for the purposes of scientific research or otherwise, subject to such terms and conditions as may be established in or referred to in the regulations to safeguard public health, agriculture, and/or the environment.

564. Apart from regulating the importation and exportation of such products, the Director is also responsible for the containment and eradication of plant pests. In fact, if the Director is satisfied that a notifiable plant pest is present at any place, he will notify the landowner of such place and others in the vicinity to take whatever measures on their land in order to eradicate, contain, or restrict the spreading of the notifiable plant pest. And if such owner can't comply with any term of a notice, the Director may authorise the Plant Health Service to enter upon the land or premises in question and to take whatever measures as may be appropriate to carry out the requirements of the notice. And where any plant material or other thing is destroyed or harmed by any measure taken to eradicate, contain, or limit the spread of a notifiable plant pest, the Minister may compensate the owner of the plant material or item destroyed or harmed from monies voted for that purpose by the House of Representatives.

565. The transgression of the provisions of the Act or any of the regulations issued under it is a criminal offence. Upon conviction by the Court of Magistrates, the offender may be subject to a fine (*multa*), which varies depending on the type of offence and whether it is a first or a subsequent conviction and/or imprisonment. In addition to this, the court may order that all income and profits from the sale of such offending article be seized; impose an additional fine equivalent to the estimated economic benefit which the convicted person derived from the commission of the offence or would have derived had the offence remained undetected; and/or revoke any permit granted under this Act and de-bar the person convicted from holding another such permit for a period not exceeding three years. Furthermore, the Minister responsible for Justice may, by regulations, prescribe that certain offences under this Act shall be scheduled offences for the purposes of the Commissioners for Justice Act and may be tried by a Commissioner for Justice as in infringement. Lastly, any person found guilty under this Act may be ordered by the court to reimburse the Director for any expenses incurred by the Director or by any inspector or other authorised officer.

§2. Protection of Fauna

I. Wild Birds and Wild Rabbits

566. Before the advent of EU legislation, wild birds and wild rabbits were protected under the same laws dealing with the hunting of these species. These are now dealt with under separate legislation, but the general regulatory and protective framework is the same and shared.

567. The first regulation of bird protection dates back to 1872, and these regulations were eventually built upon during subsequent years. The regulations in force today are the Conservation of Wild Birds Regulations.[783] This Legal Notice, published under the EPA,[784] repealed the previous regulations of L.N. 146 of 1993, except for the parts dealing with the wild rabbit. The Regulations in force are divided into three parts and with ten schedules attached. These are:

(1) Schedule I – Bird species subject of special conservation measures concerning their habitat;
(2) Schedule II – Part A – Birds that may be hunted or taken on land;

783. L.N. 79/2006 (S.L. 549.42).
784. Formerly the Environment Protection Act XX of 2001 (Ch. 435 of the Laws of Malta), and currently the EPA (Ch. 549).

(3) Schedule II – Part B – Birds that may be hunted at sea;
(4) Schedule III(a) – Bird species which are permitted to be imported or exported, sold, transported for sale, kept for sale or offered for sale, alive or dead birds or of any readily recognisable parts or any derivatives thereof, provided that any such birds have been lawfully killed or captured or otherwise lawfully acquired;
(5) Schedule III(b) – Bird species which are permitted to be imported or exported, sold, transported for sale, kept for sale or offered for sale, alive or dead birds or of any readily recognisable parts or any derivatives thereof, provided that any such birds have been lawfully killed or captured or otherwise lawfully acquired, provided these are recommended by the Ornis Committee;
(6) Schedule IV – Reporting Obligations;
(7) Schedule V – Bird sanctuaries, site maps of which were also included as part of the schedule;
(8) Schedule VI – General Licence conditions;
(9) Schedule VII – Beaches protected under the Regulations;
(10) Schedule VIII – Administrative fines;
(11) Schedule IX – Non-Schedule I species subject to special protection; and
(12) Schedule X – Administrative fees.

568. The Minister responsible for the environment is responsible for the administration and enforcement of these Regulations.

The Regulations establish the setting up of the Ornis Committee and outline its composition, workings, functions, recommendations, reporting, and studies in connection with bird protection. One of the functions of the Ornis Committee is to recommend the open seasons during which hunting and taking shall be allowed to the Minister. Its function is purely consultative; however, a substantial divergence between its recommendations and the Minister's final decision must be justified by the latter in the *Gazette*.

The implementation of the Committee's recommendations and the Minister's decisions is entrusted to the Wild Birds Regulation Unit (WBRU), as well as the enforcement of the Regulations. To this end, it can designate officers to assist the police or other authorities in inspections or prosecutions carried out pursuant to these Regulations. The Committee may also delegate any of its functions to the WBRU.

The WBRU is responsible for the administration of a Conservation of Wild Birds Fund, the aim of which is to finance activities, etc., related to the implementation of the Regulations' aims and objectives, including those organised by NGOs.

569. Part I of the Regulations deal with bird[785] conservation. All birds are protected, and it is illegal to:

785. 'Birds' is defined as any species of naturally occurring avifauna in the wild state in the European territory of the Member States of the EU, with the exception of Greenland.

(1) hunt or attempt to hunt, take or attempt to take any bird protected under the Regulations, other than as provided and subject to the stipulated licences and conditions;
(2) hunt or attempt to hunt, take or attempt to take, destroy, damage or remove by any means any birds nests and eggs;
(3) take the eggs in the wild of any bird which is protected under the Regulations and keep those eggs even if empty;
(4) deliberately disturb any bird which is protected under the Regulations during the period of breeding and rearing;
(5) be in possession or in control of any bird specimen, alive or dead, or any recognisable parts or derivatives, not listed in Schedule II and/or being a non-European territory bird,[786] subject to the Regulations.

The bird species listed in Schedule I are afforded special conservation measures concerning their habitat, particularly including the designation of SPAs. The same applies for regularly occurring migratory species not listed in the Schedule, as regards, *inter alia*, their breeding, moulting, and wintering areas.

Part I of the Regulations also deals with the import, export, sale, transport for sale, keeping for sale, or offering for sale of live or dead birds or any recognisable parts or derivatives of wild birds protected under the Regulations, except for birds included in Schedule III(a) and Schedule III(b), subject to certain provisions.

570. This Part of the Regulations also lists illegal methods for the taking and capturing of wild birds. These include:

(1) snares, limes including birdlime, poisonous or stupefying bait, hooks or any similar substances or methods;
(2) any electrocuting devices;
(3) any artificial light sources, mirrors, devices for illuminating targets or any night vision devices comprising an electronic image magnifier or image converter;
(4) any gas, or any electric or electronic device, especially the use of pre-recorded bird calls;
(5) nets, including those known as *ranja*, mist-nets, and any type of vertical net;
(6) any kind of cage trap, whether with a net or not;
(7) decoy live birds which are blind or mutilated;
(8) decoy live birds held by any means except those held by cotton string and swivel;
(9) decoys of protected birds;
(10) explosives; and
(11) semi-automatic or automatic weapons with a magazine capable of holding more than two rounds of ammunition.

786. A non-European territory bird is any bird species which, although naturally occurring in the wild in any territory outside the territory of the Member States of the European Union, does not naturally occur in any territory of the Member States of the European Union.

However, bird ringers can use mist nets and pre-recorded bird songs in accordance with the Regulations. Furthermore, no person shall sell, offer for sale, exhibit for sale, or keep any device the use of which is prohibited under the Regulations unless they are not used in connection with the taking or hunting of birds.

571. Part I of these Regulations also lists hunting restrictions. It is prohibited to hunt or attempt to hunt any birds except those in Schedule II, subject to specific derogations, subject to the Regulations and in accordance with the principles of wise use and ecologically balanced control of such species. Hunting can be carried out on land for species listed in Schedule IIA and also at sea for species listed in Schedule IIB. However, there can be no hunting of these birds during the rearing season or during the various stages of reproduction of these species, as well as no hunting of the migratory species during their period of reproduction or during their return to their rearing grounds.

The Regulations also regulate the carrying and loading of firearms, both on land and also at sea. The size of lead shot is regulated, and no person can sell, offer for sale, carry, be in possession of, hunt or use, import, or manufacture any cartridge loaded with lead shots of any size greater than 3.3 mm in diameter, except those persons authorised by the Police Commissioner for purposes other than hunting.

572. The issue of licences for hunting and taking (trapping), and conditions stipulated in Schedule VI to the Regulations, for the issue of such licences, are also dealt with by the Conservation of Wild Birds Regulations. Among these conditions is the person being a paid member of an organisation representing hunters and trappers. Nevertheless, he may not hunt if he has not paid the general licence fee and any other fees due under Schedules VIII and X. Hunters and trappers are obliged to carry with them their identity card or any other recognised means of identification and the proper licence for the activity issued to them under the Regulations or any other law. However, hunters and trappers not carrying such documents with them can, within two days, produce to the police such document at the place indicated by them. No person in search or in pursuit of birds[787] may enter property occupied by third parties against their consent. No person shall, between two hours after sunset and two hours before sunrise of the next following day, hunt or attempt to hunt, take, or attempt to take any bird by any means or carry a firearm which is loaded or out of its case. Other time limits are stipulated depending on specific dates or times of the year, along with other general prohibitions relating to times for hunting and trapping, use of firearms, etc. There are also restrictions on cage size and a prohibition on involvement in any event where captive birds are freed for the purpose of being shot at. Specific provisions are also in force regulating bird ringing. The Regulations are furthermore not intended to prohibit clay-pigeon shooting in conformity with the law.

787. Unless the contrary is proved, any person who between two hours before sunrise and two hours after sunset, or during any close season, is found in the open countryside, whether on his own land or on land belonging to some other person, or outside such land, or is found at sea carrying a firearm or ammunition for taking game, shall be deemed to be in the actual search for or pursuit of birds.

573. Bird sanctuaries are protected from any form of hunting or taking at any time and on any date, except for bird ringing and some others, and also benefit from certain measures for protection and prohibitions. The WBRU may order the owner, tenant, or other person who is making use of or is in possession of land on which any bird hide used for hunting or trapping birds or other hiding place intended to be used for shooting or taking of birds to demolish, within such time as it may determine, any such structure if it has been so constructed or built in a bird sanctuary, or within limits not in conformity with the Regulations.

574. Taxidermy is also regulated under these Regulations. No person can stuff or mount any bird or non-European territory bird or act as a taxidermist for commercial purposes without a licence issued by the WBRU. No taxidermist shall mount or stuff any bird except those included in Schedules II or III or which are captive-bred and closed-ringed. Every taxidermist shall keep a register of birds in his possession. Furthermore, it shall not be lawful for any person to possess any stuffed bird or birds whose species is not included in Schedule III to the Regulations. All those who possess protected stuffed birds have to register them within the time prescribed in the Regulations.

575. The Regulations provide for derogations from the provisions of Regulations 4, 5, 6, 7, 18 and 21, which deal mainly with trapping, hunting, taking of eggs, use of illegal methods, closed seasons, and taxidermy. Such derogations may be authorised where there is no other satisfactory solution. The Ornis Committee may make such recommendations for authorisation to the Minister. Derogations must be justified under one or more of the following reasons:

(1) in the interests of public health and safety;
(2) in the interests of air safety;
(3) to prevent serious damage to crops, livestock, forests, fisheries and water;
(4) for the protection of flora and fauna;
(5) for the purposes of research and teaching, of re-population, of re-introduction and for the breeding necessary for these purposes; and
(6) to permit, under strictly supervised conditions and on a selective basis, the capture, keeping or other judicious use of certain birds in small numbers.

However, in authorising any derogations, the following must be specified:

(1) the species which are subject to the derogations;
(2) the means, arrangements, or methods authorised for capture or killing;
(3) the conditions of risk and the circumstances of time and place under which such derogations may be granted; and
(4) the controls which will be carried out.

Legal Notices are in force providing frameworks for these derogations, as well as season-specific derogations and will be tackled separately in the paragraphs below.

576. L.N. 221/2010 is the Framework for Allowing a Derogation Opening a Spring Hunting Season for Turtle Dove and Quail Regulations.[788] The Minister may establish the period for hunting by notice in the Gazette at a maximum of three weeks which may commence in March or April of the year for which the Minister may decide to open the season. Any hunter requires a spring hunting licence, which is subject to possession of a valid general licence to hunt birds on land. Every licence shall establish the overall and daily bag limits for the season and other conditions and obligations to be adhered to by the hunter. Hunting is only permissible between two hours before sunrise to noon on weekdays, Saturdays, Sundays, and Public Holidays. The police are empowered to carry out spot-checks to ensure compliance with the conditions of the licence and relevant regulations. Interestingly, the Framework is declared to prevail in the case of inconsistencies between itself and the Wild Birds Regulations.

Each spring hunting season opened under the derogation framework is published as a separate Legal Notice, which establishes the specific dates of the open season and sets the quotas for it. Prior to its promulgation, the Wild Birds Regulations would be amended yearly to provide for the open and closed seasons for hunting and trapping of birds.

577. Live-capturing (trapping) of wild birds by any means is prohibited except by derogation. Even so, the licensee can only use traditional, manually operating selective clap-nets for capturing for the purpose of keeping the birds in captivity according to the relevant framework regulations. Live-capturing can only occur within live-capturing sites in areas clearly outlined on a site plan approved for the purpose by the WBRU and registered with the Police Commissioner containing not more than two sites live-capturing stations per licensee. Each station is limited to two pairs of clap-nets.

The relevant framework is the Conservation of Wild Birds (Framework for Allowing a Derogation Opening an Autumn Live-Capturing Season for Song Thrush and Golden Plover) Regulations.[789] The duration of the open season is capped at a maximum of seventy-three days for song thrush and seventy-one days for golden plover, which the Minister may establish for each year by notice in the Gazette. The general provisions relating to licences, enforcement, etc., are similar to those of the spring hunting derogation framework, with a few additions, such as a duty on the police to conduct daily on-the-spot inspections throughout the season in all the regions shown in the Second Schedule. There are added provisions on the live-capturing stations, the nets' mesh size is established to exclusively capture the relevant species, and each captured bird is to be fitted with a single-use ring as specified by the WBRU. The framework prevails over the Wild Birds Regulations in case of any inconsistencies.

Each autumn live-capturing season opened under the derogation framework is published as a separate Legal Notice, which establishes the specific dates of the open season and sets the quotas for it.

788. S.L. 549.57.
789. L.N. 303/2012 (S.L. 549.74).

578. The trapping of finches[790] could be legally undertaken up to 31 December 2008, according to an agreement with EU Commission prior to accession. These could be deliberately captured by traditional nets known as clap-nets exclusively for the purpose of keeping them in captivity in accordance with the intermediate targets provided for in the Accession Treaty between Malta and the EU; however, any taking as may be allowed was to be subject to any obligations arising from the said Treaty. The government re-introduced finch trapping in 2014, and it eventually established a Framework for Allowing an Autumn Live-Capturing Season for Finches Regulations by virtue of L.N. 253/2014.[791] However, this was repealed by L.N. 383/2018 after it was found to be in breach of Malta's obligations under the Treaty on the Functioning of the European Union (TFEU) by the Court of Justice of the European Union (CJEU).[792]

The Maltese Government then issued L.N. 399/2020, the Conservation of Wild Birds (Declaration on a Derogation Allowing a Research Period to Determine Malta's Reference Population for Seven Finch Species) Regulations.[793] The aim was to gather sufficient scientific information for Malta to introduce a derogatory regime in compliance with the Birds Directive and that also complies with the 'small numbers' criterion as interpreted by the CJEU in judgment reference C-557/15. It, therefore, allowed the trapping of the seven finch species in order to reach this aim. This was heavily criticised by conservationists and resulted in infringement proceedings being initiated against Malta by the European Commission before the CJEU since it was seen as a ploy to allow finch trapping by circumventing the CJEU judgment delivered against Malta. This led to the repeal of these Regulations by L.N. 387/2021 and their replacement by the Conservation of Wild Birds (Framework for Allowing a Derogation to Carry out Scientific Research on Seven Finch Species) Regulations.[794]

579. These latest Regulations establish a framework for allowing, under strictly supervised conditions and in a selective manner, a research derogation to obtain scientific data on Malta's reference population of the same seven finch species. These can be trapped through clap-nets meeting the requirements of the Regulations and are to be kept solely until they are duly controlled or tagged with approved scientific rings and/or satellite tags and their details are taken. The responsible authority for the issue of the relevant special research licences and the establishment of the research parameters, etc., is the WBRU. All specimens captured are to be immediately reported, in real-time, to the WBRU. The research period is not to be longer than sixty-four days in autumn and must be declared by the Minister by Legal Notice. The licence requirements, contents, and application process, as well as other regulations concerning research sites, are governed by these Regulations. The

790. The finches in question were *Fringilla coelebs* (chaffinch), *Serinus* (serin), *Carduelis chloris* (greenfinch), *Carduelis carduelis* (goldfinch), *Carduelis cannabina* (linnet), *Carduelis spinus* (siskin), *Coccothraustes coccothraustes* (hawfinch).

791. S.L. 549.93, now repealed.

792. Case C-557/15, *Commission v. Republic of Malta* (21 Jun. 2018).

793. S.L. 549.137. The first such season was opened in October 2020 through L.N. 400/2020 (S.L. 549.138).

794. L.N. 394/2021 (S.L. 549.145).

licence is valid only for a single research period. Furthermore, the police are to carry out daily systematic spot-checks and may request the assistance of NGOs. It is an offence to fail to comply with these Regulations, with the contents of the specific licence, or with any order lawfully given under the Regulations, etc. The penalties in Regulation 27 of the Wild Birds Regulations apply here. The framework prevails over the Wild Birds Regulations in case of any inconsistencies.

580. The new finch trapping framework has again been heavily criticised by conservationists for the same reasons. The repealed 2020 Regulations, as mentioned, resulted in infringement proceedings against Malta. In December 2020, the European Commission initiated these proceedings by sending two letters of formal notice to Malta: one for Treaty infringement and disregard of the mentioned judgment through the new finch trapping framework; the other for Treaty infringement through the general hunting and trapping derogation frameworks. Malta defended its finch trapping derogation framework, but the EU still deemed it dissatisfactory, sending a reasoned opinion in June and giving the government one month to answer. The case was referred to the CJEU on 12 November 2021, following the promulgation of the new 2021 Regulations, for failure to correctly apply the Birds Directive. In its press release, the Commission considered that 'even though the declared objective is "research", several elements indicate that the scheme – in practice – allows for a large number of birds to be captured without being reported, contrary to the strict conditions for derogations set by the Birds Directive'.[795]

581. Another derogation framework came into force with L.N. 255/2013, the Conservation of Wild Birds (Framework for Allowing a Derogation for the Control of Birds in the Interest of Air Safety) Regulations.[796] The Minister may declare a maximum of twelve calendar months as the period for such bird control for the year he decided to allow it, provided there is no other satisfactory solution[797] to disperse the birds from within the areas in Schedule V. The activity requires a specific Air Safety Bird Control Licence, valid for a maximum period of one year and regulating the bird control operation. The framework lays down the grounds on which the licence may be issued and empowers the police to perform spot-checks to ensure compliance. In case and to the extent of any inconsistencies with the Wild Birds Regulations, the framework will prevail. The Minister must publish each derogation as a separate Legal Notice. So far, they have dealt with the control of *Columba livia* (Rock dove) and *Sturnus vulgaris* (Common starling).

582. Part II of the Conservation of Wild Birds Regulations deals with offences and penalties. The penalties come in the form of a fine (*multa*), with the amount varying with the infraction and whether it is a first or subsequent conviction. A first conviction is also subject to the confiscation of the *corpus delicti* and the suspension of any licence or permit issued under the Regulations and under Part XV of the

795. *See* the European Commission's Press Release in full at https://ec.europa.eu/commission/presscorner/detail/en/ip_21_5666.
796. S.L. 549.85.
797. In terms of the relevant EU legislation.

Code of Police Laws[798] for specific periods. A second or subsequent conviction entails the alternative of imprisonment or both fine and imprisonment, the confiscation of the *corpus delicti* and the permanent revocation of any such licence or permit. There is also the possibility of the court imposing a Community Service Order[799] and other measures and special procedures.

583. Part III deals with omissions by responsible persons. Where any person or body responsible for the performance of these Regulations fails to perform any tasks or functions as are assigned to it under these Regulations within the prescribed time period, if any, the Minister may proceed to take action as he may deem expedient, without prejudice to the possibility of making any charges upon the performance by such person or body of the tasks or functions assigned to it. It also lays down that the Regulations do not exempt any person with a valid licence from obtaining any other required valid licence for any activity he wishes to undertake.

584. Part III of the Regulations also repeals the Protection of Birds and Wild Rabbit Regulations[800] except for the definition of the closed season and the provisions regulating the hunting of the wild rabbit. However, despite repealing the previous Regulations, the Regulations in force have maintained that anything that has lawfully been done by virtue of the repealed Regulations shall remain in force, except insofar as it is inconsistent with any of the provisions of the Regulations in force. Furthermore, any liability to any penalty under any of the provisions of the repealed Protection of Birds and Wild Rabbit Regulations is to continue to subsist.

585. Despite the savings for the provisions on wild rabbits, there are now in force the Protection of Wild Rabbits Regulations,[801] which protect *Oryctolagus cuniculus* in Malta insofar as the Regulations allow. No person may shoot, capture, kill or take, or attempt to perform such acts on, any specimen of a wild rabbit during the closed season for the capture and/or shooting of rabbit by means and methods other than those allowed and unless he is in possession of a general licence issued by the Police Commissioner and the WBRU and is carrying this, together with a means of identification, on his person throughout the activity. The issuing of the licence is subject to passing an exam to test knowledge of the Regulations and the use and safe carrying of firearms. The open season is from 1 June to 31 December, both days included, provided the Minister may alter or revoke its duration if relevant scientific knowledge creates concern for the rabbit's conservation status or for the maintenance of its population at a satisfactory level. The times for hunting/capturing and the capture and shooting methods are also regulated, together with certain exceptions, restrictions and prohibitions from entering certain areas while hunting/capturing rabbits. Furthermore, the licensed person must report to the

798. Chapter 10 of the Laws of Malta.
799. In terms of the Probation Act (Ch. 446 of the Laws of Malta).
800. L.N. 146 of 1993.
801. L.N. 207/2014 (S.L. 549.90).

WBRU through a game reporting system, as may be prescribed, information on the number of wild rabbits killed/captured and the geographical area where this occurred. Offences and penalties are also laid down, very similarly to those for violating the provisions of the Conservation of Wild Birds Regulations. Schedules to the Regulations determine: general licence conditions, administrative fines, restricted areas where capturing rabbits is prohibited, and applicable fees.

586. L.N. 249/2016 contains the Conservation of Wild Birds (Falconry) Regulations[802] regulating falconry. No person may practice falconry or any related activity without a licence issued by the WBRU, with the exception of persons keeping falcons[803] solely for keeping them in captivity or for static display, although they must still comply with the Regulations and the provisions of the Trade in Species of Flora and Fauna Regulations. Falconry may only be practised with captive-bred falcons covered by all permits and authorisations in terms of the Trade in Species Regulations. The importation, transport, keeping, and sale of falconry species shall be done according to both Regulations. The Falconry Regulations determine the grounds for issuing a Falconry licence and their terms and conditions. The flying of falcons purely for training and display flights is permitted all year round. The open season for the pursuit of quarry species[804] is between 1 June and 31 January of the following year, both days included, between two hours before sunrise and two hours after sunset, with certain provisions for specific quarry species. Falconry may be practised over the entire land territory of the Islands, excluding bird sanctuaries and protected beaches in the Schedules of the Wild Birds Regulations, subject to certain provisions. It is permitted to use trained dogs or ferrets to flush or retrieve quarry species. It is prohibited to: fly any untethered falcon that is not wearing a transmitter of a real-time tracking device that is able to be tracked; allow the falcon to stray outside the area where falconry may be practised; allow the falcon to escape from the control of the licensee; allow the falcon to pursue, take or injure any species other than quarry species; allow the falcon to pursue, take or injure any species outside the open season for falconry. It is furthermore prohibited to practice hunting or taking by any means while practising falconry. Practising falconry at sea is prohibited. It is the licensee's duty, without prejudice to the Animal Welfare Act,[805] to ensure the welfare of his falcons in compliance with the applicable best codes of practice, with certain duties laid down in the Regulations themselves. The Regulations lay down offences and their respective penalties on similar lines to those for the Wild Birds Regulations.

802. S.L. 549.106.
803. Defined as a captive-bred, close-ringed specimen that is used for the purpose of practising falconry, which forms part of the order Falconiformes, Strigiformes or Accipitriformes, including hybrids between such specimens.
804. These are the species listed in Schedule II of the Wild Birds Regulations and in the Protection of Wild Rabbit Regulations, and captive-bred specimens of those species.
805. Chapter 439 of the Laws of Malta.

II. Reptiles

587. All the reptiles naturally occurring in the Maltese Islands are protected through L.N. 76/1992, the Reptiles (Protection) Regulations.[806] These are listed in the Schedule attached to the Regulations, being three species of marine turtles, two species of geckoes, the chameleon, four subspecies of lizard, the ocellated skink, and four species of snakes.[807] It is prohibited under these Regulations for any person to pursue, take or attempt to take, kill or attempt to kill, possess, sell by any method, buy, exchange, import or export any of the species or any part or derivative of the species listed in the Schedule. As the shells of marine turtles are sometimes used and kept as trophies, the Regulations require any person who was in possession of a marine turtle prior to the publication of these Regulations to register the marine turtle shell with the Director for Fisheries. Similarly, any marine turtles accidentally caught by fishermen during their normal fishing activities and landed at the fish market in Valletta shall be surrendered immediately to the Director responsible for fisheries, who shall dispose of them for scientific purposes only. To ensure compliance, the Regulations provide that the fisherman shall be compensated for any loss of tackle or income, as fixed from time to time by the Director responsible for fisheries.

588. A person who is in possession of any specimen,[808] the importation of which is restricted subject to these Regulations, must retain all documentary evidence such as permits, certificates, and licenses relating to the import of that specimen for as long as the specimen remains in his/her possession. The Director may issue permits for the taking and keeping of any species listed in the Schedule if intended for bona fide scientific studies. Such permits are to be renewed on an annual basis. The Director may prohibit the importation of any species of reptiles if such trade can lead to the endangering of the biological identity of the Maltese Islands.

Any person who shall take,[809] kill, possess, sell, buy, exchange, import, or export any specimen in contravention of these Regulations; any person who contravenes any restriction, prohibition, or requirement imposed by or under these Regulations, and any person who conspires or attempts or aids, abets, counsels, or procures any other person to commit any of the above offences, shall be guilty of an offence. The person who commits an offence against these Regulations shall, on conviction, be liable to a fine of not less than EUR 58.23 for each specimen involved, in the case of a first offence, and not more than EUR 232.94 for each subsequent offence. The Appendix to these Regulations lists all the reptiles occurring in the Maltese Islands and the territorial waters thereof.

806. S.L. 549.02. These Regulations implement the obligations Malta has under the Berne Convention, under CITES and the Protocol to the Barcelona Convention on Specially Protected Areas.

807. With the exception of the chameleon, all the species are indigenous.

808. For the purpose of these Regulations, 'specimen' means 'any reptile specified in the Schedule to these Regulations, of whatever species, whether in the original form or after having undergone any transformation, wherever found in the Maltese Islands and their territorial waters'.

809. Defined as removing the specimen from the natural habitat.

III. Marine Wildlife

589. Marine wildlife and ecosystems are protected in general, albeit indirectly, through L.N. 73/2011, the Marine Policy Framework Regulations.[810] The scope of these Regulations is to establish a framework within which Malta shall take the measures necessary to achieve or maintain good environmental status in the marine environment by the year 2020 at the latest.[811] The aims of the action plan are two-fold:

(1) protect and preserve the marine environment, prevent its deterioration or, where practicable, restore marine ecosystems in areas where they have been adversely affected; and
(2) prevent and reduce inputs in the marine environment, with a view to phasing out pollution[812] so as to ensure that there are no significant impacts on or risks to marine biodiversity, marine ecosystems, human health or legitimate uses of the sea.

590. Marine mammals are protected through the Marine Mammals Protection Regulations,[813] which repealed L.N. 77/1992. The Schedule attached to the Regulations lists twenty species of marine mammals[814] declared protected according to the Regulations. The Regulations prohibit any person[815] from directly or indirectly pursuing, taking or attempting to take, killing or attempting to kill, maltreating or attempting to maltreat, possessing, selling by any method, buying, exchanging, re-introducing, importing, or exporting any specimen of species listed in the Schedule to the Regulations.[816] Any accidental catch of any marine mammal listed in the Schedule must be immediately released, and if such a release is not possible, it shall be landed at the fish market in Valletta or in Gozo and shall be surrendered immediately to the Director responsible for fisheries, who shall then deal with it in consultation with the Director responsible for veterinary services and the Competent Authority (being ERA).

591. Any person who has any specimen in his possession, the import of which is subject to these or other regulations, shall retain in his possession and, until such time as that specimen remains in his possession, all permits, certificates, and

810. S.L. 549.62.
811. It also transposes the provisions of Directive 2008/56/EC of the European Parliament and of the Council, as amended, and of the Council as regards the indicative lists of elements to be taken into account for the preparation of marine strategies.
812. The definition includes underwater noise.
813. L.N. 203/2003 (S.L. 549.35).
814. Listed are the minke whale, sei whale, fin whale, common dolphin, northern right whale, long-finned pilot whale, Risso's dolphin, dwarf sperm whale, humpback whale, Blainville's beaked whale, orca (killer whale), the sperm whale, the false killer whale, Indo-pacific humpback dolphin, the striped dolphin, the rough-toothed dolphin, the bottle-nosed dolphin, Culver's beaked whale, the common porpoise, and the Mediterranean monk seal.
815. Which includes any person or body of persons acting under the instructions of any employer, master, or owner.
816. It is also prohibited to attempt to carry out any of these activities.

licences relative to the import of that specimen. Permits may be issued by the Director responsible for environment protection within ERA for the taking and keeping of specimens of species protected under these Regulations for bona fide scientific studies or other similar purpose only.[817] They may also be issued for the import or export of any specimen; the re-introduction of specimens; the performance of any activity which would otherwise not be permitted under these Regulations to dolphinaria or oceanaria, which at the time of the coming into force of these Regulations are already in possession of live specimens, provided that such permit is limited to the replacement or replenishment of specimens. In all cases, it is provided that the Competent Authority shall not issue such a permit if, in its opinion, such activities threaten any species or lead to the endangering of the biological diversity of Malta. In issuing such permits, the Competent Authority may impose such conditions as it may deem fit, provided that a special condition may be imposed upon the applicant, to submit within a month from the expiry of the permit or at the end of the calendar year, whichever is the earliest, information relevant to the activities permitted. Furthermore, the period of validity of such permit shall also be established at the discretion of the Competent Authority, provided that the validity of the permit may not exceed one calendar year from the date of issue. Besides, the Competent Authority shall reserve the right not to issue or renew any permit if the applicant in question has not fulfilled or honoured any of the conditions and obligations arising from any other permit issued by the Director or the Competent Authority under these Regulations or other relevant regulations.

592. Persons, public entities, and other institutions having been granted a permit under these Regulations will be maintained in a national public register. Where its disclosure affects one or more of the items mentioned in the Freedom of Access to Information on the Environment Regulations,[818] the applicant may indicate the information in the permit application submitted pursuant to these Regulations that should be treated as confidential. Verifiable justification must be given in such cases. The Competent Authority shall decide after consultation with the applicant which information will be kept confidential and shall inform the applicant of its decision. Except where the Competent Authority determines that there is a threat to the safeguarding of biodiversity, in no case may certain information, such as benefits arising from the permit, be kept confidential. The Competent Authority shall not divulge to third parties any information decided to be confidential and shall protect intellectual property rights relating to the data received. If, for whatever reason, the applicant withdraws the application, the Competent Authority must respect the confidentiality of the information supplied.

593. Penalties for infringing these Regulations are: on a first conviction, a fine (*multa*) of not less than EUR 232.94 for each specimen. On a second or subsequent conviction, a fine (*multa*) of not less than EUR 582.34 but not exceeding EUR 2329.37 for each specimen, imprisonment for a term not exceeding two years, or

817. Permits are renewable annually.
818. L.N. 217/2001.

both such fine and imprisonment. Furthermore, without prejudice to the above provisions, the court may also order any person who is found guilty of committing an offence under these Regulations to pay for the expenses incurred by the Competent Authority as a result of the said offence, the revocation of the permit issued under these Regulations and the confiscation, retention, and disposal of the *corpus delicti*.

594. The stony sea urchin is subject to a two-year moratorium for its conservation, starting in the year 2023, through the Stony Sea Urchin Protection Regulations.[819] The competent authority is ERA; however, it must cooperate and collaborate with the Director responsible for fisheries, the Veterinary Regulation Directorate, and the Superintendent of Public Health in enforcing the Regulations, all four being considered as 'relevant authorities'. They must exercise their powers, *mutatis mutandis*, under any applicable legislation, including any relevant powers of delegation.

595. The stony sea urchin is protected to the fullest extent since the Regulations apply to any specimen of the urchin, defined as 'any stony sea urchin in any stage of its life-cycle, whether alive or dead, whether whole or in part, whether in the original form or after having undergone any transformation and includes any part or derivative thereof, as well as any other goods which, from an accompanying document, the packaging or a mark or label or from any other circumstances, appear to be parts or derivatives of the species'.

It is prohibited to disturb, destroy, possess, transport, sell, exchange, offer for sale or exchange, or export any specimen or to attempt to do so. There are only two exceptions. First is where the act is performed by a person in possession of a valid permit for bona fide scientific research issued by ERA pursuant to the permitting process under the Flora, Fauna and Natural Habitats Protection Regulations. Second is where a person imports, brings into Malta, transports, stores, possesses, advertises, distributes, or sells specimens when in possession of documentary evidence[820] proving its legitimate importation or transportation into Malta.

596. Any act in contravention of these Regulations is a criminal offence. A first conviction is subject to a fine (*multa*) of not less than EUR 500 but not exceeding EUR 5,000, whereas a second or subsequent conviction is subject to a fine (*multa*) of not less than EUR 1,000 but not exceeding EUR 10,000. It should be noted that the police cannot ex officio institute criminal proceedings against any such offence without a complaint by a relevant authority. Indeed, a relevant authority is entitled to impose any alternative penalty or punishment that the applicable legislation may provide, subject to prior consultation and coordination with the other relevant authorities.

---

819. L.N. 149/2023 (S.L. 549.157).

820. Which may consist in any relevant import licence or authorisation, health certificate, customs declaration, labelling which indicates that the specimen was sourced outside Maltese waters, invoices or receipts which indicate that the specimen was purchased outside Maltese jurisdiction, or any other comparable evidence.

IV. National Species

597. National species are afforded specific protection under the Species Protection (Designation of Natural Species) Regulations.[821] The national species are listed in Schedule I, these being the blue rock thrush, Mediterranean killifish, Maltese rock centaury, sandarac gum tree, and Maltese freshwater crab. The prohibitions of the 'relevant regulations'[822] apply to these species unless duly authorised by ERA or the WBRU as applicable (the competent authorities depending on the species). The competent authority may also designate further national species in line with specified criteria, such as: wild species endemic to the Maltese Islands and its waters; threatened, rare and possibly extinct species in Malta; charismatic species conducive to raising environmental awareness. The competent authority is given a number of duties in relation to the national species. These include identification, surveillance, monitoring activities and in situ conservation. It may also promote education, general information and public awareness of the need to protect these species and may cooperate with national bodies and entities to further this goal. It may also issue permits under the relevant regulations in relation to national species, which are deemed to be issued under the National Species Regulations.

598. Penalties under the Regulations are threefold. First, there are administrative fines of not less than EUR 750 and not more than EUR 5,000 for each species[823] that the competent authority believes a person has committed an offence against, provided it may only issue such fine once on the same person. No proceedings may be taken, or continued to be taken, against the offender for the offence if he pays the fine. The Regulations then list general offences, with punishments, found in Schedule II, varying on whether they are committed against species in Schedule I(a) (namely, national birds) or Schedule I(b) (namely, other national species). It is an offence to: fail to observe the provisions of the Regulations; infringe any restriction, prohibition or need imposed by the Regulations or in their virtue; fail to observe any condition of a permit or authorisation granted under the provisions of the Regulations; act in contravention of any provision of the Regulations; conspire, aid, abet, counsel procure (or attempt to perform any of those actions) any other person to contravene the Regulations' provisions, fail to comply with any of them or infringe any restriction, prohibition or need imposed by the Regulations or in their virtue. These offences are without prejudice to any applicable regulation under the EPA. The second list of penalties is for offences relating to birds listed in Schedule I(a). Any person committing or attempting to commit such an offence is liable on a first conviction to a fine (*multa*) of not less than EUR 750 and not more than EUR 5,000 for each specimen and the confiscation of the *corpus delicti*, and the court is bound to order the suspension of any general licence or permit[824] for a

821. L.N. 25/2018 (S.L. 549.120).
822. Namely: Trade in Species of Flora and Fauna Regulations, Conservation of Wild Birds Regulations, Flora, Fauna and Natural Habitats Protection Regulations and the Trees and Woodlands Protection Regulations.
823. Listed in Schedule I(b); namely, all species not birds.
824. Issued under the Regulations, the Conservation of Wild Birds Regulations and under Part XV of the Code of Police Laws.

period of between two and five years. A second or subsequent conviction is liable to a fine (*multa*) of not less than EUR 1,500 and not more than EUR 10,000 for each specimen, or imprisonment for a term of between six months and two years, or both fine and imprisonment, along with the confiscation of the *corpus delicti*. The court is also bound to order the permanent revocation of any licence or permit as mentioned above. It may also impose a Community Service Order. Hunting or taking, or attempting to hunt or take, any national bird without a valid general licence is liable to the punishment for a second or subsequent offence as mentioned, plus the disqualification from obtaining such general licence for life. If, however, the licence has already been permanently revoked as above or the person has already suffered such disqualification, the convict shall be liable to a fine (*multa*) of between EUR 7,000 and EUR 15,000 and to imprisonment for a term from one to two years.[825]

Third are penalties for offences related to non-bird species in Schedule I(b). The penalties for a first conviction and for a second or subsequent conviction are the same as for the respective offences treated under the last paragraph. However, there are no consequences relating to licences or permits, nor is there Community Service. Nevertheless, additional sanctions as laid down under sub-Regulation (5), (6) and (7) of Regulation 49 of the Flora, Fauna and Natural Habitats Protection Regulations apply.

§3. The Control of Trade in Species of Wild Flora and Fauna

599. Regulations regarding the trade in species of fauna and flora were published by L.N. 236/2004, the Trade in Species of Fauna and Flora Regulations.[826] These Regulations repealed L.N. 19/1992, which had transformed the obligations under the Convention on International Trade in Endangered Species of Wild Flora and Fauna (CITES) into national legislation. These Regulations empower the Minister of Environment to appoint a scientific authority and a management authority who shall advise the Minister responsible for the Environment to prohibit the import, export or re-export in or possession of any species of fauna and flora if, in their opinion, or in the opinion of any of them, such import, export, re-export or possession would endanger the biological identity or any ecosystem or any species of fauna and flora of Malta.

The references to a permit or certificate, an export permit or re-export certificate, and a label and expressions used in these Regulations and which are also used in the Principal Regulation[827] or Subsidiary Regulation[828] are to have the meaning they bear in the Principal Regulation unless the context otherwise requires. The import

825. In determining the gravity of the offence, the court may consider the factors laid down under the fourth proviso to Reg. 27(2) of the Conservation of Wild Birds Regulations, without prejudice to the provisions of the Schedule.

826. S.L. 549.38.

827. The 'Principal Regulation' is the EU Council Regulation (EC) No. 338/97 on the protection of species of wild fauna and flora by regulating trade therein.

828. 'Subsidiary Regulation' means the Commission Regulation (EC) No. 1808/2001 on the implementation of Council Regulation (EC) No. 338/97 on the protection of wild species of fauna and flora by regulating trade therein.

of any species which is protected at the country of origin, even if not listed in the Annexes to the Principal Regulation, and even if that country of origin is not a party to the Convention,[829] shall require an export authorisation from that country. Furthermore, any person who has in his possession any specimen the import of which is subject to these Regulations shall retain in his possession and, for such time as that specimen[830] remains in his possession, all permits, certificates, and licenses relative to the import of that specimen.

Penalties for offences against these Regulations are, on conviction, a fine (*multa*) of not less than EUR 465.87 but not exceeding EUR 4,658.75, or imprisonment for a period of not less than one month but not exceeding two years, or both such fine (*multa*) or imprisonment. However, the provisions of Article 28A of the Criminal Code and the provisions of the Probation of Offenders Act[831] shall not be applicable in respect of any such offence. Furthermore, the provisions of Article 23 and of Article 30(1) of the Criminal Code shall, *mutatis mutandis*, apply to proceedings in respect of offences against these Regulations, so however that the disqualification from holding or obtaining a warrant licence, permit, or authority shall in no case be less than one year.

600. The Maltese legislator made specific provisions for the protection of seal pups through L.N. 335/2001, the Importation of Skins of Certain Seal Pups and Derived Products Regulations.[832] The importation of all products in Annex I is prohibited, except if they result from traditional hunting by the Inuit People. The prohibited products are raw fur skins and fur skin, tanned or dressed,[833] and their articles of whitecoat harp seal pups and hooded seal pups (blue-backs). The competent authority is the Department for Environment Protection. It is an offence to: fail to comply with any provision of the Regulations or with any order lawfully given in terms of any of their provisions; contravene any prohibition, restriction or requirement imposed by or under the Regulations; act in contravention of any of their provisions; conspire or attempt, aid or abet any other person by whatever means to contravene the provisions of the Regulations, fail to comply with any such provision[834] or contravene any restriction, prohibition or requirement imposed by or under them. A first conviction is liable to a fine (*multa*) of not less than EUR 1,164.69 and not more than EUR 2,329.37 per specimen. A second or subsequent conviction is liable to a fine (*multa*) of not less than EUR 2,329.37 and not more than EUR 23,293.73 per specimen, imprisonment for a term not exceeding two years, or both fine and imprisonment. The court shall also order the convict to pay

829. 'Convention' means the Convention on International Trade in Endangered Species of Wild Fauna and Flora (Washington 1973).
830. 'Specimens' has the same definition as that used in the Principal Regulation and also includes any species, whether alive or dead, any part or derivative thereof, as well as any goods which appear from an accompanying document, the packaging, mark, or label or from other circumstances to be or to contain parts or derivatives of animals or plants of those species the import, export, re-export whereof or the possession thereof is prohibited, restricted or controlled in accordance with the provisions of the regulation.
831. Chapter 446 of the Laws of Malta.
832. S.L. 549.20.
833. Including fur skins assembled in plates, crosses or similar forms.
834. Including any order lawfully given under said Regulations.

the expenses incurred by the public entities, etc., involved in the implementation of the Regulations and for the restitution of the environment as a result of the offence, and shall also order the revocation of the permit issued by the police and the confiscation of the *corpus delicti*.[835]

§4. Control of Invasive Alien Species

601. Malta is bound by the Invasive Alien Species Regulation (IAS Regulation), Regulation (EU) No. 1143/2014, on the prevention and management of the introduction and spread of invasive alien species. This is implemented through two main pieces of legislation, discussed below. Malta also has a duty to prevent the introduction of those alien species which threaten ecosystems, habitats, or species, as well as the obligation to control and eradicate such alien species under the Rio Convention on Biological Diversity.[836]

602. The Flora, Fauna and Natural Habitats Regulations[837] place an obligation on ERA to prevent the introduction of, control or eradicate those alien species which threaten ecosystems, habitats or species, in line with the provisions of the same Regulations. It is authorised to prohibit the importation and, or keeping of flora and fauna if, in its opinion, this importation and/or keeping can harm or lead to the endangerment of the biodiversity of Malta or for other reasons of national interest. This is supplemented by an obligation to keep a list of species which are detrimental to the environment, as required under the IAS Regulation. An invasive species under these Regulations is defined as 'an alien species whose establishment and spread threatens local biodiversity', whereas an alien species is defined as 'a non-indigenous organism, which has never been a native of Malta or which has been introduced therein during the past five hundred years'. This obligation also transposes the Habitats Directive, which in Article 22 provides that MS are to 'ensure that the deliberate introduction into the wild of any species which is not native to their territory is regulated so as not to prejudice natural habitats within their natural range or the wild native fauna and flora and, if they consider it necessary, prohibit such introduction'.

603. L.N. 337/2017, the Control of Invasive Alien Species of European Union Concern Regulations,[838] implements the administrative and regulatory aspects of

835. The court is the Court of Magistrates (Malta or Gozo), as the case may be, in accordance with the provisions of the Criminal Code regulating that Court as a court of criminal judicature. The Attorney General always has a right of appeal to the Court of Criminal Appeal for any judgment in respect of proceedings for offences against these Regulations. Furthermore, the provisions of Arts 23 and 30(1) of the Criminal Code apply *mutatis mutandis* to any such proceedings; however, the disqualification from holding any permit shall in no case be for less than one year.
836. Notably Art. 8(h) of the Convention. The Convention is discussed in the introduction to this chapter.
837. L.N. 311/2006 (S.L. 549.44), discussed in the introduction to this chapter.
838. S.L. 549.119.

the IAS Regulation. ERA, as the competent authority, is empowered to take all necessary measures for the eradication, control, prevention, and monitoring of species included in the Union list[839] without prejudice to the provisions of the Flora, Fauna and Natural Habitats Protection Regulations. Official controls are to take place when goods referred to in Article 15(1) of the IAS Regulation are brought into Malta. The ERA may issue derogations from the IAS Regulation prohibitions to issue any permit[840] for any species in the Union list to allow: bona fide scientific studies; *ex situ* conservation; and scientific production, and subsequent medical use where the products derived from those species are unavoidable to advance human health. In exceptional cases, permits to carry out activities not listed above may be issued in accordance with the IAS Regulation. However, ERA may revoke any permit issued and must inform the applicant of the reasons for any permit refusal. Without prejudice to any other obligations and conditions laid down by ERA, a permit holder is obliged to submit to ERA, *inter alia*, a detailed report of the activities undertaken, the methodology employed and the outcome and results within a month from the permit's expiration or at the end of the calendar year, whichever the earlier. A copy of any published results, etc., relevant to the permit is to reach ERA within three months from their date of publication.

604. It is an offence to: fail to observe the provisions of the Regulation or the IAS Regulation; infringe any restriction, prohibition or need imposed by the same; fail to observe any condition of a permit or consent granted under the same; act in contravention of any provision of the same; make a statement or present information or documentation which the person knows to be false for the purpose of obtaining the approval of a permit or derogation in line with the same; conspire, aid, abet, counsel or procure (or attempt any of said actions) any other person to contravene the provisions of the same, to fail to comply with any one of said provisions or to infringe any restriction, prohibition or need imposed by the aforementioned Regulations or by their virtue.

Any person who commits, or attempts to commit, an offence against either Regulation is liable on a first conviction to a fine (*multa*) of not less than EUR 500 and not more than EUR 2,500 per specimen. A second or subsequent offence is liable to a fine (*multa*) of not less than EUR 1,500 but not exceeding EUR 5,000 per specimen, imprisonment for a term not exceeding two years, or both fine and imprisonment. In any case, the court shall also order the offender to remove the causes of the offence, remedy the damage caused, and undo anything done without a permit within a time sufficient for the purpose but not exceeding three months from the judgment. Non-compliance merited further daily fines for each day of default. The convicted person is also bound to pay certain expenses, such as those incurred in remedying the damage caused. The provisions of Articles 23 and 30(1) of the Criminal Code apply *mutatis mutandis* to these proceedings; however, a permit, etc., disqualification is not to last for less than one year.

839. List of invasive alien species of EU concern under the IAS Regulation.

840. Subject to such conditions it deems fit and appropriate, but for not longer than one calendar year.

Chapter 3. Fish Resources

605. The subject of fish resources will be discussed here only from an environmental perspective because there are various pieces of legislation which regulate the harvesting of this natural resource. The Fisheries Conservation and Management Act[841] defines 'fishing' as the catching or taking of fish that occur or have grown naturally in the sea, any other activity which can reasonably be expected to result in the catching or taking of fish or the farming of fish, together with any operation at sea in support of or in preparation of any one of the above-mentioned activities. The Minister responsible for fisheries has the power to make regulations for the better carrying into effect of the purposes of this Act and, among other things, for: the conservation, management, and protection of fish resources; the establishment and management of marine areas for the preservation of fish stocks; the control of the exploitation of coral and sponge resources; the protection of turtles, dolphins, and other aquatic animals; and for the landing of fish and its utilisation in the manufacture of by-products and to regulate the sale of fish.

606. The Act prohibits any foreign fishing boat to fish or attempt to do so while within the territorial waters of Malta. The Director responsible for fisheries is duly appointed by the Prime Minister, and the former may authorise any public officer to exercise any or all of the powers of the Director under this Act either concurrently with him or in his absence. One of the main responsibilities of the Director is to take appropriate measures in consultation with such authority as from time to time is responsible for the environment for the safeguard against extinction of protected species. Furthermore, under this Act, there is the setup of the Fisheries Board, which among its members there, has to be an official from the Department for the Protection of the Environment nominated by the Minister responsible for that department.

The Minister responsible for fisheries may make regulations with respect to fishing, fishing boats, and the sale of fish, as well as the grant of licences in connection therewith. Any person convicted of any contravention against any regulation in this regard shall, upon conviction, forfeit any fishing instrument in respect of which the contravention was committed.

607. Any person guilty of obstructing fisheries protection officers shall, on conviction, be liable to a fine (*multa*) of not less than EUR 1,200 but not exceeding EUR 6,000. On the other hand, those who give false information shall, on conviction, be liable to a fine (*multa*) of not less than EUR 465.87 but not exceeding EUR 2,329.37. Furthermore, any person who contravenes any provision of this Act for which no penalty is specifically provided shall be guilty of an offence and shall be liable on conviction to a fine (*multa*) of not less than EUR 150 but not exceeding EUR 80,000. Apart from these penalties, the court may also order that any fishing gear, instruments, or appliances used in the commission of such offence and any fish on board a fishing vessel or the proceeds of sale thereof, if already sold, be forfeited to the government and if so forfeited, shall be disposed of in such manner as the

841. Chapter 425 of the Laws of Malta. It repeals the Fish Industry Act (Ch. 138 of the Laws of Malta).

Director, acting in his discretion, may direct. In the case of a second or subsequent conviction against this Act, even the licence or permit and any relative entry in the record of fishing vessels made under the Act shall be forfeited.

608. The Fishery Regulations[842] regulate when fishing may and may not be practised without a licence issued by the Director of Fisheries. In particular, trawling and seine nets are prohibited. The Director can issue special licences for fishing for scientific purposes in the Grand Harbour's Dockyard Creek and French Creek, which are ordinarily not subject to fishing licences. Fishing is absolutely prohibited in certain areas. The use of 'lampara' as a fishing implement[843] is specifically regulated through the Management of the *Lampara* Fishery Order[844] pursuant to Article 26(6) of Council Regulation (EC) No 1967/2006 of 21 December 2006 concerning management measures for the sustainable exploitation of fishery resources in the Mediterranean Sea. It establishes a system of non-transferrable fishing permits for this fishing technique and regulates it accordingly. Fishing with this technique without being in possession of the relative permit is an offence liable to a fine (*multa*) of not more than EUR 10,000.

609. The Explosives Ordinance[845] prohibits the use and keeping in one's possession of any explosives by any person for fishing purposes. Whoever is found guilty in this regard shall be liable, on conviction, to imprisonment for a term from one to nine years.

610. The Territorial Waters and Contiguous Zone Act[846] regulates living resources in this area and the prevention of the infringement of any law or regulation relating to fisheries. The Exclusive Economic Zone Act[847] and Continental Shelf Act[848] do the same for the maritime zones they respectively regulate.

842. G.N. 206/1934 (S.L. 425.01).
843. This is a fishing implement comprising a strong light which is used to attract fish and a purse seine to catch the fish. It was originally prohibited under G.N. 148/135, subject to special permission in the (then) Governor's absolute discretion to ensure a supply of fish for the Islands.
844. L.N. 407/2013 (S.L. 425.11).
845. Chapter 33 of the Laws of Malta.
846. Chapter 226 of the Laws of Malta.
847. Chapter 625 of the Laws of Malta. However, no exclusive economic zone has been declared to date.
848. Chapter 535 of the Laws of Malta.

Part V. Liability and Juridical Actions

611. Liability can be both civil and criminal. Under Maltese law, as a rule, civil and criminal actions exist independently of each other and involve different actors. The civil action is instituted before the civil courts by one person (or entity) against another for the compensation of damage suffered by the applicant to be granted to him by the respondent. The criminal action is instituted before the criminal courts by the Executive Police or Attorney General (though exceptionally, it can be prosecuted by the private party) for the punishment of the offender.[849]

612. However, certain exceptions exist to the rule of the independence of the two actions. Several are found under environmental legislation, particularly legislation which is more regulatory in nature. These tend to provide that the courts of criminal jurisdiction can order a person found guilty under the same legislation to pay for the expenses incurred by the competent authority (usually ERA, particularly in the case of regulations under the EPA) as a result of the offence, including any remedial action taken for any damage caused. Therefore, criminal liability and civil liability can be dealt with in one and the same action in these cases since civil liability follows as a direct consequence of the criminal offence dealt with in the criminal action. Furthermore, the EPA provides an interesting mechanism for the recovery of criminal fines (*multi*) imposed pursuant to regulations issued under it by the Minister responsible for the environment. Despite the liability being criminal, the regulations may provide that the fine will, in all cases, be due to ERA as a civil debt and that where the person guilty of the offence is a director, secretary, or manager of a body corporate for the economic benefit of which the offence was committed, such body corporate shall be liable *in solidum* with the offender for the payment of the said civil debt. This is an interesting mechanism since criminal liability can be made good through civil procedures.

613. Likewise, juridical actions can be broadly categorised as civil and criminal. Maltese law also recognises constitutional and administrative actions; however, these are also categorised as 'civil' since Maltese law considers any action not being a criminal action to be a civil one. Indeed, the Constitutional Court is considered to be a court of civil jurisdiction.[850]

849. Criminal Code, Ch. 9 of the Laws of Malta, Arts 3 and 6.
850. Code of Organisation and Civil Procedure, Ch. 12 of the Laws of Malta, Art. 3.

614. Criminal liability has been dealt with in the previous Parts in relation to each piece of legislation since individual offences and penalties are established for each. However, this Part will review criminal liability generally and under the Crimes Against the Environment Act. It will also review civil liability and judicial remedies available both to persons (natural or legal) and the government in environmental matters.

Chapter 1. Liability

615. Civil liability can arise from two main sources. The first is under general civil law, regulated by the provisions of the Civil Code.[851] The second is under specific regulations issued under the EPA. Under the head of civil liability, one may also include the so-called administrative offences, reviewed towards the end of this chapter.

When speaking of damages, it is important to distinguish between compensation for damage to the environment as a head of damage per se and other heads falling under the general title of 'economic damages', such as removal of pollutants, clean-up costs, and costs incurred to prevent, minimise, and mitigate pollution or degradation or the threat thereof, as well as economic losses resulting from damage to real and personal property. Damages can also be claimed in this regard by individuals who depend on natural resources for subsistence or who suffer loss of revenue as a result of pollution or degradation. Under Maltese legislation, a person can only be held responsible and thus ordered to pay damages for acts harmful to the environment if he is in breach of specific laws. Nevertheless, as pointed out, most of these deal with criminal liability (though some allow the court to order the person convicted to pay for expenses incurred, as noted above).

616. The legal basis for a claim for economic damages arises in the Civil Code, where liability is based on tort.[852] The quantification of damages on a tortuous action requires the satisfaction of four elements. First, there must be an act or omission which is imputable to the person causing harm. It is, therefore, necessary to have sufficient evidence to link the act or omission with the person deemed liable. Second, that act or omission must be contrary to law. The relevant legal sources have already been discussed. Third, the act must cause damage. Fourth, the person causing damage must be either in *dolus*[853] or *culpa*.[854]

617. The Civil Code also provides that any person who makes use, within proper limits, of a right competent to him shall not be liable for any damage which may result therefrom,[855] but every person shall be liable for the damage which occurs through his fault.[856]

A person is deemed to be at fault if, in his own acts, he does not use the prudence, diligence, and attention of a *bonus paterfamilias*.[857] The Civil Code provides that any person who, with or without the intent to injure, is guilty of any act or omission constituting a breach of a duty imposed by law is liable for any damage resulting therefrom.[858]

851. Chapter 16 of the Laws of Malta.
852. That is, either as a result of malice or when it occurs as a result of negligence on the part of the perpetrator.
853. Intentional element.
854. Negligence.
855. Civil Code, Ch. 16 of the Laws of Malta, Art. 1030.
856. *Ibid.*, Art. 1031.
857. *Ibid.*, Art. 1032.
858. *Ibid.*, s. 1033.

According to the provisions of the Civil Code, the liable persons, therefore, may be the person, whether legal or natural, who committed the tortuous act or omission, any person who wilfully contributed thereto with advice, threats, and commands, and any person who is indirectly responsible. If they acted in *dolus*,[859] all persons involved are liable *in solidum*. If, on the other hand, they acted in *culpa*,[860] then each is liable up to the damage caused unless it is not possible to ascertain which part of the damage is attributable to each – in that case, they are all bound *in solidum*.[861]

618. Economic damages considered by our courts are of two types: *damnum emergens*, that is, actual expenses and losses, and *lucrum cessans*, that is, loss of potential earnings.[862] Moral damages are not awarded by Maltese courts in civil claims except in certain specified circumstances, not including environmental damage. The sum to be awarded is assessed by the courts having regard to the circumstances of the case. An action for economic damages is prescribed by a two-year limit. If the tort is a crime,[863] the prescriptive period for the civil action is the same as that established for the criminal action.[864] If the injured party is found to have contributed to his own injury by his imprudence, negligence, or want of attention, part of the damage remains at his charge.

619. The provisions of the EPA are intended to supplement the general liability for damages under the Civil Code, the former being a *lex specialis* to the latter. Article 3 of the EPA states that it shall be the duty of everyone, together with the government, to protect the environment[865] and to assist in the taking of preventive and remedial measures to protect the environment and manage natural resources in a sustainable manner. Article 4 provides for the duty of the government to protect the environment, which includes the duty to take preventive and remedial measures to address and abate the problem of pollution and any other form of environmental degradation in Malta in accordance with the polluter-pays principle and the precautionary principle. However, Article 5 renders these two provisions non-justiciable and so unenforceable in a court of law, although it does provide that they 'shall be employed in the interpretation of' the EPA and any other law relating to matters governed by it.

859. Malice.
860. Negligence.
861. Civil Code, Ch. 16 of the Laws of Malta, Arts 1049–1050.
862. Comprising both present and future earnings.
863. As it would be in the case of an offence under the EPA, Ch. 549 of the Laws of Malta, and its regulations and in the majority of other legal sources addressing environmental issues.
864. Governed by the Criminal Code, Ch. 9 of the Laws of Malta, Arts 687–694.
865. Defined as 'the whole of the elements and conditions, natural or man-made, whether together or in isolation, and in particular: (a) the air, water, land, soil and sea, including their bedrock, aquifers and subsurface features; (b) all the layers of the atmosphere; (c) all biodiversity; and (d) the landscape and its features'.

620. Nevertheless, the government, through the Minister responsible for the environment, is authorised by the EPA to issue regulations relative to environmental protection. This is one way in which the government fulfils its duties under the Act. The process of adopting such regulations includes public participation and also participation by other governmental entities exercising responsibilities in the field of environmental protection, as observed in Part I.

621. In particular, the Minister responsible for the environment may, by regulations, provide for the liability of persons for environmental breaches, pursuant to Article 54 of the EPA.

The first type of measures that may be provided for are the breach of any regulations issued under the Act.[866] This therefore need not encompass 'environmental' damages *per se*; however, the liability under such regulations is intended to be criminal. Indeed, the Minister may provide that any person who acts in contravention of any regulation under the Act is guilty of an offence and provide for the appropriate penalty, being not greater than a fine (*multa*) of EUR 250,000 or imprisonment for a term not exceeding two years, or both such fine and imprisonment. The regulations may additionally provide that a person who, having been sentenced for an offence against the same regulation by a judgment which has become absolute, commits a further offence in contravention of the same regulation within such time as may be prescribed shall be liable to pay a higher fine (*multa*), not exceeding double the fine (*multa*) which would otherwise have been inflicted. For this purpose, the maximum fine that may be established is EUR 500,000. As noted in the general section above, the fine (*multa*) may be established as recoverable as a civil debt due to ERA.

The second type of measures that may be introduced are specific to environmental damage. The Minister may introduce measures relative to the liability of any individual who is in any manner deemed responsible for any action that may cause environmental damage. The regulations may additionally provide for the prevention and remedying of environmental damage.[867] The Minister may also, by regulation, provide for norms in relation to the liability of any person who causes damage to the environment as a result of any activities regulated by or under the Act and undertaken by that person.[868]

622. As already mentioned, the regulations under the EPA are intended to supplement the general legal provisions of the Civil Code relating to damages, which were never intended to deal with such cases, by means of its Articles 54(2) and 70.

The second EPA[869] contained a very advanced provision in its Article 24, causing any person responsible for causing damage to the environment to pay a sum into the Environment Fund established by the same Act, independently of any other civil

866. *See* Art. 54(2)(u) of the EPA.

867. *See* Art. 54(2)(v) of the EPA. Identical wording is used in Art. 70 of the EPA, which specifies that such regulations can be made for environmental damage occurring through actions committed within a protected area or outside such an area.

868. *See* Art. 54(2)(v) and (x) of the EPA.

869. Chapter 435 of the Laws of Malta, now repealed.

liability to make good any damages. The sum was to be determined by the court *arbitrio boni viri*, 'to make good for the damage caused to the environment and suffered by the community in general by the non-observance of any law or regulation by such person or by his negligence or wilful act or inability in his art or profession'. The action was to be instituted by the Fund Chairman (or his delegate) and was prescribed by the lapse of eight years. No such provision is contained in the current EPA, and so it may be said that while an ad hoc action for environmental liability existed under the second EPA, this has been abolished. The provision was probably not kept because it was never availed of. The only vestige remaining is that where administrative fines are imposed pursuant to the current EPA, these do not exclude any civil liability to 'make good any damages to any person or authority or to the environment in terms of environmental liability'.[870]

However, aside from individual regulations providing for liability for a breach of their own provisions, dealt with in previous parts, regulations of a general nature have been issued that address the responsibility of persons for damage caused to the environment, reviewed in this chapter.

623. Directive 2004/35/CE of the European Parliament and of the Council of 21 April 2004 on environmental liability with regard to the prevention and remedying of environmental damage was first transposed through L.N. 126/2008, the Prevention and Remedying of Environmental Damage Regulations. These were revoked and replaced by eponymous Regulations through L.N. 280/2015.[871]

The purpose of these Regulations, aside from transposing the aforementioned Directive, is to establish a framework of environmental liability based on the polluter-pays principle and to prevent and remedy environmental damage.

624. 'Damage' for the purposes of these Regulations is defined as 'a measurable adverse change in a natural resource or measurable impairment of a natural resource service which may occur directly or indirectly'. 'Environmental damage', then, comprises three separate forms of damage. The first is damage to protected species and natural habitats,[872] which is any damage that has significant adverse effects on reaching or maintaining the favourable conservation status of such habitats or species. The significance of such effects is to be assessed with reference to the baseline condition, taking account of the criteria set out in Schedule I.[873] The second is water

870. EPA, Art. 80(9).

871. Prevention and Remedying of Environmental Damage Regulations, S.L. 549.97.

872. These are in turned defined as (a) the species mentioned in Reg. 3(3) of the Conservation of Wild Birds Regulations or listed in Sch. I thereto or listed in Schs II and V to the Flora, Fauna and Natural Habitats Protection Regulations; (b) the habitats of species mentioned in Reg. 3(3) of the Conservation of Wild Birds Regulations or listed in Sch. I thereto or listed in Sch. II to the Flora, Fauna and Natural Habitats Protection Regulations and the natural habitats listed in Sch. I to the said Regulations and the breeding sites or resting places of the species listed in Annex V to the said Regulations; (c) any habitat or species, not listed in the Schedules mentioned in (a) and (b), and which ERA designates for equivalent purposes as those laid down in the two Regulations mentioned in (a) and (b).

873. There are exceptions to what constitutes damage to protected species and natural habitats. It does not include previously identified adverse effects, which result from an act by an operator that was expressly authorised by the relevant authorities in accordance with Part III or Part XI of the Flora,

damage, which is any damage that significantly adversely affects (a) the ecological, chemical and or quantitative status and or ecological potential of the waters concerned[874] and (b) the environmental status of the marine waters concerned.[875] The third is land damage, which is any land contamination that creates a significant risk of human health or the environment being adversely affected as a result of the direct or indirect introduction, in, on, or under land, of substances, preparations, organisms, or micro-organisms.

625. Conservation status is considered separately for species and natural habitats.

In the case of species, it is considered as the sum of the influences acting on the species concerned that may affect the long-term distribution and abundance of its populations within, as the case may be, the European territory of the Member States to which the EU Treaties apply or the territory of a Member State or the natural range of that species. It is considered as 'favourable' when three factors are satisfied. First, population dynamics data on the species concerned indicate that it is maintaining itself on a long-term basis as a viable component of its natural habitats. Second, the natural range of the species is neither being reduced nor is likely to be reduced for the foreseeable future. Third, there is, and will probably continue to be, a sufficiently large habitat to maintain its populations on a long-term basis.

In the case of natural habitats, it is considered as the sum of the influences acting on a natural habitat and its typical species that may affect its long-term natural distribution, structure, and functions as well as the long-term survival of its typical species within, as the case may be, the European territory of the Member States to which the EU Treaties apply or the territory of a Member State or the natural range of that habitat. It is considered to be 'favourable' when three factors are satisfied. First, when its natural range and the areas it covers within that range are stable or increasing. Second, when the specific structure and functions which are necessary for its long-term maintenance exist and are likely to continue to exist for the foreseeable future. Third, when the sum of the influences acting on the species is favourable.

626. There are a number of other important definitions to note for the purposes of these Regulations. Both 'emission' and 'pollution' are defined as 'the release in the environment, as a result of human activities, of substances, energy, preparations, organisms, or micro-organisms'. 'Recovery', including 'natural recovery', means, in the case of water, protected species, and natural habitats, the return of

---

Fauna and Natural Habitats Protection Regulations, or Reg. 9 of the Conservation of Wild Birds Regulations, or, in the case of habitats and species not covered by Community law, in accordance with equivalent provisions of national law on nature conservation.

874. As defined in the Water Policy Framework Regulations, with the exception of adverse effects under the Prevention and Remedying of Environmental Damage Regulations.

875. As defined in the Marine Policy Framework Regulations, with the exception of those particular aspects of the environmental status of the marine environment which are already regulated by means of the Water Policy Framework Regulations.

damaged natural resources and/or impaired services to the baseline condition.[876] However, in the case of land damage, it means the elimination of any significant risk of adversely affecting human health. The Regulations define 'remedial measures' as any action, or combination of actions, including mitigating or interim measures to restore, rehabilitate, or replace damaged natural resources and or impaired services or to provide an equivalent alternative to those resources or services as foreseen in Schedule II to the Regulations.

627. The Regulations apply to: (a) environmental damage caused by any of the occupational activities listed in Schedule III and to any imminent threat of such damage occurring by reason of any of those activities; and (b) damage to protected species and natural habitats caused by any occupational activities other than those listed in Schedule III, and any imminent threat of such damage occurring by reason of any of those activities, whenever the operator has been at fault or negligent. They also apply without prejudice to the Crimes Against the Environment Act, where applicable.

They apply without prejudice to more stringent Community legislation regulating the operation of any of the activities falling within their scope and without prejudice to Community legislation containing rules on conflicts of jurisdiction. Unless otherwise stipulated in other laws, they do not give private parties a right of compensation as a consequence of environmental damage or of an imminent threat of such damage. Therefore, this law is purely regulatory in scope since it is only ERA that can act under them, as shall be seen below.

628. The Regulations are subject to a number of exceptions as to their scope. Some are substantive, whereas others are temporal.

Substantively, environmental damage or an imminent threat of such damage caused by an act of armed conflict, hostilities, civil war or insurrection, or a natural phenomenon of exceptional, inevitable, and irresistible character falls outside the scope of the Regulations. Neither shall they apply to environmental damage or to any imminent threat of such damage arising from an incident in respect of which liability or compensation falls within the scope of any of the international conventions listed in Schedule IV to these Regulations.[877] These Regulations, furthermore, do not apply to such nuclear risks or environmental damage or imminent threat of such damage as may be caused by the activities covered by the Treaty establishing the European Atomic Energy Community or caused by an incident or activity in respect of which liability or compensation falls within the scope of any of the international instruments listed in Schedule V to these Regulations. Furthermore, they only apply to environmental damage or to an imminent threat of such damage

876. Defined as the condition at the time of the damage of the natural resources and services that would have existed had the environmental damage not occurred, estimated on the basis of the best information available.

877. These Regulations also apply without prejudice to the right of the operator to limit his liability in accordance with national legislation implementing the Convention on Limitation of Liability for Maritime Claims (LLMC), 1976, including any future amendment to the Convention, or the Strasbourg Convention on Limitation of Liability in Inland Navigation (CLNI), 1988, including any future amendment to the Convention.

caused by pollution of a diffuse character, where it is possible to establish a causal link between the damage and the activities of individual operators.

In terms of temporal application, they do not apply to damage caused by an emission, event, or incident that took place prior to 30th April 2007, and even where the damage caused by the same took effect subsequently to that date but derives to a specific activity that took place and finished before the same date. They are also inapplicable to damage if more than thirty years have passed since the emission, etc., that resulted in the damage occurring.

629. The Regulations deal with both preventive actions and remedial actions in the case of environmental damage.

The Competent Authority responsible for their enforcement is ERA. It has the duty to establish which operator has caused the damage or the imminent threat thereof, assess the significance of the damage, and determine which remedial measures should be taken with reference to Schedule II to the Regulations. Any decision imposing preventive or remedial measures must state the exact grounds on which it is based. It must also be notified forthwith to the operator concerned, along with information on the remedies available to him under the relevant laws concerned and of the time limits to which such remedies are subject.

The person subject to these Regulations is the operator. This is defined as any natural or legal, private or public, person who operates or controls the occupational activity or, where this is provided for in national legislation, to whom decisive economic power over the technical functioning of such an activity has been delegated, including the holder of a permit or authorisation for such an activity or the person registering or notifying such an activity. An occupational activity is any activity carried out in the course of an economic activity, a business, or an undertaking, irrespectively of its private or public, profit or non-profit character.

630. The operator is obligated to take the necessary preventive measures without delay where environmental damage has not yet occurred but where there is an imminent threat of such damage occurring. All operators shall, in any such case, including whenever an imminent threat of environmental damage is not dispelled despite the preventive measures taken by the operator, inform ERA of all relevant aspects of the situation as soon as possible. ERA shall, in turn, require the operator to provide information on any imminent threat of environmental damage or, in suspected cases, of such an imminent threat. It shall also ask the operator to take the necessary preventive measures and give him instructions to follow upon his taking the necessary preventive measures.

631. Where environmental damage has occurred, the operator must, without delay, inform ERA of all relevant aspects of the situation and take all practicable steps to immediately control, contain, remove, or otherwise manage the relevant contaminants and/or any other damage factors in order to limit or to prevent further environmental damage and adverse effects on human health or further impairment of services. He must also take the necessary remedial measures. The remedial measures must be determined in accordance with Regulation 8, which requires operators to identify potential remedial measures in accordance with Schedule II to the

Regulations and submit them to ERA for approval (unless ERA has already taken action). Where several instances of environmental damage have occurred, and it is necessary to remedy some instances before others, ERA must make the decision taking into account, *inter alia*, the nature, extent and gravity of the various instances of environmental damage concerned and to the possibility of natural recovery. Risks to human health must also be taken into account.

ERA shall at any time: require the operator to provide supplementary information on any damage that has occurred; take, require the operator to take, or give instructions to the operator concerning, all practicable steps to immediately control, contain, remove, or otherwise manage the relevant contaminants and/or any other damage factors in order to limit or to prevent further environmental damage and adverse effect on human health, or further impairment of services; and require the operator to take the necessary remedial measures and give him the instructions to be followed regarding the necessary remedial measures to be taken.

ERA must invite a number of persons to submit their observations relative to remedial measures to be taken, and these must also be taken into account. These are the persons on whose land remedial measures would be carried out, as well as other persons entitled to request ERA to take action under the Regulations dealt with below.

632. ERA must take the necessary preventive or remedial measures itself if the operator fails to comply with its obligations (respectively for each type of measure), cannot be identified, or is not required to bear the costs under these Regulations. It can also empower or require third parties to carry out the necessary preventive or remedial measures.

633. The operator shall bear the costs[878] for the preventive and remedial actions taken pursuant to these Regulations. The Competent Authority shall recover from the operator causing the damage or imminent threat thereof, *inter alia*, via security over property, or other appropriate guarantees, the costs it has incurred in relation to the preventive or remedial actions taken under these Regulations. However, the Competent Authority may decide not to recover the full costs where the expenditure required to do so would be greater than the recoverable sum or where the operator cannot be identified.

An operator shall not be required to bear the cost of preventive or remedial actions taken pursuant to these Regulations when he can prove that the environmental damage or imminent threat of such damage: was caused by a third party and occurred despite the fact that appropriate safety measures were in place; resulted from compliance with a compulsory order or instruction emanating from a public authority other than an order or instruction consequent upon an emission or incident caused by the operator's own activities. Furthermore, the operator shall not bear the cost of remedial actions taken pursuant to these Regulations where he demonstrates

878. Defined as costs which are justified by the need to ensure the proper and effective implementation of these Regulations, including the costs of assessing environmental damage, an imminent threat of such damage, alternatives for action, as well as the administrative, legal, and enforcement costs, the costs of data collection, and other general costs, monitoring as well as supervision costs.

that he is not at fault or negligent and that the environmental damage is caused by: an emission or event expressly authorised by and fully in accordance with, the conditions of an authorisation conferred by or given under relevant laws and regulations which implement those legislative measures specified in Schedule III, as applied at the date of the emission or event; or emission or activity or any manner of using a product in the course of an activity which the operator demonstrates was not considered likely to cause environmental damage according to the state of scientific and technical knowledge at the time when the emission was released, or the activity took place.

The provisions of these Regulations on liability are without prejudice to other laws regulating cost allocation in cases of multiple-party causation, especially concerning the apportionment of liability between the producer and the user of a product.

ERA is entitled to initiate cost recovery proceedings against the operator or a third party who has caused the damage, or the imminent threat of damage, in relation to any measures taken in pursuance of these Regulations within five years from the date on which those measures have been completed, or the liable operator or third party has been identified, whichever is later.

634. Specific natural or legal persons are entitled to submit their observations to ERA relating to instances of environmental damage of which they are aware and are entitled to request ERA to take action under these Regulations.

These persons come in three categories. First are those affected, or likely to be affected, by environmental damages. Second are those having a sufficient interest in environmental decision-making relating to the damage. A person has sufficient interest if he qualifies as a stakeholder or consultee pursuant to the Environmental Impact Assessment Regulations or has declared an interest in a development pursuant to Article 71(6) of the Development Planning Act.[879] Third are persons alleging the impairment of a right emanating from a valid licence or permit. The last two categories also include duly registered environmental NGOs.

The request for action must be accompanied by the relevant information and data supporting the observations submitted in relation to the environmental damage in question. Where the request and accompanying observations

635. Where the request for action and the accompanying observations show in a plausible manner that environmental damage exists, ERA must consider them and give the relevant operator an opportunity to make his views known with respect to the request for action and the accompanying observations. ERA must, as soon as possible and in accordance with the relevant provisions of national law, inform the persons making the request of its decision to accede to or refuse the request for action and provide the reasons for it.

636. The Regulations also make provision for transboundary environmental damages. According to the Directive 2004/35/EC, which the Regulations transpose, where environmental damage affects or is likely to affect other EU Member States,

879. Chapter 552 of the Laws of Malta.

the latter shall cooperate, also through the appropriate exchange of information, with a view to ensuring that preventive action and where necessary, remedial action, is taken in respect of any such environmental damage. Where environmental damage has occurred, the EU Member State in whose territory the damage originates shall provide sufficient information to the potentially affected EU Member States. EU Member States, which identify damage within their borders that did not originate within their territory, may report the issue to the EU Commission and any other Member State concerned. They may make recommendations for the adoption of preventive or remedial measures and may seek to recover the costs they have incurred in relation to the adoption of preventive or remedial measures. The Regulations transpose these provisions.

637. The Director for the protection of the environment (and his officers acting on his behalf) is given investigative powers to ensure the prevention and remedying of environmental harm through the Environment Protection (Preventive and Remedial Measures) Regulations.[880]

The Director is given the power to inspect any place or any vehicle, ship, platform, aeroplane, or other craft in Malta, or any such vehicle, vessel, or aircraft belonging to Malta outside the territorial waters of Malta, in order to ascertain the levels of protection of the environment as well as to investigate suspected violations of the provisions of the EPA or of regulations made under it, or codes of practice issued under the EPA, and to secure proof of any such violation. He cannot accede into private dwellings unaccompanied by a police officer of the rank of at least Inspector. He can take measures, samples, and copies of records or electronic data and conduct tests on any object in pursuance of his functions. He can also issue execution orders to prevent or to minimise threatened damage to the environment, to prevent threatened violations of laws or regulations concerning the protection of the environment, or to secure evidence of such violations.

It is an offence against these Regulations for any person to: obstruct or hinder the entry of the Director into any place, vehicle, ship, platform, aeroplane, or other craft for the purposes of inspection; obstruct or hinder the measurement, taking of samples, copies, or conduct of tests; disobey any order by the Director or any of his officers within the limits established in the Regulations; refrain from giving the information required under the same or give false or misleading information on any request made by the Director or his officers; or divulge any information obtained through these powers, except as provided in the Regulations. A conviction is liable to a fine (*multa*) not exceeding EUR 11,646.87, and in addition, the court must order the revocation of any relevant licence or its suspension for a period not exceeding one year, as well as the confiscation of any object used in, or in relation with, the offence.

638. Over the past decade, it has become increasingly common for the law to authorise a regulatory authority, such as ERA, to impose so-called administrative penalties for regulatory breaches. As mentioned above, once these are not dealt with through the criminal route, they are considered to constitute civil liability, broadly

880. L.N. 1/1994 (S.L. 549.04).

understood. Indeed, they are recoverable as civil debt due to the government. However, despite this characteristic, the amounts imposed can be quite considerable, and this has led to recent challenges as to their constitutionality under Maltese law. Should they be considered criminal charges and penalties under the test developed by the European Court of Human Rights,[881] then they can only be imposed, according to Article 39(1) of the Constitution of Malta, by an independent and impartial court (which ERA, of course, is not). This is a new legal animal, and this area of Maltese law is still in flux.

In this regard, it should be noted that Article 80 of the EPA provides for the imposition of administrative fines for breaches, as discussed in the General Introduction to this publication. Furthermore, other specific Regulations, some under the EPA and some not, as well as other specific laws touching upon the environment, provide for administrative fines as well. Whether these will survive the test of constitutionality remains to be seen. It should be noted, however, that Article 80(9) provides that where the fine has been paid, no criminal proceedings connected with the same matter may be initiated or continued.

881. Notably in *Engel and Others v. The Netherlands* App Nos 5100/71; 5101/71; 5102/71; 5354/72; 5370/72 (ECtHR, 8 Jun. 1976) and developed further in *Öztürk v. Germany* App No. 8544/79 (ECtHR, 21 Feb. 1984).

Chapter 2. Crimes Against the Environment Act

639. Directive 2008/99/EC on the protection of the environment through criminal law is transposed into Maltese law primarily via Chapter 522 of the Laws of Malta, the Crimes Against the Environment Act (CAEA).[882] The Directive, in particular, seeks to enforce environmental protection through criminal law against legal persons.

In actual fact, the Maltese legal system originally introduced criminal punishments for environmental offences with the promulgation of the very first EPA in 1991, and it goes without saying that the power of the Minister responsible for the environment to establish criminal punishment for offences committed under the Act and in subsidiary legislation has been retained under the current Environment Protection Act. Consequently, all the environmental subsidiary legislation published under the various parent Acts since 1991 to date provides for criminal punishment. Nevertheless, the Maltese legislator felt it was safer and more comprehensive to have a specific Act to transpose Directive 2008/99/EC. Chapter 522 was therefore promulgated to establish heftier criminal punishment for unlawful acts that amount to the infringement of legislation falling within the scope of the same Directive. The Maltese legislator has adopted a general rather than a sectoral approach for the transposition of this Directive. Most of the environmental *acquis* is transposed via subsidiary legislation referred to as regulations. As referred to above, these regulations already establish criminal liability and punishment for various environmental offences, but the new CAEA further finetunes criminal liability and the corresponding punishments for breaches of laws transposing the environmental *acquis*, thereby ensuring harmonisation with Directive 2008/99/EC.

640. The criminal punishments provided in sectoral environmental subsidiary legislation published under the EPA are more or less the same as they were all stipulated in regulations published under the various parent Acts referred to above and constrained in the punishments that could be imposed by the enabling provision.[883] There is thus no conflict between the CAEA punishments and the sectoral legislation, as they supplement each other. The CAEA, in line with the Directive, further develops criminal punishment for body corporates and the managers of such bodies convicted for such offences by drawing upon the provisions of the Criminal Code,[884] which establish criminal punishment for body corporates and individuals acting on their behalf. It adopts the same methodology and makes a cross-reference to the applicable provisions of the Criminal Code, namely, Articles 31, 42, and 43, which refer to accomplices in criminal offences, and Articles 121D, 248E(4), and 328K, which deal with the criminal responsibility of individuals acting on behalf of a body corporate and the criminal liability of the same body corporate.

641. The CAEA is, however, only expressly applicable to those legal persons that are bodies corporate. This is because the provisions of the Criminal Code made

882. Act XI of 2012.
883. Article 54(2)(u), reviewed in the previous chapter.
884. Chapter 9 of the Laws of Malta.

applicable make reference only to bodies corporate. The Directive itself defines 'legal person' as 'any legal entity having such status under the applicable national law, except for States or public bodies exercising State authority and for public international organisations'. The CAEA is, therefore, on paper less stringent than the Directive, although Maltese law recognises as a person 'a body or other association of persons whether granted legal personality [...] or not'.[885] This is probably a question of incomplete transposition of the Directive, and so the provisions of the CAEA can be said to be applicable against other legal persons recognised under Maltese law that are not expressly mentioned in its provisions.

642. There are only criminal fines and no administrative fines for environmental offences falling within the aegis of Directive 2008/99/EC, and the same applies under the CAEA. The criminal court also has the competence to impose, in the context of criminal proceedings, sanctions other than fines and imprisonment. This is regulated by the Criminal Code and includes suspended sentences, revocation of licences, forfeiture of the *corpus delicti*, interdiction from public office or the practice of a profession, and other sanctions. The time to take action is barred by the applicable prescription for criminal offences, which varies depending on the gravity of the punishment applicable to the offence in question.[886]

643. The Directive and CAEA tie multiple offences against the environment to 'substantial damage'. This term is undefined in both pieces of legislation and the Interpretation Act. Judging by established court practice, the court of criminal jurisdiction will rely on independent expert advice of persons appointed by it for the purpose of determining whether the damage should be considered substantial or not. This would occur on a case-by-case basis. It is also up to the prosecution to prove that the damage is substantial. Judges would also assess EU case law and other sources of legal interpretation of the term but relying on local expertise is essential due to Malta's particularly unique geophysical characteristics and its extremely high population density. Practice in the local scenario calls for pitching damages as 'substantial' even if these may not be considered as such in other States.

The terms '(non-) negligible quantity', 'negligible impact', and 'significant deterioration' are also not defined under the CAEA and the terms are all literally transposed from the Directive. 'Negligible quantity', 'negligible impact', and 'significant deterioration' would be assessed on a case-by-case basis via the summoning of experts by the courts, as aforementioned. The court would then evaluate the experts' opinions. The prosecution would have to prove that criminal liability arises because quantities or impacts were not negligible and deterioration was significant.

On the other hand, the term 'serious injury' in the Directive has been transposed as 'grievous bodily harm' in the CAEA, which is a term recognised in the Criminal Code. The Code goes into various details to explain when grievous bodily harm should be deemed to lead to serious or less serious consequences. This distinction applies both for wilful offences and offences resulting from negligence and or imprudence. Depending upon the criteria established, a stricter punishment is

885. Interpretation Act, Ch. 249 of the Laws of Malta, Ar. 4(e).
886. *See* Art. 688 of the Criminal Code.

applied when there are more serious consequences. Bodily harm is deemed to be grievous if it can give rise to danger of loss of life; or any permanent debility of the health or permanent functional debility of any organ of the body. Additionally, bodily harm is also considered to be grievous and subject to such a punishment if it causes any permanent defect in any part of the physical structure of the body; any permanent mental infirmity; deformity or disfigurement in the face, neck, or either of the hands of the person injured; or if it causes any mental or physical infirmity lasting for a period of thirty days or more; or if the injured party is incapacitated, from attending to his occupation; or where the affected party is a pregnant woman, and the injury hastens delivery. Other cases of grievous bodily harm are subject to a harsher punishment under the Criminal Code. These are where the harm: causes any permanent debility of the health or any permanent functional debility of any organ of the body, or any permanent defect in any part of the physical structure of the body, or any permanent mental infirmity; causes any serious and permanent disfigurement of the face, neck, or either of the hands of the person injured; or being performed on a woman with child, causes miscarriage.

644. The definition of 'unlawful' found in Article 2(a), chapeau of the Directive, has been literally transposed in national law.[887] The general nature of the transposing legislation via the CAEA covers all offences set out in the selected EU legal acts listed in the Annexes, leaving no gaps. Non-compliance with obligations resulting directly or indirectly from the transposition of these legal acts is a criminal offence.

645. Intent, negligence, and imprudence are the necessary elements of the conduct that lead to a criminal offence under Maltese law transposing the Directive. The terms 'intentionally' and 'serious negligence' referred to in the chapeau of its Article 3 are also not defined in the Directive. The CAEA transposes 'intentionally' with the term 'knowingly'. The chapeau of Article 3 of the Directive has been transposed by Maltese law under Articles 3 and 4 of the CAEA, respectively, as follows:

> 3 (1) Whosoever shall *knowingly* commit any of the unlawful acts referred to in sub-article (2), shall be guilty of an offence and shall be liable, on conviction to the punishments set out in this Act.[888]
> 4. Whosoever, *through imprudence or negligence* shall commit an unlawful offence referred to in article 3, shall, on conviction, be liable to punishments listed in article 4.

The CAEA establishes that unlawful acts listed in subparagraph 2 of its Article 3, which are a literal transposition of the corresponding Article 3(a)–(i) of the Directive, are unlawful, and any person who 'knowingly' commits any of the unlawful acts listed in the said subparagraph shall be guilty of a criminal offence. The term

887. This means infringing: (a) the legislation adopted pursuant to the EC Treaty and listed in Annex A to the Directive; or (b) with regard to activities covered by the Euratom Treaty, the legislation adopted pursuant to the Euratom Treaty and listed in Annex B to the Directive; or(c) a law, an administrative regulation of a Member State or a decision taken by a competent authority of a Member State that gives effect to the Community legislation referred to in (a) or (b).
888. Listed in Art. 5 of the CAEA.

'knowingly' is the term used under Maltese law to denote the *mens rea* (wilfulness/intention to carry out a crime) by the perpetrator. The CAEA establishes criminal liability if the same offences are the result of 'imprudence' or 'negligence' in Article 4 of the CAEA, which makes a cross-reference to Article 3 of the CAEA, and therefore includes *all* the offences mentioned. The transposing provisions under Maltese law, therefore, go beyond the minimum required by the Directive, which refers to 'with at least serious negligence'. Article 4 also includes 'imprudence' and does not qualify as negligence. Hence, it is more stringent than the Directive's equivalent. As explained above, the terms: 'substantial damage', 'negligible impact', 'significant deterioration', 'dangerous activity', 'negligible quantity', and 'non-negligible quantity' have been copied into national law without further definition. In such a circumstance, that is, whenever a legal instrument does not define a term mentioned in the law, Article 4 of the Interpretation Act[889] applies. It states:

> In this Act and in every other Act, whether passed before or after the commencement of this Act, unless the contrary intention appears:
>
> (a) the definition of any word or expression shall extend to all grammatical variations and to cognate expressions of the word or expression so defined;

In the absence of a more precise definition, the judge has the discretion to decide on a case-by-case basis how the quantitative element will be taken into account for the setting of the sanctions.

646. Acts of inciting, aiding, and abetting in the intentional conduct are punishable as a criminal offence because such actions render a person an accomplice to a criminal act under Maltese law, precisely under Articles 42 and 43 of the Criminal Code.

Under these provisions, a person shall be deemed to be an accomplice in a crime if he:

- commands another to commit the crime; or
- instigates the commission of the crime by means of bribes, promises, threats, machinations, or culpable devices, or by abuse of authority or power, or gives instructions for the commission of the crime; or
- procures the weapons, instruments or other means used in the commission of the crime, knowing that they are to be so used; or
- not in any way whatsoever knowingly aids or abets the perpetrator or perpetrators of the crime in the acts by means of which the crime is prepared or completed; or
- incites or strengthens the determination of another to commit the crime,
- or promises to give assistance, aid or reward after the fact.

---

889. Chapter 249 of the Laws of Malta.

Article 43 of the Criminal Code provides that unless otherwise provided by law, an accomplice in a crime shall be liable to the punishment established for the principal. The CAEA does not provide for an exception, so accomplices are subject to the same punishment as perpetrators. The CAEA provides the following punishments for criminal acts that fall within its scope in accordance with the Directive.

647. Article 5 of the CAEA applies to *wilful acts* and establishes that in the case of natural persons:

- If a person dies as a result of the offence the punishment awarded to the perpetrator would be life imprisonment.
- If a person suffers from grievous bodily harm, the offender shall be liable to a punishment of a prison term with a minimum of one year to a maximum of ten years, depending on the nature of the harm.[890] The punishment may be increased by one or two degrees according to the gravity of the offence, which could lead to a maximum prison term of twenty years. If grievous bodily harm is caused to two or more persons, the CAEA stipulates that punishment shall *not* be awarded at its minimum.
- If serious damage is caused to the quality of the air, soil, or water, or to animals or plants, or to the environment in any other manner, the punishment is imprisonment for a term from eight months to seven years or a fine (*multa*) of not less than EUR 12,000 and not exceeding EUR 2,500,000, or both such imprisonment and fine (*multa*).

648. Article 4 of the CAEA applies to acts *due to negligence or imprudence* as follows:

- If a person dies, the punishment is imprisonment for a term not exceeding four years or a fine (*multa*) not exceeding EUR 11,646.87, increased by one or two degrees. Therefore the maximum term of imprisonment that can be imposed is.
- If a person suffers from grievous bodily harm with serious consequences,[891] the punishment is imprisonment for a term not exceeding four years or a fine (*multa*) not exceeding EUR 10,000. If there are less serious consequences,[892] the punishment awarded is imprisonment for a term not exceeding one year or a fine (*multa*) not exceeding EUR 5,000.
- In all other cases, the punishment is imprisonment for a term not exceeding six months or a fine (*multa*) not exceeding EUR 1,000.

649. The punishments provided by the CAEA and the Criminal Code to transpose Directive 2008/99/EC appear to fulfil the requirements of effectiveness, proportionality, and dissuasiveness of the sanctions expressed in the same Directive for the following reasons:

890. Articles 216 and 218 of the Criminal Code.
891. Article 218 of the Criminal Code.
892. Article 216 of the Criminal Code.

- Under Article 5, the CAEA distinguishes between offences that lead to death from those that lead to serious or some form of personal injury from offences which negatively affect the environment without any death or personal injury.
- Death as a result of an intentional offence under the CAEA is subject to the highest punishment under Maltese law, namely imprisonment for life.
- The CAEA makes a cross-reference to the applicable provisions of the Criminal Code when establishing punishments. These provisions relate to grievous bodily harm under the Criminal Code, and the CAEA increases punishment under the Criminal Code by one or two degrees. In this manner, offences under the CAEA carry a punishment which is one or two degrees higher when compared to criminal offences under the Criminal Code or other Acts of Parliament whose breach leads to the same results. In other words, offences under the CAEA are in themselves an aggravation under Maltese criminal law.
- When offences under the CAEA lead to serious damage to the environment and its components, punishment is imprisonment for a term from eight months to seven years or a fine (*multa*) of not less than EUR 12,000 and not exceeding EUR 2,500,000 or such imprisonment and fine (*multa*). The prescriptive period for criminal offences varies. The higher the punishment, the longer the prescriptive period. The CAEA, therefore, has lengthened the prescriptive period because it has established harsher punishments.
- The punishments prescribed by the transposing legislation, namely the CAEA and the Criminal Code, are not only compliant with the compulsory punishments proposed by the annulled Council Decisions 2003/80/JHA and 2005/667/JHA but also are at times more stringent than those included in the said Council Decisions. The CAEA, the Criminal Code, the Environment Protection Act, and administrative practices also provide for some of the 'Recommended other penalties and measures' found in these same annulled Decisions.

650. The CAEA makes the provisions of Articles 121D, 248E(4), and 328K of the Criminal Code applicable to offences under it through its Articles 6(1) and (2). These three provisions must be read together. All three articles refer to the natural person who is found guilty of offences carried out on behalf of a body corporate, establishing his/her criminal liability. Articles 121D and 248E(4) establish that such a person is deemed to be vested with legal representation of the legal person, which is still liable for a punishment also prescribed by these two Articles and by Article 328K. This demonstrates that these provisions of the Criminal Code give rise to two punishments: one for the natural person and one for the legal person on whose behalf the former was acting. In this manner, liability of legal persons does not exclude criminal proceedings against natural persons who are perpetrators, inciters, or accessories in the offences referred to. The Criminal Code provisions on accomplices in crime referred to above apply, and the natural person is not exonerated because the legal person is held liable.

651. Under Article 121D of the Criminal Code, where the person found guilty of an offence is the director, manager, secretary or other principal officer of a body corporate or is a person having a power of representation of such a body or having an authority to take decisions on behalf of that body or having authority to exercise control within that body and the offence of which that person was found guilty was committed for the benefit, in part or in whole, of that body corporate, the said person shall for the be deemed to be vested with the legal representation of the same body corporate. The said body corporate shall be liable to the payment of a fine (*multa*) of not less than EUR 1,164.69 and not more than EUR 1,164,686.17.

The CAEA provides for accessory measures that are in line with recommended other penalties and measures under the annulled Council Decisions 2003/80/JHA and 2005/667/JHA. In fact, it renders Article 328K of the Criminal Code *mutatis mutandis* applicable to offences against its provisions. Article 328K establishes that, apart from the punishments referred to above, where the offender is a body corporate liable to punishment under the provisions of Article 328J, the court may, at the request of the prosecution, order:

- the suspension or cancellation of any licence, permit or other authority to engage in any trade, business or other commercial activity;
- the temporary or permanent closure of any establishment which may have been used for the
- commission of the offence; and
- the compulsory winding up of the body corporate.

652. The law does not distinguish between wilful acts and acts of negligence and/or imprudence when establishing punishments for legal persons, but judges would usually award the minimum punishment if the act was not wilful. The body corporate shall also be held liable for an offence where the lack of supervision or control by a person referred to has made possible the commission of the offence for the benefit of the body corporate; in such cases, it will be liable for the same punishment mentioned above. In compliance with the Directive, which requires that natural persons are not excluded from criminal proceedings when they act on behalf of a body corporate, the Criminal Code in Article 248E(4) (rendered applicable to the CAEA) provides for a punishment for the natural person who is acting on behalf of the body corporate if he was an employee, or otherwise in the service of a body corporate, at the time of the commission of the offence. Similarly, the natural person is criminally responsible if the commission of the offence by him was for the benefit, in part or in whole, of that body corporate and was rendered possible because of the lack of supervision or control by a person referred to in Article 121D above. Even in this case, the person found guilty shall be deemed to be vested with the legal representation of the same body corporate.

653. The individual who works for the legal person on whose behalf he committed the offence shall be liable to the punishment established under Article 121D, but for the same offence, the body corporate shall be liable under Article 328J to:

(1) A fine (*multa*) of not less than eleven thousand and six hundred and forty-six euro and eighty-seven cents (11,646.87) and not more than two million and three hundred and twenty-nine thousand and three hundred and seventy-three euro and forty cents (2,329,373.40).

(2) The body corporate shall also be held liable for an offence where the lack of supervision or control by a person referred to has made possible the commission of the offence for the benefit of the body corporate; in such cases, it will be liable for the same punishment mentioned in (1).

654 The punishments awarded to legal persons under the CAEA and the Criminal Code are effective, proportionate, and dissuasive. It must be noted that the companies in Malta that do not fall under the category of SMEs are few. Malta does not have heavy industry, and the punishments awarded herein are the highest possible for legal persons under Maltese law.

Chapter 3. Judicial Remedies

655. Malta's legal system is a mixed legal system originally based on the continental civil law model but with very heavy English law influences (both Common law and statute law), and EU law influences.[893] The influence of English law is particularly prominent in Maltese public law.

656. The Judiciary is composed of two offices, namely the judges who preside over the superior courts and the magistrates who preside over the inferior courts and conduct criminal inquiries.[894] There is a distinction between the criminal courts and the civil courts, and in both instances, there are inferior and superior courts. The procedure before the inferior courts is less formal than before the superior courts, and they also deal with civil disputes and criminal offences of a lesser degree.

In both cases, the criminal offence or civil action is brought before the relevant courts of first instance. Both parties involved may appeal the decision of the court of first instance. The appellate court's decision is then final.[895] However, in human rights disputes, it is possible for the person aggrieved to proceed further than the appellate court since there exists the right of individual petition before the ECtHR (which is not a right of appeal per se).[896]

657. As noted in the introduction to this Part, there are two broad judicial actions available in environmental matters: civil and criminal. The constitutional and administrative actions and remedies are considered to be civil in nature. For the purposes of this chapter, 'civil' will be understood in the strict sense, referring to a civil action for damages, and the constitutional actions will be tackled separately. Administrative actions will also be reviewed separately in Chapter 4. In this chapter, particular emphasis will be placed on constitutional actions since the other two have been largely covered in the two preceding chapters.

§1. Constitutional Remedies

658. The highest court in Malta is the Constitutional Court.[897] The Constitutional Court has jurisdiction to hear and determine the validity of general elections

893. *See* Kevin Aquilina, 'The Nature and Sources of the Maltese Mixed Legal System: A Strange Case of Dr Jekyll and Mr Hyde?' 4(1) Comparative Law Review 261 (2013).
894. The independence of the Judiciary is guaranteed by the Constitution.
895. The civil and the criminal courts of appeal are separate. They are presided over by one judge when hearing appeals from the inferior courts and by three judges when hearing appeals from the superior courts.
896. Malta is a party to the ECHR and the Protocol allowing for individual petition. The ECHR is transformed into Maltese law as the European Convention Act, Ch. 319 of the Laws of Malta, and the right of individual petition is found in Art. 5 thereof.
897. Set up by Art. 95 of the Constitution of Malta: 'One of the Superior Courts, composed of such three judges as could, in accordance with any law for the time being in force in Malta, compose the Court of Appeal, shall be known as the Constitutional Court'.

and of Members of the House of Representatives[898] as well as incompatibility of office, appeals from the First Hall of the Civil Court regarding disputes involving the violation of human rights, appeals from decisions of any court of original jurisdiction in Malta regarding the interpretation of the Constitution, and appeals from the decisions of any court of original jurisdiction in Malta regarding the validity of laws except those relating to human rights.[899]

The Constitutional Court may, in certain instances, act as a court of first and last instance; that is, it has original jurisdiction, but its decision is final in the sense that the parties cannot appeal from it.[900] It acts as a court of second instance in all other cases, notably those dealing with the violation of human rights. The human rights action may be of direct interest to safeguard the environmental interests of a Maltese citizen.

659. The Constitution of Malta does not recognise the right to a healthy environment as an ad hoc human right. Until 2018, the word 'environment' did not exist in the text of the Constitution. The notion was mentioned in passing in Article 9, which imposed a duty on the State to, *inter alia*, 'safeguard the landscape'. This choice of word is probably because the Constitution entered into force in 1964, at a time when the term 'natural environment' did not form part of the common vocabulary. As noted in the General Introduction to this publication, this Article was amended in 2018 to introduce a new provision recognising the duty of the State to protect and conserve the environment and its resources and to take measures to address any form of environmental degradation in Malta. It also has a duty to promote, nurture, and support the right of action in favour of the environment.[901] However, Article 9 is rendered unenforceable in a court of law through Article 21 and, in any case, does not encompass a right to a healthy environment *per se*. Whether it may still be relied on when interpreting and enforcing other provisions of the Constitution is a debated question.[902]

Article 33 of the Constitution elaborates upon exemptions from the derivation of the right to life only with respect to the use of force. The words, 'intentionally be

898. The House of Representatives (Malta's unicameral legislature), together with the President of Malta, compose Parliament.

899. Constitution of Malta, Art. 95(2). Art. 116 of the Constitution provides for an *actio popularis* regarding the validity of laws: 'A right of action for a declaration that any law is invalid on any grounds other than inconsistency with the provisions of Articles 33 to 45 of the Constitution shall appertain to all persons without distinction and a person bringing such an action, shall not be required to show any personal interest in support of his action.' Articles 33–45 of the Constitution lay down the fundamental rights and freedoms of the individual. In this case, a personal link must exist to apply to the Civil Court, First Hall, for redress under Art. 46(1) of the Constitution.

900. It acts so when deciding upon the validity of elections to the House of Representatives, questions regarding the valid election of a member of the House of Representatives, or when the Speaker has vacated his seat and is not functioning as he should.

901. Constitution of Malta, Art. 9(2). *See* Ethan Brincat, 'The Second Republic: A Green One' (LL.B. (Hons.) dissertation, University of Malta 2019) 13–28.

902. The courts have refused such an approach: 70/1977 *Walter Cuschieri et v. Il-Prim Ministru*, Civil Court (First Hall) 29 Jun. 1977 and confirmed on appeal by the Constitutional Court on 30 Nov. 1977. Authors opine against this approach: *see* Giovanni Bonello, 'A Battery of Pointless Principles?' in Giovanni Bonello, *Misunderstanding the Constitution: How the Maltese Judiciary Undermines Human Rights* (BDL Publishing 2018) 53; Tonio Borg, 'The Constitution of Malta:

deprived of the right to life' would, however, render it difficult for judges to include the right to a healthy environment as part of the right to life by analogous interpretation because of the element of non-strict liability imposed by the term 'intentionally'.[903] However, there is a copious European Court of Human Rights case law recognising various aspects of the right to the environment under a number of Convention provisions, such as Article 2 (right to life) and Article 8 (right to private and family life). Maltese courts must therefore take these judgments into account in human rights disputes concerning the environment, in actions instituted both under the Constitution and under the European Convention Act.

660. The process of enforcing fundamental rights and freedoms in Malta is rather simple. An action for breach of human rights is generally taken by a person against the State.[904] Corporations, especially if State-controlled, can be found to have breached human rights. Furthermore, there is no a priori exclusion of a private person (natural or legal) being held responsible for a breach of human rights under the provisions of the Constitution where the wording of the same provision allows such responsibility.[905] However, it is only the person, natural or legal as the case may be, that can bring a human rights action. Proceedings commence by application before the First Hall of the Civil Court, with the possibility of an appeal before the Constitutional Court available to both parties. The applicant may then petition the European Court of Human Rights to obtain further redress.

§2. Criminal Remedies

661. The EPA, as seen, enables the Minister responsible for the environment to issue subsidiary legislation (regulations) to protect the environment, and this power includes the right to impose penal provisions in case of default.

662. The courts of criminal jurisdiction are four: Court of Magistrates (Malta), Court of Magistrates (Gozo), Criminal Court, and Court of Criminal Appeal. The first two are inferior courts, presided over by magistrates, whereas the other two are superior courts, presided over by judges. It is the Courts of Magistrates and Criminal Court that are competent to hear and determine criminal proceedings at first instance, with a right of appeal from all such decisions to the Court of Criminal

---

Anomalies and Imperfections' (2022) 32; Id-Dritt 107, 110; Robert L Zammit, 'The Enforceability or Otherwise of the Declaration of Principles in the Constitution of Malta' (LL.D. Thesis, University of Malta 2012).

903. For example, *see Darryl Grima pro et noe v. Il-Prim Ministru*, Civil Court (First Hall) 17 Jun. 1988.

904. Article 181B the Code of Organisation and Civil Procedure regulates the appropriate defendant in actions against the government. As a rule, it is always the head of the government department or entity in question that is sued. If there is no head of department, as in the case of attacking laws, the appropriate respondent is the State Advocate.

905. This interpretation was adopted in a number of cases, such as *Carmelo Buttigieg v. Albert Mizzi noe*, Constitutional Court 9 Oct. 1989 Vol. LXXIII.i.119. For further information, *see* Tonio Borg, *A Commentary on the Constitution of Malta* (2nd edn, Kite Group 2022) 298–300.

Appeal. This court is composed of one judge when hearing appeals from the inferior courts and three judges when hearing appeals from the Criminal Court. The rules concerning appeals differ between the inferior and superior courts.

663. Maltese law divides criminal offences into two types: crimes and contraventions. The latter are tried by the Courts of Magistrates unless they are accompanied by other offences subject to the jurisdiction of the Criminal Court, in which case the latter court is competent.

The original jurisdiction of the Courts of Magistrates over crimes extends to those subject to a maximum punishment of two years' imprisonment. Any crime subject to a higher punishment is determined by the Criminal Court (which ordinarily is composed of a judge and a lay jury). However, crimes punishable with a term of imprisonment of more than two years but less than twelve years may be tried by the Courts of Magistrates if certain requisites are met.[906]

However, most regulations issued under the EPA, and other legislation concerning the environment, tend to provide that the Court of Magistrates is the competent court, even where, under the general provisions of the Criminal Code, it would not be. Where the law is silent, as in the Crimes Against the Environment Act, the ordinary rules on the jurisdiction of the Code would apply.

664. The criminal remedy is, of course, available only to the State to prosecute since it is the Executive Police or Attorney General that brings the action. Nevertheless, these may act upon information, reports, or complaints by private persons who become aware of offences against environmental legislation.[907] The Police and AG may also be challenged by such persons who refuse to take action following the report, etc.[908] The Crimes Against the Environment Act makes further provisions on this, as seen in the previous Chapter. Furthermore, the EPA provides in Article 75(3) that its environmental officers can assist the police in investigations and also plead the case on behalf of the prosecution in matters regulated by or under the Act.

§3. Civil Remedies

665. The courts of civil jurisdiction are four: Court of Magistrates (Malta), Court of Magistrates (Gozo), Civil Court, and Court of Appeal. The first two are inferior courts, presided over by magistrates, whereas the other two are superior courts, presided over by judges. It is the Court of Magistrates and Civil Court that are competent to hear and determine civil proceedings at first instance, with a right of appeal from all such decisions to the Court of Appeal. This court is composed of one judge when hearing appeals from the inferior courts and three judges when hearing appeals from the Criminal Court. The rules concerning appeals differ between the inferior and superior courts.

906. *See* Criminal Code, Ch. 9 of the Laws of Malta, Art. 370.
907. *See ibid.*, Arts 535–540.
908. *See ibid.*, Art. 541.

666. The Civil Court is composed of a number of sections. In environmental matters, jurisdiction rests with the First Hall as the court of residual jurisdiction once no specific court or section is expressly vested with jurisdiction in such matters. Competence between the First Hall and Courts of Magistrates differs depending on the value of the thing subject to the dispute. If the value exceeds EUR 15,000, the First Hall is competent. If not, it is the Courts of Magistrates. However, if the value does not exceed EUR 5,000, competence rests with the Small Claims Tribunal. Furthermore, cases where the value cannot be quantified fall within the remit of the First Hall.

667. The rules on damages have been reviewed in Chapter 1. An action for environmental damage must satisfy the requisites for any other action for damages since no ad hoc action exists. Furthermore, the person must prove juridical interest in bringing such an action, this being an interest that is legal, direct, and actual. This means he must prove personal suffering of damages through the violation of a right appertaining to him and that he is acting to recover such damages. Therefore, private persons can only bring actions for damages where they have suffered the damage themselves, be it due to the acts of the government or other private persons. On the other hand, the government has its own remedies to take action against environmental damage, outlined in the General Introduction to this publication, since the action for environmental damages, never availed of under the second EPA, has been abolished.

668. However, the government, through ERA, must recover any sums due by way of administrative penalties through the courts of civil jurisdiction, depending on the amount of the sum. This procedure is regulated by Article 466 of the Code of Organisation and Civil Procedure. The Chairman of ERA must declare under oath the nature of the debt, identify the debtor, and the sum due. This declaration is made before the registrar of the court or before a judge or magistrate and must be served on the debtor by judicial act. The judicial act has the effect of a final judgment unless an application is filed within twenty days requesting the court to declare the claim unfounded. Once final, it constitutes an executive title once the time established by law lapses[909] and so can be enforced by any executive act without the need for further formalities.[910] The executive title can only be rescinded if the defendant can prove he was unaware of the service of the declaration.

909. *See* Code of Organisation and Civil Procedure, Arts 255–257. The procedure to enforce is found in Arts 258 *et seq.*

910. The executive acts are indicated in Art. 253 of the Code of Organisation and Civil Procedure. The list is not exhaustive.

Chapter 4. Right of Judicial and Administrative Review and Access to Justice in Environmental Matters

669. It is important for the public to be able to challenge acts having effects on the environment, even if, strictly, they do not suffer any direct damages as a result. To this end, Maltese law provides a number of remedies that allow the public to access to justice in environmental matters. This is done through actions for review and through access to information and participation in the decision-making process.

670. Internationally, the Aarhus Convention is the leading instrument which provides the right to members of the public to challenge decisions, acts, and omissions which breach their right to participation or access to information. Article 9 of the Aarhus Convention states:

> Each Party shall, within the framework of its national legislation, ensure that any person who considers that his or her request for information under Article 4 has been ignored, wrongfully refused, whether in part or in full, inadequately answered, or otherwise not dealt with in accordance with the provisions of that Article, has access to a review procedure before a court of law or another independent and impartial body established by law.
> In the circumstances where a Party provides for such a review by a court of law, it shall ensure that such a person also has access to an expeditious procedure established by law that is free of charge or inexpensive for reconsideration by a public authority or review by an independent and impartial body other than a court of law.

671. This Convention is given effect in Malta through the Freedom of Access to Information on the Environment Regulations,[911] discussed in Chapter 2 of Part I of this publication. Under these Regulations, access to justice is catered for in the case where the right of access to information is breached. Specifically, Article 11A states: 'In cases where the applicant decides to have recourse to the Environment and Planning Review Tribunal on matters relating to requests for environmental information, having due regard to the need for expeditiousness, the Tribunal shall hold its first hearing within six working days from receipt of the appeal.' The strength of this provision is that the right to access to justice in environmental matters is not limited to appealing any decisions which breach environmental law but also covers the rights granted to individuals, in this case, the right to access to environmental information. Moreover, the Regulations provide that this access to justice must occur in an expedited manner – six working days from the receipt of the appeal.

The Regulations also provide a further remedy, Article 12, which states, 'Any person who requests the competent authority to provide him with environmental information in accordance with regulation 3, and who is dissatisfied with the response, may apply to the Information and Data Protection Commissioner for a decision.'

911. L.N. 116/2005 (S.L. 549.39).

672. Access to justice on broader matters is afforded under specific laws, notably the Environment and Planning Review Tribunal Act, the Code of Organisation and Civil Procedure, and the Ombudsman Act. The first two offer judicial remedies, while the latter offer a purely administrative remedy. Furthermore, access under the Code is unavailable if the matter is covered by the Environment and Planning Review Tribunal Act.

673. The Environment and Planning Review Tribunal (EPRT) was established in 2010, and at that time, its set up and functions were set out under the Malta Environment and Planning Act, 2010. With the demerger of the PA and the ERA in 2016, the functions of this Tribunal were re-enacted in an independent Environment and Planning Review Tribunal Act.[912] The aim of the said tribunal is to provide an independent and impartial tribunal which is tasked with reviewing the decisions of the PA and ERA. The EPRT Act differentiates between decisions made by the PA and those made by the ERA: Article 11 lists the decisions taken by the PA which can be appealed, while Article 47 lists the circumstances where an individual can challenge decisions taken by ERA. In both cases, it is interesting to note that an appeal can be submitted by both an aggrieved party and an 'interested third party'. In this case, the person must submit reasoned grounds based on environmental considerations to justify his appeal. In line with the principles of transparency, all sittings of the Tribunal must be held in public, and decisions must also be published.

The same Act lays down the procedures and timeframes on who, when, and how an appeal can be lodged in front of this Tribunal. The Tribunal has the competence to decide on decisions taken by both Authorities, namely, those where permits are granted or refused, and also on decisions related to penalties like compensation for damages, stop orders, and compliance orders, together with appeals from decisions regarding protection and conservation orders. Finally, the Tribunal may decide to grant a permit or to modify a decision taken by the Authority.

674. An appeal from decisions of the Tribunal lies to the Court of Appeal, constituted in terms of Article 41(9) of the COCP (that is, composed of a single judge), on points of law. The appellant before the Tribunal and all other persons who participated in the appeal may appeal from decisions of the Tribunal.

An appeal to the Court of Appeal must be submitted within twenty days from when the decision of the Tribunal is delivered in public, and such an appeal is regulated by the rules of the court made under Article 29 of the COCP. Pursuant to Article 53 of the Act, these procedures shall be concluded in a timely manner. The Court of Appeal may uphold the decision taken by the Tribunal, or it may send back the case to the respective Authorities for reconsideration.

675. It should also be noted that, under Article 41A of the Environment and Development Planning Act,[913] members of the public concerned having sufficient

912. Chapter 551 of the Laws of Malta.
913. Chapter 504 of the Laws of Malta.

interest have access to a review procedure before the EPRT to challenge the substantive or procedural legality of any decision, act or omission relating to a development or an installation which is subject to an EIA or an integrated pollution prevention and control (IPPC) permit. Environmental NGOs are always deemed to possess the required interest for the purposes of this provision.

676. The COCP (Chapter 12 of the Laws of Malta) offers an additional avenue for access to justice through Article 469A. This provision allows for judicial review of administrative action, allowing the Civil Court, First Hall, to inquire into the validity of any administrative act and declare it null, invalid, or without effect. The grounds of review are where the act is in violation of the Constitution[914] or where the act is considered *ultra vires*, meaning:

(1) when such act emanates from a public authority that is not authorised to perform it; or
(2) when a public authority has failed to observe the principles of natural justice or mandatory procedural requirements in performing the administrative act or in its prior deliberations thereon; or
(3) when the administrative act constitutes an abuse of the public authority's power in that it is done for improper purposes or on the basis of irrelevant considerations; or
(4) when the administrative act is otherwise contrary to law.

This process is limited to 'administrative acts', which are in turn defined as 'the issuing by a public authority of any order, licence, permit, warrant, decision, or a refusal to any demand of a claimant, but does not include any measure intended for internal organization or administration within the said authority'. The COCP imposes a timeframe of six months to impugn an administrative act as *ultra vires* from the date when the interested person becomes aware or could have become aware of such an administrative act, whichever is the earliest. No such timeframe is imposed for actions in violation of the Constitution.

677. Article 469A does not strictly speaking apply solely to violations of environmental law: in fact, there is no mention whatsoever of the environment. It is a general provision which covers judicial review of any administrative act of the public sector. Yet, despite it being a general blanket provision, it can be considered the 'strongest' local tool when it comes to access to justice locally. Interestingly enough, this provision was used by environmental NGOs when the EPRT, or rather the fora to access to justice in environmental matters, did not exist in the Maltese legal system. Nowadays, this Article is less frequently used for environmental matters, considering that the EPRT has been statutorily established and also considering that Article 469A(4) stipulates that the provisions of this Article do not apply where the

914. Although judgments have, as a rule, interpreted this to exclude situations where an action for breaches of human rights is available. For example, 1/2003/2 *Christopher Hall v. Awtorità tad-Djar et*, Constitutional Court 18 Sep. 2009.

mode of contestation or of obtaining redress, with respect to any particular administrative act before a court or tribunal, is provided for in any other law.

Article 469A, therefore, plays a residual role when it comes to access to justice in environmental matters. It can certainly be used should a right of appeal to the EPRT under the Act be omitted for a specific administrative act committed by ERA (or by any other authority where the act impacts the environment).

678. Another important legal tool to access to justice in environmental matters is the Ombudsman Act.[915] Under this Act, the Ombudsman has the power to appoint Commissioners, one of which is the Commissioner for Environment and Planning. The function of the Commissioner is to investigate any action taken by or on behalf of the government or other authority, body, or person to whom this Act applies, being action taken in the exercise of their administrative functions.[916] Furthermore, the Commissioner may conduct any such investigation on his initiative or on the written complaint of any person having an interest who claims to have been aggrieved by any action as aforesaid or where the person aggrieved has died or is for any reason unable to act for himself, of his heir or representative.

Furthermore, any Committee of the House of Representatives may at any time refer to the Commissioner any petition that is before that Committee for consideration or any matter to which the petition relates. In any such case, the Ombudsman shall, subject to any special directions of the Committee, investigate the matters so referred, so far as they are within his jurisdiction, and make such report to the Committee as he thinks fit.

Under the EPA, the Commissioner for Environment and Planning has to issue an opinion on the State of the Environment Report, which is issued by ERA at intervals of not more than four years. The Commissioner has the right to ask ERA and other authorities and entities to furnish his office with any information that he requires in order to analyse the report and to compile his opinion on such a report. The Commissioner must deliver the report together with his opinion to the Speaker of the House within eight weeks from when the said report was passed on to him, and within a month from the tabling of the report, there shall be a dedicated sitting during which the report is discussed.[917]

---

915. Chapter 385 of the Laws of Malta.
916. Vide Art. 13.
917. EPA Art. 57(3).

Selected Bibliography

Aquilina, Kevin. *Development Planning Legislation: The Maltese Experience.* Malta: Mireva Publications, 1999.

Aquilina, Kevin. *List of Environmental Legislation in Malta.* Unpublished.

Attard, David et al. *Implications of Expected Climatic Changes on Malta.* Athens: UNEP, 1993.

Axiak, V. & C. Delia. *Assessing the Impact of Compliance with CD 76/46/EEC and Other Water Quality Directives with Reference to Marine Discharges in Malta, Ministry for the Environment.* 30 November 2000.

Azzopardi, Anton. *A New Geography of the Maltese Islands.* Malta: St Aloysius College Publication, 1995.

Barnes, Pamela M. & Ian G. Barnes. *Environmental Policy in the European Union.* Cambridge: Cambridge University Press, 1999.

Boyle, A. & Redgwell Catherine. *Birnie, Boyle and Redgwell's International Law and the Environment.* 4th edn. Oxford: Oxford University Press, 2021.

Borg, Simone. *Environment Conservation in Malta: An Ultimate Test in Sustainable Development.* Paper presented on behalf of Malta at the IMASIDS Conference, Foundation for International Studies (IMA-SIDS Document 17), University of Malta, 24–27 November 1998.

Borg, Simone. *Malta's Environmental Legislation.* Working Document at the Screening Session of Malta's environmental legislation before the European Commission. Brussels, November 2008.

De Sadeleer, Nicolas. *Environmental Principles.* Oxford: Oxford University Press, 2002.

Integrated Waste Management and Life Cycle Assessment Workshop. Malta, April 2004.

Malta Federation of Industry 2006 June – Operators required to report on VOC emissions.

Micallef, J.P. *The Likely Impact of EC Law on Ozone Depleting Substances in Malta.* BA (Hons.), European Studies, University of Malta, 2003.

Onyerikam, I. 'Achieving Compliance with the Basel Convention on Transboundary Movement of Hazardous Wastes'. http://ssrn.com/abstract=984067, 12 March 2008.

Papers presented at the Eighth Symposium on Hazardous and Industrial Solid Waste Testing and Disposal, sponsored by ASTM Committees D-34 on Waste Disposal and E-38 on Resource Recovery. Clearwater, Fla., 12–13 November 1987.

Selected Bibliography

Schembri, P.J. & A.E. Baldacchino. *Ilma Blat u Hajja*. Msida, Malta: Malta University Services Ltd, University Campus, 1992.

State of the Environment Report, 2002. Malta Environment and Planning Authority (MEPA), 2003.

State of the Environment Report, 2005. Malta Environment and Planning Authority (MEPA), 2006.

State of the Environment Report, 2005. Sub-report 8: Waste – Malta Environment and Planning Authority Malta, January 2006.

State of the Environment Report, 2018. Malta: Environment and Resources Authority, 2018.

Structure Plan for the Maltese Islands. Planning Services Division, Ministry for the Development of Infrastructure, December 1990.

Stuart, Bell & Donald McGillivray. *Environmental Law*. Oxford: Oxford University Press, 2006.

Sultana, J. & V. Falzon (eds). *Wildlife of the Maltese Islands*. Malta: Environment Protection Department, Floriana, 1996.

Websites

https://era.org.mt/legislation-policy/
http://europa.eu
www.euractiv.com/en/environment/eu-adopts-stricter-air-quality-rules/
https://sustainabledevelopment.un.org/
www.eur-lex.europa.eu/en/index.htm
www.mra.org.mt
https://mccaa.org.mt/
www.efsa.europa.eu/EFSA/ScientificPanels/efsa_locale-1178620753812_GMO.htm
https://ecourts.gov.mt/onlineservices/Judgements
https://legislation.mt/Legislation
www.wasteservmalta.com

Index

The numbers here refer to paragraph numbers.

Index

Index

www.ingramcontent.com/pod-product-compliance
Lightning Source LLC
Chambersburg PA
CBHW071414230926
51846CB00001B/91
9789403539478